The S/NVQ Book

Building a Portfolio at Level 3 for
Children's Care, Learning and Development

Sheila Riddall-Leech

Step
forward
PUBLISHING

About the author

Sheila Riddall-Leech began her career as a primary teacher working in the UK and overseas. She spent many years in further and higher education, as well as becoming an OfSTED inspector, NVQ assessor and working with the assessment team at Council for Awards in Children's Care and Education (CACHE). She has written several books on childcare and related topics and is a regular contributor to several professional journals. Sheila now runs her own training company specialising in children's care, education and playwork. She lives in North Shropshire and in her spare time she enjoys gardening, walking and music.

About the book

The aim of this book is to help you put together a portfolio of supporting evidence that will help you achieve a Level 3 NVQ in Children's Care, Learning and Development. The book explains what an NVQ is and makes clear the important technical terms and words that you should understand to help you achieve your qualification. It suggests ways in which you can collect evidence from the things that you do in your every day work with children and their families, rather than working through a set of tasks and coursework which may not be relevant or appropriate to your work situation.

Throughout the book we refer to sections of your candidate handbook, which you will have been given by your NVQ Assessment Centre when you registered for your NVQ. Don't be put off by the handbook; at first it can appear complicated and a bit intimidating. This book aims to help you work your way through your handbook and 'translate' some of the language and terms used. We also look at the important forms and documents which will need to be completed and suggest ways to do this.

This book will not provide you with all the underpinning knowledge you will need in order to complete your NVQ. Instead, at the end of Chapters 2 to 6 there is a list of additional resources, such as books, websites and publications which may be useful to help you extend your knowledge and understanding. It suggests things for you to think about and reflect on as you work your way through your NVQ.

The letters CCLD are used instead of the full title of Children's Care, Learning and Development and NVQ will be a generic term to include the Scottish version of the qualification, SVQ.

In this book the use of he, him or his is gender neutral and is intended to include both sexes.

Acknowledgment

Sheila would like to thank the many NVQ candidates whose views and opinions have been sought when compiling this book and of course their assessors. Their time and patience at answering many questions is greatly appreciated. Sheila would also like to thank her husband Peter and her family for their continued support and encouragement.

While efforts have been made to contact people whose articles are featured in this book, we apologise if any authors have not been notified

Published by Step Forward Publishing Limited, St Judes' Church, Dulwich Road, Herne Hill, London, SE24 0PB
© Step Forward Publishing Limited 2007 ISBN: 978 1904575085

Contents

Chapter 4:
CCLD 303 Promote children's development

page 114

About this unit – CCLD 303.1 observe development – CCLD 303.2 assess development and reflect upon implications for practice – CCLD 303.3 plan provision to promote development – CCLD 303.4 implement and evaluate plans to promote development – keywords and concepts relating to CCLD 303 – suggested further reading – resource material.

Chapter 5:
CCLD 304 Reflect on and develop practice

page 148

About this unit – CCLD 304.1 reflect on practice – SWOT analysis – SMART targets – CCLD 304.2 take part in continuing professional development – keywords and concepts relating to CCLD 304 - suggested further reading and useful addresses – resource material.

Contents

Chapter 6:
CCLD 305 Protect and promote children's rights

page 171

About this unit – CCLD 305.1 support equality of access – CCLD 305.2 implement strategies, policies, procedures and practice for inclusion – CCLD 305.3 maintain and follow policies and procedures for protecting and safeguarding children – key words and concepts relating to CCLD 305 – suggested further reading – resource material.

Glossary of keywords and concepts   page 205

Contents

Chapter 1

Introduction

What is an NVQ?

You have decided to work towards an NVQ, but what does this mean? The letters NVQ stand for National Vocational Qualification, and once you have gained an NVQ it shows that you are professionally competent in a specific area. In Scotland, the vocational qualification is referred to as a SVQ - Scottish Vocational Qualification. NVQs have different levels from entry (Level 1) to degree (Level 6).

A Level 3 Children's Care, Learning and Development (CCLD) NVQ is first and foremost for people who work with children and their families. They may have a supervisory role, such as a pre-school supervisor, or be a specialist, such as a SureStart Family Support worker; or they may work on their own, for example, nannies and childminders. An NVQ Level 3 CCLD will give you a nationally recognised qualification which enables you to work, unsupervised, with children and their families anywhere in the United Kingdom, or even further afield, in a variety of settings from day nurseries, nursery classes, home-based childcare, pre-school groups, schools, travel companies, multi-disciplinary teams, SureStart and Children's Centres. It will show parents, carers and society that you take your job very seriously, that you are committed and qualified. One of the great strengths of an NVQ is that it can offer a qualification for people from a diverse range of settings and job roles.

What is the difference between an NVQ and a VQ

There is a range of qualifications available to childcare practitioners and it can be confusing to decide which is the best one for you. Childcare and education, like many other professions, almost has their own language, which can be full of jargon and letters which are shortened titles for certain things, such as NVQ. Many of the qualifications are referred to by letters, such as NVQ, BTEC, VQ and it is helpful to understand what these mean as it will help you realise where your NVQ sits in the whole picture.

A VQ is a vocational qualification which involves attending a course, usually at a college or school, and successfully completing a number of set pieces of work which are marked and assessed; sometimes there can also be an end-of-course examination or test. The CACHE Level 3 Diploma in Childcare and Education (DCE) and the BTEC National Diploma - Early Years are vocational qualifications, so is an NNEB. Some VQs can be studied part-time, such as the

CACHE Level 3 Diploma in Pre-School Practice, Diploma in Home-based Childcare, so people can continue to work while studying.

Other VQs may involve full-time attendance at college or school and so it is not possible to work in a childcare setting at the same time; however, part of gaining a VQ could involve you in spending time in different settings. This part of your course is assessed. Therefore you cannot receive a wage for doing the work, as you are technically a student.

NVQs can be achieved while you are working, as you are assessed on what you do. You can get the CCLD NVQ Level 3 by proving that you know and understand why you do certain things, in other words that you are competent, skilled, knowledgeable and experienced, when working with children and their families. You will be assessed in your workplace against the National Occupational Standards; therefore you can work full-time at the same time as completing your NVQ. You can also gain an NVQ while working part-time or as a volunteer. You may not need to go to college, depending on your experience and previous training. One of the strengths of an NVQ is that it is flexible and can accommodate the needs of many different people working in a wide range of settings.

National Occupational Standards

Please don't dismiss the National Occupational Standards as technical jargon that doesn't make sense or something that you don't need to know about. To help you better understand the requirements of your NVQ, you do need to have some awareness of what National Standards are and why they are necessary.

'I thought that only people working in day nurseries could complete their NVQ, but I successfully did mine working as a volunteer in a SureStart centre. I have now completed my NVQ Level 3 and am a family support worker in the same centre.'

NVQ candidate

All NVQs are based on National Occupational Standards which are standards that have been agreed by the relevant Sector Skills Council. National Occupational Standards principally describe the various aspects and parts of a specific job. There are National Occupational Standards for all NVQs, from hairdressing and beauty, vehicle maintenance, management, small animal care or any other profession you can think of. In the case of the CCLD, the standards were revised in 2005, bringing them up-to-date with new legislation, current thinking and practice. This means that at every stage highly experienced professionals and practitioners, who work with or have expert knowledge of children, were involved in writing the standards, making sure that they are relevant to the work that you do.

The CCLD Level 3 NVQ is awarded when you can show that you are skilled in your job and have reached the National Occupational Standard, in other words that you can do your job, and you know why and how you are doing it.

Principles and values

The principles and values of the CCLD are the underpinning beliefs of the NVQ and you will need a thorough awareness and grasp of these to understand the National Occupational Standards. The principles and values are printed at the beginning of your handbook; don't just flick past them, stop and read them as they are important.

These important principles and values take into consideration the United Nations Convention on the Rights of the Child and the Children Act (1989 and 2004). Following these principles and values will ensure that you always give the children with whom you are working the best possible care. It is always helpful to talk the principles and values through with your work colleagues or your assessor, if any of them are not clear or you want a further explanation.

There are two principles which underpin everything that you do.

Principle 1
• The welfare of the child is paramount
Principle 2
• Practitioners contribute to children's care, learning and development and this is reflected in every aspect of practice and service provision.

There are nine values which go alongside the two principles:

1. The needs, rights and views of the child are at the centre of all practice and provision.
2. Individuality, difference and diversity are valued and celebrated.
3. Equality of opportunity and anti-discriminatory practice are actively promoted.
4. Children's health and well-being are actively promoted.
5. Children's personal and physical safety is safeguarded, while allowing for risk and challenge as appropriate to the capabilities of the child.
6. Self-esteem, resilience and a positive self-image are recognised as essential to every child's development.
7. Confidentiality and agreements about confidential information are respected as appropriate unless a child's protection and well-being are at stake.
8. Professional knowledge, skills and values are shared appropriately in order to enrich the experience of children more widely.
9. Best practice requires reflection and a continuous search for improvement.

It is important that these principles and values become part of everything that you do in your work with children and their families; in a way they are your code of practice. The principles and values are not just good words written in your candidate handbook, but should be evident in everything that you do in your work with children and their families, and should help you to support and meet their individual needs.

"I thought that the principles and values were not really relevant to me, but when our pre-school was inspected we used these as part of our self-assessment. As a result we had a very good inspection report.'
NVQ candidate

What makes up the Level 3 NVQ in Children's Care, Learning and Development?

Regardless of which awarding body you are registered with, for example Council for Awards in Children's Care and Education (CACHE) or City and Guilds (C&G), the structure and format of your NVQ will be the same.

You should have been given a candidate handbook when you registered with the assessment centre. Your handbook contains details of each of the units and copies of the paperwork that you will need. Your handbook is very important, so you should be careful not to lose it.

The overall structure
The Level 3 CCLD has nine units, each of which is based on the National Occupational Standards, covering the care and development of children from birth to 16 years. Five of the nine units are mandatory, which means that you have to do them. There is a range of units from which you can choose the remaining four units. Each unit describes a particular aspect of children's care, learning and development; this will be explained in more detail later on in this chapter. You do not have to start with the first unit listed in your handbook; you can start with a unit that interests

you, or with which you feel confident. You do not have to do the mandatory units first followed by the option units; you can plan with your assessor the most appropriate order for you.

If you are reading this book, the chances are that you have already decided that you want to complete your NVQ. How quickly you complete the nine units depends on a number of things. For example, if you have a lot of experience already, or have already gained an NVQ Level 2, or have an appropriate VQ at Level 3, you may be able to get your qualification in a shorter time. The length of time taken to complete will also depend on whether you work full- or part-time, or if you are a volunteer. You may find that your assessment centre sets time limits for completion of your NVQ, due to their funding restrictions, but this will be discussed with you and you should have plenty of time to complete the NVQ. The awarding body will usually register you for a period of three years, and it would normally be expected that you complete your NVQ in this time. Details of how to extend this time-frame can be found in your candidate handbook.

The difference between mandatory and option units

You have to complete five units; you do not have a choice about these, as they are mandatory units. You can choose from two groups to complete the remaining four units. These are called option units. You must do two units from group 1 and two from group 2. In group 1 there are eight units and in group 2 there are thirty-three, so you have plenty of choice.

Your choice of option units will depend on where you work, your interests and who you work with. In other words, as well as giving you a broad base of knowledge, your NVQ can be tailored to meet

'I found the first mandatory unit really quite overwhelming; I did not know where to start. However, my assessor suggested that, as I was already doing a lot of the planning in our setting, I might find the option unit CCLD 309 - Plan and implement curriculum frameworks for early education - less daunting. So that was where I started and it gave me the confidence to tackle the other units.'
NVQ candidate

'I completed my CACHE Level 3 Diploma in Home-based Childcare in December 2006. As this course is matched to the 2005 National Occupational Standards, much of my work can be cross-referenced and my assessor is confident that I can complete my NVQ in 6 months.'
NVQ candidate

your specific needs. You should talk to your assessor about which option units are best suited to you. The details of each group of option units can be found in your candidate handbook and on the CD that is included in it.

Unit titles

Each unit, whether mandatory or optional, is given a series of numbers and letters and a title. Look in your candidate handbook for the first mandatory unit. You should have found a unit that is headed up:

CCLD 301 Develop and promote positive relationships

CCLD stands for the name of the NVQ, in your case Children's Care Learning and Development.

301 indicates that this unit is at Level 3 and is the first unit in the complete list of units. (In the same way a unit numbered 201 would be at Level 2 and be the first unit listed)

Develop and promote positive relationships is the title of the unit and tells you what it is about.

Age range

The Level 3 CCLD covers the age range from birth to 16 years. However this does not mean that you must be working with children from birth to 16 years. If you work with children between these ages, or any combination of age groups, you will be able to achieve your NVQ provided that you are in a children's care, learning or development setting. Your assessor will expect you to show that you have knowledge and understanding of the age range 0-16, for example in unit CCLD 303, Promote children's development, but your actual evidence for your portfolio will come from whatever age range you are working with.

Knowledge statements and links to practice

Each unit has a set of knowledge statements which relate directly to your work with children and their families and link to the National Occupational Standards. You must show that you know and understand the knowledge statements. All the knowledge statements start with K3, to indicate that they are at Level 3. They are printed at the end of each unit in your handbook

Knowledge statements are intended to show that you understand what you do and why you do it, in others words they directly link to your practice and work. Therefore you should use real-life examples from your work. For instance in CCLD 302, knowledge statement K3H201, you could show how you evacuated the children when the fire alarm went off unexpectedly, the roles and responsibilities of the rest of the team and how the children reacted as evidence of your understanding and abilities.

The knowledge statements are not questions that you must answer. In fact many of them begin with the words 'How to'; for example look at the knowledge specifications for CCLD 301 in your candidate handbook which you will find at the end of this mandatory unit. Look at how many of these statements start with 'How' (there are six). This means that knowledge statements can be met through observation and by your assessor questioning you. What often happens is that more than one knowledge statement can be met following an observation.

Elements and performance criteria

An element is one specific part of a unit and each unit, regardless of whether it is mandatory or optional, is broken down into a number of elements. Each element describes a different aspect of the unit.

Find the unit CCLD 305 – Protect and promote children's rights in your handbook. Under the unit title you will see the words 'Elements of Competence'. Under this heading you will see:

CCLD 305.1 Support equality of access.

CCLD 305.2 Implement strategies, policies, procedures and practice for inclusion.

CCLD 305.3 Maintain and follow policies and procedures for protecting and safeguarding children.

This shows that the Unit CCLD 305 has three elements, each one describing a different feature of protecting and promoting children's rights.

The number of elements in each unit will vary, but each element will relate to the work that you do with children, and many of the everyday activities that you do will provide the evidence that you need.

Each element is broken down into performance criteria, in other words, what you actually have to do in order to achieve

'As a childminder, I do not have any minded children over the age of 11 years, so all my observations and evidence were based around younger children. However, I went on a two day course, provided by a local workforce development team, on children's development for eight to 16 years. I was able to use the knowledge gained from this course to show my assessor that I had knowledge and understanding of the full age range. I included the attendance certificate from the course in my portfolio as part of my evidence.'

NVQ candidate

the element, and eventually the whole unit. The number of performance criteria, or PCs as they are often referred to, varies in each element; sometimes there can be five, in others there may be seven or eight.

Let's look at PCs in more detail.

- In your candidate handbook find the Unit CCLD 302, Develop and maintain a healthy, safe and secure environment for children.

- Now find the element CCLD 302.2, Maintain a healthy, safe and secure environment for children.

- Under the list of performance criteria find 7, **Contribute to safety on outings, according to your role and responsibility**.

Let's break this PC down.

- Contribute to means being involved with or having a part in something, so think about an outing that you have been involved with recently.

- What did you actually do to make sure that the children were safe?

- Maybe you organised the children into small groups with a named adult.

- Or maybe you made sure that every child had a safety wrist strap.

- Or maybe you visited the place for the outing beforehand and did a risk assessment.

- Or maybe you made sure that each adult on the visit had a list of emergency contact details for each child in their group.

- Or maybe you made sure that the children held hands at certain points on the outing.

- **Safety on outings** – safety is about well-being and security of children, in this case specifically when they are not in their usual setting - an outing. An outing can be a whole day out involving coaches or public transport, a trip to the park, shops or library where children walk along the road. So what did you do to keep the children safe when they were out of the normal setting?

- **According to your role and responsibility** – you may have had the responsibility for organising the entire outing; on the other hand you may not have such responsibility, but could have had charge of a group of children. In the first case you may very well have done a risk assessment, written letters to parents and carers, organised the children into small groups and made sure that the adult leaders of each group have a list of emergency contact details. In the second instance you may have been responsible for making sure that the children in your group held hands or had wrist safety straps. What you actually did does not really matter; what the PC states is that it is according to your role and responsibility, so you have to have evidence of what you did.

You might have photographs (with written parental permission) of the children wearing wrist safety straps, which you could use as part of a reflective account. You could have minutes of meetings when the outing was discussed and decisions made about the organisation. Both of these can be used as evidence so show that you have met this particular PC.

At first some PCs may seem very complicated and difficult to understand. A common cry from NVQ candidates is 'What does it mean?' or 'What do I actually have to do?' If you break down the PC into bits, as we did with the example above, it will help to make it more understandable and will have the added bonus of making sure that you do not miss bits out.

'I really found working out what I was expected to do very difficult at first. I began to think that I wasn't good enough to do my NVQ and my self- confidence was beginning to suffer. One of the people at work showed me how to break down each PC into small bits and it suddenly all made sense. I understood what I had to do!'

NVQ candidate

Links to Key and Core skills

There are six Key and Core Skills which, like NVQs, are assessed at different levels. The key skills are:

- Working with others
- Communication
- Application of number
- Information Technology
- Improving own learning and performance
- Problem solving

Some people who are working towards their NVQ are also undertaking an apprenticeship with an employer; this usually applies to people under 25. These people take Key Skills awards as well as their NVQ. It is very possible that in the process of gathering evidence for the NVQ portfolio, evidence can also be gained for the various key skills. If you look in your handbook at any CCLD unit you will see a section headed 'Links to Key and Core Skills' which shows where there may be opportunities to gain evidence.

If you are not sure if you should be gathering evidence for Key and Core Skills, talk to your assessor.

What is an assessment centre and who's who?

When you decide to do an NVQ you will need to contact an assessment centre. This centre can be part of a training organisation, such as a college of further education, a school, or a private company. The centre has to be registered with the awarding body for NVQs, such as C&G or CACHE; this means that the centre has satisfied the awarding body that it can meet the required standards and requirements. Before starting your NVQ it is usual for the assessment centre to interview you so that they can offer you the right level of NVQ, based on your experience and current skills. Your assessment centre should offer you an induction session, when the staff will explain what NVQs are all about and how the centre operates. Also at the induction session your centre will check if you have any particular assessment requirements, learning needs or disabilities and will make sure that you are given the support and resources you need.

Each assessment centre will have its own individual operating procedures, although they all work towards the same National Occupational Standards. This could mean that you might not have a completely independent choice of ways to gather evidence, or they may ask for your portfolio to be set out in a specific way. There is usually a very good reason for these ways of working, and if you are not sure what is expected, ask at the induction session. You should not be worried about asking questions at any stage of your NVQ. The assessment centre is there to help you, not to make life difficult. At the induction session you will probably meet your assessor and other important people who will help you throughout your NVQ.

What is an assessor?

This person is suitably experienced and qualified in children's care, learning and development. He will also have a recognised assessors' award. You, the candidate, will be allocated an assessor with whom you will work very closely and probably get to know well. Your assessor will help you plan your work and visit you in your work place to observe you working with children, their families and the other adults. Your assessor will sign the paperwork to show that you have collected sufficient evidence to meet the requirements of each unit. This paperwork is in your candidate handbook.

Your assessor will meet you regularly to discuss and plan how to obtain your evidence. He will give you feedback on evidence that has been assessed and may ask you specific questions to draw out more evidence.

What is an internal verifier?

This person is also suitably experienced and qualified in children's care, learning and development. He will also have an assessor's award. The internal verifier supports your assessor, samples and monitors assessment judgements made by him and also organises meetings of all the assessors in your centre to make sure that all the assessments made of different candidates are on an equal footing, are fair and at the same standard.

What is an external verifier?

This person is not employed by your assessment centre; he works for the awarding body and so can check that all assessments made in centres across the country are of the same standard. The external verifier will visit your centre, usually twice a year, and you may be asked to meet him and let him see your portfolio.

What is an expert witness?

This person is also suitably experienced and qualified in children's care, learning and development. He may or may not be employed at your assessment centre, but could be your line manager or an experienced colleague. Sometimes in your work with children and their families you will be involved in sensitive and confidential situations, and expert witnesses can be an important source of evidence. The assessment centre will know about this person and have details of his experience and qualifications. The centre will keep a copy of this person's signature in its records.

What is a centre co-ordinator?

This person is responsible for the day-to-day running of the centre and its administration and is the link to the awarding body. Sometimes the centre co-ordinator can also be an assessor or internal verifier.

What are the candidate's responsibilities?

You are the candidate while you are working on your NVQ and as such you have responsibilities towards your assessment centre, just as much as they have responsibilities to you. You

have the responsibility for keeping your candidate handbook safe, meeting deadlines set by your centre or assessor and building and developing your portfolio. You will also have to agree to work in line with the policies and procedures of the assessment centre.

How will I be assessed?

NVQs are different from other qualifications in that you do not take an examination at the end. You are assessed all the time as you progress through each unit. The ways in which you are assessed are linked to the different kinds of evidence that you provide to prove your competence. So you could be assessed while you play and interact with children, while you assess a child's development, on how you organise and plan activities or your day, on how you meet and greet parents and on the ways that you give them information about their child, in other words in every routine, working situation.

Usually you will have the same assessor while you are working on your NVQ, but there might be circumstances, such as illness or job changes, which may mean you have a different assessor. There are two forms of assessment:

1. Assessment of competence in practice - in other words, what you do, your skills and capabilities.
2. Assessment of knowledge and understanding - in other words, showing that you know why you do things.

If you do not think that you have been fairly assessed, for whatever reason, you should first contact your centre co-ordinator. Your centre will have a complaints procedure and you must follow this in the first instance. If you still feel that your assessment is unfair, then you should contact your awarding body. The details of how to contact the awarding body are in your handbook.

Holistic assessment

Holistic means to look at, or consider all aspects or parts of something. For example, holistic is often linked to medical treatments; if you have a headache and take an aspirin, you are treating the symptoms of the headache not the reasons for it. Therefore taking the aspirin is not holistic. On the other hand, if treatment considers the reasons for the headache, such as the condition of your eyes, stress levels, how tired you are and when you last had something to eat, this is holistic. So holistic assessment considers every aspect of what you do.

Your job can be broken down into various units, but it is not intended that you should be assessed unit by unit. When your assessor is observing you at work he will see lots of evidence that will relate to different units. All this evidence must be recorded and logged by your assessor. In this way your assessor will be able to see consistent evidence of your skills over a period of time. Every PC in every element in every unit must be met at least once. It is quite likely that each PC will be observed more than once. However, assessing holistically by observing you will help this happen naturally and will avoid contrived situations. Children are not automatons and cannot be coerced into having a temper tantrum, for example, just because your assessor needs to see how you deal with such a situation. If your assessor is assessing you holistically, such a situation will occur as part of the normal day-to-day routine and so will be recorded and logged accordingly.

Building a portfolio

A portfolio is an organised collection of pieces of evidence. Most candidates use a file as their portfolio. Your assessor will help you organise your file in a structured and logical way. Each assessment centre will have its own way of organising portfolios, but every piece of evidence must be numbered and logged against the standard it meets. Your portfolio will have evidence of your competence, your knowledge and your understanding.

Cross-referencing

During the holistic assessment process you will have pieces of evidence that may meet more than one standard or PC. You can use the same piece of evidence, provided it is numbered and logged for each standard or PC. This is called cross-referencing. For example, your assessor may observe you greeting children as they arrive at your setting (PC 301.1). As you do this, a child excitedly tells you about something that he saw on the way to the setting. You listen and respond to the child in a positive way (PC 301.2), and you communicate to the child's parent or carer appropriately (PC 301.4). The observation can then be cross-referenced to all three PCs, and also in some situations against knowledge statements.

'I started my NVQ some months ago and I know I was not very organised about putting evidence in my portfolio, or logging and numbering it. It reached the point where my assessor asked me for a piece of evidence and I couldn't find it and felt rather embarrassed. I sat down one Bank Holiday, it was raining, and spent the whole day organising my file. It took ages. I learnt my lesson though, and now log and number every piece of evidence as soon as I get it. My advice to any NVQ candidate is 'get organised and keep your portfolio up to date'.'

NVQ candidate

How do I gather evidence?

Everything that your assessor observes you doing will count as evidence. As you will see later on, there are different types of evidence and your portfolio should, ideally, include different types of evidence. The main way of gathering evidence will be through your assessor's observations, but sometimes in order to assess your knowledge, for example, your assessor may need to ask you questions, or you will do a case study. All this evidence needs to be collected in your portfolio, logged and numbered. For each piece of evidence your assessor will complete an evidence record. A copy of this can be found in your handbook; how to use this record will be discussed later.

What are the different types of evidence?

(including the key letters)? Look in your handbook at the second page of each unit. You will see the heading 'Key to Methods of Evidence Gathering'. Each type of evidence has a key letter which is used when logging your evidence. If you are not sure how to log evidence using a key letter, talk to your assessor.

Key letter A - Direct observation

Direct observations are made and recorded by your assessor. Holistic observations over a period of time by your assessor will be your main source of evidence. The observations will be of what you do, how you do it, your skills and how you show understanding and knowledge. Your assessor will write down what he has observed on an evidence record sheet and you will both sign it. You must keep this evidence record sheet in your portfolio. It is also possible that your assessor may take, with your permission and that of the parents and carers of any children involved, digital photographs to back up his direct observations of you.

Key letter B - Recorded oral and written questions

Your assessor may ask you questions to show evidence of your understanding and knowledge. These questions may be asked verbally and your answers written down at the time of the assessor's visit. Sometimes the assessor may write down the questions before the visit and give them to you to write the answers at a later date, followed by discussion of your answers. In your handbook you will find an evidence record sheet on which questions and answers can be recorded. This will be explained in more detail later. Again, this evidence record sheet must be logged and numbered and kept in your portfolio.

Key letter C - Witness testimony

Witnesses are people who may have been present in a particular situation, or people who can vouch for your consistency of practice. These people have a professional relationship with you, but are not on the assessment centre's list of expert witnesses. If you are working from home, for example, you could ask a parent or other professionals who visit you, such as a development support worker, to give you a witness testimony; you may have to explain about the National Standards and your NVQ before they do this.

A testimony or a statement from a witness needs to be signed and dated and should be factual, as opposed to emotional.

For example:

'I really enjoyed watching Katie tell a story and the children did too.'

This really says very little, whereas if the testimony had stated,

'Katie kept all the children's attention while reading a story. The children could see the pictures and Katie gave lots of opportunities for the children to talk about the story and pictures. She used effective questioning to check whether the children understood the story and could predict what might happen next',
we would have a very clear picture of this candidate's performance and a meaningful witness testimony.

Key letter D - Expert witness evidence

Expert witnesses are approved by your assessment centre and copies of their signatures are kept there. Expert witnesses usually provide evidence in the form of observations and can be used when it may not be appropriate for your assessor to be present, for example in a confidential and sensitive situation. Expert witnesses can also be used for their specialist knowledge when your assessor may need help in order to assess you. Expert witness evidence is normally only used for optional units.

Key letter E - Case studies, assignments or projects

Your assessor may occasionally ask you to provide one of the above things to supply additional evidence, if he does not feel able to observe sufficient evidence during a visit. Quite often this form of evidence can be used to show your knowledge and understanding, but you should make sure that you understand why you are doing it and what the intended outcome is. For example in Unit 304 – Reflect and develop practice, Element 2, PC 2 – 'Develop and negotiate a plan to develop your knowledge, skills and understanding further' could be presented as a written assignment.

Sometimes an assignment which you have recently completed for another Level 3 qualification can be used as evidence. For example, part of the assignment for Unit 3 of the Level 3 Diploma in Home-based Childcare asks for one strength and one area for development in your practice to be identified. If you have successfully achieved this, you could use this part of the assignment as evidence for Unit 304, Element 2, PC 1.

Key letter F - Reflective account

To be reflective means that you think about what you have done, how you did it, whether it worked and was successful and how, in the light of your experience, you might change it to make it more inclusive or more effective. You should also think about what you learned and how you could use this knowledge in the future. It may be that you and your assessor talk about something observed and, during the course of your discussion, you are reflective and cover the points above. However, you will need a permanent record of this discussion for your portfolio, so you write a reflective account. Sometimes it can be a good idea to write a reflective account of something that your assessor did not observe, for example, an unexpected event such as an accident, a child having a temper tantrum, or a query from a parent.

Being reflective, reviewing what you have done and what you have learnt is an important part of a Level 3 NVQ. It shows that you are professional and willing to develop your skills and learn. Remember everything that you do can be a learning experience and nothing is ever wasted.

Key letter G - Professional discussion

A professional discussion is focussed and often pre-planned. It can be used by your assessor to assess your knowledge and understanding and is always recorded, either in writing at the time or with a tape recorder. You should be well prepared for a professional discussion, so that you remain focussed and understand why you are having the discussion and what the outcome will be. This evidence will need to be recorded, logged and numbered in the same way as all other forms of evidence.

Key letter H - Work products

Work products can be anything that you have produced, so work plans, displays, policies and procedures from your setting, photographs of children's work, children's observations and assessments, information leaflets and letters to parents can be used. Remember confidentiality must be maintained at all times, so photographs should not identify children and it is not good practice to use audio-visual records for the same reason.
It is good practice to include a short written piece to explain more about the work product. For example if you include a policy, write about how you have been involved in preparing and developing it and how you implement the policy in your everyday work. In the same way, if you include a curriculum plan write about how you are involved in the planning and implementation of the activities, be reflective, evaluate the plan and comment on what the children gained from the plans. You can include photographs of yourself carrying out some of the activities. Remember, if you are planning to use something from your workplace as evidence, such as policy or plans, if appropriate you should check with your line manager or employer before you include it in your portfolio.

Key letter I - Simulation

Simulation does not happen very often and can only be used where it is clearly indicated in the evidence requirements, and then only if no evidence naturally occurs through observation. If simulation does have to be used, it must be as realistic as possible and needs to be carefully planned between you and your assessor. For example if you have no contact with babies and never make up formula feeds, your assessor could observe you doing this in a contrived situation; you could use role-play to demonstrate how you could handle a difficult situation, for example with a parent, which it would be inappropriate to observe.

Key letter J - Experience from prior experience and learning

You may have a lot of experience and perhaps relevant qualifications when you begin your NVQ. You can use these as evidence for your portfolio. Your assessment centre will take you through a process called accreditation of prior learning (APL) or accreditation of prior achievement (APA). For such evidence to be used, you will have to prove that it is all your own work and that the information is relevant and up-to-date. For example, if you have an NNEB from before 1989, when the first Children Act became law, it is unlikely that your assessor would allow an APA or APL for this qualification, as it would not have taken into consideration current legislation on anti-discriminatory practice, child protection, rights of children and their families.

'We had a one-year-old baby starting at nursery and I was made his key person. I had responsibility for settling him and liaising with his parents. My assessor suggested that we had a professional discussion about settling this baby and attachment theory. She gave me a list of points to consider and research. We agreed to have the discussion in three weeks, so I had plenty of time to prepare. We agreed to tape our discussion, which I found very useful, although I felt I bit nervous at the start, as I really could prove to my assessor what I knew and how this knowledge related to my work. My assessor gave me a written copy of the tape for my portfolio at our next meeting.'

NVQ candidate

This type of evidence can also be used when it would be inappropriate for your assessor to carry out direct observations, for example in the case of a child's disclosure of abuse.

How do I complete the paperwork?

Copies of important recording forms can be found in your candidate handbook and can be photocopied as required. However, your assessment centre may decide not to use the forms from the candidate handbook and may have devised their own. All NVQ paperwork should be completed in ink, not pencil, and correction fluids must not be used. If a mistake is made, it should be just clearly crossed out and the correct information rewritten.

Your paperwork should be completed as the evidence is gathered and only assessed evidence should be recorded. Assessed evidence is that which your assessor, not you, has decided what it proves. Paperwork should be signed and dated by your assessor and you.

Your assessment centre has to keep copies of the assessment plans and assessor feedback forms for three years to provide evidence that the assessment process has taken place and that it was fair, safe, valid and reliable.

What is an assessment plan?

When you meet your assessor in the early stages you will need to draw up an assessment plan, an example of one such plan is included. It is a good idea, for your first unit, to work with your assessor to complete this plan. As you get more confident you may wish to do it on your own. There are two ways that you can plan your assessment:

1. You can consider each element separately and plan an activity which your assessor can observe, and include other evidence that you need for that element.

OR

2. You can plan a whole session which will cover a range of activities and so provide evidence for more than one element or PC or unit. This is holistic assessment (see page 11) and is recommended because it is more effective use of both your and the assessor's time.

A copy of an Assessment plan is given at the end of this chapter. This form will be used to record the evidence for your portfolio, and is not a mandatory form, but is still very useful in keeping track of the evidence. One of the benefits is that it allows to you see at a glance the different forms of evidence that you have gathered.

Why is the assessor's feedback to the candidate important?

Feedback between you and your assessor is the opportunity to review your assessment plan and the judgements that your assessor has made. It provides you with an opportunity to discuss ways in which you can improve your skills or, if you are judged to be competent, what the next steps are for you to progress further. The feedback should be focussed and relate to your assessment plan. You can ask questions, but a feedback session should not become a professional discussion or an oral questioning session.

What is a witness status list?

This is a list of other professionals who you may ask to provide evidence for your portfolio. This is an on-going list that you build up as you progress through your NVQ.

On the list you need to include:

• full names
• contact numbers
• whether they have an assessor's qualification
• what their professional relationship is to you
• which units, elements or PCs they have witnessed
• their signature
• the date of their evidence.

Unit assessment records (UARs) and Unit signature sheet (USS)

Each unit, both mandatory and optional, must have a UAR/USS. This form must be completed in ink and correction fluids should not be used. It is completed by both you, the candidate, and your assessor when you have successfully completed a unit. You keep the original in your portfolio and a copy is held in your assessment centre. This form is not valid unless both of you have signed and dated it.

If your assessor is asked to show part of your portfolio to an internal verifier to make sure that the assessment judgments are fair, valid and consistent; the internal verifier will also sign the UAR/USS.

One of the keys to successfully building your portfolio is to be organised with your paperwork. You are probably a busy person with both work and personal commitments and it is easy to forget to do something when you are working hard. It is good practice to get into the habit of keeping an NVQ diary, in which you make a note of important events, such as an assessor's visit, when you have to prepare for a professional discussion, or plan answers to questions that have been set by your assessor. A diary can also be invaluable in recording unplanned and unexpected incidents which happen in your setting. You can briefly record the date, time, who was involved, what happened and what you did. Later you can use this diary entry to help you put together a reflective account (Key letter F) which you present to your assessor as evidence for your portfolio.

What do the keywords and concepts mean?

As mentioned earlier in this introduction, each profession seems to have its own technical jargon and language; often there are lots of abbreviations and groups of letters which, to an outsider, can seem almost incomprehensible, for example CCLD, PC, UAR/USS. In your handbook you will find a list of key words and concepts relating to each mandatory unit at the start of each unit. You may be familiar with many of these words, but sometimes to relate to the National Standards they may be used in a particular way. It is important that you make sure that you understand what the key words and concepts mean in relation to each unit in your NVQ. A full list is provided at the end of each chapter relating to each unit, where appropriate.

'I really appreciate our feedback sessions after an observation session. My assessor sees things in the centre that I am not always aware of. For example I was not aware of a situation developing between two children until one started shouting. I realise that I was focussed on the children in the book corner, and should have been more aware of other children. Without the feedback session I would not have known that this is an area I need to develop.'

NVQ candidate

ASSESSMENT PLAN

Award CCLD (L3)   **Date** 01.10.06

Candidate's Name A. Candidate   **Candidate's PIN** 06/12345

Assessor's Name T. Assessor

Evidence Type Achieved	Date of Assessment	Date
Direct observation in day nursery Between 10:30 am and 1:00 pm (A)	01.11.06	Yes 01.11.06
Work products (H)	01.11.06	Yes 01.11.06

Arrangements for giving feedback and dates:

Orally after direct observation, 01.11.06
Written feedback 15.11.06

Units that may be covered for performance criteria, knowledge and scope:

301.1   PCs 1,2,3,4,5,6,7
301.2   PCs 1,2,3,4,5
301.3   PCs 1,2
302.2   PCs 1,2,3,4,5,6
304.1   PCs 1,2,3,4
306.2   PCs 1,2,4,5

Review of assessment plan   **Date:** 05.01.07

Agreement box

Assessment plan discussed and agreed

Candidate's signature: A. Candidate   **Date:** 15.11.06
Assessor's signature: T. Assessor   **Date:** 15.11.06

Chapter 2

CCLD 301, Develop and promote positive relationships

About this unit

This is a mandatory unit and looks at how you can promote and develop relationships with children and their families, an essential aspect of your work. Positive relationships, which foster mutual respect, create environments in which children can thrive. It is important that you fully understand the importance of positive relationships. This underpins much of your work and can be fundamental in helping children reach their full potential. Many of the activities that you carry out on a daily basis will provide evidence for this unit, and may also be cross- referenced to other units.

Everyone benefits from good, positive relationships: children, parents, you and your colleagues. Good relationships can create a welcoming and emotionally secure atmosphere for children where they feel valued and can flourish. If relationships in your setting are good with the parents and carers, they in turn will feel more able to share information with you and take a greater interest in the activities and experiences of their children. This will also benefit the children as you will be more able to meet their needs. Parents are the first educators of their children and know their child better than anyone else, so the more information that you can both share, the better the experiences of the child in the long run. Positive relationships within your staff teams and setting will lead to more job satisfaction and enjoyment of work. Another bonus is that in times of stress or difficulties adults are more supportive of each other where relationships are good.

As with all units, you will have to show and provide evidence that you are a reflective practitioner. Look in the resources section of Unit 304 for 'What makes a reflective practitioner?'. Reading this article will help you understand more about reflective practice and how it can improve the care and services that you offer to children and young people.

In relation to this unit, a reflective practitioner is someone who is able to evaluate their own attitudes and practice in connection with building relationships. This will involve asking yourself questions all the time, such as:

- 'What is the aim, or the main point of what I am doing?'
- 'How am I promoting positive relationships?'
- 'What are the children gaining from this?'
- 'Am I a good role model for promoting positive relationships?'
- 'Are the children's needs being met?'
- 'How could I do this better?'
- 'Would something else be better or more appropriate?'

You will have to show that you understand the limits of your responsibilities, and that you know when you need to refer to senior colleagues or other professionals who may be outside your setting. As with all units, the principles and values of this unit focus on the welfare of the child. This must be your main consideration in everything that you do in your work. You must be aware of good practice in relation to anti-discrimination and anti-bias and of how you meet individual needs. You must show how you respect and value children and their families with different values and beliefs and find ways of overcoming communication difficulties. You should be able to show that you are interested in everything about the child and his family. This is very important if you are to develop and sustain relationships. Children and adults can pick up the signals very quickly from a disinterested person and so will make less effort to communicate, which will have a direct impact on the quality of the relationship. You must understand how and why to keep information about children and their families confidential, why this shows respect and how it can help build relationships.

You may be already doing all of these very important things, but not recognising them and, more than likely, not using the language of the CCLD NVQ to describe what you are doing. As you read this chapter, you will become aware that many of the unit elements and PCs you are covering will help this become clearer, as will the list of suggested activities. The knowledge specifications must also have evidence to show your understanding; again this may come about through direct observations by your assessor and also by other forms of evidence, which will be explained as they occur.

This unit has four elements of competence and you must have evidence for all these elements in your portfolio. The elements are:

- CCLD 301.1 Develop relationships with children
- CCLD 301.2 Communicate with children
- CCLD 301.3 Support children in developing relationships
- CCLD 301.4 Communicate with adults.

Each one of the elements will be discussed in turn, together with suggested ways of collecting and recording your evidence. At the end you will find the resource section, plus a list of suggested further reading material.

CCLD 301.1 Develop relationships with children

Getting started

As you progress through this element, you will realise that your relationships with children are very important and underpin

TIP:

It is important, as well as being good practice, to read through the performance criteria before you begin to collect your evidence. Try to break each one down as discussed in Chapter 1. Make sure that you understand what you have to do and how you can collect the evidence. Ask your assessor if you are not sure.

It is a good idea to read through the knowledge specifications for the entire unit. These are printed in your handbook at the end of each unit. You will need to show that you know and understand the information in each specification and can show how you can apply and use that knowledge in your work place. Some of the knowledge specifications may require you to do some personal research and reading; have a look at the end of this chapter for suggested further reading, which you may find helpful.

Think about ways in which you can show your evidence of the knowledge specifications to your assessor. You may be able to include this on your assessment plan, but if this the first unit that you are doing, don't try to attempt too much on your plan. Keep it simple initially and then you will be better placed to achieve.

TIP:

Try to link the knowledge specifications to each PC or element. Mark them in your handbook. Doing this may help you to avoid repetition and make cross- referencing easier. For example:

CCLD 301.1.7	K3M158
CCLD 301.1.2	K3C160
CCLD 301.1.1	K3D161
CCLD 301.3.4	K3D179
CCLD 301.4.6	K3C186

Don't forget that you need evidence for each knowledge specification.

TIP:

When completing your first personal skills audit, try to focus specifically on the PCs relating to the element. In other words, in this case think and reflect on your relationships with children. As you become more confident, you may be able to complete a personal skills audit that covers several elements.

everything that you do with them. However, relationships will change as children grow and develop. You would not expect to have the same type of relationship with a one-year-old as you would have with a nine-year-old, as they have different needs. Similarly, how you develop and promote these relationships will be different depending on the age of the child. However, whatever the age of the child, your relationship with him will be built on trust and respect and the belief that the child's needs will be met.

This element has seven performance criteria (PCs) and you must provide evidence for all of them. In this unit you are aiming to show that you can:

- interact with children in a way that makes them feel welcome and valued.
- adapt your behaviour to the age, needs and abilities of individual children.
- negotiate with children about their needs and preferences and involve them in decision-making as appropriate to their stage of development.
- apply inclusive and anti-discriminatory practice in your relationships with children.
- make sure that your behaviour with children is appropriate at all times.
- give attention to individual children in a way that is fair to them and the group as a whole.
- respect confidential information about children, as long as this does not affect their welfare.

At this point, before you actually begin to collect any evidence, it would be useful to complete a personal skills audit. Sometimes this can be called a SWOT analysis, where you identify your strengths, weaknesses, opportunities and threats, but essentially it is the same thing. Both are very helpful to identify what you know you are already doing well, your strengths and areas that you know need to developed or worked on, your weaknesses. This will also help you become a reflective practitioner. An example of a personal skills audit is given over the page

You may feel confident enough about your strengths to start planning your assessment using the assessment plan discussed in Chapter 1. If possible, plan with your assessor initially until you feel confident about planning independently. Although you can plan your evidence for assessment for each PC separately, (initially this may help you understand what you have to do and may well be easier for you), it is better to try to plan for the whole element, in this case CCLD 301.1. You will then find it easier to cross-reference and will avoid repeating yourself.

Key Issues

In many instances, how you develop relationships with children may not be through planned activities but through the routine events and activities of the day, for example how you meet and greet children at the start of the session (CCLD 301.1.1). You must be aware of these experiences as you work your way through the NVQ.

Developing relationships with children is the basis for effective practice in all areas of your work. Children who feel valued by you and furthermore, enjoy your company and want to be with you, will respond more positively. How you develop these relationships

PERSONAL SKILLS AUDIT

Unit No _____

Element No _____

Date completed _____

1. **My strengths, things that I feel confident I can already do.**
   _____
   _____
   _____

2. **My weaknesses, things that I do not feel confident about.**
   _____
   _____
   _____

3. **Things that I do not understand, from the knowledge specifications or PCs.**
   _____
   _____
   _____

4. **Possible activities my assessor could observe.**
   _____
   _____
   _____

5. **Types of evidence that I could provide.**
   _____
   _____
   _____

6. **Things that I don't have the opportunity to do at the present time.**
   _____
   _____
   _____

7. **Things that I have done in the past that may be relevant.**
   _____
   _____
   _____

8. **What I am going to do about my weaknesses (with date for completion).**
   _____
   _____
   _____

9. **What I am going to do about the things that I do not understand (with date for completion).**
   _____
   _____
   _____

10. **What I am going to do about things that I may not have the opportunity to do (with date for completion).**
    _____
    _____
    _____

and the strategies you use will depend on the age of the child or young person. Developing relationships with babies is absolutely essential to their well-being and should be different from the strategies you would use to develop a relationship with an older child. Look in the resource section about developing attachments and the key person approach. Look also in 'Birth to Three Matters' especially the aspect 'A strong child', which places great emphasis on relationships with special caring people.

Your relationships with all children should be friendly and positive, but you must remember that you are not a member of the child's family; you are a professional and must remain so at all times. When talking to children you should not be childish or patronising, but your language should be appropriate to their needs and age and stage of development.

Suggested activities and experiences

There are activities that you can do, and you are probably doing some already, to help you provide evidence for this element, such as:

- Holding and cuddling a baby can help him feel wanted and reassured. Physical contact is important for babies and although they do need to play on the floor, or on a play mat, they should not be left untouched for long periods of time.
- Use care routines, such as feeding and nappy changing, to provide opportunities for eye contact, cuddles and lots of responses to the cues, such as smiles, babbling or cries of the baby. There is lovely sequence on the Birth to Three video where a practitioner is changing a small boy's nappy. It's clear that she uses this routine event to develop their relationship. Have another look at it and try to relate it to your practice if you work with this age group.
- Sing songs and rhymes with repeated actions to provide opportunities for a baby or young child to respond to you.
- Respond quickly and positively to a child's attempts to make contact with you, such as when they tap you or point at something. It is important that children have responsive adults caring for them; smiles, eye contact and touch can be more easily processed by young children and so help them feel relaxed and comfortable with you.
- Use a child's name when meeting and greeting them at the start of a session and, if appropriate, get down, perhaps on your knees, to the child's level so that you can have good eye contact. Ask him how he is feeling, or what he would like to do. Show genuine interest in his responses.
- Give children time to respond to you, especially when offering choices. Don't rush them or start offering suggestions as this can cause confusion, especially to young children. Children may respond with something that they think you want them to do or choose, not what they really want; so have their needs been met?
- Give children real choices, such as where they sit at the lunch table, a choice of foods and drinks, which activities or resources they use and where they can play with them or when they want to play outside.
- Use circle time for children to talk about things that are important to them; this can help the adult find out more about the child and so provide opportunities to develop relationships. Circle time should be a positive experience and an opportunity for adults and children to listen to each other. Remember that it can be difficult for young children to sit and listen for long periods of time and also some children may not be confident enough to speak in a large group. Plan your circle time carefully to make sure that you meet the needs of the children.

- Be a play partner and become involved in play activities, share experiences, listen and value the children's views. Show pleasure and enjoyment in what the children are doing and acknowledge their strengths and the things that they do well, no matter how small. Comments such as, 'You are looking very happy', 'You are listening very carefully', 'You are being a really good friend today', will help children feel valued and so promote positive relationships
- Involve children in activities that you are doing, such as putting up a display, preparing a snack, or domestic activities like shopping. Invite and value their suggestions and ideas. Older children can be involved in committees or councils where their views and suggestions can be heard and respected. Encourage older children to develop their own views and opinions and let them know that you are interested in and appreciate them.
- Give children responsibility for organising activities, their play areas, and their environment. Even young children can have a say in what they play with – we call it free play.
- Offer reassurance and approval unconditionally at all times so that children learn that they are valued all of the time and not only if they are achieving or pleasing an adult.
- Provide spaces of which children can have ownership, for example a small bag or box that contains toys or items for one particular child, such as a special toy when having a nappy change, or a named tray or peg. Encourage older children to have responsibility for the activities that they do in an after school club, where the activities take place and what resources are needed.
- Plan and provide activities which encourage children to express themselves in different ways, such as dance, music, painting, modelling. These activities do not have to have an 'outcome' as such but can be open-ended so that the children can express their individuality. These types of activities can also be completely spontaneous, unplanned and child-initiated.

- Make sure that children's records and information about them is not left lying around your setting. It must be securely stored and kept confidential. Don't engage in conversations about the children in earshot of others, don't gossip or talk inappropriately about children. Remember it is a good idea to regard all information about children and their families as confidential and as such it should not leave your setting. It could be argued that completing a child's record on the bus or train on your way home is technically a breach of confidentiality.

Types of evidence

Most of the suggested activities and therefore this element, can be assessed through **direct observation (Key letter A)** by your assessor. He will complete an evidence record sheet (this is in your handbook) of what he has seen. You will need to plan your assessment, using an assessment plan (see Chapter 1 and your handbook) and identify good times for direct observation to take place. For example, if you use circle time to develop relationships and this happens around 9.45 am each morning, your assessor needs to know to get to your setting before you and the children begin circle time. If the play scheme council meets at 4:45pm your assessor needs to know. This is a small but very important point.

It is possible that in order to assess that you understand how to adapt your behaviour to different ages (PC 2) your assessor may ask you **oral and written questions (Key Letter B)**. This is likely to occur when you are working with one age group and do not have the opportunity to work with a range of ages.

TIP:

You must remember to maintain confidentiality at all times. It is good practice to either give the child a false name or call them by a letter, such as Child A. Also, if your assessor uses digital photographs make sure that confidentiality is not breached.

Your assessor will also ask you questions to check your knowledge and link both the questions and answers to the knowledge specifications, for example 'K3C155 Relevant legal requirements covering the way you relate to and interact with children'. Evidence for this knowledge specification may be assessed through written questions which your assessor gives you beforehand so that you can write your answers in your own time. In this example you may have to read and research before you can complete your answers. Look at the end of this chapter for suggested further reading.

Your assessor will write down your answers to any oral questions that are asked, usually on an evidence record sheet from your handbook or oral questioning record sheet. This sheet will be given to you to keep in your portfolio. Don't forget to number or log it clearly and put it in the right place in your portfolio, as it may be able to be used to provide evidence for other PCs, In other words, cross- referenced. Each assessment centre will have its own record sheets, but all will record essentially the same information.

It may be that you would find it useful to undertake **a case study (Key letter E)**, of one particular child. For example you may have a new child in your setting and you could record how your

'My assessor and I spent a long time when I started my NVQ filling out an assessment plan. One of the activities, tidying up equipment, would have provided lots of opportunities for direct observation, but I forgot to put times on my assessment plan. We tidied up in the middle of the session, but the assessor assumed it was at the end of the session and so arrived when we had done it. I didn't make the same mistake again.'

NVQ candidate

relationship with this child develops over a period of time. What you do to build the relationship and the reactions and interactions of the child with you? Look in the resource section for the article 'Helping new children to settle.'

You may also want to include **observations (Key letter E)** in your case study to provide more specific detail and evidence, for example when children are discussing and negotiating issues that are important to them. Suggestions on how to observe children will be discussed in more detail in Chapter 4 CCLD 303, element 303.1.

This element could lend itself well to **reflective accounts (Key Letter F)**. You may, for example, have engaged children in negotiating about something that perhaps wasn't planned (PC3). You could write about how the situation arose, what you did, how you encouraged the children to negotiate, what your role was, what was the outcome, whether the children's needs were met and how you could have changed, improved or developed the situation.

It is quite likely that a reflective account, such as the one outlined above, could lead to a **professional discussion (Key Letter G)** with your assessor, to extend the information from the reflective account and probably cover other PCs and or elements.

> **TIP:**
>
> Don't forget to cross-reference evidence wherever you can to avoid repetition. Ask you assessor if you are not sure how to do this. For example, your reflective account could perhaps provide evidence for K3D163, K3C171, and K3D179.

CCLD 301.2 Communicate with children

Getting started

Building relationships, developing negotiating skills and allowing children to make choices all require good communication skills. You should take every opportunity to talk, listen and interact with children. The way you talk and respond, either verbally or non-verbally (body language, gestures and facial expression), will help show that you respect and value the children and so develop your relationships. Look in the resources section to see how you can improve your listening skills.

This element has five PCs and you will need to provide evidence for all of them. You will need to have evidence to show that you:

- communicate with children in a way that is appropriate to their ages, needs and abilities.
- listen to children and respond to them in a way that shows that you value what they say and feel.
- ask questions, clarify and confirm points.
- encourage children to ask questions, offer ideas and make suggestions.

- recognise when there are communication difficulties and adapt the way you communicate accordingly.

You will also need to complete an assessment plan. Remember to talk with your assessor about your plan. Try to cross-reference some of the PCs to other elements or even other units. For example, you may have evidence for PC1 that could also be used to support K3D221.10, K3D218.19, knowledge specifications for CCLD 303.4.

> **TIP:**
>
> As with the first PC described in this chapter, it may be a good idea to complete another personal skills audit, but this time focussing on your communication skills. On the other hand, you could add to and develop the first one.

Communication with children is not just about spoken language, but includes the ways that you listen, your body language, gestures and facial expressions. Communication is a two-way process. There has to be a giver and a receiver and both have to be active and involved in order for the communication process to be effective. It is important that you take every opportunity to talk with and listen to children, in all activities and routines in which they are involved. Effective communication takes time and effort and should not be rushed. Look in the resource section for the article on 'What is communication?'.

Sometimes we say one thing but mean another, for example, 'It is not a good idea to get that game or toy out now as it will soon be time to go home', what we actually mean, but do not say, is 'Please can you start to tidy up'. These mixed messages and unclear statements can cause confusion, especially for younger children, who may not yet have the cognitive skills to interpret what is really being said. This will have a direct impact on how children develop relationships. It can be very difficult to even start to develop a relationship if you cannot communicate effectively with another individual. Children who are not fluent or confident in the language being used or who have language delay may experience similar confusion and difficulty.

Key Issues

Clear communication with children that takes into account their ages, stages of development, abilities and needs is a fundamental aspect of developing relationships. Babies establish relationships in the early stages by responding to their environment through their senses, in that they recognise the smell of their primary carer, or the sound of their voice. Young babies use smiles and cries to communicate rather than words. Young children use gestures and body language to complement or expand their spoken words. Look in the resource section for the article on how children can communicate without words. Also look in the Birth to Three Framework at the aspect 'A Skilful Communicator' for more information on how to communicate effectively with babies and young children. Older children need adults who will communicate with them sensitively showing respect for their growing need for independence, people who will listen without being judgmental or dismissive (CCLD 301.2.1).

Think about the vocabulary that you use when communicating to children; phrases such as 'hang on' or 'just a minute' may not always be clear in meaning and some children may not understand what you have in mind. In the same way, sentences which contain several different ideas can be difficult for some children to understand. For example, 'When you have finished playing with that toy, please go and wash your hands, then get your coat so we can go outside'. All professions have professional jargon which may be well understood by adults within the sector, but this is not necessarily true for children. Imagine the scenario where a four-year-old asks you what you are doing and you reply, 'I'm just doing an ob on your KUW.' Not as far fetched as it may at first appear.

When we listen, we are doing much more that just hearing the sounds that the other person has made. We think about what the person has said and so make our response. We should give the other person our full attention, in other words we must actively listen to children and young people. All children need to be listened to by someone that they can talk to; older children especially need caring adults who will actively listen to them and when this does not happen they will often complain that 'no one understands me'. Children learn to listen from adults who are actively listening to them, so make sure that you are a positive role model at all times. See the resource section for the articles about listening and in particular 'Helping children to learn to listen' (CCLD 301.2.2).

There will be times when we can expand and develop a child's attempts at communication and at the same time acknowledge what they have said in a positive way. For example, a young child may say 'I dunned it,' and you could respond with 'That's great that you have done that. Where shall we put it now?' Not only does this acknowledge what the child has said, but it makes him feel an active partner in the communication process. Asking appropriate questions can show a child that you have listened to what he has to say, that you value and respect his contribution and that you are interested in his views and ideas. Asking questions also helps you to fully understand what the child means and so aids communication and reduces the risk of misunderstandings (CCLD 301.2.3).

Suggested activities and experiences
- Make sure that when you are talking with children you make good eye contact, but do not make this intimidating; some children may avoid communication with you which will affect your relationship with them.
- Make sure that spoken sentences are focussed and to the point. Avoid long rambling sentences. Children will either forget what you are saying or may lose interest.
- Ask questions which provide opportunities for children to show that they understand what is intended. These do not have do be interrogating or intimidating, but ask them in way that children can respond to confidently.
- Provide unpressured opportunities when children can practise their communication skills, for example share routine events such as wiping tables, preparing snacks or washing equipment, when children can work alongside an adult in a relaxed and unhurried way.
- Ask open-ended questions, that is those which don't have just a yes or no answer, to show children that you are interested in what they are doing, and in their ideas and views. Use questions that

begin with phrases such as 'Can you tell me about…?', 'What do you think will happen next?', 'How can we make this happen?'
- Don't interrupt children and do not allow other children to interrupt someone who is talking. It can give the impression that what you have to say is more important than the child who is talking.
- Play stop and go games. Play music and ask the children to stop moving when the movement stops.
- Play listening lotto games, where children have to listen attentively to sounds form a tape or CD and match the sounds to pictures.
- Supplement what you say with visual clues; this can be especially important for a child whose home language is not the same as the setting. Puppets, photographs, gestures, signs and symbols can all be very beneficial. Many settings put pictures of individual toys or equipment on the trays or boxes in which they are stored as well as written words. Look in the resource section for the article on resources to support communication language and literacy.
- 'Makaton' is a visual method of communication which can help children understand the meaning of the spoken word. It may be a good idea to ask your local children's and young person's workforce team if there are any training opportunities for learning Makaton. Look in the resource section for the article 'Promoting inclusion for children with communication difficulties'.
- Remember that children with hearing difficulties may respond and communicate more effectively if they are in an area that is free from distracting background noises.
- Giving children responsibilities such as handing round snacks or pouring drinks for each other helps children understand about the 'give and take' process of communication. Such situations should be non-threatening and of course achievable for the child concerned.
- Make sure that you recognise and acknowledge when children are being co-operative. This will help to build their self esteem, and children who feel good about themselves are more likely to accept and enjoy being with others.
- Encourage older children to be part of a team that is constructive not competitive, that is inclusive not exclusive. Make sure that they are aware that they are valued for their role within the team or group, regardless of what that role is.
- Take every opportunity to encourage interaction with children. Make each activity more meaningful by your own enthusiasm and positive attitude. For example, when singing songs do the actions in a dramatic way. This will help children to join in, communicate and interact with others.

Types of evidence
As with the previous element, much of CCLD301.2 can be assessed through **direct observation (Key letter A)** by your assessor. Make sure that your assessment plan clearly shows what you are planning to do and how this may provide opportunities and evidence.

Think about **making work products (Key letter H)** such as puppets, signs and symbols to extend children's communication skills. Your work product could be supplemented by a written account or reflective account (Key letter F) as to how the work product was used by the children and how successfully it met the intended aim.

A professional discussion (Key letter G) with your assessor on, for example, ways that you encourage children to ask questions, offer ideas and make suggestions (PC 4 CCLD 301.2), could provide evidence for some of the knowledge specifications such as K3D163, K3D164, K3C169.

You may want to make a recording, either audio or video, of you communicating with children to use as evidence. If you decide to do this, make sure that you do have written permission from the parents or carers to record their child and that you maintain confidentiality at all times. You may find it useful to make a transcript of the tape if you want to use it as evidence. It could be used as part of **a reflective account (Key letter F).**

Don't forget to check whether, in providing the evidence for this element and the one before, you have provided for some of the other elements, for example 'CCLD 303.3 Plan provision to promote development'. Make sure that you cross- reference at every opportunity.

CCLD 301.3 Support children in developing relationships

Getting started

The emphasis in this element is on ways to support the children with whom you work. Supporting children is about providing and facilitating opportunities and experiences that encourage, help and assist development. All children need help and support in developing relationships, not just with their peers, but with children of all ages and adults. This is a very gradual process and is dependent on many factors, not least a child's own emotional development. If a child is emotionally secure and has good relationships with the adults who care for them, then they are more likely to be able to understand the feelings and needs of others. All children are unique, and how you support them in this important aspect of their development will depend upon their individual needs.

Children, just like you, do need to understand how to build relationships with others. Children need to understand that not everyone will agree with their views and there will be times when disagreements could lead to hurt feelings and conflicts. They need help and support to deal with such situations. This element has five PCs and you will need evidence to show that you:

- support children in developing agreements about ways of behaving, according to the requirements of the setting or service.
- support children in understanding other people's feelings.
- support children who have been upset by others.
- encourage and support children to sort out conflict for themselves, according to their ages, needs and abilities.
- encourage and support other adults in the setting to have positive relationships with children.

Key Issues

In order to provide some evidence for the first PC you will have to make sure that you are very familiar with the behaviour policy of the setting in which you are working, or the service in which you work. Not only should you be familiar with the policy, but you should be confident about how it is implemented and put into practice. Policies should not just be documents that are full of good words, but they should be practical, meaningful and consistently followed by everyone involved in the setting or service, and that also includes the children (CCLD 301.3.1).

This first PC is not just about making sure that children are aware of what is right or wrong and fair play, or implementing a policy, although these are very important. It is also about helping children to understand the impact of their behaviour and their actions on others. Young children find this difficult, due to their levels of cognitive and language development. You may need to find small ways to support young children to understand the impact of their behaviour (see suggested activities and experiences, later on in this chapter).

For children to understand the feelings of others, they need to be aware of their own feelings and needs. Talking about feelings with children helps them to become more aware. Once children have some understanding of their own feelings, they will be more able to relate to others; for example, a four-year-old who says 'I don't want to play because I am feeling tired', is more likely to understand when you say to that child 'X doesn't want to play right now because he is feeling tired'. The four-year-old is less likely to feel rejected or not understand why the other child won't play. See the resource section for more information about children's feelings (CCLD 301.3.2).

Children get upset by others. It is a fact of life, and how children deal with that upset and the support that they need will be different for every child. You will also have to be aware of ways to support children who may have additional needs. For example, how would you support an autistic child, how could you support a child who is never included in a play activity? Think about the strategies you could use to support these children (CCLD 301.3.3).

Sometimes children get upset and this can lead to bigger disagreements and conflicts. Learning how to resolve conflicts and disagreements is an important skill that requires an understanding of negotiation, respecting the views of others and sometimes compromise. See the resource section for the article on what to do when children squabble.

Children who can deal with conflicts for themselves are more likely to be confident and have good self esteem. Knowing when and how to intervene and become involved in children's disagreements can be tricky and is a sensitive issue. You obviously need to become involved immediately if another child is being physically hurt or subjected to aggressive behaviour. The strategy that you use and at what stage you become involved will depend on the age of the children and their level of understanding (CCLD 301.3.4).

You are part of a team. Even if you are a home-based carer, there will be other people who you work with such as support workers or network co-ordinators. So as well as having a positive relationship with the children, it is important that you encourage the children to have good relationships with other adults. One of the main and most effective ways in which you will do this is by being a good role model, showing other people with whom you work respect, listening to and respecting their views, communicating with them clearly and

> **TIP:**
>
> There may well be many opportunities in this element for evidence to be cross- referenced to several other units, such as CCLD 304.

avoiding negative or judgmental comments (CCLD 301.3.5). Look at the article in the resource section on improving the way that you communicate.

Suggested activities and experiences

- Giving a child a small amount of responsibility such as handling round snacks can help them see that their behaviour benefits others. Also, helping to tidy away resources or equipment benefits everyone, perhaps because they can all spend longer doing the next activity. If one person were to do it alone, it would take longer and so not everyone would benefit.
- Acknowledge positive behaviour by looking for occasions when children are co-operating with others, respecting the behaviour boundaries and framework and commenting about the behaviour.
- Children become aware of the feelings of others by being able to recognise their own feelings. To do this, they need opportunities to talk about how they are feeling, again in a non-threatening way. With young children, pictures of faces displaying different emotions can be a helpful prop; older children need opportunities to talk in non-threatening or judgmental situations about how and why they feel the way that they do. Take your cues from the child and don't probe or pry.
- Older children will learn to listen to and respect other views if they are given challenges, such as organising an event like a celebration, a talent show, a competition, or choosing and ordering equipment. This provides opportunities for them to work together co-operatively and to listen to each other.
- Use circle time with younger children to talk about feelings and behaviour issues, the effects they have on others and how to understand others' feelings.
- Talk to children and acknowledge their feelings in a positive way; you could start a conversation with a child somewhere along the lines of 'you are feeling cross because you were left out of that game', and then discuss other ways of dealing with the situation.
- Think about using photographs as evidence in your portfolio, provided that you have written parental permission to do so and maintain the confidentiality of the child. These can be used to show incidences where a child acknowledges the feelings of another, for example when a child, of his own accord, puts an arm around another child to offer comfort or sympathy.
- When you intervene in children's disputes, make sure that you give children the opportunity to come up with suggestions themselves of ways to resolve conflicts and disagreements. You can do this by asking open ended questions, encouraging discussion and not imposing your solutions on the children.

Types of evidence

As before, **direct observations (Key letter A)** will be very important. Some of these PCs and elements of this unit can not really be planned. Realistically, you cannot plan for children to be upset or have a disagreement. It may well be that much of this evidence may not have been on your assessment plan, and will be gathered when your assessor is observing planned experiences and activities. This is classic cross-referencing and needs to be logged and recorded carefully as soon as possible after the assessment visit.

Your assessor may want to involve you in a **professional discussion (Key letter G)** to confirm that you understand the knowledge specifications, for example K3D162 is looking at your understanding of your settings behaviour policy and how it is implemented. This discussion could also cover part of several other knowledge specifications such as K3D167, K3C171, K3D176, K3D176, K3D177, K3D178, and K3D179.

Reflective accounts (Key letter F) may be useful ways for reflecting on how you supported children in developing relationships, looking at incidents when children have perhaps had a disagreements, resolved conflicts, acknowledged other feelings. Such experiences with children may also be recorded by **witness testimony (Key letter C)**, but make sure that your centre has the details of such people; include a signature otherwise their evidence may not be accepted as valid.

CCLD 301.4 Communicate with adults

Getting started

All practitioners work with or have contact with other adults at some point. This can of course depend on the work that you do. If you are a home-based child carer you may have contact with other professionals, apart from the children's parents, less frequently than someone who works in a SureStart Children's Centre and could be part of a multi-disciplinary team. Nevertheless, it is very important that your communication is effective and that children see adults who are co-operative and positive role models. Effective communication with adults limits opportunities for misunderstandings.

This element has six PCs and you need evidence to show that you:

- communicate with other adults politely and courteously and in a way that is appropriate to them.
- show respect for other adults' individuality, needs and preferences.
- respond to other adults' requests for information accurately within agreed boundaries of confidentiality.
- actively listen to other adults, asking questions and clarifying and confirming key points.
- recognise when there are communication difficulties and adapt the way you communicate accordingly.
- handle any disagreement with other adults in a way that will maintain a positive relationship.

Key Issues

Communicating in a polite way with others shows that you respect what they are saying and how they are saying it. Being polite is part of being professional; you can still be assertive and polite. Being polite does not mean that you have to be passive; differing views and opinions do not have to lead to disagreements. It is important to check on the views of others rather than jumping to conclusions. For example, some parents may not wish their child to join in a harvest thanksgiving, but may not object to the same child taking part in a charity fund-raising event.

How we address other adults is very important in building positive relationships. You should take time to find out how adults prefer to be addressed. For example, do not assume that all mothers of children in your care are married and are therefore 'Mrs.'. In the same way do not assume that is acceptable to call all adults by their first name (CCLD 301.4.1).

Appropriate communication for some parents can be by email or text, especially if they are very busy people. It is always good practice to check what you have put in the email or text before you hit the send button. Even though these methods can be effective, don't always use them to replace face to face communication.

Being polite and courteous does not mean that you have to agree with everything that another person says. Life would be very boring if we all had the same views. In the same way, think about how dull life would be if we all had the same lifestyles, interests and opinions. Recognising and respecting these individual differences is what anti-bias practice is about (CCLD 301.4.2 and also KS K3P159).

All information about children and their families should be treated as confidential and should not be disclosed to a third party, unless the welfare and well-being of the child is threatened. Parents will pass on and request information all the time in a variety of ways: face to face, telephone, email, texts, notes and letters. Regardless of the method of communication, it must be given the same level of importance, confidentiality and respect. This helps to build up trust and positive relationships between adults and in many cases the relationship deteriorates if that trust is broken. Settings should have a policy on confidentiality, and the procedures outlined in it should be followed at all times by both parents and practitioners (CCLD 301.2.3). Look in the resource section for the article on working with parents, 'Providing information and establishing trust'. This may help you show evidence of your understanding of the knowledge specifications, for example K3C181, K3C182, KC3183, K3C184 and K3C185.

Look in the resource section of this chapter for suggestions on improving your own communication skills, especially active listening. When talking with other adults, it is important to give them your full attention and try to maintain eye contact without staring. Remember, communication is a two-way process that requires both a giver and a receiver. Using open-ended questions can be a very effective way of clarifying points and gathering more information. If you don't understand what is being said, it is very important that you don't just carry on regardless, but stop and think. Jumping to conclusions and making assumptions that are not based on correct information and facts can be very damaging to relationships (CCLD 301.4.4).

It would be naive to think that we will never ever be in situations where there might be conflict or disagreements. What is important is that you think carefully about how or why such situations might arise and ways in which you can resolve the conflict. A useful starting point might be to think about what might cause such situations. Poor communication is often a cause of conflict, with misinterpretations of what someone has said, or mis-hearing. Sometimes if we lack confidence in our own abilities, or if we feel threatened professionally, this can potentially lead to a conflict situation. We need to be aware of what messages we are giving out, perhaps without being aware, through our body language, facial expressions and gestures (CCLD 301.4.5).

How we handle potential or actual conflict situations will have a direct impact on the quality of the relationship with then other person. Remember that children will see and take note of how we deal with conflict. They will model their behaviour on adults and so we should be positive role models at all times (CCLD 301.4.6).

Suggested activities and experiences

- When talking with work colleagues, try to make sure that your communications are clear and unambiguous. One way to do this is to use statements that start with 'I'. For example, when discussing roles and responsibilities saying something like 'If you like, I could sort out the role-play area this week' is not very clear. Are you going to do it or not? If you had said 'I will sort out the role-play area on Thursday' it would have left no-one in any doubt of your intentions.
- Take time to find out if your local authority has a translation service available for parents for whom the language of your setting is different from their home language.
- Reflect on the way that you communicate with adults and children. You might find it helpful to tape yourself talking to children, in a relaxed situation. When you play it back, ask

'I remember one time when a parent, in a desperate hurry, left a very garbled message on the telephone about a change of collection time. The child didn't know what the change was and I had to go to a training course that night. I assumed that the parent was going to be late and felt a bit cross that she hadn't given me more notice. However, the mum turned up in the middle of the afternoon, as the child had a dentist appointment. If I had bothered to call her back and ask some sensible questions, I would not have felt cross.'

NVQ candidate

yourself if the conversation was balanced between yourself and the children. Did you listen as much as you talked, did anyone individual dominate? If you wrote an evaluation of this taped conversation you could perhaps use it as evidence.

- Make sure that you are familiar with the confidentiality policy of your workplace. Even if you are working on your own, it is good practice to have a confidentiality statement or policy that is shared and discussed with parents. Think about the different ways that you can communicate with them. Newsletters may not be the most effective method for some people; the same is true of notice boards. Take time to discuss with parents different ways that you can communicate: text, email, telephone or face to face.
- It might be appropriate to use a photograph of a child to let other practitioners know about a serious allergy or medical condition, but make sure that confidentiality is not breached in such cases.
- Listen carefully to what adults are actually saying to you. If you are not sure or need to have something clarified, ask open-ended questions. These are questions that do not have just a 'yes' or 'no' answer.
- If you find yourself in a potential conflict situation, keep calm; take deep breaths, think before you speak and do not shout.
- Remember, parents are often busy people and are less likely to read lengthy letters. Try to keep correspondence brief and easy to read.

Types of evidence

We have already discussed the possibilities of doing a **reflective account (Key letter F)**. Your assessor will be looking for evidence that you understand issues of confidentiality as part of knowledge statement K3M158. This could be assessed in a variety of ways, such as a **professional discussion (Key letter G)** and **oral or written questions (Key letter B)**.

You may decide to keep a diary of a discussion that you had with a parent and the joint action that resulted. In this case, the diary could be classed as a **reflective account (Key letter F)** or as **work product (Key letter H)**, or **case study (key letter E)**.

A parent may also be prepared to give you **a witness testimony (Key letter C)** describing how you supported and communicated with them in a particular situation. When using this evidence, make sure that the details of the witness are accurately and appropriately recorded (see Chapter 1).

Key words and concepts relating to CCLD 301

adults – mature family members, such as parents, grandparents, aunts and uncles, colleagues, other professionals

anti-bias practice - taking positive action to oppose prejudice, stereotypical attitudes and unfair dealings with other individuals; making sure that you meet individual needs

anti-discriminatory practice – taking positive action to oppose prejudice, stereotypical attitudes and unfair dealings with other individuals; making sure that you meet individual needs

appropriate - suitable, fitting, apt for the circumstance, situation and setting

behaviour - what an individual does, says or shows; actions, deeds and activities of an individual

children - the children with whom you work

colleagues -the people you work with, people working at the same level as yourself or your manager

communication - different forms of contact with others in order to give a message or impart meaning

confidentiality - usually refers to information that should not be disclosed to a third party and refers to the right to privacy of the individual. (Information that would otherwise remain confidential can be disclosed to a third party, if it is suspected that a child or young person is in need of protection.)

effective working relationship - the type of relationship with your colleagues that helps the team to work well and provide a high level of service to the customer. This includes getting along well with your colleagues, being fair, avoiding unnecessary disagreements or arguments and not letting your personal life influence the way you relate to colleagues

ethnicities - refers to a person's identification and recognition with a group that shares some or all of the same culture, way of life, customs, traditions, language, religious beliefs and practices. It can also refer to a geographical region and history. Everyone has an ethnicity

individuality - what makes each person unique, the way that everyone is different from everyone else, for example because of their attitudes, appearance, behaviour

individual needs - the unique requirements and wants of a person that should be met in order for them to reach their full potential

inclusion - the process of identifying, recognising, understanding and removing barriers to belonging and participation

positive relationships - dealings, association and contact with others that are beneficial in all ways to children, young people and adults

potential - the latent capabilities of an individual that will emerge under the right circumstances and situations

provision - this includes the physical setting that a child can be in, such as a school, childminder, day nursery or a peripatetic service within the community, such as a play bus

setting - anywhere children's care, learning and development takes place and where children are normally under supervision

Suggested further reading

Birth to Three Matters SureStart/DfES

DfES (2004) Every Child Matters: Change for Children, DfES

DfES (2007) Early Years Foundation Stage, DfES

Draper, L. & Duffy, B. (2001) 'Working with Parents' in Pugh, G. (ed) Contemporary issues in the Early Years, Paul Chapman

Lindon, J. (2000) Your Child from 5 -11, NCB

Lindon, J. (2000) Growing Up: 8 - Young Adulthood, NCB

Riddall-Leech, S. (2003) 'Managing Children's Behaviour', Heinemann

Tassoni, P. et al (2005) Children's Care, Learning and Development, Heinemann

British Deaf Association – www.bda.org.uk

www.parentlineplus.org.uk

What part do relationships play in how children develop and learn? How important is it for you to feel close to the children you care for? Dr Jillian Rodd explains all about the theory of attachment

Words you need to know: Attachment

Do any of these scenes sound familiar? They all reveal different attachment levels and patterns.

■ Jordan cries when his mother drops him off but clings to you when she arrives to pick him up.

■ When she sees her father return, Hannah smiles, runs over and hugs him then carries on with her game.

■ Ahmed is quiet when his mother comes to collect him but suddenly starts to cry and looks away from her as she tries to comfort him.

■ When Tan's mother arrives and bends to kiss him, he hits out at her and pushes her away.

■ Louise bursts into tears when she sees her mother but a cuddle and kiss soon comforts and calms her.

What do we mean by attachment?

Attachment is the development of emotional connections between a child and an adult. It is one of the key factors that influence young children's development, specifically their relationships with other people, their behaviour and learning.

Children and adults who are securely attached to at least one other person feel safe. They use the trusting relationship as a secure base from which to explore the world, as a source of comfort when distressed or stressed and as a pillar of encouragement.

Why is it so important?

When children are securely attached, when they have developed warm,

affectionate relationships with adults in their care setting, they will find that learning is an enjoyable and rewarding experience. They will want to actively explore, discover, investigate, create, practise, rehearse, repeat, revise and consolidate their developing knowledge, skills, understanding and attitudes.

Young children who have developed close bonds with important adults in their lives, such as parents, carers and early years practitioners, show a healthy sense of self-esteem. They believe that the adults in their lives love and accept them, will nurture and protect them and ensure their well-being. Young children who feel unloved, unwanted and unaccepted develop low self-esteem, which can lead to learning and behaviour problems, apathy and depression and this may result in mental health problems later.

That's why it is essential to appreciate the importance of attachment and the development of genuine relationships with children, especially in the early years. It is important to understand how to encourage and respond to attachment behaviours in young children, such as smiling, eye contact, talking, touching, clinging and crying.

While some parents may at first feel uneasy about close relationships between a childminder, for example, and their child, lasting emotional and social problems can develop if young children do not have the chance to develop close ties with one or a few familiar adults. Where parents and professionals communicate and work together, young children learn that day care settings and childminders' homes are safe places where adults other than their parents care for them.

Attachment theories

It was Freud who first proposed that a baby's emotional tie to the mother was the corner stone of all later relationships. However, the importance of attachment was established by John Bowlby in the 1960s and by Mary Ainsworth in the 1970s.

Bowlby's theory of attachment argued that a child's emotional bond to the familiar caregiver was a biological response that ensured survival and that the quality of attachment to the caregiver had huge implications for the child's sense of security and capacity to form trusting relationships.

Babies (between 6-8 months and 18-24 months) who have developed secure attachment often display separation anxiety, that is, they become upset when the familiar caregiver on whom they have come to rely leaves. They may try to prevent the adult from leaving by crying, clinging, following and climbing on her. By two years of age, most toddlers begin to understand that adults come and go, can predict their return and use language to help cope with separation. Bowlby argued that the child's experience in early close relationships established a model for expectations about and interactions for future relationships.

Ainsworth and her colleagues examined the nature of attachment. They showed that, although almost all children develop attachments, including bonds with a number of caregivers, they differ in how secure those attachments are. Ainsworth devised an experiment called 'the strange situation' where observations of young children and their parents revealed patterns of attachment. These were:

■ Secure attachment – children who are distressed by parental separation and easily comforted on their return.

■ Avoidant attachment – children who are not usually distressed by parental separation and who avoid the parent on return.

■ Resistant attachment – children who remain close to the parent before departure and who display angry, resistant behaviour when the parent returns.

■ Disorganised or disoriented attachment – such children show the greatest insecurity by displaying a range of confused, contradictory behaviours on parental return, for example, looking away when being held, having a dazed expression or crying out unexpectedly after having calmed down.

Supporting secure attachment

Most young children develop secure attachments. However, when children fail to develop secure attachments, they become vulnerable. Research has revealed that pre-school and primary

children who were identified as securely attached as infants were found to be more competent and sensitive to relationships with peers and adults than their age mates who had shown signs of insecure attachment.

A number of factors appear to affect the development of secure attachment including:

■ Lack of opportunity to establish close emotional bonds with caregivers in early childhood, particularly the first two years. Consistent care from a familiar adult is essential for the development of attachment bonds, thus the importance of key workers.

■ Warm, sensitive caregiving. Attachment develops when adults respond promptly, consistently and appropriately to children's signals. It appears that children attach to those adults who are sensitive to their needs.

In the early years

In *Birth to Three Matters* relationships with other people and a key person in the setting are considered to be essential to young children's learning and well-being.

Trusted adults who are actively involved and interested in children's learning are considered to be more important than resources and equipment. Such factors provide the foundation for all types of learning, including exploration, trial and error, discovery, examination, inquiry and problem-solving.

Older children

Children whose parents and carers respond to them sensitively in later childhood also foster development and resilience.

Older children who establish at least one affectionate and secure relationship, for example with a grandparent, teacher, playworker or childminder, are more able to bounce back from adverse life circumstances and experiences. Such a relationship can compensate for the lack of secure attachment in infancy. So, if you

Important factors in attachment

■ **Commitment**
All children need at least one warm, caring, reliable, responsive adult who is available and enjoys being with them. Responsive adults help children extend their learning.

■ **Communication**
This is the vehicle for encouraging learning, sharing ideas, expressing feelings, developing emotional closeness. Adults who enjoy talking to young children help build confidence, independence and competence. Because very young children have limited ability to communicate their needs and wants, adults need to be able to recognise different signals and respond appropriately.

■ **Appreciation**
Children's self-esteem and self-worth develops when adults encourage their interest and efforts and are sensitive to their unique individual development and cultural characteristics.

■ **Coping strategies**
Teaching children strategies to cope with difficult situations helps maintain self-esteem. All children have to learn to cope with sharing, anger, frustration, conflict, disappointment and stress. Offering support and encouragement during difficult situations and, when appropriate, helping them reflect on what went wrong may help children cope better the next time such a situation occurs.

■ **Limits**
Simple, reasonable and consistent limits help young children feel safe, secure, likeable and competent. Children are more likely to use limits to guide their behaviour when they like and respect the adult.

work with older children and adolescents, you should be aware of the importance of creating warm and sensitive physical and emotional environments for them, too.

Dr Jillian Rodd, educational and developmental psychologist, independent consultant specialising in the early years.

Young children need to feel safe and secure, to know that there is someone special for them when they need help at school or nursery. Parents need that support, too, and that's why it's at the heart of the key persons approach. Dorothy Selleck explains

Introducing a key persons approach

The concept of key people as part of quality is well documented in national guidance for children from birth to six. The guidance is based on contemporary research that demonstrates the importance of this approach to care, learning and teaching in the Foundation Stage for children's mental health, their emotional well-being, as well as for children's achievements, and for the key practitioners to assess and plan the next steps in children's learning.

Why have a key persons approach?

In my work as an advisory teacher I have regular opportunities to visit day nurseries, playgroups and Reception classes and spend time observing before talking with staff teams. This is my favourite part of the job – I unobtrusively track one of the children so that I can begin to understand their particular experiences of all the opportunities and activities that have been planned. I also try to support practitioners by making documented notes of children in their groups – something that they tell me is often hard to fit into their busy programmes.

These observations highlight many rich learning involvements for the children and affirm good practices. However, they also have repeatedly revealed to me the need for a key persons approach if children are to get their full entitlement to quality learning experiences that are truly responsive to individual children.

In the notes on my morning with Jack in his Reception class (see box) there were only four occasions when he had time and attention paid to him in particular rather

than as part of the group as a whole.

It is not uncommon for a child to have only a handful of direct conversations with an adult over a morning or afternoon session. These fleeting exchanges are often brief instructions rather than more sustained conversations. It is rare for children to have the chance to contribute to an interaction where both child and adult have time to talk, time to listen and time to respond.

Observations of Jack, aged five

■ Teacher (Rosie) to Jack: 'Would you like to take the register to the office?' Jack nods and looks pleased.

■ Jack to adult (Sarah) at the outdoor water tray, squirting with syringes of water: 'I tried to get the birds and the aeroplane and I tried to put the sun out!' Jack giggles and looks to the adult to share his joke. She takes the syringe from him and says: 'Come. You may have a turn later.'

■ Jack is in a small group planting seeds. Rosie says: 'It's your turn to plant the seeds now Jack.' Jack pushes the seed he has been offered into the soil and says: 'I done it, I got the water in the tap – right?' She responds: 'That little seed will grow a long root down, down, down and then a long stem up, up, up … like in the story we had yesterday!' Jack: 'Yeah! And then like the big one in my garden!'

■ Clearing up time. The adult (Mike) says: 'Thank-you Jack for putting all the play people in the box. Go and sit on the carpet now.' Jack complies.

It's your turn to plant the seeds now, Jack.

'Babies and young children are social beings, they are competent learners from birth. A relationship with a key person at home and in the setting is essential to young children's well-being …. A strong child is understanding s/he can be valued and important to someone… so gaining self-assurance through a close relationship. A healthy child's emotional well-being includes being special to someone… developing healthy dependence.'

It is also worrying that it may be one adult who welcomes them, another who gives them comfort after a bump, and yet another who sits alongside them at an activity to cue into their play. Everyone is warm and responsive but in this scenario it is not possible to listen in any depth to each child's 'threads of thinking' (a term used by Cathy Nutbrown), and so build a programme that differentiates for children as they step along their own particular stones of progress toward the Early Learning Goals.

All other interactions will have been in groups and the conversations are mostly directed at everyone rather than the child I have been following. Not all young children are able to feel included in those conversations and can't access the teacher's attention in such groups. Even though these 'carpet sessions' are an important part of belonging in the community of the Foundation Stage class, they do not enable the intimacy and immediacy needed for children to be listened to and then to have a personal response.

We know that young children need to be in small groups and/or on their own with an adult as well as being part of whole group sessions if they are to get the chance to express their ideas and feelings, ask their own questions and share their own representations with an adult. The way to manage this change is to introduce the key persons approach to Foundation Stage classes so that children have more opportunities to be in real two-way conversations and get the support they need from adults who can enter into their jokes and creative play.

Adults in turn will be able to skilfully match their plans and scaffold children's learning in a more intimate and meaningful way.

I wonder what Jack's teacher would have said or done next, during the squirting game, to encourage his creative thinking if the structure of the setting had given her more time to be with Jack, to stay with him and really talk to him?

What if Jack had been playing in Urdu or Arabic or was using sign language? How much more important that someone has time to develop their relationship with him.

What is the key persons approach?

It is much more than the organisational strategy of a key worker system. The key persons approach is also about an emotional relationship with children and their families.

The key persons approach is a way of working in Foundation Stage settings and classes in which the whole focus and organisation is aimed at enabling

'The key persons approach leads to better satisfied and engaged staff, better care and learning for children, and a parent clientèle who are likely to develop a more trusting confidence in the competencies, qualities and devotion of professional staff.'

and supporting close attachments between individual children and individual staff. It is an involvement, an individual and reciprocal commitment between a member of staff and a family. It is an approach that has clear benefits for children and parents, the key practitioners, as well as the Foundation Stage setting or school unit.

'Children learn to trust practitioners when they have consistent key adults to relate to and when they receive consistent responses and feel valued because adults engage in their play, support their interests and converse with them. Children will develop a sense of belonging…'

'… ensure key practitioners are familiar to the children, set up a comprehensive settling in programme, and listen to parents' views… '

Curriculum Guidance for the Foundation Stage (QCA)

Benefits for young children

The key person(s) makes sure that, within the day-to-day demands, each child feels special and individual, cherished and thought about by someone in particular. It is as if there is an elastic thread of attachment that allows for being apart as well as for being together - being in their key person group as well as being with other staff and other groups of children.

The child will experience a close relationship in the setting with a particular adult as well as with a small group of other children and their families. This key person (staff) offers time and attention that is affectionate and reliable.

Benefits for parents

The key person approach ensures parents have the chance to build personal relationships with someone rather than 'all of them' in the Foundation Stage staff team. The benefits are likely to be peace of mind, and the possibility of building a partnership with professional staff who may share with parents the pleasures and stresses of child rearing and supporting their child's learning in this phase of their care and education.

For parents it is liaising with someone who is fully committed and familiar with their child and who has time to learn the important details of their family culture and understand their expectations of school and education.

Benefits for the key person(s)

The key persons approach is intense, hard work and a big commitment. This relationship makes physical, intellectual and emotional demands upon the key person, which need to be understood, planned for and supported by the school/setting policies and management. The benefits in being and

'The benefits of being and becoming a key person are feeling that you really matter to a child and their family.'

becoming a key person are feeling that you really matter to a child and their family.

You are likely to have a powerful impact on the child's well-being, their mental health, and their chances to think and learn. These powers and responsibilities bring feelings of pleasure and pain, the joy and relief of partings and reunions, and the satisfaction and anxiety of being a key person in a child's formative early years care and education.

Benefits for the setting/school

The key persons approach leads to better satisfied and engaged staff, better care and learning for children, and a parent clientèle who are likely to develop a more trusting confidence in the competencies, qualities and devotion of professional staff.

There are indications that this approach reduces staff sickness and absence - and develops involvement and positive attitudes to professional development within staff teams.

Why key person not key worker?

The terms 'key worker' and 'key person' are often used interchangeably but there is a clear distinction to be made.

A key worker is often used to describe a role that is about liaison or coordinating between different professionals or between different disciplines, making sure that services work in a coordinated way. It is quite different from the key person's role defined here.

The term 'key worker' is also used to describe how staff work strategically in nurseries to enhance smooth organisation, transitions, observations and recording stepping stones of progress in the FS profiles. This is only a part of being a key person, which is an emotional relationship as well as an organisational strategy for learning and teaching.

This approach enables further shared responsibilities for all Foundation Stage practitioners – not only the lead teacher/practitioner but all the professionals in the team (including teaching assistants and NVQ trained workers).

How does a key person approach work?

Each member of the team is assigned to a group of children and their parents so as to build up this special relationship with the family and, where possible, sustain it throughout the Foundation Stage.

In some settings this will mean that each trained and supported adult will have a key person relationship with eight children and their families in the group. In traditional Reception classes the group could be as large as 15. However, as Foundation Stage schools, children's centres and partnerships between the private and voluntary sector for Foundation Stage units become more developed for this phase of education, and as people adjust to working in new ways, they may want to think about the rationale of deploying staff in different ways.

Of course, the key person cannot be there every minute of the day - no one, even at home, can manage or even aspire to that.

Otherwise, how would a child ever learn that they could survive if left alone for a short time or be able to benefit from all the activities supported by different staff? How do children learn that the people who love them or who are concerned for them will not forget them but will come back as soon as possible?

Some children are in the Foundation Stage from around eight in the morning until six in the evening as they attend the wrap-around care of breakfast and after-school clubs. Very few staff work in all those settings; and of course the key person will go on holiday, be off sick or be attending training days.

It is at these times that a back-up key person is so important. Even so, the times when the main key person is not available must be kept to a minimum or the role starts to become meaningless.

The key person is the staff member who has begun to get to know the important adults and brothers and sisters at home, who knows the young child so well and all the special details of how they are cared for. The key person is the staff member who has planned with the family when the child will start nursery, how they will work together to introduce her and settle her in; how they will work together to make sure life in the setting, at home and in wrap-around care dovetails together.

The key person is the staff member who is there, as far as possible, to greet the child in the morning, to comfort her if she is upset, to play with her and enjoy time together, and to be the one, whenever possible, to offer intimate bodily care (helping with changes of clothes after an accident, administering sun cream ensuring any medication that is needed). A person who is available for sofa time storytelling, help with a construction or who has time to offer resources needed for a (child initiated) creative collage or dance session.

This staff member will also have other children for whom she is a key person and part of the skill of her/his job is being available to each of these children, in turn, and sometimes together, as much as she can.

If Jack had had a key person in his class - if Sarah or Rosie or Mike had key times with him (see box) it is much more likely that he would have had more sustained interactions, fewer fleeting remarks and many more opportunities for an adult to listen to him.

What is certain is that children who are enabled to feel safe and secure, who know that there is someone special for them when they seek them out - will be much more able to be themselves and try out new ideas in all the new relationships and experiences on offer in the nursery, playgroup or Reception class.

Dorothy Selleck works as an advisory teacher in Oxfordshire's Sure Start Early Years Development and Childcare Partnership and the Schools Development Service. She is co-author of the book, *Key Persons in the Nursery*.

'The key person makes sure that, within the day-to-day demands, each child feels special and individual, cherished and thought about by someone in particular.'

If you want to find out more

This approach is described in more detail with practical ideas on how to put it into practice in:

Key Persons in the Nursery. Building Relationships for Quality Provision by P Elfer, E Goldschmied and D Selleck (David Fulton Publishers 2003).

Some adults feel that children owe them respect and that is the end of the matter. So, it is refreshing to read how positively the word is used in Scotland's *Birth to Three: Supporting our Youngest Children*, says Jennie Lindon

Building relationships on mutual respect

'Each child is an individual, a person who has the right to be responded to and treated with genuine respect at all times' (page 37, *Birth to Three: Supporting our Youngest Children*).

The Scottish *Birth to Three* guidance describes what really matters for emotionally and physically healthy experiences in these vital early years. The information, advice and food for reflective practice are built around the three Rs of relationships, responsive care and respect.

The concept of respect for babies and very young children is closely linked with the other two Rs. Out-of-home care has to be built on the development of a warm, personal relationship with young children, and their families. The Scottish *Birth to Three* is perhaps even clearer than the English *Birth to Three Matters* that responsive care and a caring outlook is central and utterly non-negotiable.

Birth to Three clearly promotes respect as a two-way process. Adults need to show active respect for young children's interests and enthusiasms. Respect is not something that adults demand as their grown-up right. It needs to be shown throughout daily practice with very young children.

This stance connects with the key question now posed by Ofsted for inspections in England: 'What is it like for a child here?'

Value for care and caring

Respect for young children underpins a personal approach to their physical care needs, both what you do for them and how you steadily support babies and toddlers as they start to share in their own care. Respectful care routines are

created when you give time and make it a personal experience. Disrespectful, rude adult behaviour around care makes young children feel like just another boring task.

Very young children soon show observant practitioners their preferences in regular care such as nappy changing, how they like to be settled to sleep and mealtimes. Of course, communication through partnership with families provides your first insight into family choices and parents' unique knowledge of their own baby or toddler.

You show respect to parents when you want to create continuity between the family home and nursery, or your home as a childminder. When babies and young children see and hear you in friendly communication with their family it reassures them that the different parts of their life connect together.

Children's interests and preferences

Young children experience respect when you

notice and obviously want to give your time and attention to what really interests them.

Two-year-old Elena feels important to Becky, her childminder, in the most positive way. Becky is happy to read *Six Dinner Sid* every day this week because it is currently Elena's favourite book. Becky spends extra time

Birth to Three: Supporting our Youngest Children

The Scottish team drew on the same research and practice materials as the English team who created *Birth to Three Matters*. But in Scotland they made different decisions about how to set out a framework for good practice. The materials include an A4 publication that is just over 50 pages long, a leaflet for parents and posters. A DVD and staff development materials are in the pipeline.

on Elena's favourite pages. Because Becky avoids over-filling days, there is still plenty of time for 15-month-old Tom, who loves repeat hearings of the story Becky tells to the pictorial book *Moonlight*.

A key person system is essential for developing personal relationships in a group setting. From the beginning of the settling-in process Katie shows toddlers that she respects their possessions. Young children are welcome to bring their comfort objects into nursery. Their blanket, piece of muslin or cuddly toy is treated with care as a precious item. Children have a personal basket where such items can be safe when they are not needed.

Young children feel respected when you share their current interest and do not rush to take it over with adult questions.

Alistair shows genuine interest in what catches the attention of his key children as they enjoy a wander around the local park. Alistair has given each child a small brown carrier bag, donated by the local delicatessen. 18-month-old Glen is intrigued by stones. He likes to pick one special stone each day for his bag and take it back to place on their 'special table'. Just two-year-old Jaina wants to re-visit the corner where last time they saw all the cobwebs. Jaina cannot recall the words to describe this experience, but Alistair shows that he remembers.

The English *Birth to Three Matters* pack is full of examples where practitioners are encouraged to watch and listen. They can then join in the play and offer resources or experiences that will connect with children's preferred ways of exploring their world.

Individual children cannot feel valued if adults feel they have to control the when and how of play activities, even right down to an adult-acceptable end product. On the other hand, under threes, and older children too, blossom when early years practitioners are confident to be led by what intrigues children today. As children's spoken language skills develop, such shared experiences will be the source of happy reminiscences – 'Do you remember when ...?

How children want to stretch their skills

Respect can be shown when you give time for challenges that children choose for themselves. This can give rise to magic moments, which can be shared later with a child's parents. I saw just such a moment in an early years centre when a two-year-old girl wanted to use the climbing and balancing run set up for the older children.

The practitioner let the child take her time, offering a hand when the child looked uneasy and staying close when she indicated she could manage the next section. The practitioner was a quiet and helpful companion, who avoided imposing any help. The young girl was delighted when she completed the section and her immediate reaction was to do it again – with increased confidence.

On the other hand, young children are disrespected if their interests are ignored, hurried or highjacked by adult concerns. Children need to experience respect themselves in order to feel like showing the same behaviour to others. Adults are responsible for setting the tone, showing in action how you would like children to behave towards you and each other.

Children's feelings and their behaviour

Respect for children does not mean that you let them do whatever they want, regardless of safety or the consequences for other children. A positive approach to dealing with the words and actions of young children does show respect. You:

■ Acknowledge their feelings, while sometimes saying that it is not okay to express the feeling by hurting other people.

■ Set clear boundaries, guide children in a firm but fair way and follow your own ground rules.

■ Listen to children and give them a chance to explain what happened

• • • • • • • • • • • • • • •
• **Where to find out more**
• *Birth to Three: Supporting our Youngest*
• *Children* (Learning and Teaching
• Scotland; free for practitioners in
• Scotland, £5·00 elsewhere tel: 0141
• 337 5000 or download free from www.
• LTScotland.org.uk/earlyyears)
•
• 'Equality in the world of very young
• children' *Practical Professional Child Care*
• September 2005
•
• 'Why children want to "Do it myself"'
• (*Practical Professional Child Care* April
• 2005)
•
• 'Learning how far they can go' (*Practical*
• *Professional Child Care* July 2004)
• • • • • • • • • • • • • • •

Respect for children's feelings means taking a child-friendly approach when they are unhappy or worried. It shows a lack of respect when adults label distressed or fearful young children as 'being silly' or 'too clingy'.

Yinka needs respect, and friendly help, when he jumps back in alarm from the large worm that appears in his digging patch. Then perhaps he will give Lotty a cuddle later in the day when she looks tearful at the noisy song that delights the other twos in their nursery room.

Both Yinka and Lotty need to have a firm basis of trust and confidence that their feelings are recognised and taken seriously. This basis will be important when they are ready to make the transition from their current room to the room for older children.

Jennie Lindon is an early years specialist and author. She has worked for more than 30 years with services for children and families.

Children need adults around them who show affection and show they care. Close relationships are crucial to young children's well-being not an optional extra, says Jennie Lindon

Relationships matter: making it personal

Human babies are born ready to be social. Even newborns can lock onto your eyes with a steady gaze. These personal developments occur because babies are primed to be social and their brain is attuned to the sounds of a human voice.

Individual ways of making contact

It is not long before babies make contact by touch and you will notice individual preferences. Perhaps Eddie used to push a little hand into his mother's curls and hold on tight. But his baby sister, Kimberley, places a balled-up fist close into her mother's neck just under the ear.

Babies and toddlers show that they want to make social contact with the important people in their life. But these relationships are formed one-to-one, initially with the closest family members. Perhaps baby Kimberley is sociable and happy enough in a family gathering to pass between several grandparents and doting uncles. But there comes a point where her face crumples and she stretches her arms out, indicating she wants to be returned to Mum or Dad, or to the lap of a rather proud Eddie.

Babies come to notice familiar patterns of touch and tone of voice. They recognise facial features, ways of being held and (in the nicest possible way!) how you smell. Increasingly babies join and initiate exchanges, so that you and they together create early conversations from sounds and gestures.

The needs of babies and young children stay the same, wherever they receive their care. So it is crucial that childminders and nurseries, who share the care of under-threes

with their family, lead good practice through personal relationships.

Close relationships outside the family

Birth to Three Matters, the recommended guidance in England, highlights personal relationships within the ten key principles: 'Relationships with other people (both adults and children) are of crucial importance in a child's life' and 'A relationship with a key person at home and in the setting is essential to young children's well-being' (introduction booklet, pages 4-5).

The importance of warm, affectionate relationships with children is one of the three key features that shape the under-threes guidance in Scotland, *Birth to Three: Supporting our Youngest Children*. The other two Rs are responsive care and respect (see 'Building relationships on mutual respect', *Practical Professional Child Care*, October 2005). The guidance offers valuable materials for practitioners anywhere in the UK. The focus of birth to three advice about out-of-home care is that days have to be organised around personalised care routines and warm, affectionate contact.

Partnership with parents

Many of the examples given on the 16 cards of *Birth to Three Matters* depend upon your giving time to get to know a baby or young child as an individual. It can be reassuring for families to realise that you want easy communication to create a warm relationship with their children.

■ You might let Jessica's parents know you appreciate how they told you their

daughter preferred to sit on the toilet and not on a pot. You show respect for parents' knowledge, but also that personal details about Jessica matter to you.

■ Winston's father is pleased that you listen carefully as he says they have introduced their son to banana. You are equally attentive to his explanation that Winston likes to have the fruit mashed, not chopped.

■ Neither Jessica nor Winston will feel in a warm relationship with their out-of-home carer if their preferences are brushed away for a one-size-fits-all pattern of care.

Feeling 'kept in mind'

When young children feel secure in a relationship, they are confident that they matter to you. Under-threes do not then have

to spend precious time and energy trying to establish contact each time they come to your care. A telling phrase in *Birth to Three* is that young children 'need to feel that they are being "kept in mind" – so that even in the busiest times of the day, young children feel secure that they have not been forgotten' (page 17).

It is straightforward to give children the experience of having been 'kept in mind'; you do not have to learn complicated techniques. All it takes is a genuine smile, a swift response to their call, readiness to talk but also to listen properly to babies and toddlers.

All the little things build up over time: what Elinor Goldschmied refers to as 'the minute particulars' (a quotation from the poet William Blake). The emotional experience of being kept in mind goes alongside the physical welcome that is in your arms and on your lap.

■ The emotional warmth in Jon's behaviour lets Asif know that Jon missed the two-year-old when he was away from nursery last week on a family visit. A big hug says 'nice to have you back!' Asif can also see that his partly decorated shoe box is safe on the work-in-progress shelf, so he can continue whenever he wishes.

■ Mandy greets the two children who return from a library trip with Clement, her husband and co-childminder. Mandy is busy changing baby Josh. But she encourages the children to come alongside with, 'I've been looking forward to hearing about Tuesday Story Time. And I bet you found some good picture books for Josh'.

Key persons

Making a close relationship is not an optional extra, fitted in by practitioners after they have completed other tasks that they judge to be a higher priority. Babies and very young children are receiving poor quality care if personal attention and communication is brushed aside as something that 'would be nice to give in an ideal world but…' Practitioners, or teams, that feel this way need to consider what it is like for very young children, if they do not feel kept in mind.

The English and Scottish birth to three materials are clear that the key person system is non-negotiable for group settings. However, this way of organising is all about personal contact and continuity. The key person role is not just for the settling-in period, nor solely about who completes the paperwork.

In contrast, I have spent enjoyable days with the under-twos or threes group in centres who have really thought about how they nurture close relationships with children. Teams have established special time that Elinor Goldschmied calls 'the island of intimacy': a period of about 20 minutes before lunch when each practitioner spends time with her or his key children.

This shared time together can be different; it certainly is not a set pattern for each little group. In one centre I observed one small group settling with their practitioner onto a large sofa for child-chosen books. Another small group took their key person out into the garden for some serious clambering. The third small group gathered around a table with resources chosen, again, by these very young children.

Following children's lead

Babies, toddlers and twos do not do groups and it is poor practice to try to organise their communication, or any form of learning, through days dominated by group sessions, with activities planned by adults. Of course, practitioners can have some ideas and offer some adult-initiated activities.
But children only feel part of an equal, personal relationship when respect and time is given to their interests and ways of exploring materials.

■ On the *Birth to Three Matters* CD-Rom you will find a series of video clips. The excerpt under each Healthy Child component is a relaxed shared routine, where practitioner and children prepare food for the nursery guinea pigs. Young children look confident in their role, chat about what they are doing and then go out to feed and watch the animals.

■ Look also at the excerpt on each of the Competent Learner components. Children explore using glue and spreaders

Where to find out more

■ *Listening to Babies* Diane Rich (National Children's Bureau Tel: 020 7843 6000 or visit www.ncb.org.uk/ resources/listening-babies

■ *Birth to Three Matters: A Framework to Support Children in their Earliest Years* (Sure Start Tel: 0845 6022 260) To find the video excerpts on the CD-Rom: go into Main Menu, click on Contents, then on Index of Videos and you will see a listing by the 16 components.

■ *Relationships and Learning: Caring for Children from Birth to Three* Anna Gillespie Edwards (National Children's Bureau)

■ *Birth to Three: Supporting our Youngest Children* (Learning and Teaching Scotland; free for practitioners in Scotland, £5-00 elsewhere tel: 0141 337 5000 or download free from www. LTScotland.org.uk/earlyyears

in their own way, supported but not pushed by a practitioner.

■ Warm relationships are naturally developed when practitioners respond spontaneously to young children. I sat at a lunch table in one centre where a practitioner was chatting with young children just before lunch arrived. One boy offered his sunhat and the practitioner put it on her own head. This action delighted the children, not least because the practitioner already had a closely fitting scarf around her head and face, so the sunhat perched on top. She repeated the action several times to the children's great amusement.

Jennie Lindon is an early years specialist and author. She has worked for more than 30 years with services for children and families.

Babies and very young children let you know, loud and clear from their body language and spoken words, how much they appreciate adults who give them time and personal attention. Early learning requires firm foundations built on respectful care

Making time to show you care

Care should not be seen as somehow separate from early education. Caring is not less valuable. Some national developments value care.

■ Scotland's *Birth to Three: Supporting our Youngest Children* makes care central to children's well-being. Their guidance is built around the three Rs of responsive care, relationships and respect.

■ The English *Birth to Three Matters* pack is full of examples (on the video, the cards, the CD-Rom) that children's personal care deserves time and scope for individual choices.

■ Lesley Staggs, national director of the Foundation Stage, is leading the project to

The Scottish model

The Scottish team drew on similar research and good practice resources as the English team who created *Birth to Three Matters* but in Scotland they made different decisions about their framework. Guidance (in A4 book format), a leaflet for parents and posters have been supplemented by a staff development pack and DVD.

The materials are free if you work in Scotland, but need to be bought if you live elsewhere in the UK. However, you can download the guidance book from the Learning and Teaching Scotland website and get a taster of development materials (written pages and short video excerpts) on www.ltscotland. org.uk/earlyyears/birthtothree

develop an Early Years Foundation Stage for England to create coherence over birth to five years. One of the aims is to address the artificial care-education division that continues to disrupt some practice. the artificial care-education division that continues to disrupt some practice.

The importance of personal routines

Early years practitioners sometimes want to stress that they do a lot more than wipe noses and change wet knickers. We all know that a full day for nursery staff or childminders includes much more than this. But practitioners, who feel the need to justify, 'I do more than just care, you know!', are usually downgrading the importance of personal care to babies and very young children. When it is your nose, or your bottom, it matters a great deal how that caring attention is offered and undertaken.

Under threes (and over threes who want your help) do not show through their behaviour that they think it is right to add 'just' or 'only' to care routines or caring adult behaviour.

The Scottish birth to three guidance stresses the importance of valuing routines, so that children are not rushed. It recognises that the personal care routines of babies and young children inevitably take up a large amount of time each day. The guidance is strong (as are the examples in the English *Birth to Three Matters*), that practitioners must therefore see routines as 'valuable opportunities to be with the children and to develop relationships' (page 25), not as tedious, repetitive tasks to get through as fast as possible.

The Scottish guidance goes on to highlight

Food for thought

Most adults have memories that help them tune into the feelings and perspectives of very young children.

■ In your own childhood, do you recall a family or other carer who swooped in to wipe your face or adjust your clothing, without so much as a 'Shall I...?' How did that make you feel?

■ As an adult, what emotions well up if you are having a haircut and the hairdresser holds a long conversation with somebody else, while handling your head and your hair?

■ How have you felt at a health clinic or hospital if medical staff talk about you, but fail to include you in that conversation? In contrast, what does responsive and respectful medical care feel like?

The very youngest children notice the difference in how their care is offered. They appreciate being treated as little people with feelings and preferences. Toddlers protest when they are treated as a body that leaks from one end and needs to be refilled at the other – in ways that are efficient for the adults.

that, 'When adults become too focussed on adult-led activities and tasks, they may be in danger of forgetting about the individual child. Adults need to recognise that for the child, the process is often far more important than any end product and that allowing children to follow their own interests at their own pace is part of respectful care' (page 26). Good practice – anywhere in the UK – means behaving in ways that show young children how they are welcome to this time and attention.

Practitioners or parents who rush young children through care routines often end up taking much longer. Babies and toddlers struggle because changing time is impersonal and boring. Fed-up twos protest about not being given the time to put the books back on the shelf in their own way. As some experienced childminders once said to me: 'If you give time, then you gain time'.

to follow their own interests at their being given the time to put the books back on the shelf in their own way. As some experienced childminders once said to me: 'If you give time, then you gain time'.

Children learn through friendly routines

It was adults, not children, who created the care-education divide and made care the less valued part. Young children are potentially interested in all parts of their day and regular daily experiences are a rich source of learning. Children learn a great deal through play opportunities, but they do not only learn through those activities that adults label as 'play'.

■ Relaxed mealtimes support babies and young children as they steadily share in their own care for eating and drinking. Look at the video excerpt 'Eating together' from the Scottish staff development materials (find them on the Learning and Teaching Scotland website).

■ Another good example is provided by the mealtime sequence in 'A Healthy Child' on the English *Birth to Three Matters* video.

■ Look also at the video excerpt on the *Birth to Three Matters* CD-Rom under 'A Healthy Child' (Index of Videos under Contents). Young children are enthusiastically involved in the routine of preparing food for the nursery guinea pigs. They are busy learning about caring for others.

A caring approach

Young children's emotional security is built as they become confident that you will attend to their personal care needs, but that you also care about their personal preferences.

The Scottish *Birth to Three* offers an example (on page 30) of 14-month-old Anna who is less keen than her peers to get directly involved in the water play. But Nichola, her key person, does not pressure Anna. The toddler sits on Anna's lap and watches. Nichola asks if Anna would like to touch the water. But she does not move to take off the toddler's clothes until Anna tugs at her own top. Anna enjoys the water play for a while and then becomes upset when she is splashed. Nichola wraps Anna in a warm towel and cuddles her. Anna indicates that she has had enough and Nichola takes her time to dress Anna, commenting on each item of clothing in turn. Anna has been allowed to determine the beginning and end of her own involvement in the water play.

Nursery practitioners and childminders show a caring outlook to children when they allow scope for safe choices. For example:

■ It matters a great deal to Darren, who is just two years old, that he wipes the table with a cloth after lunch. Darren takes time with this domestic task but Abigail, his childminder, does not rush him. She expresses warm thanks for his help when Darren is satisfied with the job he has done.

■ Two-year-old Kay has looked on with interest at the hand painting that is spread out to enjoy in her nursery. But Kay does not want to get her hands into the paint. Marcus, Kay's key person, has noticed that she does not seem to like the feel of paint

. . . .
Where to find out more
● ■ 'Building relationships on mutual respect'
Practical Professional Child Care October
2005 and 'Relationships matter: making it
personal' (*Practical Professional Child Care*
November 2005).

■ *Helping Babies and Toddlers Learn:
a Guide to Good Practice with Under
Threes* by Jennie Lindon (National Early
Years Network, distributed by the National
Children's Bureau)
. . . .

and some other materials too. Despite encouragement, Kay has not got any closer to making direct contact. So Marcus has bought some textured mittens and offers Kay a pair today. Kay is enchanted and happy to work with the paint now that she does not have to touch it. Other children show an interest and soon the special mittens become yet another tool for exploring hands-on materials.

■ Young children are often keen to take simple messages within a family home or across the garden or a room in the nursery. They like to fetch something or are proud to be given a written note to deliver. The 'journey' does not have to be long; toddlers are still within your sight. But they are proud to be sent on a mission or to join you in taking some play resources from one room to another.

Jennie Lindon is an experienced early years specialist and author.

When a child first joins you, it may be the biggest change they have had to adjust to so far in their lives. Some children have no experience of being cared for by someone other than their parents or are new to social situations with other children. You need procedures in place to help them cope

Helping new children to settle

Settling in can be a time of emotional upheaval so it's important to be sensitive to children's needs. It's upsetting for parents and carers to know their child is unhappy. They may feel guilty about leaving them and worry about them throughout the day.

Planning a settling-in strategy helps families and you. It can be presented in a policy that sets out the way forward for all concerned. If practitioners are consistent in their approach it gives children a sense of security. The child's key worker should take the primary role in implementing the strategy, which may include the procedures below.

When a parent/carer books a place, the key worker:

■ Explains their strategy.

■ Explains it's best if adults show the child they are confident that they will be all right.

■ Completes a settling-in form (see example overleaf), gaining as much information from parents/carers as possible. This is in addition to the registration form.

■ Answers questions and addresses concerns.

■ Arranges for a parent or carer to pop in with their child, just for a few minutes, at a time when children will be doing an activity they like. Future settling-in sessions are also planned (see below).

When meeting the child, the key worker:

■ Greets and talks to the child on their level, but doesn't overwhelm them. Avoids asking them too many questions, so that the child can take everything in.

The next step – the first play session

The second visit is a play session. The parent or carer stays and the length of time depends on the child - an hour is enough for some children, others may want to stay longer. Parents or carers need to encourage their child to join in and interact with their key worker. They shouldn't take part too actively themselves, but should be a 'safe person' for the child to return to. The key worker:

■ Uses the information on the form to plan activities that will appeal to the child. If parents have agreed the child will bring in their favourite teddy, for instance, the home corner could be set out for a teddy bear's picnic.

■ Observes the child's progress, playing alongside if appropriate, or nearby if the child is less confident. If children are reluctant to play, plan to try again at another session with the parent or carer there. If the child does play, this indicates that they are ready for the next step.

Attending alone

Children who are used to group settings may stay for an entire session straightaway, while others may need to build up time gradually, perhaps just staying for half an hour, or less if they become distressed. They then start to trust that they will be collected, and generally settle down as the time they are left is gradually increased. Most children settle within a fortnight. The key worker:

■ Again sets out favourite activities, and makes sure there is food the child likes for snacks/meals, and their own cup if they prefer it.

■ Makes sure they are there to greet the child.

■ Establishes a routine of saying goodbye. Discourages the parent or carer from sneaking off when their child is playing. Takes the child in their arms if necessary.

■ Encourages the parent or carer to phone if they are worried, and reassures them they will be in contact if their child is overly distressed. (They do not let the child hear this.)

■ Comforts the child if they are upset and offers distractions in the form of favourite toys and activities. Encourages the child to play, joining in alongside them until they are settled, then withdrawing, but staying close by.

■ Reports back to the parent or carer at the end of the session, giving an honest account of how their child has been. Includes details about what the child/ group has done, so the parent can talk to them about it at home.

■ Tells children something that the group will do next time, so they know what to expect.

■ Says goodbye and sees the child out.

Not all children have difficulties settling – some arrive and act as though they've been coming their whole lives! Sometimes a parent or carer is more upset than their child.

Miranda Walker is an early years and playwork writer, trainer and speaker. She owns her own daycare settings in Devon.

Use this form as a prompt when talking to parents/carers to find out as much as you can about their child before they join you

Settling-in form

Child's name.. Date..

Completed by.................…......................... (Key worker) and ……….…..…………….……..... (Parent/carer)

Notes:

Child's general experience of care outside of the family, including their response to being away from their parent/carer:

Child's general experience of being in social groups with children outside of their family, including their response:

Do they have a comfort toy or object?

What are their favourite play toys?

What else does the child enjoy doing at home?

What are the names of family member/friends the child may mention?

What does the child like to talk about/show interest in?

What are their dietary like and dislikes? (Requirements and allergies should go on the registration form)

Do they need a nap during the day? If so, what is their usual routine?

Miscellaneous notes:

How do children build relationships with key adults in your setting? Is there a nappy changing rota? If so, do you change the tenth child with as much care and sensitivity as the first? Do you sit with the same children for lunch every day? Do parents know that you are their child's special person? Kate Banfield and Angela Sugden look at how to offer personalised care

Organising a key person system

In any care setting, children need someone who sees them and their family as special. They need a person who is committed to building a special relationship with them, enabling them to be themselves in unfamiliar surroundings, someone who is consistent, who they can trust and who responds reliably to their individual and personal needs. That someone is known as a key person.

There is some confusion about key workers and the key person approach. A key worker is an organisational role. You can split children up into smaller groups and give a key worker responsibility for assessing and monitoring those children. Children do not necessarily know who their key worker is.

A key person, however, is the key to a positive relationship between the setting, individual children and their parents. A key person approach enables children to feel emotionally secure. This means that they are able to learn and play and reach their full potential. The key person looks out for their key children, and feeds, changes and supports them in their personal routines most of the time.

The relationship that forms between a child and a significant person is called attachment (see 'Words you need to know: attachment' *Practical Professional Child Care*, July 2004). It is the feeling that encourages a child to feel safe, loved, confident and special. For the key person it is the feeling that encourages them to look out for that child when they come into the room, the feeling that encourages them to take a special interest in that child and be responsive to their cues, rituals and temperament.

What does a key person do?

A key person is responsible for:

■ Building a trusting relationship with the child and their parents/carer;

■ The needs of the child while they are at the setting or centre (changing, feeding, comforting);

■ Settling the child in;

■ Collecting information about the child's specific needs from their parents/carer;

■ Keeping management/coordinators informed of issues/requirements related to the child;

■ Planning for the child's learning and progression;

■ Assessing the child's learning and progression;

■ Making sure that the child's parents/carer are kept informed of the child's day and experience at the setting;

■ Working with other members of the staff team if not a lone worker to provide a stimulating and safe environment for the child;

■ Being aware of any special requirements that the child has;

■ Liaising with other professionals as required;

■ Monitoring that the setting's environment

Why do children need a key person?

Children need to feel safe, secure and confident if they are to develop to their full potential.

Their parents need a trusted person who they can talk to about their child's individual needs.

and planning meets the needs of the individual child.

To settle a child into your provision, so that they can explore and play without their parent, you need to reassure them that their parent will come back. This is best done by experience. Plan a series of small separations over a settling-in period of about two weeks while the parent is having a coffee before building up to leaving the child for a morning.

Think of a time when you were leaving someone you loved. How did you feel? Sad, excited, loss, insecure, worried, frightened? You need to deal with these emotions sensitively. Remember that you can say how

'Young children are vulnerable. They learn to be independent by having someone they can depend on.'

you are feeling - very young children can't always do this. But just because they can't explain their emotions doesn't mean they are not feeling them. It's your job to help them find the words and space to explore feelings and support relationships.

You can do this being consistent with times and manner, making time for them, listening to them, being honest and putting yourself in their place.

How do you organise a key person system?

■ Identify a key person and a second key person for a child, taking into consideration which staff are present when the child attends.

■ Agree a settling-in timetable and give copies to the key person, parent and/or previous key person. The average settling-in time is two weeks.

■ Write the settling-in times in the diary and make sure that shifts are arranged accordingly. For children moving rooms, the new key person should visit the child in their present room as part of the plan.

■ Other staff in the room need to be informed of the settling-in schedule so that they can support the key person.

Moving rooms

If a child is moving rooms within a nursery, the new key person and parent and/or current key person should meet to discuss the child and negotiate the best settling-in times and arrangements to meet the individual needs of both the child and their parents. The parent/key person is expected to remain with the child, as agreed in the settling-in plan. Transition should be seen as a shared responsibility.

Building a relationship with a new child

Building a relationship with a new child starts with the first visit. The child visits your room with their parent or close adult. Your colleagues support your settling-in time by covering your activities or taking you off the rota. This allows you the freedom to shadow the new child.

Encourage eye contact with the child, get down to their level, making suggestions about what they would like to do, modelling the unfamiliar activities that they might find. Make them feel special. Talk to the main

carer. Ask questions about the child's needs and requirements, how they go to sleep, the toilet, what they like to eat, what they don't like, and so on.

What happens when the key person is absent?

When the key person for a particular child is identified, so is a second key person. The second key person will take over the key person's responsibilities in their absence. It is also the second key person's responsibility to keep the child's record book up to date in the absence of their key person if appropriate. It is important from an organisational perspective that key persons do not take holiday at the same time.

Kate Banfield and Angela Sugden, childcare workers, Kirklees.

Babies can hold conversations long before they can say their first words. You just need to realise that they are communicating, says Jennie Lindon

Children don't need words to tell you something

All children learn to speak, unless they have a disability that affects communication or their childhood is so deprived that nobody communicates with them. Different theories aim to explain how human babies manage such an impressive task, but no single theory has come up with all the answers.

■ Human babies are primed to be social. Their brains start working before birth, tuning in to sound - which is how some young babies recognise their mother's voice.

■ Long before they can move their bodies easily, babies lock their eyes onto the human face. They use their sight as well as their vision to start communicating with important people in their life - and that includes other children, like siblings, as well as parents and familiar carers.

■ Babies need plenty of attention from affectionate adults and time given to simple communication. They need to hear spoken language and they need people to take their early communication skills seriously.

The first words are an exciting development, but spoken language arrives because toddlers have experienced months of happy early communication without words. Within the second half of their first year, babies move from making single sounds to trills of sound, showing that they can deliberately play around with what they are able to say. But babies have also been busy communicating without words through their gestures.

Babies show what they mean

Watch how young babies show what they want through non-verbal communication and share your observations with their parent(s):

■ Five-month-old Rory stretches out his hand and looks keenly at you. He seems to be saying, 'I want my cup and I can't reach it'. If you are slow to react, Rory backs up his gesture with a shout.

■ Six-month-old Kara uses a gesture of opening and closing her hand as a way to indicate, 'Give me my toy'. Kara may have watched you or her mother use this gesture and has imitated it.

■ Ten-month-old Polly is clear when she does not want any more lunch. She turns her head, pushes back into her chair and screws up her face. A firm 'No!' cannot be far away.

■ Thirteen-month-old Sam has learned the thrill of pointing with his finger and outstretched hand. Pointing

works well to show that he would like his books from the shelf. But Sam has also learned that finger pointing is a way to direct the attention of his father towards interesting sights on the street. Sam is delighted that older children he meets at his childminder's home are willing to follow his gesture to look at flowers and ducks when they are at the park.

If you watch and listen, you will notice that older babies and young toddlers often repeat waving gestures or sounds, like blowing raspberries, when this communication has made an adult or other children laugh.

Long before babies have a working vocabulary of spoken words, they are busy with communication. You just need to realise that they are communicating, not wait around for the 'real words'. Watch the baby with his childminder in the *Birth to Three Matters* video section about **A Skilful Communicator**. He is joining in with the story read to the young girl and he adds his sound-comments.

What can you do to help?

There has been a lot of publicity about children who cannot hold a conversation or struggle to listen in nursery or school. National organisations like I Can and local speech and language teams are aware of disabilities that may affect the development of communication. But they highlight that children cannot develop their potential for talking, listening and understanding without generous time and attention from adults, who also set a good example in communication.

Spoken language can seem complicated, if you take it apart to analyse vocabulary, sentence structure, grammar and so on. But very young learning, day by day, is simple and what babies need from their caring adults is straightforward - certainly not difficult 'communication techniques'.

■ Be close

You need to be close enough to touch; most babies' comfortable distance is very close. Stay on a young child's level and make friendly eye contact. Make sure you have their attention before you start, using gentle touch, eye contact and a smile. Say a child's name before anything else, rather than at the end of your sentence.

■ Use pauses

Babies need you to speak with them, but they also need you to listen. You can say something, or point out something of interest, then pause and look expectant. Wait, and even babies as young as three or four months 'say' something in that gap. Soon they pause and look expectant in their turn. The first conversations start before babies have words.

■ Look and sound interested

Use your facial expression and tone to show you enjoy chatting with this child. Babies soon pick up on whether an adult is genuinely interested. A bored tone and 'I'm fed up' expression turn babies off, and even worse they think that they are boring. Be generous with your gestures to add to the communication from your words.

■ Follow their lead

Show you are interested in what catches their attention. Then you can add words to name what a baby is holding, comment on what a toddler is doing. Make sure that your language links with what babies and toddlers can see right in front of them, then your words and gestures are meaningful.

■ Keep it simple

When the first words and short phrases come, you can sometimes repeat what a very young child says and extend a little. You say a word correctly as you reply, but do not make the child re-say it. Just like with a baby, you add a little, then pause and look expectant.

■ Set a good example

Be a good role model: pay attention with eyes and ears, take your turn and avoid interrupting. Behave in the ways that you would like young children to learn and you will soon see babies and very young children communicating well with each other.

Using infant-directed speech

Babies like communication that is personal. But they also like it lively, with a musical intonation and at a higher pitch than normal conversation. Talk at a slow pace, with pauses. Babies also respond well to simple repetitions and a circling quality to what you say. For instance, 'Rory, do you want something? Is it your cup? Yes, it's the cup you want. There you go. Well done, you're drinking from your cup.'

Researchers, who first identified this kind of speech, had observed mother and baby pairs and so they called this pattern 'motherese'. But it is more accurately called infant-directed speech. Not only mothers, or even women, talk in this way. Men, as fathers or carers, use infant-directed speech and so do some children, for instance, with younger siblings.

Infant-directed speech is certainly not instinctive or everyone would behave in this way to babies and this is not the case. Adults, and children, imitate people who are at ease with babies and the delighted reaction of the baby encourages them to continue.

Birth to Three Matters stresses the effective practice of 'Adults who interpret, give meaning to and echo young babies who are making a variety of sounds' and how, 'In a familiar context, with a key person, babies can understand and respond to the different things said to them'.

The best communication is not complicated to do, so perhaps we need to consider what stops adults from communicating as well as they might with babies and young toddlers.

■ Parents and practitioners need to recognise if they feel self-conscious. Avoid thinking that it is silly to talk with a baby or toddler who cannot yet talk back 'properly'.

■ You help babies to concentrate, in your home or a nursery, by creating peaceful times and places. *Birth to Three Matters* reminds us that, 'Babies enjoy experimenting, exploring and using sounds and words to represent the objects around them'. But they have to be able to hear clearly, as well as see familiar objects.

■ Non-stop sound, from music or the television, is not 'stimulating'. Babies and toddlers struggle to listen against continuous background sound. Choose just a few suitable programmes to watch with children. Then use the off switch.

■ If you work in a day nursery, remember that very young children communicate as one individual to another. Don't be tempted to have a group communication time.

Jennie Lindon is a child psychologist and author. She has worked for nearly 30 years with services for children and their families.

If you want to find out more

The Social Baby Lynne Murray and Liz Andrews - book and video from The Children's Project Tel: 020 8546 8750 www.childrensproject.co.uk

Relationships and Learning: Caring for Children from Birth to Three Anna Gillespie Edwards (National Children's Bureau Tel: 020 7843 6000)

Listening as a Way of Life Free leaflets from the Early Childhood Unit Tel: 020 7843 6000 www. earlychildhood.org.uk

The development of spoken language should be one of the highest priorities of pre-school education, says Sue Palmer. Problems with speaking and listening have implications not only for learning but for behaviour and social skills

Language, listening and learning

Speech matters. We need it to communicate and co-exist with others, to explore and express our experiences, to proclaim our needs, hopes, fears and passions. We need it to think and learn – not least to learn the skills of literacy. 'Reading and writing', said educationist James Britton, 'float on a sea of talk'.

How worrying, then, that over the last 20 years children's ability to speak and listen seems to have steadily declined. A combination of social and environmental factors (including the breakdown of the extended family, the speed and pressure of modern living, and constant TV and video) mean that adults spend less time than ever before talking to their little ones. Instead of bedtime stories, many toddlers now have televisions in their rooms. Instead of a family chat round the table, they have solitary TV dinners. Instead of a cuddle and a song to cheer them when they're tearful and fractious, they're treated to a video.

David Bell, Chief Inspector of Schools, has said: 'Children starting school today have never been so ill-prepared. The average five-year-old is not ready for the social regime of infant classrooms, unable to talk, not used to sitting at a table, unwilling to concentrate

'The problem of widespread delay in listening and language development is a new one, born of recent changes in our society, and there is still much to learn about the best ways to tackle it.'

even for very short periods, and without listening and response skills'.

And it's even more worrying that, while children's speaking and listening skills have waned, attention to these skills in early years settings has also been eroded. In England, many practitioners have found that emphasis on tests, targets and pencil-and-paper work in Key Stage 1 has had a knock-on effect in Reception and pre-school provision (and, despite apparently less formal regimes, this is often also the case in Scotland, Wales and Northern Ireland). Children are now expected to knuckle down to formal work earlier and earlier, and the time for developing oral language – like the time for play – has grown ever smaller.

There are signs that the educational establishment has noticed this squeeze on language and listening. David Bell's quote indicates Ofsted's concern and the National Primary Strategy, together with Sure Start, has now commissioned training materials about pre-school children's communication skills. Moves are also afoot in England to reduce the pressure of Key Stage 1 tests – or perhaps even abandon them altogether, as in Wales. However, it will take several years before these 'official' moves take effect.

Let's jump up in the air... wheeee!

In the meantime, it's up to practitioners to make the development of spoken language one of the highest priorities of pre-school education. As well as resisting pressure to introduce pencil-and-paper work, this means finding ways to support the development of oral language skills. The great question is – in such a huge area, where do you start?

The suggestions below are based on what I have learned from talking to speech therapists, educational psychologists and pre-school teachers around Britain, and also in other European countries, where oracy skills are considered an essential part of the curriculum. But the problem of widespread delay in listening and language development is a new one, born of recent changes in our society, and there is still much to learn about the best ways to tackle it.

Learning to listen

The most basic skill of listening is **discrimination**. Children must be able to discriminate a significant foreground sound against a background noise. For a one-year-old, this means being able to single out their parent's voice against the sound of the television; for a four-year-old, it's being able to discriminate the teacher's voice against the babble of the classroom.

The next key skill is **attention**, the ability to concentrate on auditory information for increasing lengths of time, blocking out other distractions. For children whose early life has been filled with visual stimuli on TV screens – and who are also used to being able to 'rewind' at will if they don't catch something first time – this can be a difficult skill to learn.

These two skills underlie **auditory memory** – the ability to remember sequences of sound. This is vital for numeracy (for example, counting), literacy (for example, remembering the three sounds /k/ /a/ /t/ in the right order to read or write 'cat') and indeed for all learning. Good auditory memory is arguably the most important factor in academic success.

Children with hearing difficulties, including intermittent hearing loss (which also seems to have increased in recent years, perhaps due to environmental changes) clearly have difficulty with these skills, and need specialist help. However, an increasing number of hearing children also need help because they have simply not learned to listen. Problems with listening have implications not only for learning, but for behaviour and social skills.

Time to talk

Children are naturally 'programmed' to learn to speak. Basically, they listen to adult models, imitate and innovate on familiar words and phrases, and go on to invent meaningful sentences of their own. However, if they don't have enough experience of interactive language with adults (or if they have hearing or listening problems) speech may be delayed. If this is the case, children need help to catch up on vocabulary and sentence construction (see box) so that they can make normal progress.

One of the main reasons for talk is social communication, which involves both listening and speaking. One key skill is making eye contact, which for many children nowadays does not come naturally. The listener must then attend, while the speaker engages attention. Both need to abide by the conventions of turn-taking and other aspects of 'conversational etiquette', including ways of disagreeing politely.

Another aspect of language is its relevance in learning and understanding – as the psychologist Vygotsky put it, 'A thought is a cloud, shedding a shower of words'. Young children often produce a spoken running commentary on what they are doing to help them make sense of the world. (Later this 'exterior monologue' is internalised, but when something is difficult, it often becomes external again, as when we find ourselves muttering tricky instructions or reading aloud to underpin understanding.) This sort of talk is nowadays referred to as pole-bridging and is an important element in intellectual development.

The greater children's command of language, the more explicit and organised their talk – and thus their thinking – will be. One time-honoured way of developing language is through reading to children, which helps them absorb the vocabulary and the more complex patterns of written language. However, for many contemporary children, bedtime stories are a thing of the past. On the bedroom TV, stories are in the form of dialogue – much simpler, spoken language patterns. We need to ensure all children benefit from hearing literate language by frequent reading and rereading of favourite books.

Tuning in to sounds

In terms of literacy, there is another essential element in early language experience. Phonological awareness – the growing recognition of the significant sounds that go to make up words – underlies the ability to read and write. It arises through exposure to

'A thought is a cloud, shedding a shower of words' Vygotsky

language in general, but especially to rhythm and rhyme.

Children who live in a language rich environment, who have no hearing problems or language delay, and who regularly hear songs and rhymes, usually start playing with rhyme naturally (for example, 'This is easy-weasy-peasy-deasy'). Once they can do this, we know they can discriminate individual speech sounds – the w, p, d at the beginning of the rhyming words – which means they're ready to learn phonics. For children who have not developed phonological awareness, phonics teaching may well fall on deaf ears.

Sue Palmer is a writer and educational consultant, specialising in literacy.

Speaking and listening are fundamental to everything we do every day. But we can't assume that children's skills will just develop naturally. It is becoming ever more important that we target these skills, and ensure daily, systematic, structured coverage

Helping children learn to listen

Most of these activities can be done with a small or large group, but children whose language development lags behind the norm also need regular one-to-one attention. This is obviously difficult to achieve, but if every adult has a list of five children a day, and tries to spend five to ten minutes of quality speaking and listening time with them, it can make a huge difference to language development.

Discriminating a foreground sound against background noise

Dodgems

Familiarise children with a particular sound (such as clapping, tambourine, bell), which is the signal both to 'start' and 'stop'. At the 'start' signal, children pretend to be cars, speeding around (avoiding each other!), and making an appropriate noise. Make the sound again to signal 'stop', and give a few moments for all children to respond. Give praise for recognising the signal. Play the game a few times.

Make a note of those children who do not seem to notice the signal and make sure they have opportunities

■ for regular one-to-one talk with an adult

■ to play the game in a smaller group.

Stop the gossip!

Gather a group of children together and tell them they are going to gossip with partners for a few minutes (they can make gossip-gossip-gossip noises or genuinely chat quietly). When they hear the words 'Stop the gossip!' they must immediately be quiet and turn to face you. To begin with, speak quite loudly to make sure you're heard. As before, praise children for recognising the signal. Then try lowering your voice gradually. Once children have played a few times, make it trickier by asking other people (classroom assistant, a child) to 'Stop the gossip!'

Discriminating sounds and building attention span

Listening walks

Explain that you are going to listen for any sounds, such as cars, birds, people talking, and so on. Tell the children they have to walk very quietly and if they hear a sound put up a hand, whereupon everyone must stop. Invite the child to say what sound it was. Once they get good at this, progress will be slow, so get them to stop every so often instead and 'collect' as many sounds as they can hear. You can do listening walks inside or outside, or use them as part of any outing.

Spot the sound

Choose a number of items with recognisable sounds, for example a music box, a ticking clock, an automatic timer, or sounds recorded on tape. Gather the children together and explain that, while they close their eyes, you are going to hide a 'sound' somewhere in the classroom. On your signal they have to listen hard and guess (a) what it is (b) where it's hidden.

If a child is consistently baffled by these activities, s/he may have a problem with hearing, rather than listening, in which case, seek specialist help immediately.

Make your own picture

Choose a short vivid poem to read to the children. Explain that you're not going to show them a picture as you read – you want them to focus on a blank area (empty whiteboard? blank wall?) and 'make your own pictures in your heads'. When you've read the poem ask what pictures they conjured. Don't be surprised if at first few respond – children who are constantly fed images on TV often do not know how to image in their heads. Repeat the activity, gradually lengthening the texts you choose.

More ideas

Children need frequent and varied opportunities to learn and refine listening skills. For many more excellent suggestions, try:

Helping Young Children to Listen Ros Bayley and Lynn Broadbent (Lawrence Educational Publications: 01922 643833)

The Little Book of Listening Clare Beswick (Featherstone Education: 01858 881212)

Developing Baseline Communication Skills Catherine Delamain and Jill Spring (Winslow Press: 0845 921 1777)

There are also many games on the market (using ready-made taped sounds) for use in free play sessions. These also provide practice in turn-taking, for example:

Picture Sound Lotto for ages four to eight (LDA: 01945 463441)

Soundtracks for ages three to six (Living and Learning: 01223 864886).

Developing auditory memory

Mr Copycat

Use a puppet to give children sequences of sound to repeat, for example:

- clapping a regular beat

- saying a silly sentence

- making a sequence of animal sounds

- saying a list of words

Start with two sounds/words to remember, and build up to three, then four.

Music and song

Involve the children in musical activities, especially song (one of the best ways of developing auditory memory) every day. Action songs, where kinasthetic memory aids memorisation of words, are particularly useful in the earliest stages. Expect the children to learn at least one new song by heart per week. Three excellent publications are:

The Music Makers' Approach (NASEN: 01827 311500)

Music in Action from Big Books Gaunt and Dunville (Lovely Music: 01937 832946)

Tom Thumb's Musical Maths Helen MacGregor (A & C Black: 020 7758 0200).

I think I'll play too – I'm making a castle!

Again and again and again...

Provide plenty of time for happy chanting! Encourage children to join in with rhymes, refrains ('Run, run, as fast as you can....'), and whole chunks of favourite books (see also 'Five a day'). Expect children to learn at least 20 rhymes between the ages of three and four (this is in addition to songs!) and another 30 between four and five.

Which instrument?

Introduce children to a number of musical instruments with distinct sounds and give plenty of opportunities for them to familiarise themselves with the sounds. Place two or three of the instruments in front of a screen where the children can see them. Behind the screen, use duplicate instruments to make a sound sequence, putting your instruments down (behind the screen) in order as you play them. Ask children to place the instruments in front of the screen in the correct order. Remove the screen to check they are right. Over time, build up the number of sounds in the sequence.

Supporting children with language delay

Make sure you know the three key ways to offer support:

■ **Expansion**, for example: Child: 'Daddy car'. Adult: 'Yes, Daddy's gone home in the car'.

■ **Offering alternatives**, for example: Child: 'Juice allgone'. Adult: 'Have you finished your juice?' 'Oh dear, have we run out of juice? Didn't you get any?'

■ **Modelling** pole-bridging talk, which is particularly useful for a shy child, for example, instead of asking the child 'What are you doing?' sit alongside them and comment: 'I see you're playing in the sand. I think I'll play too – I'm making a castle', providing plenty of silences for the child to respond/join in if she or he wishes.

> Pole-bridging talk is when you produce a spoken running commentary on what you are doing.

All of these can happen naturally throughout the course of the day, but it is also important to allocate specific time, preferably daily, for focused adult attention.

For children who need more focused help, try *How to identify and support speech and language difficulties* by Jane Speak (LDA: 01945 463441).

Puppet talk

In one-to-one sessions, try giving slow or shy speakers a puppet who can talk on their behalf. Ask the puppet to repeat a few words or a short sentence related to what you are doing (and hope the child will help him out!). Try asking the puppet simple questions, or asking for instructions on how to do something.

Social communication

Look me in the eye

Teach children how to make eye contact by using it as a selection device, for example 'I'm not going to say your name when it's time to get your coat today, I'm going to look at you'. Once they're familiar with this technique, choose children to be the 'looker'.

Make children want to look and listen to you with daily compliments! As they arrive in school, have an adult 'greeter', whose job it is to look each new arrival in the eye and say something nice, for example 'I love your hairband today!' 'What a happy smiling face – it brightens my day!' Encourage children to respond if they wish.

Circle time

Use circle time activities regularly. There are many suggestions for games encouraging social talk, listening and turn-taking in:

Because We're Worth it Margaret Collins (Lucky Duck Publishing: 0117 973 2881)

Circle Time for the Very Young Margaret Collins (as above)

101 Games for Social Skills Jenny Moseley and Helen Sonnet (LDA: 01945 463441)

Learning and understanding

Target language!
Whenever you plan a new topic, list the vocabulary you can specifically target in all activities. Think of suitable examples from each category:

■ nouns (naming words, for example 'cow', 'pear', 'shoe', 'giant');

■ verbs (doing words, for example 'run', 'sing', 'wash');

■ adjectives and adverbs (describing words, for example 'purple', 'big', 'slowly', 'quietly');

■ prepositions (showing relationships between words, for example 'on', 'under', 'behind', 'in');

■ conjunctions (words that link ideas together, for example 'because', 'when', 'after').

Make a list on a postcard that you can keep to hand to make sure no opportunity to use the new words is missed.

Talk it through
Try to model pole-bridging talk by giving a running commentary (hopefully containing much of your targeted vocabulary) when you are:

■ demonstrating how to do a task;

■ participating in an activity with children;

■ sitting with and watching a child, for example 'I can see how carefully you're rolling that pastry. That's right, press down hard with the cutter. What next? Ah, you're going to peel it off the board...'

Always make sure you leave plenty of space for children to take over the pole-bridging and praise their pole-bridging talk. Talk about how it helps with learning.

Literate language

Five a day!
Read to children every day! In fact, read at least five short picture books a day, frequently returning to favourites. Encourage children to join in:

■ first with refrains and favourite lines;

■ then with whole chunks of the book.

Aim, over 10 to 20 reads, to get the whole group joining in with the whole book. This activity has many benefits:

■ it develops auditory memory;

■ it enlarges children's vocabulary and range of sentence constructions;

■ it prepares them for reading (some children actually learn to read 'naturally' from this activity; others become familiar with the language of books);

■ it prepares them to make up their own stories, providing them with a head full of characters, settings, plots and sentence patterns on which they can innovate in the future.

Book talk
Use favourite books as the focus of creative work and talk.

■ Children retell and dramatise the stories, using puppets, props, costumes, pictures on storyboards, and so on.

■ Find or make up action rhymes to link to the plot.

■ Talk about the characters and plot – use 'hot-seating' and 'TV interviews'.

■ Use art to revisit the story – paint pictures, make models and friezes, choose favourite lines to print out on the computer and add to the display.

■ Let children help you choose a specific piece of music to introduce the story whenever you read it.

Tune into sound
Many of the activities described above involve rhythm and rhyme. As children's language develops, focus increasingly on rhyming activities.

Easy-weasy-peasy-deasy
Gather a group of children and provide a starting word (for example, grumpy, lazy, stingy – words ending in 'y' work best). Starting with a different child each time, go round the group, with each child supplying another rhyming nonsense word. It doesn't matter whether their words begin with a single phoneme (for example, 'd') or a consonant cluster (for example, 'gr', 'str'). Some children find this activity hilarious.

Make a rhyme
With an individual or group, say a familiar rhyming couplet but miss out the final word for the children to provide, for example 'Humpty Dumpty sat on a wall, Humpty Dumpty had a great....' Then innovate on the rhyme so the missing word is easy to guess, for example 'Humpty Dumpty sat on a chair, Humpty Dumpty was brushing his....' Finally, give just the beginning of the final line, for example, 'Humpty Dumpty sat on a pig, Humpty Dumpty ......

This sort of activity prepares children for learning phonics. There are many more ideas in:

Phonemic Awareness in Young Children Marilyn Jager Adams et al (Jessica Kingsley Publishers: 020 7833 2307)

Sue Palmer is a writer and educational consultant, specialising in literacy.

More ideas
Time to Talk (for Reception and KS1) Alison Schroeder (LDA: 01945 463441)

Little Book of Storytelling Mary Medlicott (Featherstone Education: 01858 881212)

Little Book of Role Play/ of Prop Boxes for Role Play Ann Roberts (as above)

A Corner to Learn Neil Griffiths (Nelson Thornes: www.nelsonthornes.com)

Storysacks Neil Griffiths (Storysack Ltd: 0161 763 6232 www.storysack.com)

If you were to record what you say over the course of a day, what would it tell you about the quality of your communications and the messages you are giving to children? Jenny Barber encourages you to think about how you talk to children

Talking to children

You talk to children in different ways:

■ to encourage language development;

■ to develop vocabulary;

■ to model language;

■ to inform and instruct;

■ to challenge and extend thought and discovery;

■ to chat;

■ to affirm what they say and do.

Humans are programmed to talk, but we have to learn how to speak and understand the vagaries of language. Adults have a vital role to play in modelling language.

Communication is also about how you encourage children to speak. It is a two-way process and you need to offer opportunities for children to talk, listen and respond. Remember not to talk *at* children, but to listen and respond *to* them. Some adults do too much talking and not enough listening.

The ability to talk and communicate opens up a whole new world to a child. As their understanding and awareness increase, they are able to express their thoughts, wants, needs and ideas.

The basic principles of good practice in talking to children are as follows:

■ make sure the tone of your voice conveys interest and warmth;

■ think about your rate of speech - are

you speaking clearly? Are you speaking too quickly?

■ show a child you are listening: get down to their level, maintain eye contact, engage in conversation;

■ give them time to respond;

■ if possible, use open-ended questions, for example 'When did you get your new shoes?'

■ contribute your own experiences in a conversation with a child to show interest and involvement;

■ encourage children to give an account of what they are doing or have done and to make predictions in real and imaginary situations. This all helps to develop creative thought and extend vocabulary.

■ make sure that children get the chance to talk to another child on their own,

an adult on their own, in a group of children and a group of children with an adult. This extends and develops their use and understanding of conversation

■ don't use sarcasm and don't patronise or belittle children in your responses.

In terms of your general chatter with children, you have to achieve a careful balance between involvement and standing back, being supportive of development and ideas, but respectful of independence.

Following the approach of silence, observation, understanding and listening (SOUL) can help and reduces the chance that you will interrupt unnecessarily. This puts the emphasis on you, the adult, spending time observing and becoming more sensitive to individual needs.Through silent observation and listening you can gain an understanding of how best to respond and support.

Some of the following methods and approaches can help you to be effective in supporting children's communications.

Self-talk
You provide a commentary labelling what they are doing, for example 'I am getting out a clean nappy to put on you'. This supports children's language development, giving words for actions and therefore making associations.

Parallel talk
This is similar to self-talk, except you are describing what the child is doing as you interact with them, commenting perhaps on where they are playing, what they are playing with and what they are doing.

Repeating

After listening carefully to a child, to clarify what they have said, you repeat their words. This also serves as an acknowledgement and is supportive of the words/language the child uses. It often has the result of keeping the child talking because it acts like a question and shows you are interested in what they are saying.

Restating

Sometimes children make mistakes with language. If you repeat what they said in a correct form, you are correcting them in a positive manner, without drawing attention to the error.

Expanding

In conversation, an adult will often add new ideas to what a child is saying. For example, the child says 'there's a spider', and you continue with 'he's spinning his web'.

Encouraging ideas

Encourage children to explain and describe their ideas and solutions to problems and challenges by asking them what they plan to do (beforehand) and what they did (afterwards). You can also ask them to help you. This indicates your respect for their ideas.

Asking open-ended questions

Open-ended questions encourage more than just a 'yes' or 'no' answer and stimulate children's thinking and use of language.

As children get older, although the basic principles remain the same, certain aspects of your approach need to change. To continue to support vocabulary extension and to challenge thinking, you need to consider your suggestions and responses and not simply ask questions. It is important to remember to:

- choose questions you know are likely to challenge children's thinking;

- give children time to prepare and consider their response to a question;

- provide models of the patterns of language and vocabulary;

What do you talk about?
- ■ How much of what you say is management talk? Do this, do that, it's time for...

- ■ How much is conversation and chatting? How much is explaining and playful talk?

- ■ Children need to be involved in a wide range of language experiences to develop their communication skills.

Developing thought
- ■ Do you ask for and give reasons and explanations when talking with children?

- ■ Do you encourage predictions?

- ■ Do you encourage children to give accounts of what they have done and what they are doing?

Who do you talk to?
- ■ A tricky question - we like to think we regularly talk to all children in the group, but do you? It is essential that you do, as they all need the chance to practise talking with different adults and have their language needs met.

- ■ vary your responses to children and debate with them to encourage explanations for greater understanding;

- ■ use appropriate vocabulary for the listener.

Accentuate the positive

If you listened to a recording of your day with children, would your talk be peppered with unintentional negative messages? How often do you tell a child not to do something, instead of saying what you would like them to do?

For example, you might say to a toddler who is sitting at a table about to have a drink: 'Careful you don't spill that!'. The consequence is that they feel under pressure and are more likely to spill the drink. If you say 'Hold the beaker with both hands', you are not only ignoring what you hope the child won't do, but are also instructing them to do something to prevent it from happening.

How many times do you say something like 'Don't spill the sand' or 'Don't run' over the course of the day? This can result in a stream of negatives, whereas 'Remember to walk' or 'Try to keep the sand in the tray' convey a different message. Sometimes what we don't say can be as influential as what we do say.

I am sure that if you were to sit down and listen to a recording of yourself, you would discover that most of the time your communications with children are positive, encouraging and developing language and vocabulary. There is no harm, though, in occasionally reflecting on what you do say and don't say, and looking to explore your practice in terms of communication.

Jenny Barber, early years and childcare trainer and consultant, Buckinghamshire.

How inclusive is your provision? Sue Fisher asks you to think about the resources you provide as well as the activities you organise. She starts by looking at the issues for children with learning and cognitive difficulties

Promoting inclusion for:
children with learning difficulties

Difficulties in cognition and learning can take many forms. Some children who experience learning difficulties may have a recognised medical condition or disability, such as Down's syndrome, but many others will not. These children may be classed as having developmental delay, general learning difficulties or cognitive difficulties and these difficulties may have been recognised or confirmed while the child is attending your setting. However the difficulties are identified, it is your responsibility to provide an environment and activities that are suitable for and accessible to that child - and all the children in your care.

Building on the child's interests

When you work with a child with learning difficulties, so much seems to revolve around what they cannot do. It is, therefore, important to build on what the child can do and what they enjoy doing. All children have individual learning styles - recognising these will help to make sure you provide the best type of resources, activities and teaching strategies to get the best from each child.

Build on their strengths. If the child is new to your setting, developing a passport style system or an 'All about me' booklet can be an effective way for parents to pass on important information about their child. This can be anything you or the parent feels would be useful but should always contain the crucial details that will help to ensure inclusion, such as how the child communicates (for example, through Makaton), how to gain the child's attention, what situations may cause distress, and so on.

It may also be possible to establish early links with other professionals if they have

already been involved with the child. For example, if the Portage service has been involved in the home environment it will be helpful to reinforce the steps they have been working towards through sharing ideas and resources.

Planning the environment

Children with learning difficulties will be at a lower developmental level and learn more slowly than most children in your care. If a child with such difficulties attends, or is soon to be attending your group, you should carry out an audit of your current provision, identifying barriers particular to that child, to make sure you are providing a safe, supportive learning environment.

For all children to learn and develop to their full potential, they need a thorough and thoughtful range of well-planned opportunities to explore, play and develop socially. Approaches will need adjusting to meet individual needs, even when groups of children have similar difficulties.

Continuous provision and defined learning areas will help to support children in becoming familiar with the layout of the setting. Children are more likely to feel safe and secure when they know where things are. They will learn that when they come back the next day, they will be able to continue or extend their play, adding ideas and equipment that is readily available. Remember this when you are thinking about moving things around. Is it really necessary?

Thoughtful organisation of resources will support the child in developing independence,

especially if you help them by providing strategies to develop memory skills.

Consider:

- Attaching a photograph of the resource (construction materials, musical instruments, small world toys) to its storage container and placing a copy of the same photo where the container is kept.

- Colour coding areas to help with tidying up. For example, everything in the role-play area has a red dot, equipment for sand and water play has a green dot.

- Photographs of objects and resources can also help children to become familiar with and name

objects within the environment and could be used to develop a memory game where the child matches a photo with an object. Keep it simple to start with, using one or two objects, and build on this as the child's confidence grows.

■ Extending this approach, photographic records of outings and events will help to develop memory and recall skills. Many settings keep photographic records of thematic work and these help children's memory development as well as reinforce learning.

Displays and posters should aim to reflect differences. For children with learning difficulties you should also think about simplifying pictures and illustrations. You may find that children respond more positively to photographs than drawn images. Clear labelling of items and displays helps all children begin to recognise familiar words. This is important to many children with learning difficulties, particularly those with Down's syndrome in their Reception year and beyond at school, as research suggests they may have more success in learning to read through whole word recognition, rather than phonetic approaches.

The outdoor environment

If a child has a learning difficulty, it can often be spotted first in poor movement and coordination and delay in reaching motor milestones. When physical skills are delayed, the child will not only need extra support but consideration will need to be given to the play equipment you provide. As this needs to offer a challenge to all children, multi-purpose resources or equipment that can be added to or simplified are most likely to help the child to experience success.

When coordination and balance are delayed, this will not only affect basic movement patterns but also skills involved in handling small apparatus, such as bats and balls, as well as running, jumping and hopping. Simple, familiar rhymes such as 'hop, skip and jump' played regularly will help children develop these skills.

Children with learning difficulties will benefit from visits out into the wider outdoor environment - real life experiences promote understanding as well as familiarity to build on.

Resources for learning

Children with learning difficulties learn effectively from real life experiences and this can be developed through the stories you read. Books provide a good starting point for helping children to learn about particular situations and new experiences, such as going to the dentist or moving on to school. Usborne publishes a good range of books on new experiences and the Topsy and Tim series (Ladybird Books) is simply written with clear illustrations. The stories are just the right length to hold most children's concentration.

Learning about everyday experiences can also be consolidated through role play. At first, a child may need an adult to play alongside them, as their social skills are likely to be immature. You will be able to gradually withdraw into an observer's role as the child grows in confidence.

Often the best resource is other children. Children learn from each other and it may be worth considering setting up a buddy system where the more confident children support the less confident ones.

You will also need to consider whether you need specialist resources. This will depend on what you have already and the age range of

'Remember that what works for one child will not necessarily work for another. The key is to provide positive opportunities for learning, ensuring all children's needs are met in an environment that supports them to experience success.'

the children you cater for. If you have a range of good quality resources covering all six areas of learning which are used imaginatively you may not need anything else. However, the child is at a lower developmental level and likely to lack specific skills (such as fine motor). You may therefore need to consider buying resources such as construction equipment, jigsaw puzzles and games with larger, chunkier pieces than usual.

Children with learning difficulties enjoy using computers but some will have difficulty with mouse control and using function keys. A chunkier mouse and touch control pads will support them in computer-based learning.

Safety may also be an issue. The child may put objects in their mouth as a means of exploration. Small beads and construction bricks can, therefore, be a hazard but still need to be made available. As a staff team, you will need to work through such dilemmas, deciding on the best solution for your setting.

Remember that what works for one child will not necessarily work for another. The key is to provide positive opportunities for learning, ensuring all children's needs are met in an environment that supports them to experience success.

Sue Fisher, early years training consultant, Hull.

If you want to promote Communication, Language and Literacy, you need to think about providing telephones, post boxes and dressing-up clothes as well as books and pencils, says Linzi Pearson

Resources to support:
Communication, Language and Literacy

Books

Try to have a variety of books available. Include:

- Cloth, bath and board books, as they are easy to handle, especially for young children or children with additional needs. They also wipe clean or wash easily and are more difficult to destroy than normal books.

- Storybooks, especially ones that the children are familiar with, so they can retell the stories using the pictures.

- Feely books, containing different textures.

- Books containing photographs.

- A selection of fiction and non-fiction books, illustrating a range of people from a variety of backgrounds, cultures and of different ages and abilities.

- Dual language books - a must if children in your setting speak languages other than English but also valuable to show native English speakers that other languages exist and are worthy of respect.

Rotate the books so that only a selection are out at any one time, to keep the children interested. Books can be expensive, so contact your local library to see if they loan out sets of books.

Create a book nook

Children need access to books. A dedicated area with somewhere comfortable for them to sit is best. The type of book area you provide will depend on your setting and the space available to you. There is a great

to one or you don't have the space, a box and some floor cushions is just as good.

Surround this area with lots of words and pictures of characters from their favourite books to make it appealing and welcoming. If possible, have a member of staff in this area to read stories to the children. If you cannot spare a member of staff, ask a parent, carer or volunteer to come in and read.

Opportunities for writing

Even very young children like to make marks. Emergent writing is an important stage of development and should be encouraged. Opportunities for writing should be provided throughout your setting, for example have a pot of pencils available in the creative area, so the children can write their names on their paintings and pictures themselves. Even if their attempt is unreadable, you can always put their names on the back

when they have finished. In the home corner, especially if you have a telephone, provide pieces of scrap paper and pencils to write messages and notes, such as shopping lists. A permanent writing table is also a good idea. Give the children forms and envelopes as well as scrap paper; junk mail is a great source of these and can be collected by parents and carers.

Once the children have written their letters they might want to post them. Several educational suppliers sell post boxes but they can be expensive because they are often made out of wood and are usually quite large. You can make your own out of a strong cardboard box. Choose a size to suit your setting, something as small as a shoebox is fine if that's all you have space for. Paint it red and decorate with black stripes and delivery times. Make sure you can retrieve the letters as children like to take their work home. They can be encouraged to collect their work at the end of each session.

The S/NVQ Book ∎ ▪ ▪

Pencils

When learning to write children need to be encouraged to hold a pencil in the correct position to enable them to form letters correctly. This position, the tripod grip, can be promoted through the types of pencils used. Look for ones that are a triangular shape. They are a little more expensive than normal pencils, but a cheaper option is to buy tripod pencil grips. These fit onto normal pencils and can be reused. They can be bought from most educational suppliers, usually in packs of ten.

Phonics and letter recognition

There are lots of different products available to help teach children phonics and recognise letters. These schemes of work can be useful resources and are often available in sets that include games, worksheets and teachers' handbooks and notes. You will need to decide which are appropriate for the age and stage of your children. Some teach children letter recognition through characters. Although these characters are appealing to children, they can confuse them, making it difficult for them to recognise the letters or say the sound without the character as a prompt.

There are also letter matching and spelling games, tapes and magnetic letters. Choose a selection of these or you could even make your own.

Make a phonic box

A good way of building links with home is to have a phonic box or display that the children can add to with items brought from home. Tell your parents and carers each letter that you are teaching the children, then they can help their child to find an item or a picture of something that begins with that letter. Ask them to bring it in to put in the box. Make sure all the items that go into the box or on the display are labelled with the child's name to prevent any mix-ups when they are returned.

Imaginative play

Giving children opportunities to use their imagination will help and encourage them to tell and write their own stories. This should be a combination of small world play, such as dolls' houses, dressing-up clothes and the home corner which can be changed into different play situations or scenarios.

Telephones

Telephones are a really useful and cheap resource to encourage language development. You can buy toy telephones from most toy shops, but try to avoid ones with lights and sounds that need batteries. It is costly to keep replacing them and toys that make noises and light up encourage children to keep pressing the buttons rather than playing with them and using their imagination and language skills. For example, if the toy telephone has a button that makes a ringing sound then the children will not pretend to make the sound themselves.

A good alternative to toy telephones is old telephones. Ask parents and carers to donate them, then make them safe by cutting off the long cord. These are usually popular with children because they are 'grown-up' telephones instead of toys. Listening to the children playing with them is often amusing because they mimic the adults they are surrounded by.

In your telephone area display words such as 'hello' and 'goodbye' and also imaginary telephone numbers. You can base your area on a topic, for example if your focus is on fairy stories you could have the telephone number for Goldilocks and the three bears, so the children can call them.

Rhymes and songs

Rhymes and songs should be part of every session. It does not really matter which ones, it is the rhythm and the rhyming words that are important. Although the children will have favourite songs and rhymes, try to introduce new ones on a regular basis, so they learn new words and different rhythms.

Labels and pictures

Label everything, from chairs and doors to toys! This teaches children that words have meaning and they will soon start to guess what the labels say. Use lower case letters for your labels, only using upper case letters when they are needed, for example, for names of people or places. Use labels on displays, using pictures to accompany the

words to help the children predict what it says. Labels can easily be produced on a computer with pictures from programs such as *Clip Art*. Choose a simple font so that the labels are clear and easy to read.

Name cards

To help the children recognise and write their names, they will need something to copy it from. Make a name card for each child in your setting. Like labels, they are easy to make on a computer using a word processing program. If you can laminate them they will last longer.

On one side of the card, use the child's first name and on the reverse put their first name and surname. This allows for progression, so once they recognise or can write their first name, they can turn it over and practise their surname. Lots of games can be played using the name cards, for example, when the children sit down around a table or mat, place their names down first and encourage them to find and sit next to their name. When played on a regular basis, these games will quickly teach them to read their name.

Linzi Pearson, play development adviser, Sure Start Brierley Hill.

Pride can be experienced in different ways, but whether a shared or a personal experience, private or public, by exploring this emotion with children you will enhance their understanding of themselves and others

Exploring emotions:
feeling proud

Feeling proud of ourselves as a result of something we have achieved is important for all of us, and especially important for young children. They are at a crucial time in their lives; a time when they are forming opinions about who they are and how they fit into the world around them, and attitudes formed at this stage are likely to stay with them!

To feel proud involves us in experiencing a sense of honour and self-respect; a sense of personal worth. It enables us to take pleasure in our own or somebody else's achievements, and as such is inextricably linked to the development of self-esteem. For this reason, it is extremely important that you devote time and attention to the ways in which you enable young children to experience this important emotion.

Celebrating children's achievements

All the time you are working with children you are consciously or unconsciously supporting

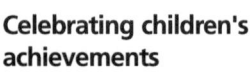

them to feel proud of their accomplishments, but when an early years team devotes a little time and attention to considering exactly how they do this, they do it even better.

The way in which you give feedback to children about what they have achieved can have a massive impact on the way they feel about themselves, so you need to think really carefully about how you do this. We all need recognition

for the things we have done, but the most important thing we can do is to help children think well of themselves, so that their feelings of pride are genuinely their own. Praise can have negative implications; in

your attempts to make children feel good about themselves you can inadvertently undermine their capacity to feel proud themselves.

In simple terms, unless you are thoughtful about the way you respond to children, it is all too easy to turn them into 'praise junkies.' You can actually make them dependent on your

approval and take away their power to evaluate their own efforts. For this reason, it is really important that you develop encouragement strategies. This means that you must work hard at being descriptive rather than evaluative and acknowledge children's work and ideas by making specific comments. You must develop the skill of asking open-ended questions, and encourage children to describe their efforts, ideas and products. In short, you must develop their capacity to express for themselves the things they feel proud about.

Using photographs

When you talk with the children about the things they have achieved you can introduce the word 'proud', and suggest that in order to celebrate their achievement you might take a photograph of what they have done. Once you have trained them to use a camera they can take the photograph themselves. These photographs can then be displayed in a special 'Things we are proud of' book or on a special display board where there is a place for every child to have a picture of something they are proud of. If the thing they are proud of cannot be photographed the children can dictate the story of what they are feeling proud about. Encourage the adults in your setting to contribute to the display, and to talk to the children about the things they feel proud about.

Using puppets and toys

If you have a favourite teddy or soft toy, tell the children that he or she is feeling proud about something they have done. Explain that your character has done something to help someone, and that they feel really proud about it. You could even introduce another toy to represent the one that has been helped. Tell the children that one toy was crying because they had no-one to play with, or because someone was doing something unkind to them. Encourage the children to generate ideas for how the other toy may have helped, and use this as a springboard for getting them to talk about times when they have felt proud about the things they have done. Simple scenarios like this help the children to understand that you can feel proud for lots of different reasons.

If you have some large puppets, put them into situations that mirror the challenges the children have to deal with, and explore the feelings of pride that are experienced when challenges are overcome. You may like to try the following story scenario. I will call my puppets Jake and Mina; you can substitute the names of your own puppets.

Jake feels proud

Jake's mum tells him that a letter has come to say that he needs to go to the dentists for a check-up. Jake is frightened and does not want to go.

He tells his friend Mina about how he feels. Mina says that she never minds going to see the dentist, and tells Jake that if he is brave and goes for his check-up she will buy him a present.

Jake says that he will try to be brave, and his mum rings up to make an appointment for him.

Once he has been to see the dentist, Jake feels really proud of himself, and his mum and Mina tell him that they also feel proud about what he has done. Jake tells Mina all about the filling he had and then asks Mina if she has bought him the present that she promised him.

Mina hands Jake an envelope, and inside the envelope there is a really special toothbrush. Each time Jake uses it he feels proud about going to see the dentist, even though he felt frightened.

Once you have shared this scenario with the children, encourage them to think about the way in which Jake and Mina felt differently about going to the dentists. Talk about whether Mina had done anything that she could feel proud about. Start a 'tag line'. Sit the children in a circle and begin by saying: 'I feel proud when ….' share your own experiences with the children, and encourage them to tell everyone about something they have felt proud about.

Using pictures and posters

Another good way to explore this emotion is by cutting pictures from magazines and collecting posters of individuals and groups of people who are feeling proud of themselves. You can then make a display and invite the children to offer suggestions for why the people may be feeling proud. You might have a picture of a climber who has just reached a summit, a football team that has just scored a goal or won a match, a mother with a new baby or a child holding their new puppy. Once you start hunting you'll be amazed how many pictures you will find, and if you get the children and parents hunting too, you'll soon have a good collection.

You could also make a collection of medals, certificates and cups and explore why they might have been presented. This sort of activity helps the children to understand that feelings of pride can be experienced in a variety of contexts.

To help the children understand that different people feel proud about different things, collect pictures of different people or groups of people, for example a jockey, an athlete, a postman or woman, a police officer, a gardener, a mum, a dad, a grandma or grandad, a choir or a football team. Encourage the children to think about things that may make them feel proud, and be prepared to challenge stereotypes - the grandma may be very proud because she has just learned to ride a motor bike!

In common with many other emotions, feelings of pride can be full of subtlety and complexity, but by beginning to explore such feelings at an early age you can really help children towards a better understanding of both themselves and others.

Ros Bayley, early years consultant and trainer, Walsall.

Using published stories
There are numerous published stories about children who feel proud about things they have done, but the Alfie stories by Shirley Hughes are among the best.

In *Alfie's Feet (Red Fox)*, Alfie is so proud of his new wellingtons, and in *Alfie Gives a Hand*, Alfie overcomes his own fears in order to help another child.

Lucy's Picture by Nicola Moon (Orchard Books) is also an excellent book for exploring feelings of pride.

A feeling that may start out as frustration can quicky move on to become irritability. With a little careful thought, you can lead children (and yourself!) towards a greater level of understanding and self-knowledge

Exploring emotions:
feeling irritable

We all feel irritable from time to time, but this is a difficult emotion for children to understand. As adults, we are usually, although not always, able to rationalise and find reasons for our feelings of irritability, which at least goes some way to helping us cope with what we are feeling. For children, who have not yet developed this ability, such feelings can be uncomfortable and distressing.

However, by giving this emotion a little time and attention you can help children to deal with their feelings more effectively and make sure that the feelings do not spiral downwards into even more extreme feelings. Irritability is a subtle emotion; less extreme than anger or sadness, but without acknowledgement it can soon turn into anger or distress.

When we're feeling irritable we can be short-tempered and easily annoyed, and whilst we find this state easy to understand in adults, we are often far less tolerant and understanding when children are irritable. It is as if we do not expect children to experience this emotion!

It is also interesting to explore the ways in which irritability can often be traced back to quite precise human dilemmas. The cause could be physical, like feeling unwell or being

unable to meet a physical challenge. It could result from feeling jealous or inadequate, or it may be because we feel that we are not equal to an intellectual challenge, such as not knowing the answer to a question or being unable to work something out.

A feeling may start out as frustration, but move on to become irritability. With a little careful thought, you can lead children (and yourself!) towards a greater level of understanding and self-knowledge.

Acknowledging feelings

Young children find it difficult to understand abstract concepts, so they will find irritability far easier to recognise if it is acknowledged when it is happening. Next time you feel irritable or short-tempered, think about whether it would be worth sharing your feelings with the children! Tell them that you feel irritable and explain why. It may be that the baby kept you awake all night or your car broke down on the way to work. When the children appear to be irritable, talk with them about their feelings and their reasons for feeling that way.

Empathise with how they are feeling, even if they cannot explain why. It is all too easy to try to distract a child from the way they are feeling in an attempt to get them to 'snap out of it', but by talking with them about how they are feeling you expand their vocabulary of feeling words and help them to understand themselves better. You also help them to see that everyone feels irritable from time to time, and that it is nothing to feel guilty about.

Using puppets and toys

Using a puppet or a toy to explore

'Next time you feel irritable or short-tempered, think about whether it would be worth sharing your feelings with the children! Tell them that you feel irritable and explain why.'

irritability enables children to think, reason and apply what they have learned from experience in a context where they are not feeling irritable themselves. Think up some simple scenarios that mirror the things that lead to irritability in the children and use them as a springboard for discussion. You might like to try the following scenario. I call my puppet Gloria; you can substitute the name of your own puppet or toy.

Gloria at bedtime

Gloria was excited because her aunty and uncle were coming to tea. She could hardly wait for them to arrive but she enjoyed herself helping her mum to get the tea ready.

When she heard the car pull up outside she ran to the gate to meet her aunty and uncle and they all played in the garden until it was time to eat.

After tea, Gloria's Uncle Jo read her some stories and then her mum told her it was time for bed. Gloria didn't want to go to bed and begged for one more story, and then one more, until finally her mum said she must go to bed. Reluctantly, Gloria went upstairs to get ready for bed and her mum tucked her up

and then went downstairs, but Gloria couldn't go to sleep!

First she got up and went downstairs saying she was thirsty. Later, she got up saying that she had a stomach ache. Then she got up again to say that there was a spider in her bedroom. By the time it was midnight and her uncle and aunty had gone home Gloria was still awake.

When morning came she did not want to get up for nursery/school, did not want to get dressed and she would not eat her breakfast! She was so tired and irritable, that her mum had to almost drag her to school.

When she got to school her friends wanted to talk to her and show her things but Gloria wasn't interested. She did not feel like playing with anyone, and when it was time to sing she refused to join in. After singing Gloria tried to build a house with the Lego, but when it wouldn't work out she threw the Lego on the floor and stormed off to the book corner. Ten minutes later her friends found her curled up fast asleep in the book corner.

Once you have shared this scenario with the children, you can use it as the basis for a discussion. Ask questions to start things off. For example:

■ Why do you think Gloria kept getting out of bed?

■ Why do you think she was so irritable in the morning?

■ How do you think Gloria's mum felt about the way she was behaving?

■ How do you think the other children felt about how she behaved?

■ What do you think will happen when Gloria wakes up?

Encourage the children to relate the story to their own experience by asking them if they have ever felt the same way as Gloria. Spend a little time thinking about the ways in which people behave when they feel irritable, for example being snappy and short-tempered, being rude to people, not wanting to join in and finding it difficult to concentrate.

Share your own experiences

Talk with the children about the things that make you feel irritable and encourage the other adults in your setting to do the same. You might consider making a book or a pictorial display. Collect photographs of adults and children and by the side of the photographs record the things that make them feel irritated. This will help the children to understand that there are some things that cause irritation to us all, but that sometimes what irritates one person will not necessarily irritate another.

Using visual images

It is amazing how many pictures you can find in newspapers and magazines of both children and adults looking irritated! Make a collection of these pictures and encourage the children to speculate about why the people in the photographs might be irritated. Mix the pictures up with others that depict different kinds of feelings, and let the children sort them out. With younger children, take photographs of some of the adults in your setting looking irritated, for example when the children haven't put things away properly or when they have left the taps running! Once you put your mind to it you will be able to think of a whole host of reasons for being irritated!

• • • • ■ The S/NVQ Book

Using published stories

There are examples of people feeling irritable in many published stories, but one that is extremely useful is *The Good Mood Hunt* by Hiawyn Oram and Joanne Partis (OUP). In this story Hannah, the main character, wakes up feeling really happy, but becomes very irritable when she remembers that she has nothing to show in 'show and tell'. Encouraged by her father, she sets off to hunt for her good mood, which returns when she has found the things she wants for the show and tell session. As you explore this text, draw the children's attention to the illustrations and get them to notice the way in which Hannah's expressions and body language change with her changing moods.

Other useful texts for work in this area are *The Bad Tempered Ladybird* by Eric Carle (Puffin) and *Where the Wild Things Are* by Maurice Sendak (Red Fox).

As a way of exploring the ways in which adults feel irritated you might read *Not Now, Bernard!* by David McKee (Red Fox) or *It was Jake!* by Anita Jeram (Walker). Talk with the children about why they think the adults in these stories look and feel irritated. If you feel brave enough, get the children to identify the times when they have noticed *you* feeling irritated!

Irritation is not an easy emotion to deal with, as it is subtler than the more extreme feelings of anger or jealousy, so for this reason, it is probably best to leave focusing directly on it until you have developed the children's understanding of the more straightforward feelings. Having said this, children frequently astound us with the things they are able to understand, and by helping them to understand the nature of irritation, we will be leading them towards a better understanding of themselves and others.

Ros Bayley, early years consultant and trainer, Walsall.

Babies show what they feel - through crying and facial expressions - before they can say. As they grow, young children need your help to develop an emotional vocabulary so that they can share their experiences and feelings with those around them. Jennie Lindon explains

How children show their feelings

Babies show emotions through how they cry. As you get to know a baby, you recognise different kinds of crying. The first message may be 'I feel a bit grumpy but I'll mutter myself into a doze'. You may listen and wait to see what happens but respond when the level of cry increases to say, 'I'm unhappy now. You are coming soon, aren't you?' Babies should not be left to reach the desperate cry that tells you, 'Where are you? I'm all alone and now I'm scared!'

But babies also show they are content and happy with big smiles and gurgles. They wave their arms and legs around in excitement and anticipation. Babies' facial expressions soon let you know they are interested, a bit puzzled or on the doubtful side but not yet worried. You will still use all the non-verbal clues of facial expression and body language after they have started to say recognisable words. Tuning in to full communication remains important even when you are listening to fellow adults.

Developing an emotional vocabulary

In *Birth to Three Matters* (**A Skilful Communicator** 'Finding a voice') you will find the reminder against the logo for two-year-olds that, 'Children use language as a powerful means of widening contacts, sharing feelings, experiences and thoughts'. But such a skill does not simply appear because a child is two. Young children need your help to develop an emotional vocabulary within their language skills.

Babies need plenty of experiences that reassure them that familiar adults notice and care about their feelings. Young children need to feel confident that adults will listen. Two- and three-year-olds are unlikely to voice their emotions if early experience has taught them that their important adults do not want to know.

The 'Making meaning' component of **A Skilful Communicator** recommends, 'Let young babies know you understand what they're saying, for example when they are hungry, tired, happy, sad, lonely'. You show your support when you put babies' likely feelings into words.

Of course, they do not understand the words but your tone acknowledges and reassures. Support your actions with words like:

■ 'Does it feel a bit scary in your baby bath? Here, let's put your feet so you can feel the edge. Do you feel safer now?'

■ 'Are you feeling a bit grumpy after your doze? Let's sit a while, there's no rush.'

■ 'Did you feel lonely over there? (which might not be very far at all!) Come and snuggle up with me.'

■ 'Oh, what can you see? You look very interested!'

■ 'You look happy! Do you like that song? Shall we sing it again?'

Linking words with experience

You build the beginnings of understanding for young children because your words link with experiences. Words for feelings, like any abstract words, need to be clearly connected with what is right in front of children. Otherwise they are mystified about what you are saying. Toddlers start with naming and then action words. It is unrealistic to expect even older toddlers to use many words for abstract ideas, and feelings are very abstract. But you help them start to learn the words for emotions by being as concrete as possible about feelings.

Give young children plenty of direct experience of emotional vocabulary and they will soon start to use the words themselves. For example:

■ 18-month-old Tanya adores a brightly coloured shawl from the dressing-up box in the drop-in centre. Her childminder takes the opportunity to say, 'Tanya, you look very pleased. Have you got your favourite shawl? Do you want me to help wrap it around you?'

■ Two-year-old Jackson is complaining about having to leave his cars to have his nappy changed. His key person has given him some more time and now acknowledges his feelings with, 'Yes, Jackson, I know you're not keen to leave the garage and the cars. But we really do need to get you out of that wet nappy. How about you hold tight to your favourite car?'

Sometimes, you will be uncertain about a child's feeling. Then you can put feelings into words in a tentative way. For instance:

■ 'You look puzzled. Have you lost something?'

■ 'Marsha, I think you have your sad face today. Are you feeling sad about something?'

■ 'Sandra, you look a bit uncertain up there (on the slide). Would you like my hand?' Then, if the child accepts your hand, you can acknowledge with, 'Does that feel safer?'

When you focus carefully on children's feelings, you can become more aware of your own. Are you tempted to say, 'Cheer up!' or jolly young children along because you feel brought down by their sadness?

Some adults fear that acknowledging children's sadness will only make them more upset. In fact, simple acknowledgement reassures children. On the other hand, children who are relentlessly jollied along and told to 'come and do a painting' can feel more distressed. They may think that you do not really care or that nobody is supposed to show they are upset.

It is unrealistic to expect under-threes to manage a sophisticated grasp of other people's feelings. But you can help them along the way through your comments about events, for example talking about your own feelings. You might say, 'What a loud noise; that made me jump!' or 'I feel frustrated. We all wanted to go to the library and I forgot it was closed today.' You can also help by commenting kindly on the feelings of other children, for example:

- 'Ivan is crying because he misses his Mummy.'

- 'I think Jessica is upset because she was playing with that bucket. Shall we ask her?'

- 'Stevie, I know you feel sad today. You're missing your friend Jamal. But it's not fair to make Rosie feel sad too. She was trying to cheer you up and you told her to go away.'

Using books and puppets

In *Birth to Three Matters,* the card for 'Emotional well being' (**A Healthy Child**) says, 'Provide stories, pictures and puppets which allow children to experience and talk about feelings'. This suggestion is made against the backdrop of plenty of personal time spent with young children. Books or puppets will not take the place of simple conversations linking to events and experiences that have meaning for young children. Play resources work well to complement your communication. For instance:

- You can read or tell stories that highlight feelings. The emotions may emerge directly through the storyline or there are opportunities to wonder out loud what a character may be feeling.

- Books that directly explore different feelings may start to support two-year-olds, so long as there are good illustrations. But twos and young threes are more likely to relate to emotions linked with a storyline.

- You can use props like puppets or simple story bags to make a narrative come alive. Twos and young threes are ready to imagine that a puppet has feelings and to speak for that puppet.

Sharing with parents

The effective practice box for 'Emotional well-being' (**A Healthy Child**) recommends that you 'Establish shared understandings between home and setting about ways of responding to babies' emotions'.

Open communication with families can show up any potential differences. Perhaps you need to reassure parents, who feel they must take a tough line on crying, that you are not spoiling their baby or toddler. But you can also share examples of a child's experiences and likely feelings.

- It might be that Stevie's father needs to know that his son misses Jamal.

- You can tell Sandra's mother that her daughter was thrilled to manage the slide with a guiding hand.

- You can share with Damian's grandmother, who is his primary carer, that Damian was fascinated by the emotions felt by the characters in the story you read today.

Jennie Lindon is a child psychologist and author. She has worked for nearly 30 years with services for children and their families.

Do you want to find out more?

- *The Social Toddler* Helen and Clive Dorman (The Children's Project Tel: 020 8546 8750 www.childrensproject.co.uk)
- *Listening as a Way of Life* (free leaflets from the Early Childhood Unit Tel: 020 7843 6000 or download from www.earlychildhood.org.uk)
- *Childwatching: a Parent's Guide to Children's Body Language* Susan Quilliam (Ward Lock)
- www.talktoyourbaby.org.uk: A useful website for practitioners as well as parents – information and downloadable resources

When a child behaves in a way that shows there may be underlying emotional problems it can be useful to set aside time for play therapy sessions. Eleanor Patrick explains what this means and how children can benefit

Exploring feelings through play

There is always a reason for how children behave, often related to unacknowledged or unprocessed feelings. By learning to use play therapy skills on a one-to-one basis, you not only gain insight into possible reasons for a child's behaviour but also offer them an opportunity to resolve difficult feelings through play rather than verbally.

Using play therapy skills doesn't mean you are providing therapy - although it may be therapeutic for the child. It does not replace professional counselling with a trained play therapist. In the 1960s, Bernard Guerney, who had the idea of training parents to play therapeutically with their children in this way, called it filial therapy. Professional carers are also well placed to do this.

A special kind of play

Some forms of play are adult led: 'Try turning the piece round – see if it fits the other way', 'I know - let's drape this over the table and make a lion's den!'.

Non-directive play therapy is quite different.

■ The child leads the play.

■ You concentrate on the child and have no other activity on the go.

■ You join in only in the way the child asks.

■ You offer no suggestions/ encouragement/ praise/ criticism/ teaching.

■ You accept the child's feelings as valid.

■ You reflect the child's feelings and actions verbally to raise awareness of them.

Why use these skills?

Children need to process their daily experiences. This usually happens unconsciously, but with constant new input, it can be neglected. For example, if children experience or hear about a burglary, they need to process the information to gain understanding about the events, the fear involved, and how safe they really are. If there is no time for processing, the event lurks in the background, producing floating fears that show up in other areas of life.

Play is where children do this 'work' of coming to terms with life. When they are assured of acceptance, whatever their feelings, children are able to re-run troubling events, make meaning of them, face their fears, work out alternatives and come to terms with the world they live in.

Most of this is done symbolically: the tiger may represent mother, an illness or a fear, for example, perhaps even the strong, brave person the child wants to be. The child gains control and mastery ina way that is appropriate for their age and stage of development as the various symbols interact in their play scenario. Setting aside a regular session and giving it your exclusive attention communicates that what is being done is worthwhile and important. Where a child has specific problems it is an invaluable investment of time.

Who can benefit?

Play therapy is usually appropriate for children from four to eleven who show:

■ Problems with expressing feelings appropriately.

■ Difficulties in relating to others.

■ Symptoms of unhappiness or insecurity, maybe bedwetting or nightmares.

■ Confused or distressed reactions to events such as family splits, bereavement or loss, change of school, hospitalisation.

Running the session

When preparing to spend some time using play therapy skills, consider:

■ **Place** – preferably private and uninterrupted. In a community setting it is still possible to allow visibility (for child protection) without undermining the child's need for privacy.

■ **Time** – half an hour is ideal. Consistency and commitment are more important than how long.

■ **Toys** – generic rather than brand names (for example, a bea, not Pooh Bear) and exclusive to the session, but not expensive or numerous.

■ **Limits** – basic limits include not breaking

toys or hurting you, not leaving the play space, not bringing favourite toys to the session or taking yours away, and any other rule necessary in the particular location. Within these limits, the child is allowed to play as he wishes. Children quickly understand that these are special circumstances.

Explain to the child that they can play with whatever they want but wait quietly while they decide what to do. While the child plays, reflect *content* and *feeling* from time to time (total silence does not convey interest). Comments like 'You've decided exactly how you want them lined up' (reflection of content) or 'That gorilla looks really angry with hippo' (reflection of emotion) show the child you are paying attention. You may even say, 'I wonder how that baby feels?' It doesn't matter if no answer comes. That's the child's choice. You are simply aiding their emotional processes.

Reflection of emotion should always be kept within the storyline and not interpreted as

referring to the child – the child has a right to keep at a safe distance to feelings. However, if the child openly owns the feeling - 'I'm sick of you' (said to the doll) - this is rightly reflected as 'You're really fed up with her'.

If the child asks you to play a part – 'I'm having this puppet, you have leopard', 'Help! Fetch an ambulance, quick!' or 'I'm making a sand storm, will you help?' - do just that ('Okay, the ambulance is coming: der-der der-der') and either wait or ask for further instructions ('What do you want leopard to do?'). Keeping quiet and waiting for the child to make decisions is the hardest part of all! Reflecting the content and feelings and playing your part at the same time does take practice, but the child is not aware that this play is meant to be therapeutic intention and a few 'errors' will not be disastrous.

Common themes

If you have been worried about a child's behaviour, you will almost certainly find specific themes played out repeatedly with a changing cast of characters, perhaps:

- ■ aggression

- ■ crashes/accidents

- ■ family and nurturing

- ■ safety and control

- ■ exploration of a particular event

- ■ sexuality

- ■ fixing/rescuing/making things better.

If you watch for themes you will be able to understand more of the cause of a child's behavioural problems. The evidence is that children can usually sort out the problem feelings themselves through this type of play. If not, you will at least know what to keep track of, what to help with, or what to talk to parents about. Your own ethical guidelines will dictate what should or should not be shared.

As well as helping children to express emotions appropriately and master difficult circumstances, the use of non-directive play therapy skills contributes to children having

more confidence and self-esteem, taking responsibility for decisions, and gaining in emotional resilience. This will serve them well in future.

Eleanor Patrick is a qualified counsellor trained in working with children and young people. She uses counselling and play therapy with primary school children.

Toys you can use

Choose a few toys that can be used in many ways – ones that encourage emotional expression:

- ■ Paper and markers.

- ■ Clay/playdough.

- ■ Miniatures: bendy people (various families, including those from minority ethnic groups), animals, cars.

- ■ Sand tray – damp: for building/demolishing/burying, and (used with other toys) for miniature fights, race tracks, town/school stories and so on.

- ■ Dolls plus feeding bottle, shawl, clothes.

- ■ Tea set, doctor's set, two telephones.

- ■ Dolls' house (or small open boxes for rooms)

- ■ Animal glove puppets (can serve as people or animals).

These toys leave the child free to go where need and imagination lead. If privacy is ensured, both boys and girls will use any of these toys.

Children of all ages squabble. Toddlers snatch and grab, school-aged children shout and teenagers bicker! It drives parents insane and can take up so much of your time each day. So what is squabbling about and do children gain anything from it? Penny Tassoni explains

What to do when children squabble

Squabbling can appear quite early on. Mobile babies can descend and take toys from their sitting peers. Sometimes the snatch and grab raid goes unnoticed but, as babies become more aware of objects, they tend to hang onto them or get upset. These early squabbles are quickly over and an offer of an alternative toy usually calms things down. It is worth reassuring parents that such squabbles are not signs of delinquency, but merely the result of a baby's curiosity and desire to explore.

Push me, pull me

Tears and falling out over toys continues with toddlers. This is in some ways understandable. Toddlers, like babies, are attracted to interesting activities and toys, but whilst babies can be distracted, toddlers remain focused. A toddler will go over to another child and try and grab whatever is of interest. This sometimes results in a push me, pull me contest which can, if you are not quick off the mark, quickly get out of hand. Scratches and bites are notoriously common in this age range and so careful intervention is important to avoid some toddlers becoming serial biters!

However you decide to intervene or manage the situation, it is always important to remember that toddlers are victims of their own needs. They don't yet have the language to express themselves nor the social skills to understand about ownership. But they do, on the other hand, have impulsive desires that often prove impossible to rein in. For adults this is a testing time! You may have to learn to be patient and use avoidance strategies to prevent squabbles and tantrums for the next year or so. The dreamed for co-operative play and turn taking gradually comes along when children are about three years old.

Beginning to get along?

From around three years, you should find that most children are able to get along with others, although this does not mean an end to squabbles. Squabbles, from this point onwards, can have a variety of causes and are not always just about possessions. Learning to think about the true source of the squabble can help you to respond sensitively.

Power and jealousy

Power mixed with a dose of jealousy is often a root cause of some squabbling, particularly between siblings and children of different ages who spend a lot of time together. It is not uncommon to see an older child taking a toy away from a baby or toddler. The toy is not often wanted for play and once the younger child begins to cry, the toy is returned. A point has been made: remember, I'm boss!

Whilst this behaviour is not acceptable, thinking about the child's need for power should make you reflect on how secure the child is feeling. Is the younger child's presence a threat, even though the child himself may not consciously realise it? If power and insecurity is the issue, then the way you deal with it needs to reflect this. Look for ways of 'empowering' the older child by giving them particular responsibilities that only they can do. Encourage them to choose the toys to put out and ask their advice about the toys needed for the baby or toddler. Consider involving them in some of the care for the younger child if they are interested and, above all, make sure that they do get some special time with you where they can just cuddle up or play a game.

You need to think about the way in which you might intervene when a squabble has occurred. Whilst going straight in and telling a child off may seem the most straightforward action, unfortunately, if jealousy is part of the cause, it is unlikely to help in the longer term.

Consider instead going for a lower profile. Ask the older child gently if they can help the other child to stop crying, which usually entails the return of the possession. Once calm has been restored, you could tell the older child how much the younger one counts on them, as this is usually the case. Point out to the older child how the younger one often looks to see what he is doing. This can come as a revelation as many older children do not realise that their younger sibling's interferences in games and toys are often a result of admiration.

Different points of view

Squabbles often break out when children have different opinions of how best to manage a game or activity. This can sometimes come as a surprise to adults as one minute children are happily playing together and the next their voices are raised and one is pushing another

around. Here, it is important to monitor the situation. Going in too quickly may prevent children reaching their own solution, but always standing back may mean that some children simply learn to shout and impose their will on others. A good tactic can be to amble over and simply ask children how their game is getting along and whether they need anything. Taking this approach can calm things down and also help children to articulate what is happening. If possible, avoid becoming the referee as this can teach children that only adults can sort out their problems. Try instead to ask them about how they might resolve their dispute and give pointers as hints such as 'Will everyone have the chance to join in?' or 'Do you have enough things?'

Boundary disputes

Children can be protective of their space and the activity they are engaged in. One child may reach over and take more dough than is considered fair or

a group of enthusiastic track builders may encroach into the space of the toy farmers. Again, thinking about the cause of the dispute can be helpful before intervening. Have children just become over enthusiastic? Or is the layout and set-up of materials part of the problem? A low-key response which enables children to find their own answers can be helpful. You might ask, 'It looks as if you have a problem here. Can you think about how you might share this space?' Tools such as egg timers and rotas can come in useful as children can see the fairness of such organisation.

It is also worth looking afterwards at how much equipment you have provided and the way in which it is laid out. Individual mats each with a lump of dough can help children to see how much dough is available. Equally, developing good-bye routines when leaving an activity can be helpful for children who come back only to find someone else playing in 'their place'. Rolling the dough back into a ball or putting the jigsaws into the middle of the table can help children to sign off from an activity.

Boredom, hunger and tiredness

Never forget children's key needs. Boredom from waiting in a line or for a snack can mean that children can begin to jostle uncomfortably. You may need to think about whether you have put out enough materials and appealing activities, especially if you have several children milling around, all wanting to do the same thing at the same time. Think too about whether children are basically tired or hungry as this can lead them - and even some adults - into fractious behaviour.

Finally, think about yourselves as role models. Children need to learn the skills of negotiation and thoughtfulness from you. You, too, need to be ready to listen, take your turn and compromise!

Penny Tassoni, author and educational consultant.

Communication is part of everything we do, and poor communication can cause problems. It is worth taking the time to consider the most effective strategies to use when communicating with parents, with colleagues and with your team

Improve the way you communicate

You should always communicate in a way that is easy to understand and remember that sometimes you need to be explicit and state the obvious to avoid assumptions being made.

We have a tendency to hear what we want to hear and we learn to expect certain communications in certain situations. This can lead to confusion when these expectations are not met. When you want people to take notice of anything new or different you want to communicate, you need to highlight it so they will take notice and expect the unexpected.

Communication is a two-way process involving the person delivering the message and the person listening. The deliverer or sender is responsible for engaging the listener and needs to communicate in a way that is easy to understand. The listener may choose not to listen if the message is delivered inappropriately or at an inconvenient time.

So what can you do to make sure your communication skills are up to scratch? Firstly, remember communication is not just about what you say but how you say it. Research has shown that communication can be broken down as follows:

- 55 per cent body language

- 38 per cent your voice

- 7 per cent the content

So you could be telling someone a juicy piece of gossip, but if your voice has no expression, your facial expression disinterested, your body slumped, no one is going to be interested in what you have to say. Put expression in your

Better communication means that:

- you approach work in an organised way;

- you have a setting that runs smoothly;

- staff and parents are informed and happy;

- you work better as a team because there are clearly defined roles and responsibilities;

- problems are dealt with quickly and effectively.

voice, lift your face up and appear animated and it is a different story.

In any verbal exchange, there is a sender and receiver. While two people in a conversation will take on both roles, the person who started up the conversation is always the sender. For the sender and receiver, there are some simple rules to follow.

As the sender, you should :

- Be clear about what you want to say.

- Look at the person you are speaking to, so it is easier for them to understand you and pick up on any non verbal clues.

- Speak clearly.

- Consider the feelings of the person you are speaking to. This is particularly important if you are telling someone something which may cause upset.

- Choose carefully the time and place you speak, a mutually convenient time, not when a parent is rushing, for example.

- Check that the person has understood what you have said. This ensures you know you have got your message across.

- Make sure your words match up with the way you are sounding.

- Vary the tone and pace at which you speak so that your voice is interesting to listen to.

Don't:

- Complicate what you are saying with too much detail or difficult language. It is easy to slip into jargon with parents, be considerate.

- Talk so much that the other person has no chance to comment or ask questions.

- Be vague. Give concrete examples.

- Put down, attack or ridicule the person you are talking to.

- Use particular ideas you know will irritate the other person.

- Ignore signs of confusion, resentment or disinterest in the person to whom you are speaking. If this is the case you need to stop and get some clarification.

- Speak in a detached, remote fashion; keep them interested.

For the receiver:
- Look at the person who is speaking to you and give them your full attention. Then they know you are listening.

- Recognise how the speaker feels about what they are saying. This is particularly relevant when there is obvious distress.

- Look for points to agree with rather than to argue with. Always start your response with a positive.

- Give a quick summary of what you have heard. This tells the sender you have listened and understood.

Don't:
- Interrupt the speaker to give your views. Letting them finish gives you a clear picture of the point they are trying to make.

- Let your previous experience of the person put you off.

- Be negative about or belittle what the person is saying.

- Change the subject, even if you are disinterested!

- Fidget or distract the speaker.

The six steps of communication

By following these steps and incorporating the rules for the sender and the receiver, you can make it easier to communicate and feel confident.

Step 1: Know your purpose
Be clear in your mind what you want to get across and what you would like the outcome of the exchange to be. This ensures you get to the point quickly and don't ramble.

Step 2: Decide the best method
What would be the most effective way of delivering your message or getting a piece of information across? On a one to one, in a meeting, with a group, over the phone?

Step 3: Overcome barriers
There can be many barriers - nerves, lack of confidence, a previous bad experience with a person. These need to be put aside otherwise they will affect the fluency of your communication.

Step 4: Choose your time and place
This can make the difference between understanding and misunderstanding.

Step 5: Transmit the message
Say what you need to say.

Step 6: Obtain feedback
Was the communication received and understood? Don't make an assumption - check.

Are you a good communicator?
So now you know the theory, is there any way you can check how effective your communication skills are?

The best thing to do is to begin by analysing someone else's communication skills. This helps you to focus on identifying positives and areas for improvement.

Firstly, identify a speaker. This could be a television presenter or a trainer on a course. You then need to:

1) Establish the aim of the communication, for example explaining, reminding, asking, informing, recounting.

2) What is the speaker's verbal manner? Angry, patient, insistent, friendly?

3) Describe the speaker's physical manner, facial expressions, gestures, body language, and so on.

4) Who is the communication aimed at?

5) What is the speaker's relationship to the person/people identified in answer to question 4?

Once you have answered these questions you need to decide if the speaker communicated effectively and achieved their aims? What aspects of their delivery made them successful/unsuccessful?

Having identified positives, you can then relate them to yourself when you are communicating with an individual or a group. Do you employ these strategies? Are there any other positives you use? Can you identify any areas for improvement?

Remembering and using all these basic principles of effective communication can make life in your setting much easier for you and those with whom you come into contact, and help in the smooth running of the setting. The more you put these principles into practice, the more skilled you will become.

Jenny Barber, early years and childcare trainer and consultant, Buckinghamshire.

Background reading
Managing Staff in the Early Years Setting A Langston and A Smith (Routledge)

Working with parents, we start by looking at the information that you should give them, and how to establish trust

Providing information and establishing trust

Parents and carers are of central importance to children and their lives – they are the prime source of love and affection, and the providers of basic necessities such as food and a home. They are also children's primary educators and influencers. It is good practice for you to work in partnership with parents and carers, and a requirement under Standard 12 of the National Daycare Standards. Partnerships help:

- Families to feel confident that children are properly cared for by trustworthy practitioners.

- You understand the needs of individual children and families.

- Children to settle as the transition from home to setting is eased – children often sense when parents or carers are anxious and they may feel insecure as a result.

- Create a relationship where personal, confidential information about families and children can be shared in confidence.

- Create a relationship where support and help can be asked for and received by both you and the parents/carers.

- Key adults in the child's life to share the same childcare strategies, promoting consistency and helping children to learn. For example, when toilet training or when managing challenging behaviour.

- Create a forum where problems or issues that arise can be openly discussed and worked through.

Creating a culture

Childminders and nannies working alone are the only point of contact for parents and carers and so it is vital that they recognise how important partnerships are. Working with parents and carers is also a critical aspect of the job for key workers in childcare settings, who have the primary responsibility to form and maintain good relationships with individual families.

But for a culture of working in real partnership with parents and carers to thrive, everyone within an organisation must understand the importance of establishing trust and maintaining good relationships with adults, as well as with the children themselves. A setting should whole-heartedly value and respect parents and carers, and all staff should consistently ensure that their words and actions promote these values.

It takes everyone to work effectively with parents and carers because:

- **Everyone contributes to the atmosphere of a setting**

For instance, when everyone present greets parents and children as they arrive, it makes them feel welcomed. If only a family's key worker acknowledged them, the atmosphere would be less welcoming. Only one person is required to receive the child, but everyone in the room can call hello and contribute to positive relations.

- **The key worker will not always be free**

Parents and carers may need to talk to someone else to pass on information, and

they must be confident to approach other members of staff.

- **The key worker will not always be in attendance**

There will be times when the key worker is sick or on holiday – families need to feel confident that their child is still well cared for, and that they will still have a point of contact within the setting.

- **Other staff will work with the child day to day**

Parents and carers will want to know all the staff that work alongside their child and are therefore important within their child's life, whether they are a supervisor or a trainee.

- **There may be an issue with the key worker**

In which case, a parent or carer may prefer to discuss the situation with a senior member of staff, whom they should feel confident to approach.

Initial information

When parents and carers first register their children, you have a good opportunity to start to build a relationship based on trust. The routine of gathering information about an individual child should be used positively to assure adults that you understand and respect that each child and family is different, and that they will have different expectations, requirements and needs. (See 'Settling-in procedures' *Practical Professional Child Care* August 2005). However, it is equally crucial for parents and carers to be given information about the setting in return.

Welcome packs

To avoid overwhelming parents and carers with more than they can take in at one time, you may find it helpful to compile a welcome pack that contains useful written information (parents may sign a form to confirm that they've received it). This may include copies of policies, an explanation of the setting's routine, and how a child's learning and development is planned for and assessed. It may also include practical guidelines, such as the procedures to follow to book holidays, and how and when to pay fees or use childcare or education vouchers.

However, although information packs can be a future source of reference for parents and carers, handing them out cannot replace explaining things in person. For example, we often find people's names and job roles difficult to remember at first, so it is helpful for staff to wear badges or for labelled photographs of staff to be displayed somewhere prominent. But this should not replace introductions - families are generally keen to meet the staff who will be working with their child. Introductions break the ice and are the first step to establishing a rapport.

Key points

It is helpful to explain the key points of important policies and procedures - how you handle inappropriate behaviour for instance, or what happens if a child becomes ill. You can then assure families that full details are included in their pack. Invite any queries that may occur later on once adults have had a chance to read all the information provided.

Accessible information

Remember that parents and carers may have differing requirements when it comes to receiving information. You should ask families about these, and take the relevant steps to make sure your information is accessible to everyone. For instance, you may need to arrange for print to be enlarged, your home language to be translated into a foreign language or Braille, or for an audio tape to be made. You should also consider the best way to pass on different pieces of information.

You may use a combination of:

- One-to-one scheduled meetings with key workers;

- Group meetings held for families (perhaps specifically for new families in settings where there is a scheduled intake);

- Brief conversations held when parents/carers drop off/collect children;

- Current newsletters;

- Display boards;

- Welcome packs.

Parents and carers need initial information about:

- Staff – names and job roles, particularly the role of the key worker;

- Routines – what happens when each day, including information about meals, snacks, rest periods and toileting;

- The overall ethos of the settings – the principles that are promoted;

- Policies and procedures – that inform the way the setting operates;

- Curriculum or activities – how the setting promotes the Early Learning Goals where appropriate, or otherwise plans playful activities to stimulate children's learning and development.

- Current themes or topics if used – and how families can become involved in children's learning;

- Records – how children's current learning and development will be assessed and how progress will be tracked;

- Special events – already planned for the future;

- Day-to-day information – the methods by which they will be informed about

Building trust

Parents and carers come to trust practitioners over time when practitioners:

- Consistently behave professionally;

- Do the things they say they will do;

- Promote the policies and procedures of the setting, including the maintenance of confidentiality;

- Are honest and open, particularly if a problem occurs;

- Establish a caring relationship with their child.

Where to find out more

www.standards.dfee.gov.uk/parentalinvolvement

www.early-years.org.uk/eyos/weblinks/html/parents.htm

www.daycaretrust.org.uk

www.care.org.uk/family

www.parentalk.co.uk

www.parentsonline.gov.uk

www.parentlineplus.org.uk

www.oneparentfamilies.org.uk

www.disabledparents.net

A Practical Guide to Working with Parents and Carers by Hobart and Frankel (Nelson Thornes) 0-7487-3906-8

how children have been, what they've done and the friends they've made.

Miranda Walker is an early years and playwork writer, trainer and speaker. She owns daycare settings in Devon.

Communication, of which listening is part, is an exchange of ideas, contact between individuals and interaction; so if these are to be effective both the speaker and listener should be involved.

Listening skills for practitioners

Listening is a basic and fundamental communication skill. It is not a passive activity; so it just does not happen. To be a good listener requires time, effort and concentration. Being a good listener does not come naturally to some people. They find that they are easily distracted, or that their feelings about a person can affect how well they listen.

You should be aware that listening is a two way skill, involving a giver (speaker) and a receiver (listener). Both have to be equally active in order for effective listening to take place. There are skills that you can learn to make you a more effective listener and therefore a better communicator, with children, colleagues parents and other professionals.

Be aware of triggers that stop you listening.

Sometimes we can react negatively to certain words and this will have an effect on how well we are listening. These words are sometimes called 'red-flag' words. When we become upset or irritated we stop listening. What are your 'red-flag' words?

Jen had arranged a meeting with the parent of a child in the after school club, as the child's behaviour was giving the staff cause for concern. Jen said that when the parent came in she was pleasant enough and we talked briefly about the weather and what was going on in the club. 'When I started to talk about her daughter, the parents became quite agitated and started using four letter words, which I hate. I found that I stopped listening to what she was saying because I was getting upset with her language. The meeting was a complete waste of time from my point of view as we didn't talk about the child. I know that I will have to set up another meeting but I will have to think very carefully what I will do if she starts using my' red-flag' words.'

Give the person who is speaking your undivided attention.

Let them know that you are listening attentively. Try not to be distracted by other things going on around you. If the situation you are in is noisy and there are distractions suggest to the speaker either that you find somewhere quieter or that you continue the conversation at a better time.

We live in a noisy world, many of us will get into a car and the radio or music will come on as soon as the car is started. We go into supermarkets with piped music, or lifts in shops. Frequently we can't actually remember what music was playing; we seem to have developed a skill for blocking out sounds and not listening. Whilst this can be good in a busy supermarket, it should not happen when you are talking on a one-to-one basis with another person.

Try to maintain eye contact, without staring, which can make people and children feel uncomfortable. Use appropriate body language and gestures, such as nods of the head, perhaps saying,' yes' or 'mmm'.

Be careful that in your attempts to maintain eye contact that you do not become 'glassy eyed'. Sometimes when we look intently at someone we can appear to be listening although out minds might be on other things. However it is usually quite easy to see when someone is doing this!

Focus on the person speaking.

This is especially important if you are discussing a problem or cause for concern. Make sure that when you are listening you are giving your attention to the speaker, taking into account their body language, facial expressions and gestures. It can be quite easy to focus on the problem or cause of concern rather than the person and this will make you a less effective listener.

Whilst the content of what the person is saying is important you should not fall into the danger of concentrating on a

'Make sure that when you are listening you are giving your attention to the speaker, taking into account their body language, facial expressions and gestures.'

few facts to the detriment of everything else. Often when we want to remember something we go over facts in our minds so that we do not forget them. While we are doing this, the speaker had often moved on to something new and we have missed it.

Ask questions of the other person.

This shows that you have listened to what they were saying and that you either want more information or perhaps clarification of some points. Don't be afraid to ask the speaker to repeat something; it is better to make sure that you have heard correctly rather than guess and run the risk of misunderstandings or misinterpretations.

Ask questions that are open-ended and don't just give a yes or no response. Open-ended questions give the speaker the opportunity to develop what they were saying, especially if you say something like, 'Can you tell me more about....?' Or 'Will you explain to me what you meant by....?' Asking open-ended question doesn't mean that you haven't listened but rather that you want more information and are interested in what the person has said.

Sometimes when a speaker challenges our views or opinions we can feel uncomfortable. When this happens, we can appear to ask many questions, but what often happens is that we stand firm to our own opinions and in effect stop listening to the other person's point of view. We use the questions as a way of getting the other person to change their mind and agree with us. This can be called 'matter –over-mind' listening.

Summarize what the other person has said.

This makes you listen carefully and lets the other person who was speaking know that you have understood what they have said. Summarising also reduces the possibility of misunderstandings. Sometimes however we make decisions

about what has been said, or about the person speaking before they have finished. This often means that we stop listening and so can not summarise what ahs been said. This can also happen if the speaker says something that we find boring or does not make sense. This is sometimes called 'open-ears, closed mind' listening.

· · · · · · · · · · · · · · · · ·
Ash is a student in a day care setting; he is the only male practitioner. His mentor is female and unfortunately Ash does not seem to get on very well with her. 'All she can talk about is clothes and where she is going that night, she is so boring. Also her voice is so high all the time she gives me a headache.' When asked by his assessor what support the mentor has given him, Ash could really give a proper answer and admitted that when she started talking he 'switched off'.
· · · · · · · · · · · · · · · · ·

In the same way, now and again people will talk about something that we think is too difficult or complex for us, so we don't ask question because it might make us feel stupid and so we stop listening and switch off.

Sheila Riddall-Leach, Educational Consultant, Trainer and Author

CCLD 302, Develop and maintain a healthy, safe and secure environment for children

About this unit

This is a mandatory unit and considers how you develop and maintain an environment which promotes children's and young people's health and safety and ensures that they are protected. You will need to show that you understand how to keep all children safe and secure while they are in your setting, both indoors and outside and also when you take them out. This is not something that you would do once a week; it should be a vital part of your work, for every moment that you spend with children.

The word 'environment' covers a wide range of things; it is not only about what we can see, hear, touch and smell, but also about the atmosphere that exists in your setting. This means that, as well as making sure that physical environment is safe, healthy and secure, we should make sure that children and their families feel wanted and welcome when they enter (see Chapter 2). It is also about making sure that all people who work in the setting are at all times ensuring that every child is benefiting from being there (CCLD 302.1).

It is vital that the children's environment is healthy, safe and secure, so make sure that you know the current health and safety legislation requirements. These are covered in the knowledge specifications K3P189, K3H193 and K3H246. As always, you should try to cover them in your other observed evidence and you can cross-reference with other units where appropriate. Health, safety and security requirements are frequently up-dated and modified to meet the needs of all children, so it is crucial that you keep your knowledge current. Look out for relevant training courses and events provided by your local Children and Young People's Workforce Development team; not only are these excellent ways of keeping up-to-date, but also provide good opportunities to meet with other like-minded people and share ideas and expertise (CCLD 302.2).

When accidents, emergencies or illnesses occur in your setting you must know how to respond in line with the agreed policies and procedures. You should have a current first aid qualification and although it may not technically be a requirement of your position, it is good practice and this qualification should relate to the age of the children with whom you are working. There must be at least one member of staff on site who is a qualified first aider. Of course, if you are working as a home-based carer, a first aid qualification is essential. This is covered in the knowledge specification K3S198 (CCLD 302.3).

Developing and maintaining a healthy, safe and secure environment is an essential part of your role for all the children and young people in your care. It is even more important if you have disabled children or those with special educational needs. It does not

'I had the opportunity to get a Basic Food Hygiene Certificate through my local authority. Although some of it was common sense, it did make me think about how food is handled in our setting, and I have to admit that sometimes we didn't get it quite right. We do now though!'

NVQ candidate

necessarily mean that these children are at more risk, but they may need more adult support at certain times.

This unit has three elements of competence and you must have evidence for all three elements in your portfolio. These elements are:

- CCLD 302.1 Establish a healthy, safe and secure environment for children.
- CCLD 302.2 Maintain a healthy, safe and secure environment for children.
- CCLD 302.3 Supervise procedures for accidents, injuries, illnesses and other emergencies.

Each one of the elements will be discussed in turn, together with suggested ways of collecting and recording your evidence.

As suggested in the previous chapter, it is a good idea to read through the knowledge specifications for the entire unit. These are printed in your handbook at the end of each unit. You will need to show that you know and understand the information in each specification, and can show how you can apply and use that knowledge in your work place. Some of the knowledge specifications may require you to do some personal research and reading; for example, those relating to health, safety and security requirements and regulations. Make sure that you are familiar with the relevant policies and procedures in your setting.

OfSTED has launched a website around two of the five outcomes for children – Stay Safe and Be Healthy. The website is called Safe and Sound and has information showing how you can help children to be safe and healthy. Further details of this website are given at the end of this chapter. Also, look at the end of this chapter for suggested further reading, which you may find helpful.

CCLD 302.1 Establish a healthy, safe and secure environment for children

Getting started

As a childcare practitioner you have a key responsibility for the safety of the children in your care. You are put into a position of trust by the parents. They trust you to care for and look after their children all the time they are with you. Safety is a basic element for sustaining life. Unhealthy environments can cause the spread of disease, infections and illness that could threaten children's well-being, and children who feel secure are more than likely to be emotionally secure as well. This reinforces the belief that overall CCLD 302 is a very important unit.

This element has six PCs and you must provide evidence for all of them. In this unit you are aiming to show that you:

- have up-to-date and accurate information about the health, safety and security requirements for your setting.
- check all areas of your setting and identify and record hazards.
- identify and remove those hazards that can be eliminated.
- assess the levels of risk for all other hazards and establish procedures for managing these risks to an acceptable level.
- make sure that all children and adults using the setting have information about the health, safety and security procedures relevant to them.
- review and revise your health, safety and security procedures in line with changing circumstances and requirements and make improvements.

Key Issues

Many of the legal and regulatory requirements for health and safety will be covered in your setting's policies and procedures (CCLD 302.1.1). All policies should be reviewed regularly, at least once a year as a minimum or if circumstances change, such as a new room being added to the setting or if a child with specific health and safety needs starts at the setting. Everyone who works in the setting should be involved with the review of policies. It may also be appropriate to involve children and young people in the review process. Children can see things from a different perspective to adults and will have very relevant views that should be considered (CCLD 302.1.6).

Risk assessments should be regularly carried out, not just for rooms or buildings, but on equipment and toys, and outside as well as indoors. Once you have identified hazards, make note of the possible risks and what action you can take to remove those hazards. Sometimes it may not be possible or practical to remove these risks, and in such cases you must decide how they can be managed. For example, almost every activity carries some risk, even something a simple as drawing with wax crayons - a young child could put a crayon into his mouth and choke, or push a piece up his nostril, or down his ear. However, if the activity is well planned and effectively organized, with consideration given to possible dangers, the risk of injury or accident should be negligible.

Look in the resource section of this chapter on risk assessment to help you carry one out effectively (CCLD 302.1.2, 302.1.3 and 302.1.4).

TIP:

Try getting down on your knees and looking at a room in your setting. You are now seeing things from a small child's perspective and it can be surprising how many things you will notice that you thought at adult height were safe, but at this new level could be quite the opposite.

You must make sure that all the adults and children in your setting are aware of and follow the health and safety procedures of your setting. This includes security arrangements for children's arrivals and departures and for outings. It does not necessarily mean that, because a setting has a security system for entry to the premises, everyone who comes in will be known and familiar. Do not be afraid to check and ask if you are not sure if someone should be allowed in. It is good practice to ask all visitors to sign in and out. This is not just to check their identity, but also in case of an emergency such a fire or accidents while they are on the premises (CCLD 302.1.5).

Suggested activities and experiences

- Find out which legal and regulatory requirements cover health and safety in your setting. Make a list and cross-reference it to your setting's policies. This can then be included in your portfolio as evidence type E.
- Look at your setting's health and safety policy. Find out when it was last reviewed and who did it. Where is the policy displayed? Do you think it covers everything or are there gaps? What can you do about this?
- Make sure that all health and safety policies and procedures are reviewed whenever there are changing circumstances and decide whether improvements can be made. If these are discussed at staff meetings, keep copies of the agenda and minutes to use as evidence in your portfolio.
- Undertake a risk assessment of your setting or, if working from home, all the rooms and areas, both indoors and outside that the children can access. Look in the resource section for the chapter on risk assessments.
- Choose one room in your setting and check how many items have a Kite mark, the CE symbol, or both. Choose five or six

TIP:

Pieces of equipment that you use everyday will often have the Kite mark from the British Standards Institution (BSI). This means that the equipment has been independently manufactured and tested to make sure that it meets the relevant standard and is safe and reliable. However, the Kite mark does not mean that equipment will always be safe; it will wear out and deteriorate so you must always check. Some products will have a European mark - CE. This shows that the item meets European rules, but it is not a safety or quality mark.

Kite mark and European mark   C E

items and look at them carefully. Decide whether they could be considered safe and reliable.
- Find out about training courses that you could do to help you establish a healthy, safe and secure environment. Look for Basic Food Hygiene, Manual Handling and, of course, First Aid.
- Think about creating a display area for parents, carers, children and visitors that looks at health and safety issues. Remember to change it regularly to maintain interest. You could think about topics such as why some products have a Kite mark and what it means, how you check outdoor equipment, food storage and handling, or fire safety.
- Start a collection of fact sheets on health, safety and security issues. These can often be found in health centres, large supermarkets or DIY centres. Think of an innovative way of storing them that could allow easy access to the information.

Types of evidence

It is likely that your assessor will ask you **oral questions** and may set you **written questions (Key letter B)** to assess your competence for this performance criteria. This is especially the case for PC 302.1.1.

You may also think about writing **a reflective account** of a training course that you have attended – for example on Basic Food Hygiene or Manual Handling **(Key Letter F)**. Don't forget to include in your account how the training will impact on your setting and practice.

Your assessor may **observe** a policy review meeting where you have suggested improvements to policies **(Key letter A)** or suggested ways to make sure that everyone in the setting is aware of health and safety policies. Such direct observation sessions will need careful planning, so don't forget to include these meetings on an assessment plan and ensure that you ask your manager, supervisor or officer in charge if it is acceptable for your assessor to observe the meeting. As mentioned earlier, keep copies of the agenda and minutes for your portfolio **(Key letter H)**.

If you have developed displays for children and adults, ask permission to take photographs, if appropriate. Mount them and put them into your portfolio with annotated comments of how they were used, how children and adults reacted to them and how effective you think the displays were **(Key letter E)**. You could write a **reflective account of how** you put the display together, any difficulties that you encountered and any things that you would change in the future **(Key letter F)**.

CCLD 302.2 Maintain a healthy, safe and secure environment for children

Getting started

This element has seven PCs and you must provide evidence for all of them. In this unit you are aiming to show that you can:

- assess the health, safety and security of the setting before starting, during and at the end of work activities.
- follow health, safety and security procedures yourself.

- make sure children and adults in the setting are following health, safety and security procedures, providing them with help and support when necessary.
- maintain supervision of children appropriate to the levels of risk and the child's age, needs and abilities.
- encourage children to help manage risk for themselves.
- encourage children's awareness of their own and others' safety and their personal responsibility.
- contribute to safety on outings, according to your role and responsibility.

Key Issues

Everyone working with children and young people has responsibility for their safety. It is therefore important that all areas where you work are checked before, during and after activities. When planning an activity, health and safety issues must always be considered and should be clearly identified on any plans that are made (CCLD 302.2.1). An example of an activity plan which considers health and safety issues is given over the page, but it is by no means complete.

Recommendations

Make sure that you know where the health, safety and security policies are kept and that you have a sound working knowledge of them (CCLD 302.2.2). Be a positive role model to the children and other adults you are working with so that they are encouraged to follow health, safety and security procedures (CCLD 302.2.3).

Children need opportunities to learn how to manage risks for themselves, depending on their age and needs; they will become more confident at doing this if you are able to offer appropriate supervision and support (CCLD 302.2.4 and 302.2.5).

Children develop an awareness of their safety and that of others as they grow and mature; therefore you will need to make sure that you provide opportunities, experiences and activities which encourage this and also know what responsibilities children have with regard to safety issues (CCLD 302.2.6).

Outings should be fun and enjoyable for all concerned and offer enriching experiences. This will happen if safety issues have been assessed, planned and managed (CCLD302.2.7).

Suggested activities and experiences

- Carry out a safety check of your setting. You could do this a as a chart that shows what points or areas to check, and what to look for. For example, one point could be to check equipment for any sharp or broken edges, or to check that the nappy changing area is clean and well stocked.
- Make a note of any changes or improvements that you think could be made in your setting with regard to health, safety and security. Talk to your line manager, if appropriate, about your ideas. Perhaps you could take them to the next staff meeting
- Find out how many accidents there have been in your setting over the last year. Can you also find out what caused them, and can you think of anything that could have been done to avoid these accidents?
- Make sure that you have a food hygiene certificate, even if you do not handle food at the moment.
- Encourage and support the children you are working with to wash

their hands before handling food, after using the toilet, after playing outdoors and after touching animals. Be a positive role model and make sure that you and the other adults in your setting also wash their hands on these occasions.

- Make sure that medicines and other medical products are stored safely.
- Provide opportunities for children to make decisions about their own safety in an environment that is controlled and has been risk managed. Talk to them and discuss their decisions and ideas. Increase the level of risk and challenge as children grow and mature.
- Put together an information sheet or leaflet for parents and carers about how risk is managed in different areas of your setting and how children are involved in assessing and managing potential risks.
- When planning an outing, put together a checklist that either you or another adult could complete to make sure that children are safe. Think about the following points:
- How many adults will be needed to make sure that all the children have adequate supervision?
- Will there be a register of the children's and adults' names?
- Will children and adults wear name badges?
- Will the children and adults be organized into groups with a nominated and named leader?
- Has a letter been sent to all parents?
- Have parents returned the letter and given their written consent?
- Do parents know the arrangements for the outing, such as the venue, start time, time that children will be back, time for collection and place?
- What arrangements have been made if a child is not collected at the agreed time?
- Have arrangements, policies and procedures been discussed and agreed for emergencies or if a child becomes lost?
- All children need to explore their environment and in doing so will probably put themselves at risk in some shape or form. It is important that you strike the right balance between safety and allowing the children to manage the risk for themselves. Take time to discuss with children what risks there might be in the environment and how they could manage them for themselves. This could also be turned into an art, IT or craft activity, where children could make posters or leaflets to alert each other of potential risks in certain areas of their environment.

Types of evidence

Your assessor will get much of his evidence from **observing** you directly **(Key letter A)** as you go about your everyday work with children in your setting, for example how you manage the security arrangements when children are left and collected, how you assess the health, safety and security of children before, during and at the end of activities.

Make sure that you keep copies of all agendas and minutes from meetings and discussions where health, safety and security issues have been raised. These can be used to support **professional discussions (Key letter G)** or be used to help you put together reflective accounts (Key letter F). You could write a reflective account about an outing in which you have been involved.

If you have parental written permission, you may wish to use digital photographs of children on outings which show how they were

'My manager always insisted that before we took the children anywhere out of the setting we first visited the venue ourselves without the children. We all thought that this was a complete pain, especially as we had to do the visit in our own time. However, during one visit to an adventure park a child fell from the climbing frame and we had to call an ambulance. Because we had visited the place before, we knew where to take the other children to play safely while the ambulance staff dealt with the injured child.'

NVQ candidate

grouped and managed. Such evidence would require annotations to explain what you are attempting to show, and could be used as **a case study (Key letter E)**. Make sure that you maintain confidentiality of the children at all times.

You could also use photographic evidence of any displays that you made, again with annotations. You could include copies of activity plans that you have implemented which show how health, safety and security issues are considered and assessed before, during and at the end of activities. These would count as **work products (Key letter H)**.

CCLD 302.3 Supervise procedures for accidents, injuries, illnesses and other emergencies

Getting started

This element has six PCs and you must provide evidence for all of them. In this unit you are aiming to show that you can:

- make sure that accidents, injuries, signs of illness and other emergencies are quickly identified.
- follow the correct procedures in a calm and safe manner to deal with accidents, signs of illness, injuries, and other emergencies.
- make sure that you and others are not put at unnecessary risk.
- provide comfort and reassurance for those involved in accidents, illness and other emergencies.

Example of Activity Plan considering Health & Safety issues

Activity	No of children and adults involved with ages	Resources needed	Health & Safety issues
Making shadow puppets. Children to look in books for pictures to copy. Draw or trace picture onto black paper, cut out and stick on lolly stick. Hold puppets in front of lamp to send shadow onto wall. Evaluation of plan.	3-5 children 3.5-5.9 years 1 adult	black paper lolly sticks pencils scissors sellotape pictures lamp blank wall	Check tables are level, stable and clean. Check there are enough resources for children doing the activity. Check heating, light and ventilation. Cutting paper and sellotape. Flex from lamp must not trail across where children are walking. Heat from lamp: make sure children do not touch lamp.

- make sure that medication and first aid are provided, following the correct procedures.
- follow the correct procedures for reporting and recording accidents, signs of illness, injuries and other emergencies.

Key Issues

Accidents can occur to all children at any time, but there are certain ages and stages of development when some accidents may more commonly happen. For example, babies under the age of six months are more likely to suffocate than older children, as they cannot push covers away from their faces. In the same way, toddlers are full of natural curiosity and are not old enough to understand the concept of danger; therefore they are at risk of falls.

It is vitally important that safety checks of the outdoor and indoor environment are carried out every day (CCLD 302.3.1). It also very important that everyone working in your setting has knowledge of, or knows where to find, signs and symptoms of common childhood illnesses and can promptly identify them. When accidents, illness or emergencies occur there should be a procedure that is followed by everyone in your setting. This procedure should ideally be written down and should also include details of how to make a record of such incidents (CCLD 302.3.6).

You should have a first aid certificate that is current and appropriate to the age of the children that you are working with (CCLD 302.3.2). You must also remember to respect a child's privacy and if you are treating a child, administering medicine or dealing with a child who is ill, you should avoid having other children around if at all possible.

There is always the possibility that infections and viruses can be carried in body waste matter and blood. Therefore it is good practice to wear protective gloves when dealing with a sick child, soiled clothing and also when changing a nappy or dealing with a child who had diarrhoea and sickness. All soiled items, whether dressings or clothes, must be disposed of carefully and hygienically (CCLD 302.3.3).

Sometimes children who are sick, injured or involved in accidents and emergencies can become fearful and anxious. It is important that you remain calm and can deal with the situation in a reassuring manner. In this way you will be able to comfort the children and not add to their distress (CCLD 302.3.4).

Your setting should have a policy on first aid and administration of medicines. Make sure that you are fully aware of this policy. As with any policy, it should have been regularly reviewed and be up-to-date (CCLD 302.3.5).

Suggested activities and experiences
- Research and find out the signs and symptoms of common childhood illnesses. You could make either a chart or file which is easily accessible to everyone in your setting, including parents.
- Make sure that all medicines are kept in a locked cupboard and clearly marked with the child's name and the dosage required. When medicines are given out make sure that the dosage is recorded, with the time, date and who gave the medicine. If your setting has not already got a simple record sheet to record this information, then devise one.

'We thought that the seven-year-olds playing on the climbing frame were quite skilled and competent, but one child over-estimated his abilities and responded to a challenge from the others to hang on the bars by one hand. The bars were still wet from rain earlier in the day and he didn't have a strong enough grip and fell; fortunately he had a sprained wrist rather than a broken one.'

NVQ candidate

- Produce a clear information chart for parents and adults on the legal requirements for the administration of medicines.
- Make sure that the first aid kit in your setting is complete and accessible. Find out who has responsibility for ensuring that used items are replaced regularly.
- Younger children may find role play sessions help allay their fears of illness, but make sure that such sessions do not create unnecessary distress and plan them carefully.
- After an accident or emergency has occurred, take the opportunity to discuss it with the children, perhaps at circle time. Talk about what happened, how they felt and how the situation was dealt with. Some children might find drawing pictures or painting help them deal with anxieties.

Types of evidence

The chart or file of childhood illnesses could be used as evidence as a **work product (Key letter H)**. When there has been an accident, illness or emergency which has been dealt with either by you or other adults, write **a reflective account** of what happened, how the accident, illness or emergency was identified, the roles and responsibilities of other adults involved and what the outcomes were **(Key letter F)**.

Illness, accidents and emergencies cannot be contrived, so if something happens when your assessor is present, even if he has come to observe something else, he will take the opportunity to observe how you deal with the children and the situation in general. Your assessor will of course be able to directly observe you checking the environment, and if your have planned a circle time to discuss an incident, that can also be **observed (Key letter A)**.

Because we can not plan illness, accidents and emergencies it is quite likely that your assessor will either ask you questions or write some down for you to answer. This will check your knowledge of the correct procedures and provide evidence for the knowledge specification statements **(Key letter B)**. Here are some questions that your assessor could ask you to research, not just for this element, but for the whole unit CCLD 302:

- What are the legal and regulatory requirements covering health and safety?
- How do the different stages of children's development impact on health, safety and security in your setting?
- What are your setting's procedures for safety and security on outings?
- What is a risk assessment and why is it important to carry it out?
- How would you assess a casualty in a medical emergency?
- What are the signs of (a specific childhood illness, eg chicken pox or meningitis)?

Key words and concepts relating to CCLD 302

antibiotics - medication which kills bacteria

bacteria - pathogenic organisms that can cause infections

children - children and young people with whom you work

chronic illness - a prolonged illness where the signs and symptoms change very little from day to day

communicable diseases - diseases that can be communicated or transmitted

correct procedures - those that are required by law, inspection agencies and the organisation or setting

COSHH - Control of Substances Hazardous to Health regulations (1994)

emergency - an urgent situation that is unplanned

environment - all aspects of the indoor and outdoor surroundings for which you, the candidate, have responsibility

hazard - something that is likely to cause harm

HIV - human immuno-deficiency virus; the virus that causes AIDS

risk - the danger or seriousness of a hazard and its likelihood to actually cause harm to an individual

Suggested further reading
Birth to Three Matters SureStart/DfES

British Medical Association (2000) Complete Family Health. London, Dorling Kindersley.

Child Accident Prevention Trust (CAPT) www.capt.org.uk.

DfES (2004) Every Child Matters: Change for Children, DfES

DfES (2007) Early Years Foundation Stage (2007), DfES

HMSO (1995) Manual of Nutrition. London, HMSO.

National Standards for Under Eights Day Care and Childminding, www.childcarelink.gov.uk/standards.asp.
Royal Society for the Prevention of Accidents (RoSPA) www.rospa.org.uk.

St John's Ambulance www.sja.org.uk.

Tassoni, P. et al (2005) Children's Care, Learning and Development. Heinemann

Terence Higgins Trust (THT) for information on AIDS and HIV www.tht.org.uk.

www.ofsted.gov.uk/safeandsound

Carrying out a risk assessment

Safety management is all about identifying hazards, assessing risk and controlling that risk to reduce the possibility of accidents involving people or damage to property. You cannot control risk unless you are aware of the hazards.

The Management of Health and Safety at Work Regulations 1999 require that every employer shall:

'Make a suitable and sufficient assessment of the risks to the health and safety of his employees and the risk to the health and safety of persons not in his employment arising out of or in connection with his undertaking, to enable him to identify the measures needed to comply with the requirements and prohibitions imposed by or under health and safety law'.

In other words, people at work must not be put at any risk of injury or damage to their health because they are not aware of hazards to which they are exposed or because they have not been told what they must do to minimise risk.

What are hazards and what are risks?

A hazard is anything that has a potential to cause harm. Serious hazards include toxic substances or machines, but even a chair in a dimly lit corridor has a potential to cause harm.

A risk is defined as the likelihood that harm will be caused by an identified hazard. We all take risks occasionally but what is important is that we are able to control risk and avoid damage. Risk control is about minimising danger and risk assessment is about recognising what is likely to cause damage or injury.

An assessment of risk is nothing more than a careful examination of what, in your work, could cause harm to people, so that you can weigh up whether you have taken enough precautions or should do more to prevent harm. The aim is to make sure that no one gets hurt or becomes ill. Remember, accidents and ill health can ruin lives and affect your business, too, if custom is lost, equipment or property is damaged, insurance costs increase or you have to go to court.

If you do not feel confident carrying out the process yourself, get help from a competent source such as a professional association or a consultant, but remember that you are responsible for seeing that it is adequately done.

Five steps to risk assessment

It is a good idea to assess distinct areas, for example premises and activities. You should also carry out separate assessments for fire, outdoor play equipment, trips and outings and swimming pools. It is generally accepted that there are five steps, or stages, that must be gone through. These apply in all areas.

Step 1 – Look for the hazards

If you are doing the assessment yourself, walk around your home/workplace and look at what could reasonably be expected to cause harm. Ignore trivial hazards and only concentrate on significant hazards that could result in serious harm or affect several people. Ask your employees (or family if you're a childminder) what they think; they may have noticed things that are not immediately obvious. Manufacturers' instructions can also help you to identify hazards and put risks in their true

perspective, so can accident and ill-health records.

Step 2 – Decide who might be harmed and how

Think about people who may not be in your home or the workplace all the time, such as parents, cleaners, contractors and maintenance staff. Include members of the public, or people you share your workplace with, if there is a chance that they could be hurt by your activities.

Step 3 – Evaluate the risks

Evaluate the risks arising from the hazards and decide whether existing precautions are adequate or whether more control measures are needed.

Even after all precautions have been taken some risk usually remains. What you have to decide for each significant hazard is whether the remaining risk is high, medium or low.

First, ask yourself whether you have done all the things that the law says you have got to do.

Then ask yourself whether generally accepted industry standards are in place. Do not stop there; think for yourself, because the law also states that you must do what is reasonably practicable to keep your workplace safe. Your aim is to make all risks low by adding to your precautions if necessary. Improving health and safety need not cost a lot - it could mean, for example, using Blu-tack instead of drawing pins or staples to fix pictures on noticeboards.

If you find something that needs to be done you will need to consider the following control measures:

- Is whatever is causing people to be put at risk really necessary? If not, get rid of it.

- Can you find a suitable, safer alternative? If so, use it.

- Is there a safer system of work that would reduce the likelihood of people being put at risk? If so, adopt it.

- Is it possible to move people or the hazard so that fewer people are affected? If so, move them.

- Can you reduce the risk by providing mechanical means such as guards or extraction systems? If so, provide them.

- Is there a need for more training to reduce risk? If so, provide training.

If the hazard only puts people at risk occasionally or if the consequence of exposure is minimal it might be appropriate, for example, to use personal protective equipment (PPE), such as latex gloves or plastic aprons. PPE must only be used as a last resort; the other controls must be considered and used first.

Step 4 – Record your findings
If you have fewer than five employees (an employee is classed as being paid, unpaid, full-time, part-time, volunteer, trainee or work experience participant) you do not need to write anything down, but if you have five or more employees you must record the significant findings of your assessment. This means writing down the more significant

hazards and recording your most important conclusions. You must also inform your employees about your findings.

There is no need to show how you did your assessment provided that you can show that:

- a proper check was made;

- you asked who might be affected;

- you dealt with all the obvious significant hazards, taking into account the number of people who could be involved;

- the precautions are reasonable; and

- the remaining risk is low.

Assessments need to be suitable and sufficient, not perfect. The main points are: are the precautions reasonable, and is there something to show that a proper check was made?

Keep the written document for future reference or use; it can help if an inspector questions your precautions, or if you become involved in any action for civil liability. It can also remind you to keep an eye on particular matters and it helps to show that you have done what the law requires you to do.

Step 5 – Review and revise
You will need to review your assessments and check that they are still an accurate reflection of the hazards and risks in the working environment. You will also need to review a particular assessment if:

- a new procedure has been introduced;

- an accident has occurred involving an area or activity which has been assessed;

- new equipment or substances are introduced; and

- when employing someone under the age of 18.

Mike Waters, managing director, Safety UK.

Safety check-list

Do not block doorways, fire exits or access to children's activities.

Do not leave external doors open as children may run out.

When opening doors, watch out for children running past.

When going up or down stairs, always make sure that an adult is on the lower side of the child to catch them if they fall.

Fit safety gates at the top and bottom of stairs.

Make sure children cannot fall through banisters or become trapped in them.

Do not make hot drinks near children and do not put cups of tea or kettles anywhere a child could reach.

Warm baby bottles in the kitchen.

Wipe up all spills immediately.

Make sure that radiators are covered or that the water temperature is maintained below 43°C at all times.

Check toys regularly to make sure they are safe.

Clear up toys as soon as children have finished playing with them.

Get rid of any small objects that a child could choke on.

Check that tables and chairs are not next to windows where a child could climb up and fall out.

Fit safety catches on all upstairs windows.

Fit safety glass in doors and windows.

Make sure that children in high chairs are wearing a five-point harness.

Do not leave bags where children can rummage in them.

Keep all cleaning and art materials under lock and key when not in use.

Keep all plastic bags and plastic sheeting away from children.

Do not use pillows, duvets or bean bags for children under one year old.

Check gardens for toxic plants and if any are discovered remove them.

Cover or fill in garden ponds.

Pets can play a positive part in children's lives, but whether you share your household with a family dog or keep a rabbit in a hutch at the bottom of the garden, you need to pay careful attention to hygiene and safety. Sue Griffin outlines good practice

Good practice when keeping pets

The RSPCA advises against keeping pets in centre-based childcare and education provision as it is difficult to ensure the welfare of the animals (for instance, over weekends), but in many home-based settings, pets are part of the household. If you work in your own home, you decide if and how animals share your space. If you work in a family's home this may not be within your control. But in either case, there are a few simple aspects of best practice to remember - and implement - every day.

The benefits

Having pets can benefit the children you work with. They are likely to find the animals attractive and interesting, and it is important for them to learn that pets are different from stuffed toys - they are living creatures who will suffer if they are not cared for properly.

Involving children in caring for animals – making sure they are fed and given clean water, kept clean and groomed, kept in appropriate conditions and exercised – helps them to develop an understanding of taking responsibility for another creature and making sure it does not come to harm. Learning to be gentle and considerate to animals can be part of learning the same lessons about how to behave to each other. If a pet is ill or dies, you can sensitively introduce emotional learning.

Exotic species

If someone in the household keeps snakes, spiders or other creatures which are venomous, you will need to insist on very tight security.

Stroking or talking to an animal helps to calm and sooth children who are unsettled or troubled, making them relaxed in unfamiliar surroundings or giving them an outlet for their anxieties. Helping with the feeding, cleaning and exercise routines of animals can help to provide predictable patterns to the day and stability for children.

Some parents will choose a childcare setting where there are pets to give their children the chance to enjoy animals and to learn these important lessons.

Cleaning up your act

Where children come into contact with animals it is important to maintain scrupulously careful hygiene precautions at all times. There is some evidence that children who spend most of their time in 'too clean' an environment are actually more prone to picking up infections (because their immune system does not develop natural barriers). But childcare professionals must always be aware of the vulnerability of children (especially the youngest) to infections which can have unpleasant, even dangerous, effects and avoid unnecessary exposure to potential sources of disease.

Make these hygiene precautions part of your everyday practice:

- Keep animals' feeding dishes out of children's reach.

- After a pet has been fed, clean up the surrounding floor carefully (otherwise bacteria can multiply or pests can be attracted).

What the National Standards say

Registration standards in England and Wales require you to make sure that any animals on your premises are safe to be near children and do not pose a health risk.

The Scottish Standards make no reference to keeping animals.

In Northern Ireland, check with your local registering social worker.

- Wash up and store pets' feeding bowls separately from utensils used by humans (and keep the dishwasher closed so pets can't lick the contents).

- Cover pet food carefully when it is stored in the fridge.

- Never allow pets on to working surfaces where food is prepared.

- Keep animals' litter trays out of children's reach, and wash your hands thoroughly after emptying used litter trays.

- Never let dogs lick children's faces or hands (remember how they clean their rear ends!), and don't let children kiss animals.

- Make sure that children wash their hands thoroughly when they have been handling animals, and discourage them from putting their fingers in or near their mouths while they're handling them.

- Keep animals clear of fleas, wormed and inoculated – have them checked regularly by the vet.

- Always exercise dogs away from the garden.

- If you have a sand pit, cover it when it's not in use to prevent animals getting into it.

- Keep dogs off settees and beds used by children – exposure to pet hair in the early years can cause sensitivity later, or aggravate any tendency to asthma and allergies.

Playing safe

Children should learn to respect animals and not treat them as toys. Make sure they understand that they must not tease pets, and must leave an animal alone when it's resting or sleeping. It's better they don't learn this the hard way when a cat scratches or a dog bites them in retaliation.

If you're caring for a baby, use a cat net over the pram or cot.

If you keep rabbits or similar small animals in hutches, make sure you supervise children when they are nearby. A finger poked through the wire is likely to get a nasty nip.

You and your family may be confident around your large and sometimes boisterous dog who has grown up with you and knows you all well. But will this be safe for children who are less familiar to the dog and might unsettle it? Some dogs are best kept away from the children you care for, in a secure separate area.

Out and about

Whether there are animals in your childcare setting or not, the children you care for will encounter animals when they are with you outside and you must maintain your attention to safety and hygiene.

Explain to children that they must never approach a strange dog, because not all dogs are friendly and some are frightened by strangers and may become fierce. If a child is interested in a dog they meet, always ask the owner whether it is all right for the child to come near and stroke. Explain, too, about guide dogs who help people with sight, hearing and other impairments. These dogs are working, and are not to be petted and stroked.

Help children enjoy and pursue their curiosity about animals, but help them too to learn about potential danger. Remember, even that serenely beautiful swan gliding along can harm you if she thinks her precious cygnets are threatened. Animals must be respected and their place in our shared environment understood, even by the youngest children.

Meeting more animals

One way to introduce children to a wide range of fascinating animals is to visit a farm or other centre with animals. It is wonderful to go at lambing time, or to see a new litter of piglets (but be aware of the danger to pregnant women of contact with lambs). There are opportunities to learn about where eggs and milk really

Sources of disease

Zoonoses are diseases which can be transmitted from animals to humans. They include cat scratch fever and mite infestations.

- *Toxoplasmosis* can be contracted from cat faeces. It causes sore throat, swollen glands and other flu-like symptoms – and is extremely dangerous for pregnant women and unborn babies.

- *Toxocara* results from a roundworm in dog faeces. The eggs can be picked up on fingers unnoticed and passed to a child's mouth. This can cause lung infection or even blindness. It can be avoided by regular treatment with worming tablets.

- E coli 0157 is found in the faeces of pets, wild birds and farm animals. It causes diarrhoea which can be severe (and even fatal).

- Ringworm is a fungus common in dogs and farm animals. It leads to nasty sores.

- Salmonella is found in the faeces of farm animals and exotic pets such as terrapins. It causes stomach pains and diarrhoea.

- Psittacosis can be caught from parrots, budgerigars, chickens, ducks or pigeons. It is a virus which causes fever and sickness.

come from (not just the supermarket!) When you are choosing somewhere to visit, make sure that that there are good hand-washing facilities (with soap) so children can wash their hands easily after touching the animals, before eating their picnic and before they set off for home. Make full use of these facilities, explaining to the children why hand washing is so important.

Sue Griffin, early years and childcare consultant.

When drawing up fire safety procedures, you should take the advice of fire safety officers. Miranda Walker talks you through the registration process and how to ensure ongoing compliance

Fire safety procedures

Legislation is in place to make sure that employers generally, and childcarers specifically, fulfil their duty of care to staff, to the public and children regarding fire safety. The Fire Authority and Ofsted work in partnership - both inspect to make sure that settings comply with the legislation.

Essentially, providers are required to carry out and act upon a fire risk assessment (see 'Risk assessment: fire safety', *Practical Professional Child Care*, October 2004) for their premises, addressing the following seven main areas:

1. Fire ignition sources and risks from the spread of fire

2. Escape routes and exits

3. Fire detection and early warning of fire

4. Fire fighting equipment

5. Fire routine training for staff

6. Emergency plans and arrangements for calling the fire service

7. General maintenance and testing of fire protection equipment

The Fire Precautions Workplace Regulations came into force in 1997 and were amended in 1999. They apply to most places of work, and must be considered in addition to Ofsted's regulations, the National Daycare Standards, which also extend to fire safety.

- -
Remember

- Adults are children's role models.
- Keep calm on hearing the fire alarm.
- Panic spreads quickly and leads to a loss of control of a situation, making it much more dangerous.
- -

The Fire Precautions Workplace Regulations do not apply to workplaces where there are only self-employed workers, or to domestic dwellings, which means that most childminders are exempt from these particular rules. However, childminders must still comply with Ofsted's requirements.

To clear up any confusion, the Chief and Assistant Chief Fire Officers' Association (CACFOA) has produced two helpful documents called *Fire Precautions for Childcare Facilities that are Places of Work*, and *Fire Precautions for Domestic Dwellings used for Childminding Activities*. These can be downloaded from www.ofsted.gov.uk/publications /index. The information helps practitioners to check that their premises and practices meet the legislation appropriate to their individual circumstances.

The inspection process

When a setting first applies for registration (or when there are significant changes to the premises of an existing provider), Ofsted informs the Fire Authority, and will not register the applicant until the authority states that they have no objections.

New premises will be visited by a fire officer who will judge whether the fire regulations are met. This process includes evaluating the effectiveness of any existing fire prevention features, and making further recommendations as necessary. The setting must comply with these recommendations and keep records of them.

The fire officer's visit is important. Since premises and therefore fire risk assessments vary greatly, it is crucial that an expert approves each setting's individual procedures, and gives the registered person the unique advice that they need. If a building is already known to the fire officer (for instance, an out-of-school club may be applying to open on school premises that have been previously inspected), approval may be granted without a visit.

Fire officers consider many factors including the number, location and working order of fire extinguishers, fire blankets, smoke detectors, fire alarms, fire doors and emergency lighting in addition to escape plans, risk assessments, training drills and records.

Fire drills

■ Staff and children must know what to do in the case of a fire.

■ Nominated staff must understand their role fully.

■ People are more likely to respond automatically in a highly stressful emergency situation when they have practised, preventing panic.

■ Reading or being told about fire procedures cannot compare to the practical experience of a drill.

■ The difficulties of evacuation may not be highlighted until the event – how will babies be transported out for instance? (Evacuation trolleys are now available that allow up to six babies to be wheeled to safety at once).

It is good practice to:

■ Carry out drills at varying times of the day, not just at the most convenient times, and on different days of the week.

■ Practice evacuating from different parts of the premises – from the bathroom and playground as well as the playroom for instance.

■ Occasionally divert people away from the nearest exit by indicating that the imaginary fire is there! They will then need to use alternative routes.

■ Display the evacuation drill clearly and express it in simple language and symbols.

■ Explain the fire safety procedures to all staff, students, volunteers or trainees as part of their induction.

■ Fully record all fire drills, and carry them out monthly or during each half-term and holiday.

■ Ensure registers are always up to date and taken to the assembly point.

Once the fire officer has given their initial approval to a setting, ongoing compliance with the National Daycare Standards concerned with fire safety is monitored by Ofsted during the normal inspection routine. Inspectors consider:

■ The registered person's ability to plan for and practise fire safety. (Standard 1: Suitable Person)

■ Whether the premises are safe, secure and suitable. (Standard 4: Physical Environment)

■ Whether the provider has fire-fighting equipment in accordance with BSEN (British Standard European Norm) standards, smoke detection equipment, emergency escape plans for the event of a fire, correctly stored flammable materials, guarded against potentially harmful sources of heat, and recorded and carried out any recommendations made by a fire officer. (Standard 6: Safety)

Maintenance matters

Ongoing checks and maintenance are required to make sure fire safety standards are kept up. You can carry out and do as much of the necessary actions yourself while others require specialist attention.

Joe Redfearn is the managing director of Ace Fire Equipment UK, based in Plymouth. Childcare providers are useful amongst his clients. He says, 'Each month, practitioners should visually check fire extinguishers themselves, documenting their checks. They should check that fire-fighting equipment is where it should be, and that the tamper seal, pin and discharge hose are undamaged. The extinguisher gauge should read "pressurised".

'Visual checks should also be made to fire exits and escape routes to make sure they remain clear, and to emergency lighting to check they are in good working order. Fire alarms and smoke detectors should be audibly checked. Whenever a check reveals a problem it should be addressed immediately – this may require emergency specialist maintenance. However, once every 12 months a trained engineer should conduct

fire extinguisher safety checks in any case, carrying out maintenance if necessary – an annual certificate will be issued to be retained by the setting.'

Escape plans

The registered person is responsible for making sure that staff receive training on what to do in the event of a fire. This means staff must be taught the setting's escape plan, and must practise executing it during regular fire drills. (The plan itself will have been approved by the fire officer.)

Legislation also requires the nomination of staff to undertake special roles included in the setting's escape plan, such as taking the register or dialling 999.

Miranda Walker is an early years and playwork trainer, speaker and consultant. She owns her own settings in Devon.

Where to find out more

Fire Management in the Workplace, A Guide for Employers – a book and video from Fire Protection. (Tel: 0181 207 2345)

Fire Safety, An Employers Guide – published by the Home Office, ISBN 0-11-341229-0. (Tel: HSE Bookshops on 01787 881165)

Fire Risk Assessment, a guide to complying with the Fire Precautions Regulations - published by the Fire Industry Council. (Tel: 0181 549 5855)

Useful websites

www.firekills.gov.uk Has a useful section for childcarers and links to children's information pages.

www.dlf.org.uk The Disabled Living Foundation - information about fire safety for disabled people.

www.capt.org.uk Child Accident Prevention Trust - download safety fact sheets

www.welephant.co.uk Fire Service's mascot Welephant - children's site.

Immunisation is the process by which children become resistant or immune to certain types of childhood diseases. Audrey Farley looks at the role it plays in protecting children from infections

Protecting children against infections

Government policy has led to immunisation programmes being offered at health clinics throughout the UK. These programmes help to reduce the incidence of childhood diseases. For example, diphtheria, tetanus, pertussis (DTP) was introduced in the 1950s and the MMR (measles, mumps and rubella) vaccine was introduced in 1988.

The World Health Organisation (WHO) introduced multiple immunisations against diseases, such as diphtheria, tetanus, pertussis (DTP) and measles, mumps and rubella (MMR). The aim of the WHO is to eradicate infections which have the potential to be dangerous and cause disability and death. Scientific evidence shows that vaccination is a proven method of giving protection against many childhood infections.

The term vaccination is generally used to refer to the process of injecting or vaccinating people for immunity. Vaccination strengthens immunity and that is why its uptake is so important.

What is immunity?

The ability of the body cells to protect against disease is called immunity. It can be gained in a natural way or artificial way.

Immunity occurs when antibodies present in the bloodstream neutralise or destroy poisons and disease-carrying organisms. For example, when a child catches an infectious childhood disease, such as measles, the body produces antibodies which attack and destroy the organisms that cause measles. The symptoms then disappear and the child recovers. If the child is exposed to the same organisms later, the antibodies produced will destroy the organisms before they can cause any symptoms. They give

the body immunity to that particular disease and this helps to prevent a further attack. This is called natural immunity.

Artificial immunity can give protection that is temporary, called passive, or permanent, called active immunity. An example of passive immunity is when antibodies pass across the placenta to a baby's blood from the mother. Further protection is also provided from the mother's breast milk.

Passive immunity can also be gained when serum from a sick person, with antibodies, is given to prevent a child at risk from developing that disease. This protection is short term. Although some experience of infections can also induce immunity, it wears off as babies develop and at the age of two months immunisation is recommended to provide antibodies to replace those of their mother's. This is done by injecting a vaccine into the body.

Vaccines are doses of germs which are either dead or harmless versions of a particular organism. They work by stimulating defence cells in the body that are able to fight diseases without causing them. When a dose of vaccines is given, defence cells are produced in a larger quantity by the body and this gives protection against disease. This active immunity gives permanent protection.

Protection by vaccination

Children and communities need to fight diseases to stay healthy. Vaccinations are generally carried out at health clinics. They are given at various stages of children's development.

Children should have various recommended vaccines (see box overleaf) and the five-in-one vaccine (DTaP/IPV/Hib):

- DTaP - diptheria, tetanus, acellular (less cells) pertussis (whooping cough) vaccine
- IPV - inactivated polio vaccine
- Hib - haemophilus influenzae type b

These give protection against five different diseases, namely diphtheria, tetanus, whooping cough, polio and meningitis (caused by hib). The first injection is given when the child is two months old. The second is given at three months and the third at four months. The time between enables the vaccines to work effectively.

Meningitis C (Men C) vaccine is also given when the child is two, three and four months and protects against meningococcal group C, a type of bacteria that can cause meningitis and septicaemia. The Men C vaccine does not protect against viral or bacterial meningitis.

Suggested ages	Diseases	Method
2 months	Diphtheria	
	Tetanus	
	Pertussis (whooping cough)	
	Polio	
	Hib (viral meningitis)	5 in 1 injection
	Meningitis C (bacterial men)	1 injection
3 months	As for 2 months	
4 months	As for 3 months	
13 months	Measles	
	Mumps	
	Rubella	3 in 1 injection
3 years 4 months to 5 years	Diphtheria	
	Tetanus	
	Pertussis	
	Polio	1 injection
10-14 years	Tuberculosis (or at birth in high-risk babies)	1 injection
13-18 years	Tetanus	
	Diphtheria	
	Polio	1 injection

If you want to know more

www.immunisation.nhs.uk

www.doh.gov.uk

Children of pre-school age should be given a vaccine for protection against diphtheria, tetanus, pertussis and polio (DTaP/IPV) at ages three years four months to five years. This is a booster dose before starting school.

The triple vaccine, three in one, which protects against measles, mumps and rubella (MMR) is usually given at 13 months.

The BCG (Bacille Calmette-Guerin), which protects against tuberculosis, is usually given between the ages of ten and fourteen and is sometimes given to new-born babies if they are high risks. In addition, protection from tetanus, diptheria and polio (Td/P) is given between 13 and 18 to boost earlier doses (see recommended immunisation chart).

Safety of vaccines

Public concerns were raised about the MMR vaccinations after a researcher, Andrew Wakefield, claimed in 1998 that it may account for a rise in diagnosed cases of autism. A high level of media coverage caused anxieties and there was a low uptake of the MMR vaccine. It was thought that the three-in-one vaccine could overload the immune system and trigger autism and inflammatory bowel disease. Some parents preferred the option of single vaccines.

But the WHO supported the use of the MMR vaccine in its report in 2001 and various studies, according to the Department of Health, showed that there was no change in children who had the vaccine. There was no scientific evidence to support the claim.

The most recent report is based on a study in Japan. It provided the strongest proof that the MMR did not cause autism by demonstrating that there continued to be a rise in autism even after the triple vaccine of measles, mumps and rubella was stopped.

Sharing information

It is understandable for parents to worry about the safety of vaccinations but the diseases they are designed to prevent have a greater risk of causing harm to children. In the UK parents can choose whether to have their children immunised or not. Staff in nurseries and childminders should be aware of the facts and parents' likely concerns as your advice, based on factual information, could help parents/carers to make informed choices.

Parents can be reassured that immunisations will not be done if their child is unwell but they must speak to healthcare professionals. It may also be postponed if there was a reaction from previous vaccinations, if the child is taking medicine such as antibiotics or has a history of convulsions (fits). This also applies if the child suffers from allergies, is having treatment for cancer or has an illness that affects the immune system, such as leukaemia.

Some parents may also express concerns about the side effects of vaccinations on their child. A red lump or patch may appear at the site of the injection or the child may feel off colour the following day. This should not last but if the child continues to feel unwell or has a raised temperature then their GP must be consulted.

Children should be vaccinated at specific ages according to the childhood immunisation programme. These may differ slightly in different areas. Discussions with a GP, practice nurse or health visitor will clarify any misunderstanding. Parents/carers should give you information, for example, on their children's immunisation uptake and travel arrangements - special immunisations may be required before travelling abroad.

Reviewing information helps you to have up-to-date information at your fingertips. Sharing information is an important part of protecting children from the risk of illnesses that have the potential to be serious.

Audrey Farley, former lecturer in health, childcare and education.

Effective hygienic measures are critical in safeguarding the health of both children and staff. Audrey Farley looks at the habits that should be part of your daily routine

Preventing the spread of infection

Good hygiene standards in any childcare setting, whether homes or nurseries, help to prevent the spread of infection and therefore reduce illnesses in young children. Basic routines can reduce the risks of an outbreak in diseases but only if they are practised on a daily basis and consistently.

Practising good hygiene will also help children to learn good habits. Young children who have not yet developed good hygiene habits will be guided by their carers who should be positive role models.

An outbreak of an infection may be caused by any types of bacteria, viruses and other germs. For example, impetigo is a skin infection that is usually spread by direct contact with an infected child. It is caused by the bacteria staphylococcus or streptococcus, which can be present in the noses of both children and adults. This highly contagious infection can spread rapidly when handwashing is relaxed or forgotten.

To prevent an outbreak requires taking hygienic precautions, reminding children about hygiene and not sharing towels, keeping the infected child away from nursery after the start of antibiotics and until the blisters have healed up.

It is worth remembering that even though children contribute to the spread of infection, there are times when staff may do so too, for example by not ensuring sufficient ventilation and a controlled temperature in rooms. Diseases, too, can be spread by carers, for example through activities such as changing nappies and feeding children. Effective hygienic measures are critical in safeguarding the health of both children and staff.

Personal hygiene

Hands are usually covered with bacteria and can contaminate anything they touch. Good practice should include frequent washing of the hands. Wash hands:

- before starting work whether at home or in a nursery;

- when moving from one child/group to another;

- before and after cooking, eating, drinking and preparing food and feeding a child;

- after using the toilet and helping a child to use the potty/toilet or changing a nappy;

- before and after attending a sick child;

- after disposing of waste/spilled vomit, blood, urine, faeces and mucus;

- after removing gloves;

- before and after giving medicines.

Other aspects of hygiene involve cleaning and taking care of skin, teeth, hair and hands. Good habits such as covering cuts on hands with waterproof plasters, tying back hair and wearing disposable gloves when dealing with body fluids, vomit and hanging out nappies are promoting good personal hygiene.

Children need to practise personal hygiene, too. Encourage them to learn how to take care of themselves so they can become independent. Children's hands should be washed as often as necessary:

- before meals and snacks;

- after playing outside;

- after sticky or messy activities;

- after going to the toilet and after play with pets.

Handwashing should be made fun -sing while washing, for example. Younger children will need to be supervised but older ones need encouragement to do this. Praise them when they remember.

Effective handwashing involves a thorough washing of both hands by rubbing them vigorously with warm water and liquid soap, so that wrists, backs and fronts of hands, between fingers, around fingernails and thumbs are clean. Rinse in running water and dry thoroughly, preferably with a disposable towel.

Hygiene in the nursery

Preventing the possible spread of infection involves not only personal hygiene but also providing and maintaining a hygienic environment, indoors as well as outdoors.

Some nurseries have cleaners who come in regularly but the National Standards stipulate that part of your role is to keep the environment clean and safe. This involves dealing appropriately with toileting accidents or sick children in a way that does not undermine children's privacy and self- esteem.

A high standard of hygiene is required and cleaning and tidying should be done in all areas on a regular basis to maintain this. The kitchen, playroom and rest room as well as furniture, floors, walls and equipment must be kept scrupulously clean.

Changing areas must be cleaned daily and

changing mats for nappies cleaned with wet wipes or soap and water after each use. Soiled nappies should be disposed in a bin that is lined with plastic, with pedals operated by foot. It should be cleaned and emptied regularly. Surfaces and storage areas should be cleaned on a regular basis.

Bacteria multiply in damp conditions so bathrooms are ideal for spreading infection caused by bacteria. Clean bathrooms at least once a day with special care given to toilet handles, sinks, taps and doors. Potties must be emptied in the toilet straight after use and thoroughly washed (but not in the basins used for handwashing) with clean soapy water, and placed upside down to dry.

Children with headlice can easily infect others. Parents should take responsibility for treatment - either by wet combing or with lotions. But sharing hairbrushes, hats and other hair items should not be encouraged. Each child should have their own combs and brushes to use daily. Care must be taken to prevent the spread of infection at sleep times and rules about this should be in the setting's policy.

In the home
Cleaning and tidying on a regular basis applies to homes as well as nurseries. All areas must be clean and safe. This includes hard floors, particularly in the kitchen, which must be cleaned every day and immediately after any spillages. Wipe tables at the start and finish of a meal or at the end of an activity. Chairs and tables, too, should be frequently wiped over.

Regular washing of bedding, cuddly toys and cushions is necessary as bacteria can be found on fabrics. Effective washing and disposal of used linen is important to prevent cross-contamination.

Routines in hygiene should be in accordance with parents' wishes and discussion with parents will help to suit the needs and preferences of individual children. Child-rearing preferences can be adapted without compromising good hygiene practices.

Food hygiene
Food hygiene is about preventing bacteria

from contaminating food or drink. Bacteria such as salmonella can cause food poisoning.

Keep food safe by thoroughly cooking, keeping at the right temperature and never reheating more than once. Avoid cross-contamination by using a separate chopping board for meat and vegetables. Place raw meat at the bottom of the fridge to stop blood dripping on other foods.

Good food hygiene involves taking measures to store food correctly, preparing and cooking food properly and keeping the kitchen safe. Careful and regular cleaning should be done in the kitchen and any area where food is prepared. It is also important to clean utensils for cooking and eating, the floor, cupboards and shelves and towels, cloths and brushes and other similar kitchen items. Keep food covered and empty bins to discourage infestation. A certificate in basic food hygiene is required by law for handling food.

Isolation
Isolation means keeping an infected child away from others. Make sure that a child with an infection does not come in contact with other children until the infected child is better. A child can easily spread an infection, especially as immune systems are not yet fully mature and children are still learning to wash their hands regularly.

Barrier nursing may be needed depending on the type of infection. Avoiding contact

with others will reduce the risk of spread. The absent child can return when the worst symptoms are gone and are not able to infect others.

Disinfection
Disinfectant will destroy germs and is generally used on equipment and toys. Toys and equipment for play should be disinfected with antiseptics on a regular basis; disinfect toys for babies daily. Blood or vomit must be cleaned immediately with paper towels.

Use an appropriate disinfectant and dilute according to manufacturers' instructions. Hypochlorite, a dilute bleach but a detergent, can be used on surfaces such as carpet, which can be damaged by bleach. Remove contaminated clothing and give to parents to take home. Disinfect floor mops used to clean up spillages and allow to dry. Plastic gloves and aprons should be used when disinfecting and appropriate bags and containers used.

Preventing infection is also about education and training. Nurseries and childminders can do so much to ensure that infections are reduced or controlled. All good early years settings should have written documents on policies for dealing with relevant aspects of health and hygiene.

Audrey Farley, former lecturer in health, childcare and education.

As well as meeting the National Standards you now need to help children to achieve the outcomes set out in the Children Act 2004. Liz Wilcock explains what each outcome means and suggests how you can adapt your practice to help children meet them.

Every Child Matters: Being healthy

The 14 National Standards are now grouped under five outcome headings. 'Being healthy' covers National Standards 7 (Health) and 8 (Food and drink). You need to consider the following:

■ What does this outcome mean and what do you need to do?

■ What will the inspector want to see?

Standard 7 – Health

It is expected that the registered person will promote good health, take positive steps to prevent the spread of infection and take appropriate measures when children are ill.

Hygiene

Hygiene must be a priority. Beyond personal hygiene, you are responsible for ensuring that children are cared for in clean surroundings. Ofsted will need to be kept informed of any significant health matters that a qualified medical person considers notifiable.

Staff should maintain good hygiene practices. Personal hygiene for staff as well as children needs consideration:

■ Washing hands after using the toilet, and before handling any food.

■ Encouraging children to blow their noses and dispose of the tissue in a lidded bin.

■ All staff should be aware of procedures to deal with bodily fluids, and their disposal.

A rota system will ensure that all necessary cleaning and checking is carried out. Whilst it is important for your setting/home to be kept clean, the cleaning should not interfere with the time that children are being cared for.

■ Do you have notices around your setting to remind adults to wash their hands?

■ Do you keep nailbrushes and clean towels near washbasins?

■ Are staff familiar with your health and safety policies and procedures? More importantly, do they follow the procedures? It is the responsibility of the registered person to ensure that staff are aware of all procedures, and adhere to them. A poster showing common illnesses can be placed on the noticeboard, with any other health/hygiene information.

Environmental health officers will expect a good standard of hygiene. They can be contacted for advice if you have any queries about environmental health.

Giving medicine

Administering medicine to children takes organising. Who should be responsible? A room senior, deputy or manager should be overall responsible for all medications - never allow an unqualified person, or student, to give medication to a child.

Dosages, and the child's details, must be recorded, with a parent's signature written on the day, agreeing to you giving their child the prescribed medication. Consider the following:

■ When liquid medicine is given to a child, do you pour from the opposite side of the bottle to the instructions? That way, if any liquid spills down the side of the bottle, the wording on the instructions will not be smeared.

■ Do you check the medicine has not passed the 'use by' date?

■ What procedures are in place for children to be given their medication on outings?

■ Are parents in agreement that you will only give prescribed medication? The only time you may administer another medication is for a teething baby. Parents sometimes ask carers to give their baby Calpol, or similar, for 'when you need it'. You must not give Calpol to a baby or young child in your care, without the parent giving you written agreement first. Your medication consent form should be worded to allow for this. Usually, if a baby is unwell, and you are concerned about teething, you may have to contact the parents - the baby may have a high temperature and need to be taken home. Think about the baby's needs first.

First aid
There should always be a first aider on site. A current certificate must be available for them – the certificate is current for a maximum of three years.

Sick children
You should consider that a sick child will be unsettled and perhaps frightened. One person should care for the child until either their parent or an ambulance arrives. The child will need plenty of love and reassurance.

You should have clear policies and procedures about how to deal with a sick child. The documents should show the system you have in place to contact parents. Are your contact details up to date? Do you have emergency contact numbers? Check regularly with parents that contact numbers are correct. Do you have a sick room or quiet area for a sick child? This is important if the child has an infectious illness that you are trying to contain.

Good practice
Encourage children to understand about good health by:

■ Spending time with children on topics related to health - teeth, food, exercise.

■ Overcoming fears of going to the doctor /dentist /hospital.

■ Using the home corner/role play to promote healthy living.

■ Letting children tidy up and 'clean' - they enjoy this, when they are young!

■ Making good use of any newsletters you

send out to advise parents on current health issues, such as:

1. Infectious diseases

2. Head lice, conjunctivitis - and similar issues, when a child is not ill, but should be at home until treatment has been given.

3. How parents can get involved. Do any of your parents work in a health environment? Perhaps you can enlist their help.

■ Invite health professionals to be involved with children directly.

Inspectors will want to see your written accident records (with parent signatures), medication and emergency record forms, your first aid box, and will want to discuss your arrangements for dealing with sick children.

Standard 8 – Food and drink
The registered person needs to make sure that children are provided with regular drinks and food in adequate quantities for their needs. Food and drink should be properly prepared, nutritious and comply with dietary and religious requirements.

Meals
You may provide up to three meals a day, with mid morning and mid afternoon snacks as well. As young children grow, they need a well balanced diet. Remember that children need to eat regularly.

There are four main groups of food to consider when you are meeting a child's dietary needs. These are:

Bread, cereals and potatoes

Fruit and vegetables

Milk and dairy foods

Meat and fish

Remember the vegetarian alternatives, such as pulses and soya. If a parent tells you that their child is vegetarian (not eating meat or fish) or vegan (not eating foods of animal origin - meat, fish and diary produce), it will be a challenge to ensure that the child still has a balanced and nutritious diet to enable healthy development.

Good practice
■ Whenever possible, try to keep to the child's own routine for meals.

■ Babies who are bottle fed should be held and have warm physical contact during feed times.

■ Parents should be advised daily if their child has not eaten the meals provided that day and told of any amounts left.

■ Allow time for children to eat – let children eat slowly, as this is better for the digestive system.

■ Make mealtimes a social time. If possible, staff should eat and drink with children to set a good example. If staff have separate meal breaks, they should still sit with children at the table and talk to them.

■ Encourage good table manners.

■ Children should go to the toilet and wash their hands before sitting to the table.

■ Never leave children alone while they eat in case they choke.

■ Store food correctly. Do not leave perishable food at room temperature for more than two hours.

■ Your home corner could become the local fruit and vegetable shop. Some settings invite people in to cook with children, and talk about healthy ways to cook.

■ The inspector will note from your booking/admission forms that children's dietary needs have been recorded. Your menus will show what meals are provided over a period of time, and should indicate a well balanced diet for all children.

■ It is important that you regularly discuss children's changing dietary needs with parents.

Liz Wilcock, under-threes development officer, West Berkshire.

The outcome 'Staying safe' means protecting children from harm and neglect. Liz Wilcock looks at the related national standards and birth to three guidance

Every Child Matters: Staying safe

The 14 National Standards are grouped under five outcome headings. 'Staying safe' covers Standards 4 (Physical environment), 5 (Equipment), 6 (Safety) and 13 (Child protection).

Standard 4 – Physical environment

The premises in which children are cared for should be safe, secure and suitable for their purpose.

> You must notify Ofsted if any changes are made to the premises or their use. This is a Children Act Regulation – a requirement that you must comply with.

There is much to think about in respect of the premises or physical environment and the registered person cannot do it on their own - it must be a shared responsibility. Parents, for example, should always close and lock the gate when they arrive and leave. Staff need to make sure that the premises are clean, well-ventilated and should check the whole area - indoors and outside - before the day starts.

Whether you work in a day nursery, on school premises, in a village hall, a house converted for nursery use, or your own home, as a registered childminder, your primary consideration is for the safety and well being of the children in your care. Your premises need careful consideration, depending on the ages of the children. Security must be uppermost in your mind.

Quality of care will be affected if premises are not well planned. Think about the layout of your building to ensure that there is a welcoming feel, inviting play areas, pride in staff appearance, and recognition of children's achievements.

Think about the space available for children to play. In a group setting, individual rooms are preferable to open plan areas. This is where children are being cared for - make it homely and inviting. Are the sleep rooms separate for the youngest children? Peace and quiet is necessary. Does your space allow for babies who are becoming mobile? Put yourself in the place of the children. What would you like?

Inspectors will want to discuss how you meet space requirements and organise play space, your toilet facilities and arrangements for nappy changing, staff facilities and where confidential discussions can be held with parents.

Standard 5 - Equipment

Furniture, equipment and toys must be appropriate for their purpose and help to create an accessible and stimulating environment. They should be of suitable design and condition, well maintained and conform to safety standards.

Toys and play equipment must conform to (BS) British Standards. If in doubt, check with the manufacturers before you buy. When choosing toys, look for the lion mark (a triangle with a lion face) which means that the toys have been made to a high standard for this country and Europe.

You will need to have a policy on replacing toys and play equipment. An inventory of all play equipment is the best way to keep track of what is available for all the children.

The registered person needs to be satisfied that furniture is sturdy, and not likely to break easily. Fittings such as stairgates should be available where necessary, for

Birth to Three Matters

You need to consider how to apply your practice to keeping children safe. Babies and young children will develop if they feel secure in their environment. They will be able to make choices, explore and experiment, cope with new situations, express their feelings and take 'safe' risks.

Consider how you work towards enabling children to become capable and confident, self assured, enthusiastic and interested in their environment.

Keeping children safe is a priority, and with the framework, practitioners are guided towards ways in which they can provide an environment in which all under-threes can develop.

example to prevent children from entering the kitchen.

If you have any questions about the safety of equipment in your setting, you can ask advice from your support worker, or call ROSPA (Royal Society for the Prevention of Accidents) on 0121 248 2000.

Standard 6 - Safety

It is expected that the registered person will take positive steps to promote safety within the setting and on outings and ensure precautions are taken to prevent accidents.

Your policies and procedures will state how you intend to ensure the safety of everyone connected to the setting but you also need to keep up to date with changes in the law that affect you. The main legislation is the Children Act 1989, and the Care Standards Act 2000. These state your responsibilities in caring for young children.

You will not be expected to recite the Children Act or let the inspector know about your understanding of the Care Standards Act.

The National Standards and Guidance Book, and the amendments to those booklets, give you the relevant information you need to have to comply with the requirements of the Children Act.

You are not alone in finding out about the legislation. Other than contacting your local support worker, you will find a useful appendix at the end of your guidance book - Organisations and Publications, which can provide useful sources of information.

Your parent's information leaflet should state that the welfare and safety of the children is of paramount importance in your setting. Parents should be made aware that they have a part to play in this also. Safety issues could be discussed at parent's evenings.

All staff working in your setting should be aware of their responsibility to ensuring the premises are safe at all times, and a risk assessment is the way to achieve this.

How do you record your risk assessments? You could provide a book that is kept in one place for everyone to access and report hazards.

It is the responsibility of the registered person/people to ensure the safety of all. It is the responsibility of people working and using the setting to report any safety issue for the registered people to address. If a written format is used, as well as verbally informing a senior person of the problem, action can be taken quickly.

Inspectors will want to discuss with you about how you have complied with all health, fire and safety requirements / recommendations, how you assess risk, and your policies and procedures relating to safety.

Standard 13 – Child protection

The registered person must comply with local child protection procedures approved by the Area Child Protection Committee (ACPC) and ensure that all adults working and looking after children in the provision are able to put the procedures into practice. Local Safeguarding Boards now oversee child protection procedures in each local authority, and will replace ACPCs.

Children are vulnerable and need adults to protect them. It is the adults' responsibility to help them understand when they may be facing a dangerous situation, and guide them towards thinking of their own safety. This seems simple enough if you are considering, for example, water safety or using a climbing frame. Children will come to understand that they may get injured in certain situations.

But you must also be aware of child protection issues. The information under this standard is not enough – training in this sensitive area is necessary for all staff, so that they fully understand their responsibilities.

You should also be aware of the importance of protecting yourself against allegations of abuse.

A designated person responsible for liaison with local child protection agencies should be appointed. This will not be an easy role, and it is likely that training will be required. Appropriate support will be needed for this person at times. The designated member of staff will need to have good working relationships with all staff, as he/she will be the person to whom concerned staff will need to speak.

The responsibility of the staff is to be aware of each child, and be able to recognise when there is a problem. If a child gives cause for concern, the member of staff will need to tell the appropriate person, who may be the group SENCO, manager/supervisor, or the child protection designated person. The course of action can then be discussed.

The inspector will want to see your statement on child protection, your procedures for allegations of abuse made against a member of staff or volunteer, your arrangements for complying with local procedures, and to confirm who your designated member of staff is.

Liz Wilcock, under-threes development officer, West Berkshire.

Advice for childminders
The NCMA childminding course, Introduction to Childminding Practice, has useful guidance for you in respect of allegations:

'You need to be aware that you are vulnerable to such allegations because you work alone in your own home. One important way of protecting yourself and your family is to keep records of accidents and also of incidents such as a child arriving at your house with signs of an injury, and asking parents to sign your record to show that they accept what has happened or what you have noticed.

'If an allegation is made against a childminder or their family, an investigation must be carried out.'

What part do you have to play in helping children to be healthy? Miranda Walker looks at the guidance set out in the birth to three framework

Birth to Three Matters: A healthy child

The 'Healthy child' aspect of *Birth to Three Matters* features four components:

■ Emotional well-being

■ Growing and developing

■ Keeping safe

■ Healthy choices

Although having nutritious food and being free from illness are important to children's overall physical health, this aspect acknowledges that young children need much more than that. Being cared for and special to someone is also vital to children's physical, social and emotional well-being.

Emotional well-being

This component focuses on young children needing close, warm and supportive relationships. They need to be able to express positive feelings such as joy, confidence and achievement, and negative feelings such as sadness, frustration and anger. This enables young children to recognise emotions and to develop strategies to cope with situations that are new, stressful or challenging.

Already social beings, 'Heads up, lookers and communicators' (aged 0-8 months) need to feel close attachments and special bonds with their carers. To build the loving relationships that babies crave, it's important that they have a key worker.

Key workers should interact with individual babies and regularly attend to their needs, both emotional and physical. Whenever possible, parents and key

workers should hand their child directly over to one another at the beginning and end of sessions. This allows the child to move from the care of one person who is special to them to another, promoting feelings of emotional security.

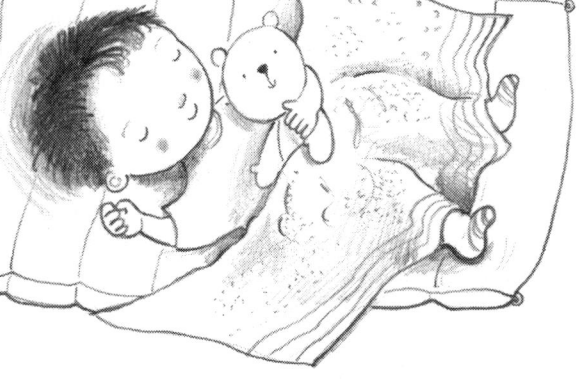

'Sitters, standers and explorers' (aged 8-18 months) enjoy mutual, warm relationships with adults and other children. They may be affectionate and demonstrative, instigating cuddles for example, or coming to sit on a carer's lap.

Children increasingly express their feelings, which will be confusing and overwhelming at times. It's good practice for key workers and parents to liaise on how to respond to displays of strong emotion, such as anger. A consistent approach helps children to understand their feelings and learn how to cope with them.

Children may react badly to inevitable times in a group setting when their key worker is not present. It helps to prepare them by ensuring that they interact with other carers as well as their special person.

'Movers, shakers and players' (aged 18-24 months) have hopefully experienced several months of loving, responsive care, developing the confidence to move

from a place of safety and security (the environment of their special adult) to explore the wider world in terms of environment, activities and people, happy in the knowledge they can return to their place of safety and security at any moment.

For instance, a child may leave their key worker to explore events across the room. After a few moments or minutes they may come back briefly, then set off again. The practitioner can support the child by acknowledging them and their adventure on their return visits – 'Hello! Have you been playing with the balls?'

'Walkers, pretenders and explorers' (aged 24-36 months) continue to grow in confidence. They will increasingly be able to do things independently, such as going to the toilet. However, children still need to know they can depend on carers to be close by.

The knowledge that a trusted adult is on hand to give help and support if needed, boosts children's confidence to attempt independence and try new things.

You can help by encouraging and praising children's efforts, as well as their achievements.

Growing and developing

'Growing and developing' focuses on meeting children's physical needs, which is essential for health and well-being. This component acknowledges that children who are physically well will have the energy and enthusiasm to benefit from the activities available to them.

'Heads up, lookers and communicators' can thrive only when their nutritional, physical and emotional needs are met. At this stage it's important that key workers and parents liaise closely about feeding and sleeping details, so that the overall picture of a baby's daily routine is not lost. Practitioners can also encourage and help mothers who wish to continue breastfeeding their babies.

'Sitters, standers and explorers' will increasingly become more independent in feeding themselves. It's beneficial to make mealtimes an enjoyable, social occasion, which encourages children to enjoy both their food and the experience of sitting around the table, even if they're in a highchair.

Children are also likely to be settling into new sleeping routines. Regular rest is still important, but children will begin to sleep less in the daytime.

This component tells us that 'Movers, shakers and players' 'have a biological drive to use their bodies and develop their physical skills'. These children need plenty of opportunities and space to run and play. To enable children to practise and develop new physical skills, you must provide access to appropriate resources and equipment, such as low slides, balls and large interlocking bricks.

'Walkers, talkers and pretenders' are increasingly gaining control of their own bodies. Their large and fine motor skills are becoming more refined, and they are ready to tackle more sophisticated physical movements, such as turning the pages of a book and riding large wheeled toys. They will also be gaining control of their bladder and bowels. Encourage independence but offer support and help when it's needed.

Keeping safe

This component stresses that to keep safe and protected, young children need a developing sense of when and how to ask for adult help. It's closely linked to the component 'Healthy choices' (see below).

'Heads up, lookers and communicators' already make purposeful movements and this component points out that babies 'tend not to stay in the position in which they have been placed'. It's the responsibility of carers to ensure that children have an increasing choice in their environment, within safe and supervised limits.

'Sitters, standers and explorers' often have little awareness of danger. This is the time when young children are beginning to walk, run and climb, and so striking a balance between challenge, freedom and safe boundaries is paramount. It's important to be consistent and to acknowledge that children of this age are more focussed on what they want to do, than on their own safety.

This component reminds us that the need 'Movers, shakers and players' have for attention and affection, coupled with their increasing independence, makes them particularly vulnerable. All those involved in their care should be aware of how to promote safety, including good practice in the area of child protection.

Healthy choices

Children gradually learn to make healthy choices in regards to their own bodies and what they can and can't do. 'Healthy choices' is closely linked to 'Keeping safe'.

This component tells us that 'Heads up, lookers and communicators' 'show preferences for people and for what they want to see, hear and taste'. Practitioners can become responsive carers by taking note of, and acting upon, these preferences.

A strong child

The concept of 'A strong child' runs throughout the framework. Being a holistically healthy child will enable children to be strong - meaning capable, confident and self-assured.

By the time they are 'Sitters, standers and explorers', children and their carers will be developing a clearer picture of their individual likes and dislikes. Simple choices and decisions will be made frequently and these can be supported by adults. Encourage considered behaviour by presenting options during this stage – 'Would you like water or juice today?'

The increasing exploration by 'Movers, shakers and players' may mean their choices involve risk. While taking risks shouldn't be inhibited, carers must ensure that children's safety is not compromised – this is something of a balancing act that becomes easier with experience and expertise.

'Walkers, talkers and pretenders' start to understand more clearly that the choices they make have consequences. They're beginning to consider the consequences of their behaviour before and during their actions. At this stage it's beneficial for practitioners and parents to use the same strategies consistently to promote positive behaviour, so that children develop a clear understanding of consequences and are not confused.

Miranda Walker is an early years and playwork trainer, writer and speaker. She owns her own day care settings in Devon.

Accidental injury is one of the biggest single causes of death for children over the age of one. More children die each year from accidents than illness. So how do you make sure that you are prepared if a child has an accident while in your care?

First aid: are you well prepared?

All employers are required by law to carry out an assessment of first aid needs within their workplace. This requires an identification of the level of risk to their employees in carrying out their work duties and considering what first aid equipment, personnel and facilities they need to make available to meet the needs. (Health and Safety First Aid Regulations 1981 and approved code of practice and guidance, L74 1997 www. hse.gov.uk)

Amazingly, there is no similar legislation regarding the assessment of first aid needs of children in childcare settings. Although Ofsted specifies in the National Standards (Under Eights Full Day Care and Childminding) that:

7.8 There is a first aid box, the contents of which will be determined in the first aid training course, and checked frequently and replaced as necessary. This is kept in an accessible place out of reach of the children.

7.9 There is at least one member of staff with a current first aid certificate on the premises or on outings at any time. This qualification includes training in first aid for infants and young children which is consistent with the Secretary of State.

7.10 Written permission is requested, at the time of placement, to the seeking of any necessary emergency medical advice or treatment in the future

7.11 A record is maintained, signed by the parents, of any accidents.

(This standard is the only mandatory requirement in regulations.)

How do you assess your first aid needs?

A first aid assessment should include:

- The size, layout and location of your setting in regard to the nearest Accident and Emergency Department. A large inner city day nursery will have different needs to that of a small rural playgroup.

- The number of employees, their physical, medical needs and distribution. A childminder or nanny will have different needs to that of a large day nursery.

- The number and distribution of children and their needs. Identify the needs of children with a medical or physical disability.

- Known staff annual leave and training days - so you can make arrangements for first aid cover for both adults and children.

- Known occurrences of accidents or illness. This will give you a good idea of the common trend of accidents or illnesses within your setting and what to prepare for.

Although it is considered good practice to record your assessment it is a legal requirement if there are more than five employees in your setting, under Regulation 3 of the Management of

Health and Safety at Work Regulations 1999.

What is the minimum first aid provision for any childcare setting?

- A suitably stocked first aid box.

- An appointed person to take charge of first aid arrangements (for adults).

- One member of staff with a current first aid certificate (for infants and young children).

First aid kits

Each setting should have at least one fully stocked first aid kit (HSE 1-10). Additional smaller kits for children will be needed for split levels, playgrounds and off-site activities.

All kits must be marked with a white cross on a green background and made easily accessible. Extra supplies must be available for immediate refill of kits.

Kits should be routinely checked by a named individual to ensure they hold all the equipment they should.

Appointed person
The Health and Safety Executive (HSE) states that the appointed person course should last for at least four hours and is widely available from many first aid training providers

An appointed person is someone who:

- Looks after the first aid equipment (for example, restocking the kit).

- Can take charge when an adult is injured or falls ill, including calling an ambulance if required.

An appointed person should not attempt to give first aid for which they have not been trained. They represent the minimum of first aid provision in any setting and as such there must be at least one on duty at every session.

First aid training for infants and children

The Sure Start Unit amended the requirement for first aid training in the revised National Standards for Under Eights Day Care and Childminding, which were circulated to all registered childcare providers in September 2003.

The standards now require that childminders and day care providers hold a current first aid training certificate which includes training in first aid for infants and young children, consistent with any guidance issued by the Secretary of State.

In January 2004 the Department for Education and Skills identified a need to clarify the duration and depth of first aid training which is appropriate for the childcare sector. Guidance on this amendment was issued to all local authorities and training providers and came into effect from April 2004.

It was identified that the course should be specially designed for early years workers caring for children aged from birth to eight in the absence of their parents and that a general first aid certified course with protocols for resuscitation and choking with small children and babies would not be adequate.

The following criteria were set:

1 Training should be designed for workers caring for children in the absence of their parent.

2 The training leading to a certificate or a renewal certificate should be a minimum of 12 hours.

3 The first aid certificate is renewed every three years.

4 Resuscitation and other equipment should include baby and junior models as appropriate.

5 Training should cover appropriate contents of first aid kits for babies and children.

6 Training should include recording accidents and incidents.

7 The course should include learning outcomes covering the following areas:

- Planning for first aid emergencies involving babies and children.

- Dealing with emergencies involving babies and children.

- Resuscitating babies and children.

- Recognising and dealing with shock in babies and children.

- Recognising and responding appropriately to anaphylactic shock in babies and children.

- Recognising and responding appropriately to electric shock in babies and children.

- Recognising and responding appropriately to bleeding in babies and children.

- Responding appropriately to burns and scalds in babies and children.

- Responding appropriately to choking in babies and children.

- Responding appropriately to suspected fractures in babies and children.

- Responding appropriately to head,

neck and back injuries in babies and children.

- Recognising and responding appropriately to cases of poisoning in babies and children.

- Responding appropriately to foreign bodies in eyes, ears and noses of babies and children.

- Responding appropriately to eye injuries in babies and children

- Responding appropriately to bites and stings in babies and children.

- Responding appropriately to the effects of extreme heat and cold in babies and children.

- Responding appropriately to febrile convulsions in babies and young children.

- Recognising and responding appropriately to the emergency needs of babies and children with chronic medical conditions including epilepsy, asthma, sickle cell, diabetes.

- Recognising and responding.

Useful links

Sure Start: www.surestart.gov.uk

The Health and Safety Executive: www.hse.gov.uk

The Association of First Aiders and Trainers: www.aofa.org

St John Ambulance: www.sja.org.uk

Meningitis is the infectious disease every parent dreads. In the early stages symptoms can be mistaken for colds, flu, even teething problems, so it's vital to know the signs, to be vigilant and trust your instincts. If in doubt, seek medical help immediately

Meningitis: know the signs and symptoms

Meningitis is the most common infectious cause of death among children under five years of age. There are around 3,000 cases of meningitis reported each year in the UK and Ireland. The best defence against it is knowledge – knowing how to spot the signs fast.

What is meningitis?

Meningitis means inflammation of the meninges, the lining surrounding the brain. There are two main types. Viral meningitis is more common than the bacterial form, and it's not usually serious. It's often unreported or even undiagnosed because it feels like flu.

Bacterial meningitis is the type we all dread. Although uncommon, it is fatal in one in ten cases and one in seven survivors is left with a serious disability, such as deafness, brain damage or in the case of septicaemia (blood poisoning), loss of limbs.

What causes bacterial meningitis?

The most common cause of bacterial meningitis is a bacteria called the meningococcus. There are two main groups of this bacteria in the UK: group B and group C. Both children and adults can carry the bacteria in the back of their nose and throat without developing the disease. Other bacteria that cause meningitis include pneumococcal and hib.

Why are children more at risk?

Children and babies are more susceptible to meningitis because their immune systems are immature and their resistance hasn't fully developed. However, anyone can get meningitis or septicaemia, regardless of age, gender or ethnic group.

How do you catch it?

It is difficult to pass on and develop bacterial meningitis because the bacteria cannot live for more than a few seconds outside the body. The bacteria are transmitted through coughing, sneezing and intimate kissing. It requires close prolonged contact, for example, living in the same household, sharing the same bed.

Is there a cure?

Bacterial meningitis can be treated with antibiotics, but it needs to be treated extremely quickly as the illness can cause long-term damage. Urgent hospital treatment is vital.

What about vaccines?

A vaccine for meningococcal group C meningitis (one of the most common forms) does exist and is part of the Childhood Immunisation Programme. It can be given on request through GPs to everyone aged under 25. But there's currently no vaccine for meningococcal group B meningitis – the most common cause of the disease in the UK. The hib (haemophilus influenzae type B) vaccine, routinely given to all babies, prevents another type of the disease, hib meningitis.

Signs and symptoms

It is important not to panic and to remember that meningitis is a relatively rare disease, however it can develop very quickly and can be life-threatening. The best thing to do is to know the signs and symptoms and to trust your instincts. Refer to the check-list overleaf.

If you are at all concerned about someone, you must seek urgent medical attention. If you need to talk to anyone for support and information, you can call the Meningitis Trust's helpline day or night on 0845 6000 800 or visit their website www.meningitis-trust.org

You can obtain symptoms cards and leaflets by calling the Helpline or emailing info@ meningitis-trust.org

The rash

The sign most associated with meningitis is the rash; this is actually a feature of meningococcal septicaemia (blood poisoning).

Patients with septicaemia often develop a rash which may appear anywhere on the body as a cluster of tiny blood spots, which look like pinpricks in the skin. This rash will not disappear when pressure is applied or a glass is pressed against it.

If a child develops the rash, take them straight to hospital. But if you have concerns, do not wait for the rash, as it does not always appear.

If you think a child may have meningitis, every second counts and you should seek medical assistance immediately - this could be your local GP surgery or Accident and Emergency at your local hospital.

What is the treatment?

This depends on the type of meningitis. A throat swab will reveal if meningococcal bacteria are present but the only sure test currently available is a lumbar puncture to test spinal fluid.

Bacterial meningitis must be treated quickly with antibiotics. Viral meningitis will not respond to antibiotics; it can be treated with fluids, painkillers and plenty of rest and is rarely life-threatening.

However, both types of meningitis should be treated as a medical emergency in hospital.

Information supplied by Meningitis Trust

Young children and babies are prone to infections and vulnerable because their immune systems are still developing. This means that you need to know how to spot the signs of a range of illnesses and know what to do if they are a notifiable disease. Audrey Farley explains the procedure

Health and safety: notifiable diseases

Notifiable diseases are monitored in Britain and the government produces an up-to-date list for England and Wales (see box). Information on these notifiable diseases must be given to public authorities. This is a statutory requirement and therefore enforceable by law.

It is important, therefore, that you have health policies to meet the needs of the children you care for and that you refer to these policies regularly. Include these named notifiable infectious diseases, as well as other infections, and set out

Relevant legislation
Public Health (Control of Diseases) Act 1984

Public Health (Infectious Disease) Regulations 1988

Notifiable diseases

- Acute encephalitis
- Acute poliomyelitis
- Anthrax
- Cholera
- Diphtheria
- Dysentery
- Food poisoning
- Leprosy
- Leptospirosis
- Malaria
- Measles
- Meningitis
- Meningococcal septicaemia (without meningitis)
- Mumps
- Opthalmia

- neonatorum
- Paratyphoid fever
- Plaque
- Rabies
- Relapsing fever
- Rubella
- Scarlet fever
- Smallpox
- Tetanus
- Tuberculosis
- Typhoid fever
- Typhus
- Viral haemorrhagic fever
- Hepatitis
- Whooping cough
- Yellow fever

procedures that comply with health and safety laws and regulations.

Policies must also include what actions to take, for example getting help, reporting the disease, informing parents, raising the level of hygiene and keeping up-to-date records. Such actions help to avoid the risk of cross-infection and promote children's health.

The procedure for notification

Suspected cases of notifiable diseases or their symptoms must be reported to a qualified medical practitioner or doctor. They are required to report cases of notifiable diseases to their local medical officer in environmental health, usually the 'proper officer' or consultant in communicable disease in the public health department of the local health authority. It is their job to check on the number of cases that are reported and take measures to reduce their spread.

The doctor must notify the authorities of the name, age and sex of the affected case, and other relevant details such as when symptoms were first displayed.

Information on each case is collected to contribute to the calculation of disease epidemics. Health campaigns, such as immunisation programmes, may be carried out.

Health and safety policies

The Children Act requires you to have policies regarding the health and safety of children. There are also regulations that underpin good child care practices.

The National Standards for Under Eights Day Care and Childminding explain what to do to meet children's needs. Your policies need to link to these standards. Standard 7 is aimed at promoting the good health of children, helping to prevent infection and taking care of sick children.

Yearly Ofsted inspections are set against these national standards. Inspectors expect you to achieve them to make sure quality care and service. They will ask to see the policies you write to help you.

Written policies must include safety as well as health and relate to:

- **First Aid** - the Health and Safety (First Aid) Regulations 1981 require that there is a first aid box and contents, a trained first aider and a record of giving medication in the setting.

- **Hazardous materials** - these come under the Control of Substances Hazardous to Health Regulations 1994 (COSHH) which relate to storage, use and disposal of hazardous materials, such as cleaning products like bleach. The risks must be assessed and procedures for managing them must be written and in place in the setting.

- **Injuries, diseases and dangerous occurrences** - under the Reporting of Injuries, Diseases and Dangerous Occurrences Regulations 1995 (RIDDOR). An accident book must be provided for reporting injuries to children (The Children Act 1989). Injuries to workers that must be reported to the Health and Safety Executive include: a fatal accident; serious injury, such as a fracture; any accident resulting in a hospital visit; a dangerous occurrence, such as collapse of a piece of equipment.

RIDDOR require you to report incidents which result in:

- absence from work for more than three days;

- death of an employee as a result of a reportable accident within one year of that accident;

- specified incidents or conditions resulting in occupational disease, for example hand cramp through typing.

You must also report:

- Certain poisonings, for example from chemicals;

- Some skin diseases, such as skin cancer and oil folliculitis/acne;

- Lung diseases including occupational asthma and asbestosis;

- The infections listed, for example leptospirosis, anthrax, tuberculosis;

- Other conditions such as occupational cancer and cataracts.

What you need to do

Children with recognisable infections or whose illness raises concerns may be infected with a notifiable disease.

You should be able to recognise the signs and symptoms which might indicate these diseases, and inform other professionals at once, according to your policies. Then reassure, comfort and monitor the child.

An emergency plan should include giving first aid treatment (by a qualified first-aider) and seeking help and advice from a medical practitioner. They will consider a diagnosis of notifiable disease, the specific treatment, and prevention of any complications.

You need to inform the parents/carers about their child's condition and ask them to collect the child to reduce the risk of cross-infection.

You also need to contact the parents of other children recently in contact with an infectious disease in your setting, but within the boundaries of confidentiality.

Information on significant changes or events should be passed to Ofsted. These include any notifiable infectious disease that a qualified medical person considers is for reporting, as stated in the Children Act regulations. Serious accidents that result in injuries or fatalities must also be reported to Ofsted.

Your record keeping should include an accurate record of the sequence of events. For example, what took place from the start of symptoms (for example, fever) to actions taken (such as taking temperature) and the child's progress. There must also be a record of all prescribed medicines given to children.

Parents may worry about infections, infestations, skin complaints and other conditions/diseases. It is important that they share information about their child's health, what they have done about it and the medical advice they have been given.

You must endeavour to recognise illnesses and take the necessary actions to help prevent infections, conditions and incidents that put the health of both children and staff at risk. Reporting disease is an important part of your work in promoting good health.

Audrey Farley, former lecturer in health, child care and education.

Do you want to know more?

- A Guide to RIDDOR (HMSO) is available from the Health and Safety Executive. Call 020 7242 6408 / HMSO 0870 600 5522

- *Child Health and Surveillance* by Judith Moreton and Aidan Macfarlane (1991 Blackwell Scientific Publications second edition)

Owners and managers of premises should undertake a risk assessment of the outside environment as well as inside. Why do you do it? How do you do it? What happens afterwards? Gail Ryder Richardson sets out the steps

Assessing risk outdoors

In everyday life we all face situations that include some risk; every time we use scissors, climb the stairs, or go for a swim we are assessing and coping with a potentially hazardous event. We learn to accept and manage these risks because we see that the benefits of these experiences are valuable. Learning to manage risk and to cope with challenge is a vital part of growing up.

David Yearley, Play Safety Manager for the Royal Society for the Prevention of Accidents (RoSPA), believes that:

- Risk taking is essential to play.

- Play provision should offer risks.

- A lack of risk hampers children's development.

RoSPA believes that exposure to risk is acceptable and should be encouraged since otherwise children may seek the thrill of risk elsewhere in unsupervised situations. However, they are also quite clear that children's contact with unacceptable risk should be avoided.

Early years practitioners support children to learn how to be aware of and deal with risks – both indoors and outdoors.

The *Curriculum Guidance for the Foundation Stage* recognises the importance of the outdoor environment for young children yet many adults feel it is a place with unacceptable dangers, for example high climbing equipment, potential for access to ponds or busy roads, as well as stinging insects, prickly plants, sharp sticks and jagged stones.

To provide a stimulating and challenging outdoor environment that supports children's play and learning you will need to find the balance between children's need to take risks in their play, the concerns of adults about potential dangers, and your responsibility to protect

children from unacceptable levels of risk.

The Health and Safety Executive has the following message which is a useful starting point when you begin to think about assessing the safety of your own outdoor environment:

'… safety must be considered at all stages of play provision… inevitably, there will be risk of injury when children play, as there is risk of injury in life generally. We must not lose sight of the important developmental role of play for children in the pursuit of the unachievable goal of absolute safety.'

Why do you need to carry out a risk assessment?

The Management of Health and Safety at Work Regulations (1999) (www.hse.gov.uk) recommend that owners and managers of premises should undertake a risk assessment of their facilities – this includes the outdoor environment.

The risk assessment procedure allows you to look closely at the whole outdoor area and think carefully about the potential for harm, and then to work out the possibility of harm occurring to children or adults using the space.

How do you do it?

Hazard and risk - don't let these words put you off! According to the Health and Safety Executive leaflet, *Five Steps to Risk Assessment*, a 'hazard' means anything that can cause harm. The 'risk' is the chance – high or low – that someone will be harmed by the hazard.

■ Look for the hazards

Walk round the outdoor space and look carefully at the existing features – both natural and manufactured. Concentrate on identifying significant hazards that could result in serious harm rather than minor hazards that children and staff can learn to cope with. For example,

a plant with prickles is a much less significant hazard than one that is poisonous.

Talk to colleagues and children about their views - they may have noticed something that you haven't. Try bending down to see everything from the children's height and perspective.

Parents can provide a useful insight, too – they will know their child's particular interests and may be able to spot potential hazards that you are unaware of.

Look at how children and adults are currently using equipment. Check back through the Accident Record Book and look for repeated incidents involving specific pieces of equipment or areas.

■ Examples to think about

Play equipment: Is it in good condition? Is it used appropriately? Is it in a good position?

Surfaces: Are there any broken or uneven surfaces? Are there icy patches in winter? Do drain covers fit securely?

Plants: Are the plants non-poisonous? Are there any plants with berries? If so, do staff talk to children about the importance of checking with an adult before picking a berry?

Boundaries: Are fences and gates secure? Are they in good condition? Where will children find themselves if they slip through? Are there adequate systems in place at entrances and exits? How is emergency access maintained, for example for fire service vehicles?

Water: Are water features and ponds adequately supervised? Are they securely protected when unsupervised?

Storage areas: Is equipment stored safely? Are adults and children at risk from equipment stored above head height? Do staff and children lift and carry heavier items correctly?

■ Decide who might be harmed

Once you have identified each hazard, think about who might be harmed and how. Try not to over estimate the likelihood or seriousness of the harm.

Think about the different users of the space and how the hazard might affect them. For example, a prospective parent visiting with a toddler may be more at risk than a child who knows the layout and procedures.

You will need to use your judgement to decide whether the existing safety measures are adequate or whether more should be done to reduce the risk. Remember that the benefits of an experience will often be greater than the risk of harm.

■ Evaluate the risk

Next you need to think about how likely it is that someone will be harmed by the hazards you have identified.

Do you need to take further action or are the existing arrangements providing adequate protection? For example, in a nursery in Kent staff noticed how much children liked hanging from low level branches in the bushes. They considered that the risk of serious harm was low and the benefits were high. However, they felt that they could reduce the risk of harm further by checking the branches and removing weaker ones, and by removing stones from the ground underneath the bushes.

'We should have as much play value as we can possibly afford, but only as much safety as is necessary.'

Julian Richter, Environmental Play Designer and Manufacturer

will remain. For each significant hazard you will need to decide whether the level of remaining risk is high, medium or low.

If you decide that something needs to be done to further reduce the risk you have two options:

1) to remove the hazard altogether;

2) to control the risk so that harm is unlikely.

Again, you will need to consider each hazard and decide on the most appropriate option. For example, you could remove the hazard caused by poorly positioned play equipment by removing it. But then children would not have the benefit of the play experiences it provided. So you would probably decide to control the risk by putting the equipment in a different place.

However, if the hazard was a broken fence that gave children access to a busy road you would want to remove the hazard altogether by replacing the broken fencing – rather than just controlling the risk, for example by propping something against the gap.

What happens afterwards?
■ Record your findings

If you have fewer than five employees in your workplace you are not required to write anything down – although it would be a sensible precaution to keep a written record of what you have done.

If you have five or more people in your workplace you should record the significant findings of your assessment. Record the hazards and your conclusions.

You need to show that:

- a proper check was made;

- you considered everyone who might be affected;

- you dealt with all the obvious significant hazards and thought about the number of people who could be affected;

- the precautions are reasonable and the remaining risk is low.

■ Further information

Five Steps to Risk Assessment Health and Safety Executive leaflet INDG165 (rev1)

Health and Safety Executive

HSE Infoline Tel: 08701 545500

Email: hseinformationservices@natbrit.com

www.hse.gov.uk

Royal Society for the Prevention of Accidents (RoSPA)

General Information: 0121 248 2000

Email: help@rospa.com

Learning through Landscapes (LTL)

An educational charity supporting schools and early years settings who recognise the value of educational outdoor spaces. Members can access free advice and support about specific issues relating to their outdoor space, for example lists of non-toxic plants and information about surfaces.

Enquiries: 01962 845811

Email: eyo@ltl.org.uk

www.ltl.org.uk

Too safe for their own good? by Jennie Lindon (National Children's Bureau)

Advocates the importance of helping children experience risk and challenge and provides useful advice and information.

www.ncb.org.uk

emailbooksales@ncb.org.uk

Keep the record for future reference. It will provide evidence of your actions as well as being a useful reminder to you next time you review your procedures.

■ Review your assessment and amend it if necessary

It is good practice to review your assessment at regular intervals to make sure that the systems and procedures you have in place are working effectively. Similarly, if you make a change to the outdoor environment that is likely to introduce a new significant hazard, such as a new water feature, you will want to consider what you need to do to keep the risk of harm low.

Gail Ryder Richardson, Senior Development Officer (Early Years), Learning through Landscapes.

Water play in paddling pools should be fun for all ages and it can be if you are vigilant, supervise children at all times and take all the appropriate precautions. Sheila Riddall-Leech looks at what you need to do

Health and safety: paddling pools

Water holds a special fascination for young children, especially those under five, and they want to investigate it whether it is in a paddling pool, a bucket or a puddle.

This natural curiosity can lead to tragic consequences. According to the Royal Society for the Prevention of Accidents (RoSPA), 111 children under the age of five have drowned in the last ten years in paddling pools and water features in gardens. In all cases, the adult supervising the child has been distracted, often only for a few seconds. Children between one and two years are at greatest risk of drowning, with the risk decreasing as age increases.

There can be no compromise with pool safety; you are literally dealing with a life and death situation.

From a child's point of view, 500 mm (19 inches) of water in a paddling pool is equivalent to an adult falling into 1800 mm (6 feet) of water. The difference is

that a child would not be able to climb out; an adult probably could. Children can drown in less than 300 mm (approx 11 inches) of water and there are reported drownings in less than 100 mm (approx 3.5 inches).

Being able to swim does not mean that children will be safe. Most paddling pools are for paddling not swimming in - children jump in and out of them and up and down. It is these actions that can cause accidents. You want children to have fun and enjoy their play but you must be vigilant and never let up on supervision.

Supervision

Supervision is vital when children are playing in paddling pools, with hosepipes, water slides or any other equipment that involves water.

Children should never be left unattended and older children should, under no circumstances, be asked to 'keep an eye' on younger ones.

Clear boundaries

It is good practice to establish clear boundaries for play in paddling pools , that all children can understand and stick to. For example, the area around the paddling pool often becomes slippery when wet and there is the risk that children will fall into the pool or on the ground around it. Make sure that children do not run around the pool area.

Types of pool

Paddling pools come in all shapes, sizes and colours, from simple round inflatables to animal shapes and pools

with integral seats and shades. Some need inflating with an electric pump. Many pools are made of rigid, heavy duty PVC and have a European manufacturers' standard of EN 1176. This gives some reassurance that the pool has been manufactured to a high standard, but does not mean that it is safe. Safety comes from the way the pool is used and how the children are supervised.

In the same way, a kite mark label (British Safety Institute) on a paddling pool

---

Lorraine, a registered childminder has always had water play in the garden, especially during the summer holidays when she has children of different ages.

She says: 'I find that all the children play brilliantly together when the paddling pool is out; there is lots of laughter and fun and hardly any squabbles. I spend quite a bit of time laying the ground rules before going out and I have written a paddling pool policy for parents. I don't join the children in the water as I think I can supervise them better from the side of the pool'.

Sample paddling pool policy

I want all children to have fun and enjoy themselves in the paddling pool, and their health and safety is paramount. Please read the following policy, sign and date the return slip and please add any comments that you feel are relevant.

■ The pool will be filled with fresh, clean, luke-warm water each time it is used.

■ The pool will be emptied after each play session and will be left upside down to dry after being wiped out using an antibacterial spray.

■ Children will be supervised at all times from the side of the pool. They will be asked not to run around the perimeter of the pool or jump in the water.

■ Please provide appropriate swimwear and a towel for your child. Children who are not toilet trained should be provided with swim pants.

■ Although the pool will be kept in the shade, please provide sunscreen cream for your child, and loose light clothing that will protect them from the sun.

means that it has been manufactured to a British manufacturing quality standard, not that it is safe.

Some pools need inflating before use and may be supplied with an electric air pump. Water and electricity do not mix. The pool should be fully inflated before any water is put in and children should not be allowed to play around or in the pool while it is being inflated.

Some pools have rigid sides which stay upright when water is in the pool, but collapse when empty or if children lean heavily on them. This can be dangerous as water will spill out and make the surrounding area wet and slippery.

Staying safe in the sun

Many paddling pools have shades attached to protect children from the sun. Remember that children can become sunburnt even on cloudy days and wet skin can be more susceptible to sun damage. The danger from the sun's ultraviolet rays is still not fully understood although the current advice is that children should be covered up and kept out of direct sunlight.

Babies have sensitive skin and so you should avoid using sunscreen or

- Staff at a day nursery have decided to put their paddling pool on the patio, because there is a large blind offering shade.

- Some practitioners are concerned because the pool is on paving slabs and so every child has to hold hands with an adult and walk around the pool area, or the adult carries the child to the water.

- The officer in charge says that the staff feel that they can manage the risk of the hard surface and that it was important for children to be in the shade when playing in water.

similar products; it is better to keep them out of the sun and wearing loose light clothing. For older children, sunscreen of at least factor 15 should be applied 30 minutes before going outside, reapplied generously every two hours or even more if children are in water.

Place your paddling pool in the shade and not direct sunlight. A paddling pool full of water is heavy and difficult to move, so even if there is an integral shade the water area may not always stay in the shade. It might be better to consider using a large portable garden umbrella or gazebo to provide shade.

When not in use

There are many products available to cover pools when not is use. Paddling pool covers must be secure and rigid. The cover should be able to support the weight of a child and not sink under the water surface.

Wire or plastic netting is not suitable or safe as these are not rigid and a child could crawl underneath them and become trapped or stuck. A cover that does not remain above the water surface at all times is not safe and does not remove all risk of drowning, especially to young children and crawling babies who could still become face down in the water and not able to get themselves upright.

You should completely empty paddling pools when not in use and turn them upside down.

National water shortages and hosepipe bans may make you reluctant to empty away the water every day but the life of a child is more important. Also, water left in paddling pools can become contaminated with plant and garden debris, or by pets and animals. Children may have urinated in the pool as well, so you should always start with clean water each time.

Wiping inside the pool after use with an antibacterial spray can help to prevent the spread of infection.

It is not necessary to add a mild disinfectant to the water - clean, fresh water each time should be enough, provided that the paddling pool is clean in the first place. Some children could have an allergic reaction to the chemicals in disinfectant or they might accidentally get water in their mouths.

Sheila Riddall-Leech, educational consultant and trainer.

Where to go for advice

RoSPA has informative fact sheets on water safety which can be downloaded from www.rospa.com

The Health and Safety Executive offers advice on health and safety issues relating to paddling pools run by local authorities. Their website address is www.hse.gov.uk

and they also have a public infoline: 0845 345 0055.

Infection can spread rapidly in childcare settings as children play together. It is therefore important to know how to identify infections and to have policies and procedures in place to reduce their spread. Audrey Farley offers some advice

Infection: what it is and how it spreads

Practitioners must always be alert to all infections because they have the potential to cause problems for the infected child, other children and staff. Therefore clear policies and procedures should be in place to care for sick children and the passing on of infection to others.

The problem is that if children have bouts of infections regularly their overall growth and development may be affected. Furthermore, they may develop diseases with complications that may lead to serious outcomes down the line.

A healthy view among both nurseries and childminders is that bouts of infection are to be expected in childhood and children will succumb to them. So complacency may set in because many children usually recover anyway from these bouts as their immune system gets stronger with age.

Various infections that affect children include diarrhoea and vomiting (tummy bug) coughs and colds, classic childhood illnesses diseases (such as mumps, measles, and rubella - and similar), skin condition, head lice and threadworms. The list goes on. So you. need to know the signs and symptoms of infection in children, particularly certain signs that indicate the need for immediate attention. Knowledge will enable you to help prevent and control infection which is essential for protecting both children and staff in the setting.

What is infection?
Infection occurs when micro-organisms or germs, microbes or small living organisms, enter into the tissues of the body, multiply and grow. These organisms are called pathogens because they cause diseases. They prevent the normal functioning of the tissues they invade and produce poisons or toxins in the bloodstream which harm cells in the body. Consequently the damaged cells cause illnesses and diseases, as the body reacts to them. Infection follows a basic pattern (see 'pattern of infection' on page 10).

As infection spreads rapidly throughout the setting children become infected. But infective micro-organisms need certain essentials to survive - moisture, warmth, food and time and sometimes, oxygen. Also there must be a source of infection, for example, a child who is already infected or a carrier of the disease; a medium where organisms can multiply such as mucus; then via a route, such as inhalation then spreads either directly or indirectly to the vulnerable host, for example, other pre school children around the infected child.

Types of infection
Bacterial infections are caused by bacteria which are in the air, water and food, and inside and outside of plants and animals' bodies. Bacteria are micro-organisms with single cells and of different types and different shapes. Good bacteria can turn milk into cheese and some convert organic matter (eg urine, leaves) into fertilisers. Some are used to make antibiotics, while others live in the lower gut and helps in the proper absorption of food.

But some bacteria are harmful and cause diseases if they invade the body and resistance is lowered. They reproduce at a quick rate if the conditions are right. Bacteria can directly damage the body tissues and certain ones can produce toxins or chemical poisons too. Antibiotics are effective against bacteria.

Pattern of infection

Entry: Harmful germs enter the body by a variety of routes such as what is breathed in (inhalation); what is swallowed (ingestion); through the skin (inoculation). Germs survive, grow and multiply.

Incubation period: The time between germs entering the body and the appearance of symptoms caused by toxins.

Symptoms: What is felt or experienced, such as pain and feeling unwell.

Signs of illness: Signs that can be seen, for example, a rash. Signs and symptoms are used to help determine a diagnosis.

Onset: The start of the disease.

Infectious stage: The time when germs can be easily transmitted from one person to another.

Quarantine: The amount of time that the child is in contact with the disease, advised to stay at home or isolated.

Recovery: The time taken to get well, usually within a specific time scale if there are no complications.

How is it spread?

Infection can be spread directly or indirectly.

Direct spread is where a child is within the range of the infected person, for example, in the same room. This includes:

- Droplet or airborne infection. Small drops of moisture are expelled in the air when sneezing, coughing or talking and inhaled by another person. Coughs and colds are spread this way.

- Touching infected people or material when the skin becomes broken (cuts or grazes), for example impetigo and athlete's foot.

- Directly from mouth to mouth, for example, glandular fever.

Indirect spread is where a child can be infected by using toys, towels, cups and other equipment that has been used by an infected child or adult.

- Hands can be contaminated by urine and faeces around the toilet area. These hands can be licked, used to eat or to prepare food and drink.

- Incorrectly stored or cooked food may harbour germs. Food can be contaminated by dirty hands or prepared in a unclean area. These can all cause food poisoning and gastroenteritis.

- Contaminated drinking water can cause gastroenteritis and bacillary dysentery and even typhoid fever. Infection can also occur if infected water is inhaled as in Legionnaires' disease.

- Rats can cause Weil's disease or leptospirosis bacterium which is excreted in their urine and passed on to humans.

- Insects, such as flies, spread germs if they land on food. Serious diseases can be spread by bites from mosquitoes, for example malaria.

Whooping cough and diptheria are examples of bacterial infections.

Viral infections are those caused by viruses, also single celled micro-organisms that are even smaller than bacteria. They can live on surfaces for a long time. Some types live on plants and animals. Antibiotics are ineffective against viral infections so the body's defence mechanism is important to fight infections. Good health will ensure this. Examples of viral diseases are chicken pox and measles.

Fungi are another type of infection. Some are harmless, such as those that help the production of antibiotics, bread and cheese. But there are those that cause ringworm - not a worm as the name suggests.

Protozoa are simple animals with a single cell, such as amoeba, which causes amoebic dysentery.

Other infections caused by parasites are known as infestations. Parasites, which get their food from humans, can be a problem in childcare settings. They include fleas, small insects which feed on the blood of human beings. You will be familiar with those that live in human hair, called head lice. Threadworms are also in this group. They are worms that live in the bowel. Scabies are very small mites that burrow under the skin.

Recognising signs and symptoms

If is a child is unconscious, has vomiting and diarrhoea, a raised temperature, breathing difficulties, excessive bleeding, serious injuries, burns, convulsions/fits or poisoning you must dial 999. This will mean the child will get immediate diagnosis and treatment. You must always inform the parents or carer.

Otherwise always look out for general signs and symptoms of an infection. This can be feeling unwell, pain or discomfort, clinginess, loss of appetite and not wanting to play with others. Don't leave the child on their own. Keep them comfortable in a quiet room until their parent comes to collect them.

Observing the child and taking their temperature is all part of good practice. It gives information that may be shared with the parent or doctor. This is in addition to the usual record keeping.

Reassure and keep the infected child away from others. Check with parents about immunisations uptake, history of infectious disease and recent travels abroad.

Fighting infection

The body protects against infection through its immune system. It fights infection by increasing the blood's white cells, for example, the swollen glands seen or felt in a case of throat infection. Other protective mechanisms include the skin, which forms a natural barrier until it is cut or broken; the stomach which produces hydrochloric acid to destroy germs that are eaten with food; the nose which has hairs for excreting micro-organisms; and tears which act as antiseptic protection for the eyes.

You also play an important part in protecting children and yourself from infection and disease. Your basic practices to encourage the prevention and control of infections mean that there should be specific procedures to follow. This must be in keeping with policies based on national standards and regulations for health and safety.

Your policies and procedures should cover what to do when a child becomes ill in your care, first aid and giving medicines. Your setting should be clean and well ventilated.

All nurseries and childminders should enforce a high standard of hygiene to prevent the spread of infection. This means personal, food and general hygiene. This is of particular importance as many strains of bacteria are becoming resistant to antibiotics.

Your own good health record means that you are taking care of yourself which is equally important in the prevention and control of infection.

Common sense dictates that you continue to update your information on childhood infections/illnesses and first aid skills.

Audrey Farley, former lecturer in health, childcare and education.

Threadworm infection: spotting the signs

Threadworm infection is common in children with up to 40 per cent of children under ten getting threadworm at some time. Fortunately, threadworms (*Enterobius vermicularis*) are easy to treat with over-the-counter treatments.

However, health care professionals believe that most parents do not know how to recognise the symptoms of threadworm. This, combined with the fact that threadworms may be considered embarrassing, means that it is not always an easy subject for parents and carers to talk about.

What are threadworms?

Threadworms are parasites that resemble little pieces of white thread and are sometimes seen in the stools or around the anus at night. Although common in children, the worms can spread to the whole family.

Adult male threadworms are 2 to 5 mm in length and females are between 8 and 13 mm long. Threadworms come from eggs which are so small they can't be seen by the naked eye. After the eggs have been swallowed, they hatch in the duodenum and the adult worms reproduce in the large intestine. At night, pregnant females come out of the anus and lay up to 15,000 eggs on the surrounding skin while the child is asleep.

The sticky eggs may cause itching and so the child scratches around their bottom, collecting the eggs on their fingers and under the nails. The eggs may then be swallowed, and the threadworm lifecycle continues. Breaking the threadworm lifecycle is the key to eliminating them.

Symptoms

The main symptoms of threadworms are:

- Tiny white threads in the child's stools;

- An itchy bottom;

- Bottom scratching at night;

- Occasionally bed-wetting.

However, 90 per cent of children will not even get the tickle or itch in this area, and 20 per cent do not get any symptoms at all.

Diagnosis of threadworms is generally straightforward. Examining the skin around the anus using a torch or bright light usually reveals the worms. The best time to do this is a couple of hours after going to bed or in the morning, but the worms can still escape detection.

Treatment of the infection

Everyone in the household, whether or not they suffer symptoms, should be treated at the same time and adopt hygiene routines to break the lifecycle of the worm.

Drug treatment

Treatment is easy and available over the counter from any pharmacy.

Treatment is in the form of mebendazole (chewable tablets)

Treatment is in the form of mebendazole (chewable tablets) or piperazine phosphate (sachets). Studies suggest that both piperazine and mebendazole produce cure rates of about 90 per cent (National Prescribing Centre, 1999).

Mebendazole can be taken by children (and adults) over two years of age. In the form of chewable orange tablets, it is given as a single dose with a follow-up dose taken 14 days later. Mebendazole works by preventing the worms absorbing sugar and they die a few days later.

Mebendazole can not be taken by pregnant or breast-feeding women.

Piperazine phosphate (Pripsen Powders) is the only drug treatment for threadworms that can be given to children under the age of two years old (from three months of age). Available in a sachet, the powder can be stirred into milk or water. Piperazine works by paralysing the adult worms and, combined with a laxative, expelling the worms in the faeces. A second dose of piperazine is given after 14 days to ensure that all worms are cleared.

Both drugs are well tolerated and side effects are uncommon. If symptoms persist after the second dose, parents should consult their GP. Pregnant women should not take either drug, but use the hygiene measures described below, which will usually eradicate the infestation in six weeks.

Hygiene measures

Threadworms are not the result of a dirty home or an unhealthy diet, so there is no need for parents to feel ashamed or embarrassed.

However, strict hygiene measures are essential to help prevent the spread of threadworms.

- Keep the nails short.

- Wash hands and scrub nails before every meal or snack.

- Wash hands and scrub nails after using the toilet.

- Bath or shower every morning (removes eggs laid at night).

- Wear pyjamas or pants in bed (clean ones every night).

- Change underwear every day.

- Disinfect the toilet seat, toilet handle and door handle regularly.

- Damp dust and vacuum bedrooms daily.

- Towels should not be shared.

- Discourage children from scratching their bottoms, biting their nails or picking their noses.

Threadworm infection is a common infection in children and can spread quickly to the whole family. However, it is generally harmless and can be easily treated with a combination of hygiene measures and drug treatment for the whole family.

Tina Green, practice nurse, Robin Hood Health Centre, Sutton, Surrey.

Fact file

- The Royal College of General Practitioners [1996] estimates that about 40 per cent of children less than ten years of age suffer from threadworm infestations (*E vermicularis*) at least once.

- Threadworms live in the rectum of humans.

- Female worms lay their eggs on the skin around the anus at night.

- 'Itchy bottom' is the most common symptom, but symptoms may be absent.

- Eggs on the fingers and under nails transfer to people and clothing and are swallowed.

- A female threadworm can lay up to 15,000 eggs before dying.

- Eggs can survive for up to two weeks on clothing, towels, bedding, in carpets and in dust.

- Piperazine and mebendazole are both effective treatments.

- All the family must be treated at the same time to prevent re-infection.

Reference

Prodigy (2004). Guidance on the treatment of threadworm infection in the UK. Last update September 2004 www.prodigy.nhs.uk/guidance. asp?gt=Threadworm

It is necessary and right that you should keep the children in your care safe and the training you do always gives examples and ideas for safety, but are you allowing children to take enough risk? Sarah Mutch asks you to think about your approach

Safety vs risk: getting the right balance

There is a lot of media hype about health and safety. Everyone is wary of the possibility of insurance claims being made against them. Professional childcarers must meet both the requirements of Ofsted/Care Standards Inspectorate of Wales/Care Commission in Scotland as well as parents' expectations.

But if children are always kept completely safe and free from any risk, how will they learn to manage and understand risk?

This does not mean you should let a toddler jump off a 10-foot wall or out of a tree but perhaps you should look to see how much you manage and balance the risk with the play value of an activity or item.

If you explore the items beforehand you can identify what the potential risks are while looking at how much fun children can have playing with and exploring the equipment. It is then possible to look at how risks can be minimised instead of trying to get rid of them completely.

Adapt your approach

Even small changes to your practice can improve children's play experience and opportunities, building on their own risk management skills while still keeping children safe.

For example, a treasure basket is filled with natural materials for young babies to explore. It offers sensory experiences, language opportunities and the chance for representational use as they get older. However, some of the items may be

potential choking hazards, spiky or rough.

To minimise these risks, explore the objects with children in very small groups or even one to one, depending on age and stage of development.

Another example is the plastic toddler slide. Normally you expect toddlers to climb up the couple of steps and slide down on their bottoms. What about the two- to three-year-olds that start walking or climbing up the wrong way? They may decide that they want to slide down on their knees or stomachs or even backwards. Is that okay?

When looking at the potential risks it might mean managing the surface that they bounce down onto or closer supervision to make sure you can catch them if they fall or take a bigger risk than they thought.

By quietly letting individual children explore their own boundaries then most toddlers will decide for themselves what they are capable of. You need to allow them space to explore for themselves to try those first hesitating steps, much like when they first stand up and walk.

Learning from forest schools

When young children take part in forest

school experiences, for the first few sessions some of them spend most of their time falling over. Ofsted/CSIW may be worried about uneven surfaces in settings but it does have benefits. Children need to have the whole range of experiences, so provide smooth, flat surfaces like tarmac, concrete, paving, wet pour or decking but also think about having some wilder areas so that children get used to finding their own sense of balance.

Den building with older children using pallets, branches and tarpaulin, and tying them together to get a stable structure is a really useful experience. Extending this using loppers or small handsaws to cut branches to the right length allows children and young people to develop skills they may never try. This will also help them to use adventure play sites to the full and build the tree houses that many of you would have built as children.

It would not be responsible to attempt this without proper training but it is not something that should be shied away from. Forest Leader and Adventure Play Worker courses offer plenty of opportunity to take these experiences to a wide variety of settings.

If you do not want to do the qualification then it might be possible to link up with other professionals through childminding networks, local Forestry Commission Rangers or through local schools who have access to a site and the trained personnel.

Try something new

Another risk-taking opportunity is the idea of trying something new. By building a child's confidence so that they feel comfortable and able to attempt new activities, games or experiences and to embrace them with both hands you are enabling children to take risks they may have missed otherwise.

This is one of the ideas of the Foundation Stage and Foundation Phase programmes. By building confident children they will take greater responsibility for their own development and learning and so be more motivated as lifelong learners.

The Foundation Phase in Wales sets great store by encouraging children to develop their own experiments or exploration according to their individual interests. This will need confident children feeling safe and secure in their setting who feel they are able to explore as they wish and feel confident that the adults will support them in their quest.

Looking at balancing the risk or potential hazard with the play value and deciding how you can manage the risk rather than completely remove it, will develop a far more holistic practice.

Your goal should be developing confident children who are prepared to try new ideas and explore their environment fully to their own evolving limits so they get the most out of life.

Every child should be encouraged to develop their own personal limitations to taking risks, set their boundaries themselves and therefore enable them to grow with the child.

Sarah Mutch, integrated children's centre coordinator, Caerphilly.

What's happening in Wales?

The United Nations Convention on the Rights of the Child recognises the importance of play for children.

The Welsh Assembly Government now has a Play Policy and a Play Policy Implementation Plan which says it believes that play is the process by which humankind has developed and is critically important to all children in the development of their physical, social, mental, emotional and creative skills.

This Play Policy has also become a part of other policies and strategies including the Foundation Phase in Wales, Forest School initiative and Flying Start.

Adventure play and staffed play provision has also reached higher status with the launch of integrated children's centres. This provision is aimed at children and young people. Integrating this ethos about play within all childcare provision means that all children are building on their previous play experiences.

It has also been identified that the high safety conscious culture in which we live may potentially cause problems at a later date because young people are frightened about taking risks. The Welsh Assembly Government is therefore looking at current legislation and policies to redress the balance.

If you'd like to read the Play Policy, visit: www.wales.gov.uk/subichildren/content/play-policy-e.pdf

For the Play Policy Implementation Plan, visit: www.learning.wales.gov.uk/pdfs/play-policy-implementation-plan-e.pdf

Playhouses have become a popular piece of outdoor play equipment. But whether they are a simple wooden shed or an elaborate purpose-built design, there are several issues relating to health and safety that you need to think about when putting a playhouse in your garden

Health and safety playhouses

Playhouses come in many different shapes, sizes and materials. They can be set on the ground, on platforms or even in trees. Some are so big that they can be used safely by adults!

Adults keen on DIY may want to have a go at building their own playhouse, but they must be careful that the materials they use are safe and do not present hazards to children.

Most plastic playhouses are for young children, up to about four or five years old. They range in price from £100 to £250 depending on the design. Wooden playhouses are for older children and prices can vary tremendously depending on the size and design. Some tree houses cost thousands of pounds and have a wide range of accessories such as swings, slides, ladders, fireman's pole and monkey bars.

Some companies will design a playhouse to your specific requirements, even to match the design of your own house or setting. What you spend will depend on your budget, but you also need to think about why you are providing such equipment. How will you use it?

Is it to provide a private place for children to play away from adult supervision where they can engage in imaginative play, role play or just have a quiet place to be? If you just end up storing outdoor toys in it, it defeats the object of having a playhouse - why not just buy a cheap shed?

All playhouses designed for children under 14 years of age should be made in accordance with Trading Standards and comply with Trading Standards Regulations 1995, with a CE mark on the label. The CE mark does not guarantee that the product is safe; it shows that it has been manufactured to agreed standards. For peace of mind that your playhouse has been manufactured to the highest standards, look for labels on the equipment that have BS 5665 (British Standards) or EN71 (European Toy Standard).

What you need to think about

There are several issues relating to health and safety that you need to think about when putting a playhouse in your garden.

Surface
■ Where are you going to put it? The surface should be flat and level, so that there is limited or no risk of it falling over. Some plastic playhouses are light and may topple over, especially if children lean through the windows, for example.

■ Think about the surface itself. Grass may be ideal in dry weather and easy to knock fixings into, but can become slippery and hazardous when wet. Hard surfaces such as concrete or paving slabs may be level and provide stability, but need drilling to house fixings firmly in the ground. With hard surfaces there may be a risk of children falling and injuring themselves.

Position
■ Look carefully at the position of the house. Is it close to a fence or wall that could tempt some children to climb

onto the roof? Generally, the construction of playhouse roofs is not substantial enough to bear the weight of a child, and even if it were, children are at risk of falling off the roof. Playhouses with an upstairs can encourage adventurous, risky play and challenges which need to be assessed.

Material and design

■ Plastic pre-moulded playhouses are not necessarily durable as the plastic may chip or split after a couple of years outside. The material could warp which may affect the hinges and how the door and windows open and shut and potentially become finger traps.

■ Some playhouses attached to metal or wooden frames are more like tents. The frames should be securely fixed in the ground and the material cover firmly attached to the frame. These playhouses are not particularly durable and should be taken down and stored when not in use.

■ Look at the design of the playhouse from a child's point of view. For example, does the roof have an overhang which is at head height and therefore increase the risk of head injuries? Do the windows open out in such a way that a passing

child could knock against them? Is there room for several children to play inside together?

Wooden playhouses

Wooden playhouses can have particular potential hazards:

■ The wood should not have any holes or knots in it as this can lead to the wood splitting, leading to the hazard of splinters and chips.

■ Nails and screws must not protrude either externally or internally. This can be a common fault when the manufacturer has used a pressurised nail gun. So it is good practice to run your fingers over all fastenings and joints.

■ The hinges on doors and windows should be of the one piece piano type, not the strip type. Any part of a playhouse that opens is a potential finger trap so again it is good practice to check that there is nowhere in the playhouses where small fingers could get trapped.

■ Your playhouse may have to be painted or treated with preservative before children can play in it. Check the manufacturer's instructions to make sure that you are not using any harmful chemicals. Remember that creosote, once a popular wood preservative, has been found to contain carcenogenic chemicals and should not be used.

Doors

■ All of the doors on playhouses, regardless of material, should allow a child to open them from both inside and out. There should be no delay between operating the handle or fastening and the door opening. It should not be possible to lock the door from the inside.

Windows

■ Any glazing material that is used should be either hardened or laminated glass or Perspex. Silicone is a safer substance to use to fix glass or Perspex rather than tacks or nails. Cracked glass is a hazard and should be replaced straightaway.

Ladders

■ Strangulation and suffocation hazards are more common when the playhouse has a second storey reached by a ladder of some kind or spacer bars. However, a naturally curious young child could get their head stuck in the window frame or between ladder rungs. Similarly, a badly secured tent-like structure could be dangerous.

■ You also need to make sure that ladders or bars are securely fixed. Rope ladders should be firmly attached at the top and make sure that the surface below the ladder is safe should the child fall.

Inside

Think about the maximum number of children who can safely play inside. This could be discussed with children and they could also be involved in deciding what to put inside. Sometimes we can unwittingly restrict a child's imagination and play by the resources we provide. For example putting in tables, chairs, play cooker and sink, may imply that only pretend domestic play is allowed, while big cushions, boxes and stools could be whatever children want them to be.

We all want children to play in safety and enjoy themselves when in playhouses. Children need private places but they must still have some discreet supervision, maybe from the garden or from a window.

With older children, you could agree how often you will look in the house and check on them. Younger children, especially those under four years, should not be left unsupervised and you could let them play in the house but stay in close proximity.

If you are at all concerned about the safety of your playhouse you can get further information from your local Trading Standards office; ask for the Toys (Safety) Regulations 1995.

Sheila Riddall-Leech, educational consultant and trainer.

Chapter 4

CCLD 303, Promote children's development

About this unit

This mandatory unit is about the observation and assessment of children, young people's development and how you can plan to promote that development. This means that you must have a good understanding of how children develop, grow and learn from birth to sixteen years.

Some of the knowledge specifications for this unit focus specifically on one age group, for example:

- birth to three years
- three to seven years
- seven to twelve years
- twelve to sixteen years

Depending on where you work, you can choose the age group that is most appropriate for you.

However, you will need to have detailed knowledge and understanding of the expected patterns of development, including the order and sequence of development in the following areas and across all four age groups:

- physical development
- communication, intellectual (cognitive) development and learning
- social, emotional and behavioural development

You can learn so much about children's development just by watching and observing them. In many cases we may find ourselves observing and making a mental note of children's development without really being aware. It is almost instinctive, but observations are vitally important in meeting individual needs and their value should never be underestimated.

Undertaking observations also encourages you to be reflective, to evaluate and question your practice and provision (CCLD 303.1).

Once you have carried out observations, you must understand what to do with the information that will allow you to make realistic and valid assessments about the child's development and to be reflective. You must remember that all children are different, and when making assessment you must be very careful not to make assumptions, jump to premature conclusions or label a child. Observations should inform your planning and provision, as well as giving vital information to parents and other professionals if required (CCLD 303.2).

'When it was suggested that I wrote observations of the children who I care for, my first thought 'was what a waste of time, I should be playing and interacting with them, not writing notes'. But, I have to admit, I have used the observations so much, in planning and evaluating planned activities, informing parents and to resolve some problems, especially with behaviour.'

NVQ candidate

Using observations to help inform planning will help you look at influences on a child's development, such as self-esteem, educational opportunities or social interactions. Observations should also help you identify patterns of development and so plan activities and experiences that are developmentally appropriate at any given time. It is very unlikely that you will only carry out one observation of a child; you will probably carry out several, depending on the child's needs. Doing this will help you to review and update your plans for the child (CCLD 303.3).

Plans should not rule your life, or that of the children. It would be unthinkable to not carry out a spontaneous activity just because it was not in your plans. Plans must be flexible, taking into account a child's needs. Plans should be inclusive, making sure that all children are valued and that their needs are met. In order to do this you will need to review and evaluate your planning, making sure that the intended outcomes are positive, realistic and achievable (CCLD 303.4).

This unit has four elements of competence and you must have evidence for all four elements in your portfolio. These elements are:

- CCLD 303.1 Observe Development
- CCLD 303.2 Assess development and reflect upon implications for practice
- CCLD 303.3 Plan provision to promote development
- CCLD 303.4 Implement and evaluate plans to promote development

Each one of the elements will be discussed in turn, together with suggested ways to collect and record your evidence. Don't forget to read through all the knowledge specifications for this unit, including the ones that may not relate directly to the age group you are working with. You may find it helpful to draw up a chart or table such as the example given below, to cross-reference the knowledge specification with the performance criteria for each element. In this way you will make sure that all knowledge specifications have appropriate evidence for your assessor.

CCLD 303.1 Observe development

Getting started
Observation, both as a technique and method of assessment, is so important that it is the main way in which your assessor will gain evidence to show that you are competent. Observing children should become a vital part of your work, so that you can plan effectively to meet their individual needs.

There are many different ways to observe and you will have to use your professional judgment and expertise to decide which is the most appropriate method for each situation. You must also remember to maintain confidentiality at all times. It is good practice

Performance Criteria	Knowledge Specification Statement
303.1.1	K3M202
303.1.2	K3D206
303.1.3	K3M202
	K3D204
	K3D207
303.1.4	K3M202
	K3D203
	K3D204
303.1.5	K3D307
303.1.6	K3D206
303.1.7	K3M202
	K3D204
303.1.8	K3M202

TIP:

If you already carry out assessments, use daily diaries or checklists as part of your work. You can then use them as evidence for your portfolio, but you must remove any surnames or family names and get permission from the child's parents and your line manager, if appropriate, before including them.

not to identify children by their real names; use a pseudonym or initial letter.

This element has eight PCs and you must provide evidence for all of them. In this unit you are aiming to show that you:

- identify the reasons for observing and assessing development.
- select appropriate techniques of observation and types of recording format.
- obtain necessary permissions to observe children from appropriate adults in the setting.
- discuss the observation with the children to be observed and respond appropriately to their views, according to their needs, age and abilities.
- minimise distractions and observe children without intruding or causing unnecessary stress.
- use appropriate techniques to observe children, covering all required aspects of their development behaviour.
- maintain confidentially according the procedures of your setting.
- implement data protection procedures.

Key issues
You need to think about why observations are important and consider all the different ways in which the information can be used. Observations are not just about providing evidence to help you plan appropriate activities, although this is very important. Observations can help to provide other professionals, such as a speech therapist, with specific information. More and more children with additional and special needs are being integrated into main stream settings, so it becomes particularly important to observe these children as many of them will need individual education or play plans (IEP or IPP). These plans have to be based on sound judgements about the abilities and needs of the children (CCLD 303.1.1).

There are several different ways of observing children and it is good practice to include a variety of methods in your portfolio and in the child's records. For example:

- written or narrative, including diaries
- checklists
- time sample
- event sample
- charts, such as pie charts, bar charts, sociograms, flow charts

Using a range of different techniques when observing children will help you to develop your own professional skills and become a more meticulous practitioner. Using a range of techniques over a period of time will help you build up a more holistic picture of the child. This is because some techniques lend themselves more to certain aspects of development; for example a checklist might be a more effective way of recording specific physical skills than a written or narrative account (CCLD 303.1.2 and 303.1.6).

Confidentiality is an essential aspect of observing children. All records must be kept in a secure place and the information contained therein should not be shared with anyone, unless the well-being of the child is threatened, for instance if the child is suspected of being in need of protection. A sure test of confidentiality is whether another person, such as your assessor, could identify the child and your setting by reading the observation. Your line manager should sign observations that you intend to use as evidence in your portfolio to indicate that they are true and accurate records. In some settings you may need to get the permission of the parents before carrying out observations that are to be used for purposes other than the assessment of the child. Some settings get parents to sign a 'blanket' permission letter which covers observations carried out by staff and students (CCLD 303.1.3 and 303.1.7).

The Data Protection Act (1998) is designed to prevent confidential and personal information from being passed on without the person's consent. Your setting should have a policy that complies with this act and which you must follow (CCLD 303.1.8).

You should discuss your observations with the child, both before and after making them. Some children will respond positively to being observed and may even feel special. Other children can react quite differently and so behave in ways that you would not normally expect. Once children become used to seeing you and other adults undertaking observations, they are less likely to react in unusual ways. Observations should become an everyday activity in your setting. Sometimes children can provide you with additional information as to why they did something in a certain way (CCLD 303.1.4).

You should respect children's privacy, and any observation that you carry out should be unobtrusive. Children should not become distressed by being observed and if they do, you should stop immediately (CCLD 303.1.5).

Suggested activities and experiences
* Check that your setting is registered with the Data Protection Commission and find out if you have a privacy and confidentiality policy.
* Check if your setting has 'blanket' written permission from parents for observing children. If not, you will have to put together a suitable letter, reassuring parents of issues of confidentiality.
* Before you start to observe, remember to check with other adults in the setting that it is a convenient time to do so.
* Make sure that any information you use from other adults in the setting or parents is factual and is not based on hearsay.
* Observe children over a period of time and in a wide range of situations. In this way you will build up a holistic picture of the chid and it will make your assessments more valid.
* Avoid making assumptions about how children will play or how an activity will develop. Allow children to make choices and to take responsibility for their play.
* Even though you may not be working across the full age bands,

try to observe one child from each of the following age bands, and look at the same aspect of development, such as physical skills:
* 1-3 years
* 4-7 years
* 8-11 years
* Over 11 years

By doing this you will get a broader picture of patterns and sequences of development.

* Although you may observe children focussing on one or two specific areas of development, it is important to remember that development is holistic and all areas dependent on each other are interlinked and interrelated.
* If you are uncertain or unsure about doing observations, practise on members of your family in familiar situations. You can also use DVDs or videos of people; one of the benefits of this is that you can always rewind the tape or DVD and check if your observation was accurate.
* Observe one child on six separate occasions. Try to use at least two different techniques for recording your evidence. Write a summative assessment, using the information you have gathered, which takes into account the child's holistic development, their interests and some suggestions for future activities and experiences to extend and stimulate their development.

Types of evidence
As well as your assessor **directly observing you (Key letter A)**, you will have to produce observations you have made of the children. These can be used by your assessor as the basis of a **professional discussion (Key letter G)**, or to set **written or oral questions (Key letter B)**.

It is also a good idea to ask you line manager or another appropriate adult to write a **witness testimony** giving details of how you went about observing the children, whether you were discreet, maintained confidentiality and used an appropriate method for the observation. This would count as evidence for **Key letter C**.

You can write a **reflective account** after you have observed a child, thinking about the method or technique that you used, how the children reacted to you, what you could have done differently and what you could change **(Key letter F)**. As you undertake more observations, use your reflective account to improve the way that you do things and then write another account to reflect on the changes or differences and decide if they were effective.

It is possible that you may have made observations of children to provide other evidence, for example in CCLD 301.2.4, CCLD 302.2.3. You can cross-reference such observations to provide evidence for this unit.

CCLD 303.2 Assess development and reflect upon implications for practice

Getting started

Sometimes it can be difficult to remain objective when carrying out observations. It can be hard to write everything down, especially when doing written observations, and you may miss something important. You also have to make on-the-spot decisions about what is important and relevant to note down and what is not. Because of all of these factors it is very important that you carry out several observations of a child, using different methods to record the information, before making any assessments. It is also good practice to observe a child engaged in different activities, at different times of the day, in group situations or alone.

You should only use the information from the observations and other reliable sources to help you assess development. Be careful that you do not jump to conclusions which are not based on fact, or make assumptions.

This element has seven PCs and you must provide evidence for all of them. In this unit you are aiming to show that you:

- can undertake formative and summative assessments.
- make sure that your assessments are based on information from observations and other reliable information.
- can use information from colleagues, families, children and other appropriate adults to inform your assessments.
- record your assessments, maintaining confidentiality as appropriate to your setting's policies and procedures.
- share your findings with children and family members as appropriate.
- refer concerns about children to relevant external agencies when required.
- reflect upon your assessments of children's development and identify implications for practice.

Key Issues

Formative assessments are those which are ongoing. Summative assessments, on the other hand, pull all the information together so that you can draw a conclusion and assess development. Formative observations and assessments that you carry out each day will give you information about a child's strengths and needs at that point in time and you carry on observing them as well as planning appropriate activities. You may be asked to put together a report for parents about their child and so will use all the information that you have gathered. This will then become a summative assessment. A series of formative assessments can contribute to a summative assessment of a child (CCLD 303.2.1).

All children develop, learn and grow at different rates and it is vitally important that you do not jump to conclusions because a child does not fit the normal patterns of development. You must make sure that any assessments you carry out are based on what you actually see and not what you think you know about the child (CCLD 303.2.2).

Most parents are comfortable with the idea of another person, such as you, observing their child, provided that the information

'At first I found it difficult to observe and make notes and know that I was missing information. I asked a colleague to do a couple of observations of the child for me. They didn't know the boy as well as I did, so I felt that their observations together with mine would give me a more objective and balanced picture of his development.'

NVQ candidate

gathered remains confidential. They are also usually eager to know the results of your observations and can often add valuable and useful insights into the development of their child. It is important that you do involve parents in your assessment so that you get an all-round picture of the child. Many settings use a home/setting diary for parents and carers to record important information, all of which can support assessment for development (CCLD 303.2.3).

Issues concerning confidentiality were discussed in element CCLD 303.1, but it is very important, and worth repeating, that all information held about children in your care must be stored securely and the identities of the child and his family protected. In many settings children's records are stored in a locked cupboard or filing cabinet (CCLD 303.2.4).

Children do not always behave in the same way when they are in different situations. Sharing information with parents will help you understand these changes in the child behaviour and so avoid making assumptions or labelling a child (CCLD 303.2.5).

Rani, a home-based child carer, was caring for Josh aged 2 years 8 months. His parents were concerned that he didn't talk very much at home and had asked Rani for her opinion on his language development. Rani's observations showed that Josh talked freely to the other children, until his elder sister joined him after school. Rani did a series of event samples over several days which showed that Josh talked a lot less when his sister was around. These observations were shared with Josh's parents and his sister.

In England and Wales it is a requirement of the Special Educational Needs Codes of Practice that any concerns that you may have about a child, using evidence from observations, be discussed with a child's parents. It is up to the parents to decide with you if further action, such as involving other professionals, is required (CCLD 303.2.6).

There is no point in undertaking observations of children if you do not intend to do anything useful with them. The information should be used to assess a child's development and so plan activities and experiences that will stimulate and extend his growth and learning. This is all part of being a reflective practitioner, which will be discussed in greater detail in element CCLD 304. It is only through being reflective that you will be able to meet a child's individual needs and be flexible when planning activities (CCLD 303.2.7).

Suggested activities and experiences

- Find out where and how children's records are stored in your setting, who has access to them and what are the reasons for access.
- Choose one child in your setting and observe him on several different occasions, doing different activities and in both group situations and alone. Use a range of different methods for your observations (formative).
- Using the information from the observations above, produce one report on this child which you can share with the parents (summative).
- Ask a colleague to do some observations of this child for you and compare your findings. This will help you remain objective and factual.
- Make sure that you are familiar with patterns of children's development. This will involve you in undertaking personal research and reading. See the list at the end of this chapter for suggested books and other materials which could help you.
- Try to do two or three checklist observations of a small group of children playing. Pay particular attention to their physical skills, such as kicking a ball, throwing and catching, balancing, or social skills, such as how they share, co-operate and play together. When you have completed the observations, you could write a summative report which compares the development of the children and helps you learn more about expected patterns of development.
- Look at an observation that you have carried out using the written method. Make a list of what you think were the advantages and disadvantages of this method. Make suggestions as to what other methods you could have used and whether you would have achieved the same or a similar result. You will then be able to use this reflective account in your portfolio as evidence of your understanding of some of the different methods of recording observations.

Types of evidence

As for the previous performance criteria, much of this element will be assessed by **direct observation** and cross-referenced pieces of work from other units **(Key letters A and H)**. Again, **witness testimonies** from other adults with whom you work will play an important part **(Key letter B)**, as will **questions either written or oral** from your assessor **(Key letter B)**. You can use reflective accounts as suggested above **(Key letter F)** to consider the benefits of different observation methods.

Your assessor could ask you questions based on the knowledge specifications, so it is important that you read them through. You will find it helpful to indicate on your assessment plans where you think there will be evidence of the knowledge specification statements. Your assessor could ask you:

- to explain the difference between formative and summative assessment (K3D208).
- to explain how your setting assesses children's development (K3D208).

- to explain why you chose one particular method or technique to record observation (K3D206).
- how you maintain confidentiality and why it is important to do so (K3M202).
- many other questions depending on your setting and the age of the children with whom you are working.

CCLD 303.3 Plan provision to promote development

Getting started

Plans of all kinds, whether long-, medium- or short-term, should be based on children's needs, their interests and on assessments that you have made. At the same time, however, plans should not be written in tablets of stone, never to be changed, they must and should be flexible; if they are not, you will not be meeting individual needs. Observations should help you to identify children's needs at any one time and so plan appropriate activities and experiences for them.

Plans can be produced in a wide range of formats; there is not really one correct way to do planning. Many settings devise and develop their own plans which can involve the children, or young people; some planning formats are developed by local authorities for all settings to follow; some can be brief, some contain a large amount of detail. However, all plans should be based on factual evidence gathered through the observation process.

This element has three PCs and you must provide evidence for all of them. In this unit you are aiming to show that you:

- can plan provision for individual children, based on your assessments of their development and your reflections on your practice.
- regularly review and update your plans.
- ensure plans balance the needs of the individual children and the group in settings where this is appropriate.

Key Issues

All children are unique, individual and different and, while it can be helpful to you to compare developmental progress, it is not a good idea to compare one child with another. For example, some babies sit up at six months, some at five months and some at seven months; it does not mean that one is more or less well developed than another; it means that they are all developing at their own individual rate. When you begin to look at your observations you will need to take into consideration these unique and individual differences and plan accordingly (CCLD 303.3.1).

Children develop at varying rates and it is good practice to review your plans for them at very regular intervals. It is not really possible to say that you will review plans every four weeks; although this will be better than no review at all it may not be appropriate, as the child may not have progressed significantly. A sensitive, reflective practitioner reviews plans when he or she notices progression, whether that be four weeks, fours days, or even two months (CCLD 303.3.2).

Children with special educational needs, difficulties or statements are quite likely to have individual educational plans, or individual learning plans, or individual play plans (IEP/ILP/IPP). Such plans will often set precise and specific targets for a child over a specific period of time. It is possible to incorporate these plans in plans for groups, where appropriate; for example, a child with emotional and social difficulties may have targets aimed at raising their self-esteem. All children will benefit from a positive self-esteem and so the specific targets can be built into activities planned for all the children (CCLD 303.3.3).

Suggested activities and experiences

- Find out about the different areas of development and the skills that children can acquire in each area. Look at the section at the end of this chapter for suggested further reading.
- Make a display or leaflet for parents and other staff members about expected developmental progress. You could do this either for each area of development, or for a specific age group. Remember, however, that development is holistic and each area of development is interrelated and dependent upon another. For example, a problem, temporary or long-term, with hearing which is an aspect of physical development, can affect a child's learning and language (cognitive and communication skills) and how they interact with others (social skills).
- Devise a system to record when you review your plans. If you are a key person with responsibility for a specific group of children, you can do this as a checklist, chart or table. Some practitioners working in their own homes use the child's home/ setting diary to record this information. This also helps to involve the parents and kept them informed. With older children you should consider involving them in when and how their plans are reviewed.
- Find out what influences there may be on a child's development. Think about how these influences could affect your plans, observations and assessments, for example, if a child is repeatedly absent from the setting.
- Make sure that you allow in your planning for spontaneous play, allowing children to make choices and take responsibility for their play. Don't make assumptions about how children will play with the resources you provide. Remember that play is never developmentally wrong.
- Use the time when you are observing to allow children to naturally develop their activities. Do not intervene or start directing the children.

Types of evidence

Again, your assessor will directly **observe you, question** you and look at **work products** that you have produced **(Key letters A, B and H)**. It is quite likely that much of the evidence for this element will be cross-referenced to other units and elements, so remember to make this very clear in your portfolio. It can be quite annoying and time consuming for an assessor to have to explore a complete portfolio to find a piece of cross-referenced evidence. The more organised and structured your portfolio is, the better it will be for you in the long term.

Remember, if you have completed another award or training that is recognised at Level 3, you may be able to use some of the work as evidence in your portfolio; for example, if you have completed

CACHE Level 3 Diploma in Pre-school Practice or CACHE Level 3 Diploma in Home based Childcare, your assessor may agree for some of the assignments to be used as **case studies, projects and assignments (Key letter E)**. In the candidate handbook for such courses you will find that the syllabus has been mapped to the NVQ units.

CCLD 303.4 Implement and evaluate plans to promote development

Getting started

Implementing plans with children and young people is a significant part of many practitioners' work and probably the part that they most enjoy. It has to be recognised that a lot of hidden work and preparation lead to successful activities and experiences. There are four main ingredients which lead to successful activities and these are:

- planning and preparation
- consideration of the layout of the activity (if appropriate)
- health and safety issues
- the role of the adult

Whatever method you use to plan activities and experiences for the children, it is important that the plans are implemented in a flexible way. Rigid plans do not allow for children's interests to be included, for example a child may bring something into the setting that is of special interest to him, but which is not included in your plans. It will not make your plans any less effective if you can accommodate such an event. Indeed it is important that you learn from any unplanned activities or experiences and reflect on the effect that they may have on your future planning.

Think about ways to evaluate your planning and preparation, who should be involved and what you intend to do with the evaluations. Planning is a 'circular' process. Plans that are evaluated after they have been implemented should lead to new plans being drawn up which will in turn be implemented and evaluated, and so on.

You will also need to evaluate whether you set out the activity in an appropriate way and reflect on ways to change or improve it. You will need to think about the health and safety aspects of your activities and experiences and how the adults were deployed before, during and after the session.

This element has four PCs and you must provide evidence for all of them. In this unit you are aiming to show that you:

- implement plans in a flexible way and evaluate their effectiveness in promoting development.
- evaluate the implementation of your plans.
- evaluate the outcomes of planning for individuals and groups, in settings where this appropriate.
- regularly review practice in terms of positive developmental outcomes for children.

Key Issues

Before you can evaluate how effective a plan may be in promoting development, you need to know what development you are hoping to promote. It is good practice to indicate somewhere on the plans exactly what it is you are hoping to achieve in terms of development. You cannot evaluate something that does not exist. An example of part of an individual learning plan is given opposite, and this clearly shows the developmental aspects it is designed to encourage.

There are clear developmental goals on the above plan which can be evaluated after the activities have been carried out. In addition, it is also clear what is expected of the adult and Charlie's parents and this can also be evaluated (CCLD 303.4.1).

When you evaluate your plans, you will need to reflect on the four main aspects as described earlier in this section. Evaluation involves thinking about the strengths and weaknesses, or positive and negative aspects, of any activity, so you will need to think about the actual preparation and planning, the layout of the activity (if appropriate), the health and safety considerations and the role of any adults involved (CCLD 303.4.2).

All four main aspects of successful activities may be different if your planned activities or experiences are for an individual or for a group. For example, to ensure health and safety in a group activity, you may need to change the layout or have more adults involved (CCLD 303.4.3).

As with policies, developmental goals for children should be reviewed regularly. In the case of Charlie in the example given above, it could be that after three weeks or so of playing with one other child and one adult, he has successful outcomes and so the developmental goal would need to be reviewed and changed, perhaps to playing in a small group (CCLD 303.4.4).

Observations can also challenge our assumptions. For example, if your carefully planned activity generates little interest and those who do take part say things like, 'Can I go now?' or 'Have I finished yet?', you should be getting a very clear message that you have not met the children's needs. In the same way, if you walk over to a group playing and ask a question, at which point all the children walk away, you should know that you have cut across the children's intentions.

Name of child	Date of birth
Charlie	05.01.2003
Date of plan	**Date of next review**
28.02.07	20 April 2007

Aim of plan

Charlie to play co-operatively with other children (Social development)

Learning Goal	Strategies
• To share materials and take turns • To work co-operatively with one other child	• Adults to verbally praise and use positive facial expressions and body language when Charlie takes turns or shares • Parents asked to play simple board games with him at home • Structured activities to be planned such as simple board games with another child and one adult 3 times a week for 20 minutes at a time

Suggested activities and experiences

- Think about using observations as an aid to communication between yourself, parents and colleagues.
- If you work in a setting with other adults, try to make time to discuss some of everyone's observations and ideas for planning.
- Make sure that you are familiar with the expected patterns of development.
- Draw up a health and safety checklist which you could use before you implement your plans. This could be used as evidence for your portfolio as a work product (Key letter H).
- Try to respond positively to unexpected learning opportunities, even though they are not included in your plans. You can add the information in your evaluations.
- When planning activities and experiences, it can sometimes be difficult to judge exactly how long they will hold the children's interest; so try to recognise when you need to change activities

and do not prolong one just because you have planned for it to take a specific length of time.
- Be prepared to adapt or extend an activity to meet a child's interests and needs. You might need to make it easier for some children or more challenging for others. You may have to approach the activity in a different way from that which was planned. Varying an activity to meet a child's needs and interests is part of flexible implementation and will mean that the children are more likely to enjoy learning; they will not get bored nor will they feel that they may have failed.
- Even though you have planned the activities and experiences for the children, you should encourage the children to take ownership of the activity. Sometimes children's ideas may not be very practical, but you should support and encourage them rather than discourage or make them feel inadequate. Remember that very formal structured activities can actually hinder a child's creative development and stop him using his imagination.

- Encourage the children to comment on the planned experiences and activities, as this can give you a different point of view and so help with you own evaluation and reflection.
- Try to put together an evaluation checklist to help you make realistic and meaningful evaluations. Consider general ideas such as:
  - the level of enjoyment
  - if the children concentrated or were distracted
  - was there any spontaneous learning?
- Think about the practical issues such as:
  - did you have enough preparation time?
  - did you have enough resources?
  - was the activity appropriate for the time of day?
- Think about how you could extend or reinforce the learning; were there any children who could not cope?

Don't forget, you should give reasons for your answers and suggest what you could do to change or modify something. This checklist could be used as evidence for your portfolio as a work product (Key letter H).

Types of evidence

Two types of checklist have been suggested and both could be used in your portfolio as **work products (Key letter H)**. You could also **write reflective accounts based** on your evaluations of **planned activities (Key letter F)**. Your assessor will also undertake **direct observation of** you implementing your plans and will look at how flexible you are and how responsive to unplanned events **(Key letter A)**.

Minutes and agendas from staff meetings where observations and planning have been discussed can be used as supporting evidence. These would also be classed as **work products (Key letter H)**.

Key words and concepts relating to CCLD 303

adolescence - the period of social and psychological transition between childhood and adulthood – the teenage years

assess - to measure, consider, or weigh up

assessment - making an informed judgement about something or a measurement of it, for example the development of a specific skill

children - children with whom you work

cognitive - also intellectual, related to how children think, understand and learn

communication - all forms of interactions with another individual or individuals, including body language, facial expressions, gestures, speaking, listening, writing and electronically, eg. e-mails, texts

creativity - an individual response; ways in which children can express their own original ideas. Children can express creativity in all areas of learning

creative play - play that encourages and enables children and young people to explore, experiment and discover, in their own unique ways. Sometimes called imaginative play

development - ways in which children grow and acquire skills and competences

developmental needs - those things that are required to enable children to progress and move forward in their development

emotional responses - how children and young people express their feelings

evaluate - to find out, judge, assess, measure the value of something, look at strengths, weaknesses, positive and negative points

family - a social unit that includes adults and children and which provides a home and care for children

formative assessment -initial and ongoing assessment

holistic - whole or complete development, not looking at specific areas

inclusion - the process of recognising, understanding, and overcoming obstructions or barriers to participation

learning - ways in which children and young people obtain new knowledge and understanding about something or acquire new skills or change behaviour as a result of experience

mental health - the well being and strength of the mind

observation - watching, studying, examining or scrutinising the actions of others

pattern of development - the sequence of   development, what development would be expected to be observed and the rate at which it takes place

rate of development - the time frame in which development takes place

sequence of development - order in which development occurs

stereotyping - to label, put into artificial categories, to type-cast

summative assessment - assessment which summarises, reviews and goes over the main points of findings

Suggested further reading

Bee, H. (1992) The Developing Child, Harper Collins

Birth to Three Matters, SureStart/DfES
DfES Early Years Foundation Satge (2007), DfES

Foundation Stage Curriculum Guidance, DfES

Meggitt, C.(2006) Child Development – an illustrated guide, 2nd Edition, Heinemann

Pound, L. (2005) How Children Learn. Step Forward Publishing Ltd.

Riddall-Leech, S. (2005), How to observe children, Heinemann

Tassoni, P. et al (2005) Children's Care, Learning and Development, Heinemann

Observation is the term used to describe the process of noticing what individual children do. Through observation, you can analyse children's behaviour and evaluate their progress. Miranda Walker looks at the different ways you can do it

Carrying out observations

When you first make observations of a child, you will be finding out about their current stage of development. You will also draw on information from other sources including parents and carers. This is known as 'baseline' information.

Over time, you make further observations, which you analyse to help you monitor the progress that that child is making. This reveals how they should be supported and what they should learn next.

You use this information to inform future planning and make sure that children's individual needs are met. Observation records will help you to share accurate information with parents, carers and other professionals.

Informal observations

You make informal observations every day. Although these are valuable, they are complemented by regular, formal (or planned) observations.

Formal observations

Formal observation helps you to take a step back from the children you work with and be objective about their behaviour and development. Planned observations allow you to:

■ Think about why you are observing;

■ Choose a suitable way of observing;

■ Schedule time to observe;

■ Make sure each child is observed regularly.

Being objective

When you're observing, it's important to record exactly what you see and be objective. Because you want children to have favourable outcomes, it can be tempting to record that

a child can do something they can nearly do. Or, perhaps you think you have seen a child do something before, and want to give them the benefit of the doubt.

But this would be unprofessional and may lead to inappropriate activities being provided for the child. You should analyse your observations after making them, when you have time to deliberate and even consult with colleagues. At the time you must remain objective.

Observing for a purpose

The reason for carrying out a formal observation should be decided in advance. The purpose will influence the method of observation you choose, and often the activity that is observed. For instance, if you want to observe a child's gross motor and social skills, you might observe them playing outside with friends. Over a period of time, purposeful observations can be used to build up a picture of a child's learning and skills in all areas of development.

Sometimes practitioners carry out general observations of whatever children happen to be doing at the time. This can be a good way to observe children's behaviour and their social relationships with both adults and their peers. Such observation records can highlight changes in behaviour patterns. This is valuable if a child becomes withdrawn or angry for instance.

The role of the observer

As well as choosing how to observe, you must decide whether to be a participant observer or a non-participant observer.

Participant observer

You can interact with the child, so they know they are being observed.

> Always seek written permission from parents and carers before carrying out observations. Many settings ask for this on their registration form. Treat observations as confidential and store records safely in line with your setting's confidentiality policy.

Advantages:

■ You can ask or encourage a child to do things you want to observe.

■ You can ask questions to find out the reason for a child's behaviour – 'Why are you doing that?'

■ It is suited to the check-list method of observation (see below) often used with babies and young children.

Disadvantages:

■ You may need to record your own actions or words.

■ Children may behave differently because they are being watched – they may try harder than usual or give up sooner as adult help is on hand. They may become anxious or excited.

Non-participant observer

You stay unobtrusive. You don't interact with the child or let them know they are being observed.

Advantages:

■ You don't need to record your own actions or words.

■ It's easier to be objective and to record

what is happening when you are not involved in events.

- It is suited to the free description and target child methods of observation (see below).

Disadvantages:

- Can be difficult to find somewhere to see and hear everything without being intrusive.

- If you don't encourage children to carry out particular activities you may not see certain aspects of development or behaviour that you want to observe.

Ways of observing

The main ways of observing are:

Free description

This is helpful if you want to focus on areas of difficulty, for instance working out why a child struggles to get dressed alone.

These observations are generally short, often covering a time span of around five minutes. This is because free descriptions require intensive focus. Using the present tense, write a detailed description of everything the child says and does during the time. Describe the child's actions, behaviour, facial expressions, speech and gestures.

> **Example:**
>
> Joshua watches an adult get out paper and crayons. He frowns and shakes his head. He walks away and goes to the book corner...

Check-lists

These are helpful when assessing children's stage of development, especially babies and toddlers.

Check-list forms can be bought but you can easily draw up your own. The forms consist of lists of skills. As they are seen, you tick them off. Check-lists may be completed over a series of observations with the non-participant observer ticking off skills as they are naturally observed. A participant observer may ask older babies and children to carry out specific tasks, or lead an activity to encourage participation.

Example of the check-list approach:

Activity comments	Yes	Date	Observer's
Picks up objects using tripod grasp	√	1/11/05	Secure grasp
Picks up objects using pincer grasp			

Time samples

These help you track activities that children participate in. Record what a child says and does in the free description style. However, carry out short observations of a minute or so at intervals over an allotted period of time. For instance, at 15-minute intervals over a three-hour period.

> **Example:**
>
> 2.15pm
>
> Kyle pulls on his Wellington boots, puts on his coat and fastens it independently.
>
> 2.30pm
>
> Kyle jumps along the stepping stones in the playground, both feet together. He follows Jemima who is also jumping.

Event samples

These are helpful for observing when/how often a certain aspect of behaviour occurs (such as crying or aggression). Whenever you observe the behaviour you are looking for, record the details on a form. The observation may take place over a session or several sessions, depending on the purpose of the observation.

Target child

This approach enables you to track what children do and say over a longer period of time. It is similar to the time sample method, but there should not be gaps in the duration of the observation, so you need to use a short-hand of codes. It's not possible to record everything seen for more than a few minutes, so record what you consider to be significant. This method can take some getting used to, and there are a number of different versions of codes used by settings. For more information, refer to *A Practical Guide to Observation and Assessment* by Christine Hobart and Jill Frankel, (Nelson Thornes).

Miranda Walker is an early years and playwork trainer, speaker and consultant. She owns her own settings in Devon.

Key information

Include the following information on all observations:

- The name of the child or alternate method of identifying them (some settings prefer to use children's initials)
- Date
- Time and duration
- Location
- Name of observer
- Participant or non-participant observer
- Activity observed/purpose of observation
- Details of other children/adults present

Example of an event sample:

Event No	Time	Event	Circumstances
1	11.20am	Jamal starts to cry. He goes to the door, sits down and continues crying.	Jamal was engaged with a book when Kiri's mum arrived to collect her. Jamal started to cry when he saw her.

It is important for young children to become confident speakers and listeners. They need their full repertoire of communication skills to access a wide range of learning experiences and enjoy the pleasures of companionship with adults and other children. Jennie Lindon looks at what you can do to help them

How to help the skilful communicators

There is growing concern that some children have limited communication skills. It is not because they are coping with a disability that affects this aspect of development. The problems seem to arise from several sources and we need to focus on what helps young communicators and what gets in the way.

Some children undoubtedly spend too long watching television. There are some good programmes for twos and older, but children should not be allowed to watch non-stop. Even programmes that aim to engage children in an active way cannot offer the skills of a real person who knows them.

Early communication is strongly linked to social development and human contact. Yet some adults feel they are too busy to relate to young children in a one-to-one way.

Babies need personal attention and toddlers need familiar adults (parents, their childminder or key person) who respond as one individual to another.

- Parents may be genuinely stressed by combining work and home responsibilities. Some may welcome a friendly

reminder that their child just wants to be with them, whatever they are doing.

- Some early years practitioners have lost their sense of priorities and value planned activities over spontaneous chats with babies and young children. Shaky knowledge of child development also leads to the unrealistic expectation that under-threes will manage turn taking within group 'communication activities' or should tolerate large group story time sessions.

There are plenty of positive ideas within guidance materials on good practice with under-threes. The English *Birth to Three Matters* devotes a quarter of its content to 'A Skilful Communicator'.

The Scottish guidance focuses strongly on the power of communication through a personal relationship and responsive care giving. Written examples and visual materials all home in on what works for very young children, wherever they spend their days

What makes the difference?

What helps young communicators is simple. Parents and early years practitioners who tune into babies and young children make the difference.

Young children do not need special language programmes unless they are coping with a disability that affects the development of communication. Family life and out-of-home care has to be organised so that personal communication is highly valued, because under-threes (and over-threes too!) all need:

- Time to look, listen and make their contribution. They need relaxed opportunities to engage with interesting resources, to recognise a familiar song or rhyme and to stare at an intriguing sight. Young children cannot relish and practise their communication skills if they are rushed from one experience to another. Avoid over-filling your days and aim to manage time in a child-friendly way.

- Familiar, communicative adults who show that they are genuinely interested in what this baby or child wants to communicate at this moment. Helpful adults share communication with young children. It is not always the adult who starts the conversation with words and body language and it certainly is not the adult who asks all the questions in an exchange. Avoid rushing to fill the gaps – use the power of the pause and look expectant.

- The security of close, affectionate relationships. Young children need to spend enough time with their own families so that their attachment to parents and other family members is strong and enduring. Children need plenty of enjoyable communication within their family life. Address any situation where parents begin to believe that nursery, or their childminder, will 'teach my child' everything, including their skills of communication.

- The security and confidence of a warm, personal relationship with their out-of-home carer – their childminder or key person in a nursery. You need to get close to young children – emotionally and physically – and to ensure through partnership with parents that there is continuity for children between different parts of their daily life. When children are very young, your conversations with their parents will bridge the gap of what children cannot express fully in their own words.

- An interesting learning environment, with flexible play resources that they can explore at their leisure and with adults who follow children's interests. The best resources, indoors and outside, are often simple. Avoid commercially produced toys, targeted for under-threes that promote the message that these very young children should be 'learning their letters' or that a battery operated toy can actually teach a child to speak.

What works best is simple

Young communication progresses when adults take time and have created a relaxed atmosphere. Show real pleasure in the give and take of conversation with children.

For example, 14-month-old Naomi has already learned how to use sounds and gestures to get the attention of Tess, her childminder. Naomi manages simple turn taking with Tess as she points and

looks at the waddling pigeon that has caught her attention. Triumphantly, Naomi says, 'Bir' and Tess replies, 'Yes, Naomi, it's a bird. A big bird' and as she bends down to toddler level, Tess adds, 'Ooh, look. I think the bird wants to eat the bread.'

The foundations for strong communication skills rest on personal relationships with young children and their experience that you are genuinely interested in what they want to show and say.

Young children need you to connect with their current focus. Sometimes the focus will be something right in front of both of you.

For example, two-year-old Ned has new shoes and wants to show Dave, his key person at nursery. First thing this morning, Ned has run up to Dave and, wobbling a bit with the balance, has thrust a foot out for Dave to admire. Dave bends down to look and says, 'Ooh, are they new shoes?' Ned vigorously nods his head and echoes, 'New shoes'. Dave points and adds, 'I like that swirly bit on them.'

However, language connects with thinking and memory and soon young children are able to access and talk about familiar experiences that are currently not right in front of their eyes.

For example, Ned has a long-term relationship with Dave and they share memories of regular events. Later in the day they go out in a small group for a trip to the local library. Ned, and another two-year-old, both become excited as they go through the main doors and start calling out, ''Tory time, 'tory time!' Dave comments, 'Well done, Ned and Jake, you remember. The library is where we come for our special story time. Do you remember where we go now?'

Alert adults notice that young children communicate with each other - even babies exchange communicative looks and touch.

Nine-month-old Katie and nearly three-year-old Jamal are sitting together on a rug out in the garden. Jamal is having fun offering Katie different items from a simple treasure box. Bahar, who is Katie's key person, is sitting on the rug watching. At one point she comments,

'Jamal, you're good at choosing what Katie likes'. At one point Katie holds an egg whisk out to Jamal and Bahar helps with, 'Jamal, I think Katie wants you to take the whisk. Is that what you want Katie?' A game of I-give-you-and-then-you-give-me-back develops and both children are soon giggling.

Jennie Lindon is an early years specialist and author. She has worked for more than 30 years with services for children and families.

If you want to find out more

■ Learning and Teaching Scotland *Birth to Three: Supporting our Youngest Children* (2005) www.ltscotland.org. uk/earlyyears/birthtothree

■ Sure Start/DfES *Birth to Three Matters: a Framework to Support Children in their Earliest Years* (2002) www.surestart. gov.uk/resources/childcareworkers/ birthtothreematters

■ Talk to Your Baby: many resources and discussion papers, including Liz Attenborough and Rachel Fahey (2005) 'Why do many young children lack basic language skills?' www. talktoyourbaby.org.uk

■ See also 'Children don't need words to tell you something' by Jennie Lindon (*Practical Professional Child Care* December 2004)

Babies and young children are interested in the world around them. They are ready to be delighted in almost anything because everything is new. You need to share in this delight, giving time and attention, says Jennie Lindon

How children find out about their world

Young children learn through direct experience, the chance to look, listen, touch, smell and taste, when it is safe to use that sense. But even rising threes still don't understand much about risks, so you need to protect them in ways that avoid making everyday life boring.

Unfamiliar sights and sudden or loud sounds can startle babies, rather than interest them. That's why you stay close by, to reassure a baby or toddler who has been disconcerted by the bang of a door slamming or a bird that swoops by without warning in the park.

Young children use their senses to explore what is in their world and how it all works. As their spoken language develops, they start to ask questions. At first, toddlers let you know that they want to find out the names of things that interest them: little creatures, flowers or what they can see from their buggy on a busy high street. Soon they will want to know more, asking questions such as 'What is that for?', 'Where is that man going?' and 'Why?'.

Look and learn

Under-threes like to look, even stare, at people or objects of interest. Their comfortable personal space is much closer than adults' or even older children. So very young children may explore you up close - feeling your face, perhaps stroking your hair.

You support young learning by giving time and attention. Young children are ready to learn a bit about what has caught their interest right now. Relax and look with them; try not to rush. What else is more important than sharing a child's motivation

to learn? When very young children stare at a wiggling worm or a scuttling spider, they are showing how they can really concentrate on what interests them.

This is the time to let young toddlers know the wriggling creature is called a worm. Two- and young three-year-olds will make sense of the description of 'wriggling' and will soon want to know, 'Where is the worm's home?' or 'Why do spiders make webs?'

For toddlers it's a thrill to see the twinkling moon and stars when darkness falls before they are tucked up in bed. They need to know that you are interested as well and will look and share the delight. This is how they learn about 'light' and 'dark' and 'getting dark', how they learn the words for 'moon' and 'stars'. They have no concept of 'space' - their general knowledge is not at that stage. So bear this in mind if you work in a group setting that plans activities relating to different topics.

Finding out through touch

Young children stretch out a hand and want to touch. You make sure that what they can reach is safe. Guide children about when to keep a safe distance, such as 'We just look at the swans. They get cross if people try to stroke them.'

Toddlers and two-year-olds really enjoy playing with natural materials. Water is fun

Everyday observations to share with parents

You share the care of other people's children, so partnership includes letting parents or other family carers know about current interests.

- Perhaps Teja does not have the words to tell her mother about the exciting shop with all the old-fashioned clocks, and how looking in this shop window is an important part of every high street outing.

- Twos and threes are more able to talk about the excitement of the crane they saw on the building site. You can help children share with their parents through photos.

- Sometimes you might all put together a story book with photos and writing that you have scribed for children. It might be 'how the goslings grew up', but could just as well be 'how they build the new block of flats'.

- It will help parents to know that their toddlers were fascinated by a visit to the local garden centre and would love to go again.

- to feel and splash as well as to pour or sweep around with a big brush outside. Younger ones will still sometimes put things in their mouth. But that's why you stay by them when they explore a pile of rose petals or the smooth beach stones that you collected.

Don't hold back their learning because exploration means they might get a bit grubby or damp. Talk diplomatically with any parents who expect children to keep their clothes neat all day.

In *Birth to Three Matters*, the component card 'Being together' gives the case study of 11-month-old Tariq, who is sitting in a pile of autumn leaves. Tariq is fascinated and his carer notices. She realises that Tariq needs to be changed but that this can wait a little while. She takes the time to be with Tariq, accepts the handful of leaves that he scoops up for her, and chats a bit about the leaves. Then she suggests that Tariq brings a leaf with him as they go for his nappy change.

Ways to join in

You help young children to learn about their world by listening with them, as well as looking.

- Be ready to say, 'Can you hear the birds?' or 'I think that's the sound of a police car. Can you see it yet?' You can

acknowledge that your high street is busy and still help them to distinguish the different sounds.

- Make sure that you experience more peaceful corners of your outdoor space and the neighbourhood. Alert children to sounds by touching your ear and saying, 'Can you hear that sound? Is it a dog barking?'

Babies and toddlers are aware of smell, a sense that adults often overlook or divide into 'nice' or 'unpleasant' smells.

- Share their interest in how apple crumble smells when it is cooking or that the new soap dispenser smells 'just like the bush in our garden' and let them know the smell is of lavender.

- You can recognise together the nice smell of earth that has just been dug over or freshly cut grass.

- And, yes, the slightly older children will let you know that 'pooh!' the baby needs changing.

Young children feel valued and happy when you share in what has enchanted them. It is discouraging for them to hear dismissive remarks like, 'What's the fuss, it's just a fire engine' or 'Don't touch the snail, it's dirty'.

Rhythms and routines

Young children learn a great deal through feeling involved in the rhythms of their day. They are genuinely interested in babies: why they need their nappies changed and when 'our baby' will be able to feed himself. They are intrigued by changes in the weather and the different seasons.

Under-threes focus on the current season through what there is to see, touch and smell. They do not need to 'do autumn' as a topic. They collect leaves, admire and stroke the shiny conkers and understand about putting on a coat because it is getting colder. They learn about springtime by looking at the crocuses pushing up through the ground and asking you questions about the baby ducks in the park.

Children learn about the weather by looking, but also by being outdoors and experiencing it - and that means bad weather as well as good. The best way to learn about rain is to put on a pair of wellingtons and step in the puddles!

Birth to Three Matters highlights the importance of direct experience in **A Competent Learner**, 'Making connections': 'Thoroughly investigate environments with children, for example when outside, consider how to shift leaves off a path, enlarge a puddle, collect water dripping from a tap.'

The ideas in **A Healthy Child** ('Healthy choices') remind how simple resources can support children's understanding. The component card says, 'recognise that outdoor provision presents rich choices for babies and children and include this opportunity in your planning, for example streamers, bubbles and windmills in a windy day box'.

Jennie Lindon is a child psychologist and author. She has worked for nearly 30 years with services for children and their families.

Do you want to find out more?

- *The Great Outdoors* Margaret Edgington (Early Education).

- *Questions and Answers Learning Together* leaflet Jennie Lindon (Early Education Tel: 020 7539 5400 www.early-education. org.uk).

- *Birth to Three Matters: a framework to support children in their earliest years* (Sure Start/DfES Tel: 0845 6022 260).

How do babies brains work? The findings of brain research can guide you towards helping babies and young children to learn. Jennie Lindon explains

Developing brain power

Human babies are physically uncoordinated, but their brains are poised to take in information from their senses. Unlike baby lambs, our newborns cannot stagger to their feet. They are vulnerable because nature has made a trade-off.

Full-term babies are born when their bodies are just mature enough to cope with life outside the womb. Babies' brains have the huge potential of the skills of thought and language that distinguish humans from other mammals. If newborns were physically more independent, along with all this intellectual potential, their brain would need a larger head capacity and normal birth would be impossible.

Ready to learn

Babies' brains are busy even before they are born. Through the last three months before birth, the brain of a human foetus develops rapidly. Brain activity before birth seems to prime the system, especially those parts that deal with vision and hearing. This incredibly early learning means that some newborns recognise familiar sounds, such as a parent's voice or their older sibling's favourite song, which they heard many times while still in the womb.

Newborn babies cannot move independently or reach out accurately, but they can direct their eyes towards anything that interests them, such as faces. It has been calculated that by four months of age, babies have already made more than three million eye movements. The part of the brain that controls and plans eye movements gradually takes over within the first year. But babies have already taken in vast amounts of information, that their brain is busy processing.

A newborn's brain contains a staggering 100 billion neurons but their immature brain has not yet made many connections between these neurons. The brain of a full-term newborn weighs about 350 grams. This weight trebles over the first 12 months to reach about 1000 grams. This impressive growth is unique to humans. Babies' experiences create neural connections and their brains also develop in complexity. All their efforts with physical movement and early communication develop the neural networks within their immature brains

– often described as the cells that fire together wire together.

What do babies need?

It is complicated to explain how our brains develop and neuroscientists do not understand everything about brain function. However, the implications from research for practitioners and parents are straightforward. The research confirms what caring adults

have long believed: the early years of a child's life are really important. Babies and very young children need positive experiences; deprivation of any kind can be especially damaging.

Attuned to language

Babies are ready to be social and appear to be programmed for the sounds and rhythms of spoken language. Babies' brains are attuned to the sound of the human voice but, of course, this voice needs to come from a real person who responds to the baby's actions and sound-making. Electronic pads and battery-driven toys are not interactive for babies and toddlers - no matter what it says on the packaging or company website!

Babies need happy opportunities to repeat experiences so that they become familiar. Young babies' eyes light up as they recognise the start of a peep-bo game or touch-and-sing with 'Round and round the garden'. Sharing books with babies and toddlers will work as 'really early literacy', when it is a warm, personal experience. The brain connections are as much, if not more, emotional as intellectual.

Those neural connections that are not strengthened by repeated experience are less strong and may fade away. This process, called 'pruning', is not necessarily a problem. For instance, babies are born with the potential to learn any language, but by about 12 months they can no longer distinguish sounds that they do not hear in speech. It would be impractical for a young child to continue to learn English, when they are hearing only Japanese. However, the early years are a vital sensitive time for learning language. It is important that babies and young children experience rich oral communication in the language(s) that are normal life for them.

Babies and toddlers need practice

Babies' repeated physical actions, such as crawling, lead to an established neural pathway in their brain. You can observe this pathway in action as confident crawlers spot something of interest, go on all fours, crawl at speed across the room, sit back and reach out their hands.

Once they are independently mobile, older babies and toddlers engage in a great deal of physical play and sheer joy in using their skills. Very young children do not need to be told to practise. Toddlers happily build their own brain connections when they have relaxed time and a safe space in which to move.

Babies and toddlers learn through their senses and by getting their hands on interesting play resources. The clear demands of very young children for 'do it again!' are ideal for their learning. Babies and toddlers find out their version of cause and effect when they drop the same object on the ground many times. They need an adult or cooperative older child to keep replacing the object.

Emotional experiences affect the brain

Early years professionals have long been concerned that young children are deeply affected by harsh treatment and unpredictable daily lives. Research into early brain development offers an explanation of what happens and further evidence that young children need to experience emotional security within family life and out-of-home care.

Repeated experiences of harshness and unpredictable adult behaviour (not the odd 'off day') create higher than average levels of cortisol in young brains. Cortisol is a steroid hormone important in the biochemistry of the brain and it is valuable to help us focus when we are at

risk. But the presence of cortisol disrupts other neural connections and high regular levels block children's ability to learn in positive ways.

Equally important, young brains make other connections that show through uncertain or aggressive behaviour. Young children start expecting normal life to be full of emotional or physical threat.

The early years are a vital time for learning, but babies and toddlers can be over-stimulated and harassed; more is not necessarily better. Human babies need to feel emotionally secure, to receive generous, personal attention. They benefit from simple play experiences and suitable resources for their level of understanding. Anxious parents or practitioners will not help very young children by putting them on a treadmill of activities designed to hurry along the course of development.

Sensitive adults notice the body language messages of a child under stress. Research into brain development provides an explanation for what is happening. Learning unfolds best when positive emotions experienced by young children facilitate chemical secretions in the brain that help the messages to cross the synapses - the gaps between neurons. These substances, called neurotransmitters, seem to help learning because children feel emotionally secure and able to go at their own pace.

In contrast, feelings of exhaustion or anxiety shift the chemical balance, so it is harder for the neurons in a child's brain to send or receive the necessary signals.

Babies and very young children need to make meaningful connections with what they already understand and can do. Too many companies are promoting toys that claim to teach written letters and numbers to toddlers, even babies. At best, such 'pre-school rat race' materials waste the time of very young children. At worst, persistent attempts by adults to take developmental short-cuts will lead young

brains to make disruptive social-emotional connections - for instance that 'adults always make you do boring things' or 'I can't do it, so I must be stupid'.

Brain development continues

Our brains continue to develop and make new connections throughout our lives; we could not learn in adulthood otherwise. By puberty an average human brain weighs about 1300 grams and by adulthood about 1500 grams. The early years are very busy, but there is another significant burst of brain activity in adolescence.

Teenage brains are working hard to integrate the different areas of the brain, especially those concerned with self-control, emotional judgement, organisation and planning. It would have been very useful to have the excuse of 'my brain hurts' as a teenager!

Jennie Lindon is an early years specialist and author. She has worked for more than 30 years with services for children and families.

If you want to find out more

- *How Babies Think: the Science of Childhood* Alison Gopnik, Andrew Meltzoff and Patricia Kuhl (Phoenix)
- *Your Child's Growing Mind* Jane Healy (a US publication by Doubleday available from Community Insight 01793 512612)
- *Brain Games for Babies, Toddlers and Twos* Jackie Silberg (Hamlyn)
- www.zerotothree.org Zero to Three has an informative Brain Wonders section

How do you know whether a child is developmentally delayed or just a bit slower than their peers? Without experience and knowledge of recognised age-related milestones, it is sometimes difficult to decide, says Amanda Kirby

Developmental delay or just lack of experience?

If you want to help a child you need to know about the stages they are likely to go through and the order that these developmental milestones come in.

It's a bit like building a house - if you don't get the foundations in place then you can't build the first floor. The same analogy works for children as it is harder to learn to write, for example, if pre-writing skills are not in place or if a child cannot balance on a chair or listen to an instruction.

How can you decide if there is a difficulty that needs addressing or that encouragement will be enough?

Defining the terms

■ **Delay** – this means the child's performance is significantly below average in a given area or skill. For example, most other children of a similar age are catching the ball but one child still keeps dropping it, or most of the children can put on their coats to go out to play but one child still needs help doing up the buttons and knowing which way around the coat goes.

■ **Deviance** - this means that development is atypical, such as a developmental milestone occurring out of sequence. For example, a child walks but does not crawl. This may not be abnormal but can be a sign that they should be observed to see if other areas of development are out of sequence as well.

■ **Dissociation** - this means there is a substantial difference in the rate of development between two streams. For example, a child can move like other children of their age but has speech and language delay. A child may be a great athlete but has difficulties with recording information on the page.

How can you tell the difference?

Most children who arrive at nursery or school have played with other children, learned to dress and undress and feed themselves. However, some children may have parents who do these things for them or they may have suffered neglect or experienced social isolation.

Usually by the end of the first term, after these children have been shown a skill (which is age appropriate for them), they will have caught up with their peers. It may take them a little longer, as they may not have the same level of practice at home, but they are usually able to manage. However, there may be a few children who are still struggling to put on their coats the right way around, take themselves to the toilet, be able to draw a circle or sit quietly for ten minutes at story time, for example. These children continue to have difficulties despite support. It is these children who may be showing a level of developmental delay.

It is important to check out other possible reasons before making this assumption.

■ Is the task suitable for the age of the child?

■ Are you giving the child enough time to do the task?

■ Are there other influences that could be affecting the child's behaviour or motivation such as social circumstances at home?

■ Is the environment noisy and distracting so they cannot concentrate, listen and follow you?

■ Is the child's hearing or vision okay? Do they need to be checked out?

■ Do you know if the child has had any past illnesses that may be affecting their learning, such as glue ear?

Check the developmental milestone chart overleaf and see if you are expecting too much from the child you are working with.

Make sure that the child's foundation skills are in place, in other words that they can do the skills required before the age band you are looking at. If not, then start at a younger age level to work out what developmental level the child is operating on for social, language and motor milestones. This is your starting point to work on foundation skills.

Amanda Kirby, medical director, The Dyscovery Centre, Cardiff.

There are signs that respect is growing for outdoor learning – or more accurately, that practitioners are rediscovering the power of the outdoors, says Jennie Lindon

Why you need to get outdoors

How did so many adults come to believe that young children just let off steam when they go outdoors?

Part of the problem was that a school view pressed down on early years practice. Time outdoors came to be seen more like school playtime, a break from the 'real learning' that was done inside, with children sitting still and led by adult plans.

In recent years, more and more primary school teams are creating 'outdoor classrooms' and taking a more child-centred view of the importance of break times.

There is great potential in even a small outdoor space. There is always something of interest for young children – adults just need to join in their curiosity and enthusiasm.

The *Birth to Three Matters* video provides many examples of how young children learn outdoors – from a happy singing time to 'posting' balls down tubing and having

adventures on a climbing and clambering area. The message is clear that practitioners need to get outside with children.

Space to move

The early years are the very best time for young children to form healthy habits. The importance of physical skills has often been devalued, along with outdoor play, and this has serious consequences.

Young children need to build strong bones, develop the capacity of their lungs and work their muscles. Without this healthy foundation, there are limits to the repair work that is possible in later years. There is good reason to worry that too many children have turned into sedentary 'couch potatoes'. But ask yourself how this can have happened, when very young children are so keen to use their physical skills to the full.

The easiest way to ensure the crucial foundation for later health is to open the doors, get outside with children and join in

their play. A sense of greater space is one of the pleasures of the outdoors, and that space stretches upwards – the sky really is the limit.

- Two-year-old Duncan loves to run in the garden of his nursery – sometimes to nowhere in particular. He loves a game of chasing with Gayle, his key person, and the game often pauses as Duncan, and his friends, stop to look down at a snail or up to a plane. In dry weather the painting easel and other materials go outside. In wet weather, the children go out with their umbrellas.

- Gayle is relieved that her nursery recognises the value of local outings. (Her previous nursery saved money on insurance by refusing to take children out and about.) They take regular trips for children to discover the pleasures of walking. Gayle and her colleagues take care to engage with babies who travel in the buggy.

- Yasmin and Harry (a young and older two-year-old) show perseverance and great concentration in the garden of their childminder, Jeff. Yasmin loves trundling the little wheelbarrow and transporting leaves. Harry works on his steering skills for the trike. The children also relish the small outdoor spaces created by the hidey-hole under the big tree and the tent that Jeff puts up regularly.

- Jeff gets out into the local neighbourhood every day. Yasmin and Harry now recognise their route to the market and park. The children have little brown carrier bags (from Matt at the local delicatessen) for treasures, like Harry's special stone and Yasmin's feather.

Children can use and practise their physical skills in a large inside space. But this experience is as well as, not instead of, generous amounts of time outside.

As a childminder, you may take children to a drop-in or regular session with mini-gym equipment. Such special experiences can be fun, but they should never become the only time when young children are seriously active.

A nursery team might welcome visits from someone who brings special expertise, perhaps with dance. But please think carefully if you are tempted to buy in a physical programme that could be better achieved by simply opening the doors to the garden and going outside with the children.

The natural world

The best way for young children to learn about little creatures or the changing seasons is to get out into the garden, or local open space, and enjoy direct experiences of the natural world.

Under-threes do not make any sense of topics on spring or minibeasts. But three- and four-year-olds also learn more effectively when they can see, smell and get their hands onto the flowers of springtime. They learn through real experiences of growing bulbs or vegetables.

Young children's knowledge has to build through direct experience of sunlight through the trees or ice on the puddles. Meaningful conversation follows on naturally for children who have spotted a huge spider under the log, or piece of carpet, that you all lift for a regular check on the resident creepy crawlies.

Follow children's interests. It has to be their choice if they want to collect leaves for a display table or draw a picture of the baby ducks.

Sometimes Harry or Yasmin do want to make a leaf print from the one they have carried back in their treasure bag. But Jeff also provides a low shelf where Harry's stone can be seen and a sheet of white paper as a backdrop for Yasmin's

feather. Their parents can then easily see what has been important for these young children today.

In colder weather, Gayle and her colleagues carry well-wrapped babies and young toddlers out into the garden. They walk them round and stop to look and listen. The three- and four-year-olds like to create interesting sights for the babies, like ribbons, wind chimes and other sound makers dangling from the tree.

In summer time, Gayle creates comfortable outdoor spaces for the very youngest children with blankets or rugs. Play resources are then provided on that soft surface. Materials like sand or water are placed in smaller containers – suitable for one or two babies and easier to carry to and fro. Baskets and other containers go outside with the children and a large plastic shape (designed for sand or water) works well as a safe place for three toddlers and their chosen books or toys.

Enjoyment of the senses

The outdoors is a rich source of sensory experiences.

- Young children are encouraged to look closely, when they have time to enjoy the outdoors and you show genuine interest in what has caught their attention.

- Sounds may be quiet or noisy, obvious in their origin or a mystery. Young children are often fascinated to track down the source of a sound or to wonder, with you, about what an unknown sound might be.

- There is plenty to touch in the outdoors and, of course, you help children to develop a safe outlook on what is all right to touch and what 'we look, but we don't touch…'

- Look at the colours of the natural world; they are an important reminder that everything is not about bright, primary colours. Your garden or local park will have some reds or blues,

especially from springtime onwards. But the outdoors is full of muted colours, many shades of green, brown and yellow.

- Children will learn about weather when adults let them get out in it, rather than use weather as an excuse to stay indoors. The UK, especially the southern parts, has a friendly climate, free from extremes. It is easy to protect children appropriately from wet, cold or sunshine. Their bodies also need the experience of adjusting to different temperatures.

- Rain is interesting, as are puddles and water running in the gutters. Wind moves leaves and branches and sunshine creates lovely, dappled effects through the trees. Snow is magical for children, especially in those areas of the UK that rarely get a snowfall.

If you want to read more

- *Understanding Children's Play* Jennie Lindon (Nelson Thornes)

- *The Great Outdoors* Margaret Edgington (Early Education)

Jennie Lindon is an early years specialist. She has worked for more than 30 years with services for children and families.

Planning is always a challenge - especially if you look after children of different ages and abilities. What's the best approach? What do you need to remember? Miranda Walker offers some advice

Planning: why you do it and how

There are three stages in the planning cycle:

- **Planning:** You plan enjoyable activities to help children learn and develop.

- **Implementation:** Children take part in planned activities.

- **Review:** You assess what learning has taken place so that you know whether activities need to be adapted (things may be done differently with hindsight), and what children should learn and experience next.

Many practitioners refer to this as the 'Plan, do, review' cycle.

Considering children's needs

When planning, it's important to meet the needs of individual children. You should think about:

The child's current stage of development

What have children learned and experienced to date, and what should they learn and experience next?

Impairments

Do you need to make any adaptations for children who have impairments and/or special educational needs? Are individual children having difficulties learning particular skills or concepts? If so, you can plan appropriate activities and support to help them.

Interests and preferences

What are children interested in and what do they enjoy? Do they show preferences for certain learning styles, such as visual, auditory or kinesthetic?

Curriculum planning

You must also take account of the requirements of the relevant curriculum/ framework for the children you work with, such as the *Curriculum Guidance for the Foundation Stage* or *Birth to Three Matters*. Curriculum plans should be:

Purposeful

Children should have the chance to take part in activities that benefit them in terms of learning and experience.

Supportive

In addition to providing appropriate support for individual children, activities should be planned sensitively, with children's sense of confidence, self-esteem and general well-being in mind.

Challenging

To motivate progression and learning, stimulating activities that are sufficiently challenging should be planned alongside activities that promote consolidation of learning.

Varied

A range of activities should be offered, such as free play, adult-led and child-initiated activities. There should be active, busy pursuits and quieter activities requiring concentration. Activities should take place indoors and outdoors.

Balanced

Activities should be planned to promote all areas of children's learning and development. When each daily programme of activities is varied and balanced, you are providing a 'differentiated approach' to learning and development.

Vibrant and exciting

One of the most valuable things you can do for children is to foster a love of learning. Provide activities that are interesting, exciting and fun to stimulate, engage and motivate children.

Planning to promote development

If you don't need to follow a curriculum or framework (with older children or in out-of-school clubs for instance), it's still beneficial to plan a range of fun activities that will promote each area of children's development - physical development, social and emotional development, communication and intellectual development, and behavioural development. This extends children's opportunities to learn and develop through play, and ensures a balanced programme.

Step by step

Most settings share something in common in the way that they plan. There will also be some aspects of planning which are unique to them; there are numerous ways of recording plans for example. Many early years settings like to plan activities around a central theme which is adopted for a period of time – perhaps a fortnight or a month – but not all settings use themes, and they are less relevant to younger children.

You may like to try the following technique:

Step 1

Working in consultation with colleagues (in group care settings), make long-term plans by compiling a list of 12 themes for the coming year, which will each run for one month. 'All about me' is a popular theme for example.

Step 2

Focussing on just one of the themes, make medium-term plans. Divide the theme into sub-categories where appropriate - week one may focus on 'My body' for example, and week two on 'Where I live'.

Step 3

Using reviews from previous activities to inform planning from now on, decide on and record a range of activities and experiences related to the sub-categories, which will promote children's learning and development in each area. If following the *Curriculum Guidance for the Foundation Stage*, refer to the Early Learning Goals and cross-reference them to the activities on your written plans.

Step 4

Make short-term plans by deciding on a timetable of activities and experiences for each day of each week. These must fit around general routines. Remember to use a differentiated approach for a balanced and varied programme. Make sure there are alternating times for physical activity and sufficient rest.

Step 5

Plan the detail of each activity, listing the resources and preparation needed. Include the role of adults. In group settings, identify who will do what and how children will be grouped and supported. This ensures the implementation is organised.

Step 6

Plan how you will assess or observe children's learning and experiences. It's important to keep an eye on what children actually do as they don't always choose to take part in the activities you offer or do them in the way you had planned.

Step 7

Plan for the review stage of the planning cycle by deciding how your finished plan will be monitored and/or evaluated and used to inform future planning.

Flexibility

Although planning is essential to good practice, there are many benefits of spontaneity, which needn't be lost if a flexible approach is taken to implementing plans. Children are sometimes so absorbed in an activity that it's appropriate to extend the time you'd scheduled. On other occasions an activity may run its course sooner than expected and may be brought to a close.

Children sometimes ask questions or play in such a way that activities develop unexpectedly. Following children's interest can lead to wonderful, naturally occurring discovery and learning. You can always reschedule the intended learning or experience for another time.

Occasionally an event arises for which it's worth straying from the session plan. For instance, if the sound of hailstones hitting the window captures children's interest, what better thing is there to do than to investigate?

Broad age ranges

Planning to meet the needs of children of a broad age range is a challenge for some providers, including childminders and out-of-school clubs. Flexibility and attention to safety are the keys to success. Involving older children in the planning process is the most effective way to make sure that you provide activities they find interesting and stimulating.

Group settings will find that many themes can operate on several levels to suit children of different age ranges. For instance, during a holiday club's beach theme, younger children may enjoy playing with sand and making collages with shells, while older children enjoy playing beach volleyball and creating surfboard designs. When a broad range of activities are offered to the whole group flexibly, children can follow the natural interests they have at different ages.

Naturally, safety is paramount. Often children of differing ages can participate in similar activities as long as the level of supervision is adjusted accordingly. For instance, older children may use some tools independently, while younger children require one-to-one help.

When working with children in the home, childminders may care for babies and toddlers alongside older children. It can be helpful to carefully schedule the timing of activities. For instance, an older child may want to make jewellery. This involves small pieces and possibly one-to-one help. A childminder may plan this activity during a younger child's nap time, when it's safe to get out the materials and full attention can be given to the older child.

It also makes sense to plan free play activities that require no adult assistance during the times when a younger child's care needs, such as feeding, are attended to.

Under-threes

Themes such as 'Under the sea' have little meaning to most children until they're around three years of age. However, linked activities can be used effectively to extend skills, knowledge and understanding. For instance, water activities could be linked giving young children opportunities to dip their hands in the water tray, splash their feet in puddles, pour out a drink of water and water the plants.

Miranda Walker is an early years and playwork trainer, writer and speaker. She owns her own day care settings in Devon.

If you look after school-aged children, whether after school or during school holidays, you may find it useful to have an insight into how you might expect them to develop and behave as they grow older, so that you feel able to meet their changing needs.

Understanding older children: social development

Once they are out of early childhood, older children usually have a social network of familiar children and adults. They can tell you the names of their friends and may have a 'best friend'. They have an equally clear idea of who is not their friend or groups of children whom they avoid. But their social network also includes relationships with important adults. Children feel the strongest attachment to their family, but they need to feel valued by key adults in their daily life: their childminder, playworkers at their breakfast or after-school club and familiar staff at their school.

Choosing friends

By five years children are active in choosing their own friends from the circle that is available. Some of these early friendships last for years, even into and through adulthood. Some friends drift apart as the children move on to diverging interests. Other friendships are disrupted because families relocate or children are moved to another school. One of the concerns about children whose family moves on a regular basis (probably because of the nature of a parent's job) is that eventually children may give up trying to make friends in yet another new school.

Children can be reasonably tolerant of social details over which they have no control, for instance, the children who also attend their after-school club or childminder's home. However, children want and need there to be at least a few peers with whom they like to play and chat in settings where they spend a lot of time. Children distinguish between

peers that they know as acquaintances and those to whom they feel closer. They can be swift to correct an adult who presumes to say another child is 'your friend', when this is not true. Within the family, older children sometimes firmly tell their parents that they do not like the children who visit with Mum or Dad's adult friends and they are no longer willing to play with these boring or troublesome peers.

Even close friends fall out temporarily and maybe just as swiftly make up again. Depending on the source of the argument or misunderstanding, mending the fences of friendship may need some outside help. Supportive adults need to approach any problems with respect and see if they can help children to talk, and listen to each other, about whatever is the problem. However, sometimes one child wants a break from a peer, who maybe seeks an exclusive 'best' friendship that the other child feels is restrictive. Neither child is wrong and, if you are involved with either child, they may both need help to empathise a bit with their peer. The social skills of friendship can include loosening the bonds, ideally without hurting someone else's feelings, as well as finding ways to join peers and get closer.

The importance of friendships

Adults usually recognise that friends matter to children, but sometimes we lose touch with just how much sustained friendships make the difference for a reasonably happy childhood.

■ A consistent message from children

over this age range (and from young people too), is that being with your friends and doing what you want to do (rather than being organised by adults) is an important part of leisure time.

■ Being without friends, even temporarily, is lonely when everyone else seems to have company. Wanting to be alone, for a bit of peace and quiet, is not necessarily a sign of emotional problems in childhood.

■ Children explain very clearly that a school playground is a grim place to be if nobody will play with you, even just for a day. For a range of different reasons, some children find it hard to get into existing groups or games. Misplaced tactics can lead children being even more excluded, and needing discreet adult help.

■ The experience of bullying for children is so distressing because, not only do these other children not want to be your friend, they are going out of their way to make you miserable.

Children and young people regularly comment that the significant transition of moving into junior or secondary school is more manageable if you have friends who move with you. Eleven and twelve-year-olds often have sound advice to offer younger children who are about to make the move. One regular suggestion is to make the effort to talk with other pupils, who are unfamiliar at the start, to create the opportunity for making new friends. As young secondary school pupils explain, friends who go together to the same, large school do not necessarily end up in the same class. Some children find that their school year of pupils is the size of their entire, small primary school – they face an entirely new social situation.

Even six and seven-year-olds can be very insightful about the situation of a 'new' child joining a school. I have heard children describe with empathy that it is hard when everyone else already has friends and that it is important for other children to make a 'new' child welcome. This social and emotional awareness means that these younger primary school children are open to a 'buddy' system to help a child feel at home. Some children do not have to be asked, but choose to stay by a child who is settling in where everyone else is already part of a social network.

Children spend a lot of time in school and they understand that a significant aim of this setting is that they 'have to learn and do their work'. However, children are also clear that school is much better if they get some time to be with their friends. So any consideration of social development over childhood needs to include adult sensitivity to what happens over the many hours that most children spend in school (more on this topic in a later feature about play).

Problems between peers

Friendships with other children become increasingly central to daily life. But adults remain important, not least for emotional support when relations between children become fraught, or a child struggles with the social skills necessary in childhood.

Adults often use the phrase 'peer pressure' to mean children tempting each other into unacceptable behaviour, or the risky effect of physical dares. Yet peer pressure can be a positive force, when ground rules are clear and adults are firm yet fair, supportive and not simply punitive.

So long as children feel emotionally secure for themselves, they are often ready to make the effort for other children. For this reason it is possible to encourage different kinds of peer support initiatives in primary school. Children are able to learn skills of conflict resolution to ease some common playground troubles. Class representatives on a school council are able to speak up for their peers on relevant issues, including social and play problems that need resolving.

If you want to find out more

■ Jennie Lindon (2001) *Understanding children's play* Nelson Thornes.

■ Hilary Stacey and Pat Robinson (1997) *Let's mediate: a teachers' guide to peer support and conflict for all ages* Lucky Duck Publishing.

■ The *Peer Support Manual* on www. mentalhealth.org.uk gives many examples of peer listening and other school projects.

How to be a helpful adult

■ If you work in a school, then be a champion for children's need to have decent length breaks through the day and over lunch. Proper playtimes give children time to cement their friendships through freely chosen play, shared interests and social conversation.

■ Proper time off from classroom work is also essential for children to clear their head and get some physical exercise through informal play. Children do not 'learn' more in a day by having their breaks severely reduced.

■ Before and after school provision works best when children's needs and interests are to the forefront. Breakfast clubs get set up to meet the need for care. But a friendly atmosphere attracts children because they find that the social breakfast is a relaxed transition into the school day.

■ If you work in an after school club, make sure that the pattern of care does not slip into a sneaky extension of classroom activities – more of a potential risk when provision is located on a school site. Respect children's wish to relax after a hard day at school and maybe do 'a lot of nothing much' with their friends.

■ Children will enjoy the company of pleasant adults, who also have some ideas for activities. Some children want a chat with you as well as their friends, some need some lively physical activity and others want to enjoy a book, some drawing or a board game.

■ If you work as a childminder, you may have more flexibility about late afternoon activities. You will support children when you respond to today's request to come back from school via the park, play a card game or make scones for tea. During this time, children will often tell you about their day - you listen perhaps to how someone was 'so horrid' in the playground and offer a few ideas about what could be done tomorrow.

Jennie Lindon is an experienced independent consultant and author who has written on many aspects of child development.

If you look after school-aged children, whether after school or during school holidays, you may find it useful to have an insight into how you might expect them to develop and behave as they grow older, so that you feel able to meet their changing needs.

Understanding older children: emotional development

Children's continued emotional development through the years of middle childhood depends so much on their early experiences. Children have feelings – there is no question about that – but five and six-year-olds have already learned a great deal from the key adults around them. Their early years have laid the foundation for what happens through childhood to the brink of adolescence. There has to be a great deal of 'it all depends...' within any discussion about how children understand their own emotions and their insights into the likely feelings of other people.

Emotional awareness

Some five to eight-year-olds are very able to express their own feelings. They have learned the words to say, 'I'm so excited that we...', 'I'm really cross with you, because...' or 'That story is so sad'. Ten and eleven-year-olds can have extended their abilities to be able to explain – at least sometimes – what they feel, with a wide range of words and an underpinning of why. Of course, sometimes children, just like adults, are uncertain of their feelings or do not want to talk at this time, or to this person, about the emotions shown clearly on their face.

Children who are able to put internal states into words show you several aspects of their emotional development so far.

■ They understand the idea of feelings and that they themselves have different reactions to what happens during daily life.

■ The children have developed an emotional vocabulary of words that enables them to communicate their feelings to other people.

■ Their experience so far – in their own family and/or in early years provision – has created a confidence that other people will welcome hearing about what they feel, as well as what they know.

■ Emotionally secure children are sure that you want to hear about their excitement and the thrill of new knowledge just as much as their feelings of doubt or distress.

■ Children's willingness to put feelings of frustration or irritation into words can also show you that they have learned to use words, even under times of stress, rather than take the physical option of shoving or hitting.

However, children do not automatically learn to express their feelings by words, if the adults around them have not provided a good model of using their emotional vocabulary. Children learn to use words rather than fisticuffs because patient adults – practitioners and/or parents – have created a supportive atmosphere and appropriate ground rules. In this way emotional development is closely intertwined with a positive approach by adults to guiding children's behaviour.

Boys and girls may learn a rather different pattern of expressing feelings. Different is not necessarily a problem, so long as children are not restricted by the unwritten rules. However, in

some cases boys seem to be given less support in expressing a range of feelings, because adults believe that boys are less emotionally aware than girls. Familiar adults may also give firm messages about emotions to children, although the adults may not be entirely aware of what they are doing. Some adults communicate in subtle ways that it is not alright for boys to appear sad, in which case older boys sometimes use an expression of anger to cover distress. Girls are sometimes given the message that it is not acceptable for them to be angry, in which case that emotion sometimes gets muddled up with a fierce version of 'being upset'.

Awareness of the feelings of others

Part of raising children within a social community is to guide them towards an awareness of the feelings of other people. Children who are only aware of their own feelings can operate in a very self-centred way. The personal, social and emotional strand of the primary school curriculum has a strong focus on the development of empathy: an awareness of the feelings of other people and a willingness to use that knowledge in a positive way.

■ Children of primary school age, and

even younger, often show that they notice how familiar children or adults are feeling at the moment. They have experience of how familiar emotions appear through facial expression and other aspects of body language.

■ The other child or adult does not necessarily have to express the feeling in spoken words. When children feel comfortable in the situation, they may comment to a peer, or an adult to whom they are close, 'you look really happy', ask, 'are you alright?' or guess, 'are you upset?'

■ Children can be confused, even by familiar adults, if the latter are less than honest about their current emotions. At times of stress within a family, children usually sense something is wrong. But they puzzle to make sense of an unfamiliar situation, especially if the adults deny that anything is the matter.

Through middle and late childhood, the thinking power of children supports them in the leap of wondering how someone else might feel – someone who is not standing in front of them right now. Eight and nine-year-olds, and even younger children, can be very thoughtful about the likely feelings of characters in a story, either in a book or told with props. Children can talk about what somebody might be feeling or how they themselves might feel in a similar situation. I have enjoyed conversations with seven-year-olds, who were very able to speculate on the feelings of a child who came to their school after everyone else had started. Boys and girls talked fluently about the likely emotions and what would probably be helpful to this imaginary child.

Offering emotional support

Children who feel sufficiently supported for their own emotional needs are often willing to make that extra effort to support their peers. On the other hand, if children judge accurately that it is every child for him/herself, they are far less likely to show kind consideration to others. In schools and after school clubs where adults create a positive emotional atmosphere, five to elevens can be adept at a wide range of what comes under the title of peer support.

■ Children will agree – they sometimes spontaneously offer – to act as a buddy to a child who is new to the school or club, or who is struggling with the social situation.

■ Friendship benches work in primary school playgrounds because children are ready to take their turn in watching out for a peer using the bench to signal they need some company.

■ Supported by an ongoing PSE programme in some primary schools, some nine and ten-year-olds are keen and able to operate as playground mediators, helping their peers to defuse conflict situations.

Any playground initiative works because it is carefully developed and adults do not give up their responsibilities. However, children are able to learn basic skills to bring down the emotional temperature and resolve arguments. There is significant potential for children's emotional development, but it all depends on adult awareness of how to make the best of the possibilities.

If you want to find out more

■ Bayley, Ros (2006) More than happy or sad: young children and emotions Early Education

■ Social and Emotional Aspects of Learning (SEAL) www. standards.dfes. gov.uk/primary/ publications/ banda/seal

■ Lindon, Jennie (2005) Understanding child development:

How to be a helpful adult

■ Be aware of your own emotional vocabulary. Reflect on whether you use opportunities to show children when it's appropriate to feel 'proud of our efforts', 'disappointed, because we tried so hard' or 'puzzled about why…' and other feelings.

■ Are you ready to use a range of words for feelings, so that children can extend their own vocabulary? For instance, it may be very helpful for some children to understand the gradations between being a bit irritated through to very angry, or from being a bit sad through to feeling very distressed.

■ Provide opportunities for children to voice their feelings but do not insist, especially in a group situation. The ground rules for any kind of group work or circle time have to include the right not to speak up, as well as the other rules that ensure fair listening and respect.

■ Whether in a small group, or cosy corner with you, children are sometimes more comfortable talking through a favourite puppet or saying that the 'talking bear' (used by their class as a whole) has something to say on their behalf.

thinking theory and practice Hodder Arnold

Jennie Lindon is an experienced indepenent consultant and author who has written on many aspects of child development.

If you look after school-aged children, whether after school or during school holidays, you may find it useful to have an insight into how you might expect them to develop and behave as they grow older, so that you feel able to meet their changing needs.

Understanding older children: communication skills

If children have had rich experience of communication in their early childhood, five-and-six-year-olds can show you wide-ranging skills of communication. Their abilities continue to develop over middle childhood, into early adolescence.

What children say

Children past early childhood have an extensive vocabulary – some four-year-olds are already impressive. Researchers disagree on a likely total of words by middle childhood, but it is certainly into the thousands. It would be a very tough task if you wanted to write down all the words that individual children use within their spontaneous conversation. Additionally some children will be able to speak in more than one language, perhaps with equal fluency, while other children will have a broader vocabulary in one language than another.

You would face a major, although very interesting, project if you also wanted to gather a representative sample of children's own phrases and sentences. When five to eleven or twelve-year-old children feel at ease, they use their spoken words to express a wide range of comments, opinions, feelings and questions. If children feel at ease, then they use words for a range of purposes in communication.

Older children should have the thinking power and the vocabulary to talk about what is right in front of them now. But they are also able to recall what has happened in the past and make connections. They often enjoy reminiscing along the lines of, 'do

you remember when' with familiar adults. Children sometimes volunteer comments in reply to adult queries. But you do not want a situation where children believe they have to wait to be asked, nor where adults always determine what is important and worth the time to express.

Children learn about communication in different situations. So they learn about holding onto their contribution in a group situation like the classroom. But waiting for their turn is hard for children when they have something really interesting to say. It is important that children have plenty of less organised, really informal conversation times with adults, as well as with their peers. When they do not feel rushed, children often talk over snack time with their childminder, at breakfast club or in after school provision. In school, children may chat with staff supervising the playground. With plenty of informal communication, children can learn a different style for more formal situations. For instance nine-and-ten-year-olds can

• • • • • • • • • • • • • • • • • • • •
This series aims to support practitioners working with older children from five to twelve years.

The articles will also be useful for students gaining their S/NVQs, since the development units at each level require a basic knowledge of children beyond the early years.
• • • • • • • • • • • • • • • • • • • •

become familiar with the pattern of a group meeting in club, or how to talk and listen at a school council session.

Older children are well able to use their words to ask direct questions and this use of their language is a handy focus for adults' attention.

■ Some questions will reflect children's wish to confirm details of routines like, 'when are going to the park?' or of permission like, 'can I have the last piece of cake?'

■ When children ask a lot of routine questions, this pattern can let an alert adult know that he or she does not feel at ease yet in class, club or your home.

■ Questions sometimes combine with a fair challenge from children as they ask for an explanation with, 'why do we have a time limit for playing on the computer?' or 'why can't we play on the grass?' Sensible adults have a better answer than, 'because I say so.'

■ When children have interesting experiences and the time to explore and reflect, it is normal that they ask some searching questions. Children are using their speaking and thinking skills in a deliberate way. They want to extend their knowledge, by asking questions like, 'how does the library know when our books are late?' or 'am I going faster if I run up the aisle when I'm on a train?'

It is also very likely that some boys and girls will use words that are especially important to them, because of their personal interests. Children allowed to have the time, space and resources can be very knowledgeable about marine life, motorbikes, how you grow tomatoes – anything that has caught their attention. Many older children have sufficient understanding to ask, 'what do you mean?' when adults use unfamiliar words. However, roles are sometimes reversed and it is pleasant for children to explain the meaning of a word to the grown-ups or share underpinning knowledge about volcanoes.

Listening, looking and understanding

Of course, communication is not only about what children say. They have also learned a wide range of skills around listening and understanding. Their early experience has also created a foundation of attitudes about listening: Is it important to listen to other people? Do adults and other children listen to me? How does anyone know you are listening? What can happen if you don't listen? And many more practical questions.

■ Children who listen can follow instructions and information, although they sometimes (like adults too) appreciate repetition when something was not clear or their attention

wandered. But listening skills are not limited to children's ability to cooperate when an adult says, 'please listen to me'.

■ Five-and-six-year-olds can already be adept at listening involving turn taking. Many of them are able to hold a conversation with familiar adults and their peers. A proper conversation includes saying something, listening to what the other person has said and then making your next contribution link up in some way with a common thread. There is a pattern of turn taking, having a reasonably equal share of the conversation time and showing respect for what the partner in conversation wants to contribute.

■ The conversational skills of some children also show that they have grasped the social skills that underpin conversation rather than simply jockeying for position to get in what they want to say. Children learn initially from an experience with familiar adults who give time and attention and who model these skills.

The attentiveness of older children is not only about listening. They look as well and they have a grasp of the messages of body language, especially of familiar adults and children. Seven-and-eight-year-olds can show, even surprise, adults with their sharp awareness of the non-verbal music that accompanies the lyrics of spoken words.

Children have different kinds of conversations with their peers. Sometimes they realise that adults, however hard they try, are not that interested in lengthy conversations about a computer game or television programme. Children talking to each other also cover angles that they do not want you to hear, including gripes about adults that are not ready, if ever, for more general announcements, and jokes that are too rude or obscure for your ears. Children of

nine-to-ten-years of age also support each other more than some adults believe to be possible. In a warm emotional atmosphere – school, club or family home – older children will sometimes talk and listen to help a friend feel better. Girls and boys need to be able to use their words to talk through worries with trusted adults. But they sometimes talk with other children about family troubles or school worries.

What helps children's communication skills?

What helps children is not complicated, nor does it require 'techniques' of communication. They need:

■ Adults in school, club or a family home who are genuinely interested in talking with and listening to children. They need to experience a good model of paying attention to other people, the turn taking of a real conversation and ways to contribute without interrupting.

■ Time and attention form the essential basics, supported by comfortable places and spaces where children can happily talk with other children, as well as enjoy relaxed time with adults.

■ Adults who are ready to recall interesting times with familiar children. You show that you value your shared past together and you encourage children to enjoy reminiscences.

■ Further experience of vocabulary. Do not worry about using new or long words; confident children will ask you, 'what does that word mean?' Be aware that children juggling more than one language may need to build up their vocabulary in their least strong language. They are thinking like a six, eight or twelve-year-old but they may have the total number of words of a younger child and this situation is very frustrating for them.

Jennie Lindon is an experienced independent consultant and author who has written on many aspects of child development.

If you look after school-aged children, whether after school or during school holidays, you may find it useful to have an insight into how you might expect them to develop and behave as they grow older, so that you feel able to meet their changing needs.

Understanding older children: Thinking skills

Children's experiences in school should support the growth of their thinking skills. There is concern that some young thinkers are disheartened by curriculum pressures in the classroom that do not allow enough time for discussion – bouncing around ideas and trying them out.

However, there are some exciting projects in primary schools that encourage children to stretch their thinking muscles through exploring stories (fiction and non-fiction), getting their hands on interesting items, long-term projects and having enough time to explore ideas through the give-and-take of conversation and guided group discussion. For more information have a look at the suggested resources at the end of this feature.

But of course children do not only build their skills of thinking and reasoning during their hours in school. You will see evidence of their understanding and can definitely help during your time with them.

Thinking and knowing

Children build their thinking skills from being encouraged to think and through the friendly support of adults who realise that 'odd' ideas, from their grown-up perspective, often arise because children still have significant gaps in their knowledge. Sometimes you realise that children are puzzled, because they ask, 'is it true that...?'. At other times they seem certain of information which is wrong, for example, when you hear them tell another child, 'snakes definitely have little legs – how else could they move?'.

Sometimes children's logical mistakes are shown by what they do in the spirit of scientific enquiry. Some of these misunderstandings lead to a certain amount of mess. Try to recall your own childhood mishaps and, as the grown-up now, find the patience to ask, 'how did this happen?' rather than assume a child intended to create the damage.

As a curious eight-year-old, I decided to see what would happen if I ironed a plastic bag. I discovered in double quick time that plastic melted on to the iron. I am still impressed with how calm my mother was about what I had done to her iron. She was more concerned from my screech that I had hurt myself, but I was unharmed because she had taught me to iron safely.

My next scientific experiment was less dramatic. I knew that if you whisked cream with a hand beater, it got thicker. So I predicted that any liquid would change in an interesting way. However, I whisked a bowl of water till my arms ached and the most I managed was some bubbles.

Talking and thinking

The skills of communication are closely linked with children's cognitive development. Thinking does not depend completely on spoken communication. Ideas and the explanations underpinning ideas can sometimes be communicated in visual ways as well as by sound. However, talking and listening are powerful

• This series aims to support practitioners working with older children from five to twelve years.
• The articles will also be useful for students gaining their S/NVQs, since the development units at each level require a basic knowledge of children beyond the early years.

ways in which individual thinking becomes explicit and is shared with other people: Children as well as adults.

Children often show you what and how they think within ordinary conversations. They are also sharp observers, so sometimes you are ambushed by eight-year-old logic with, 'but yesterday you said...'. Helpful adults listen,

explain if necessary and apologise if appropriate. It undermines young thinking skills if this kind of comment is met with, 'don't be so cheeky!'. But just as importantly – recall your own childhood – children lose respect for an adult who is unable to deal with a fair challenge.

Observant adults notice that over middle childhood, girls and boys grasp the philosophical concept of fairness, although often first in the negative version of 'it's so unfair!'. They begin to understand fairness as a practical principle, and the basic ethical idea that the ground rules of club or your home rest upon a moral stance: Perhaps that 'everyone here deserves kindness' or 'has the right to consideration'.

Children are able to do the thinking that emerges from that abstract idea, because it makes sense in their social world. If you ask them to stop playing football in a certain area because it is unsafe, they will be motivated to problem solve by finding an alternative space. It is only fair to find and agree on a solution that lets those children enjoy a favourite activity, yet ensures non-players are safe from being hit by the football.

Thinking and problem solving

Children are often willing to talk around a problem – minor or major – and you will hear out loud their ability to weigh up possibilities. With adult support, they also become skilled in the steps of problem solving. It is important to talk about 'what is the problem' before 'what might we do about it?' and then to discuss 'what is the best idea on the list we've made?'.

Wise childminders or practitioners in after school clubs do not trap themselves into always being the ones to solve a practical social problem. Children learn a great deal if you create the time to talk around issues important to children, for example: 'How do we make a fair decision about what we watch for our afternoon television programme?' or 'some children never do any tidying up – what can we do about that?'.

A discussion around problem solving, or agreeing on some ground rules is not a free-for-all, although it can get lively and noisy from enthusiasm. I have known really helpful adults in after-school clubs who set a consistently good example to the children by regularly having these discussions. It gradually becomes easier for everyone to listen to other people and older children start to bring in quieter children, inviting their ideas. Keen interrupters slowly accept the strategies for turn-taking in groups, because they are 'fair'.

If you want to find out more

- Marion Dowling (2006) *Supporting young children's sustained shared thinking* Early Education.

- Jennie Lindon (in press 2007) *Understanding children and young people 5-18 years* Hodder Arnold

- Liz McGuiness (1999) *From thinking skills to thinking classrooms* DfEE Research Brief RB115 in Publications section of www.teachernet.gov.uk

- Diane Rich et al (2005) *First hand experiences: What matters to children* Rich Learning Opportunities www.richlearningopportunities. co.uk

- Examples of good classroom practice for thinking skills www.standards.dfes.gov.uk/ thinkingskills

How to be a helpful adult

Children are inquisitive – the human species seems to be innately curious – and ready to wonder. Something discouraging has to happen to dampen children's desire to explore, to be an amateur researcher. Whatever the situation in which you work with children, there will be productive ways for you to support the development of their thinking skills and active discovery.

- Make sure that they have interesting experiences and objects. Children talk, and think, and talk again when they can get their hands on authentic materials. A great deal more talking and listening will emerge from trips into real woodland, rather than nature tables set up by the adult.

- Of course you answer children's questions, but also look for the opportunities to pause and say honestly, 'that's a very good question. I need to think a moment…. Right, I think the answer is…'.

- Searching questions from children sometimes approach from the direction of, 'is it true that you always see lightning before you hear the thunder?'. This kind of exchange with children gives you the chance comment, 'I can hear you've been thinking' followed by whatever is appropriate to the question.

- Adults show respect for children's thinking with comments like, 'you're right because…' or 'you've got the correct idea about…., but the bit about… works like this…'. Older children's questions will sometimes lead you to say, 'I don't know but I'm sure we can find out…'.

- Resist the rush to fill a silence in a conversation or a group discussion. Look attentive and wait for the reply from a child who looks as if they are busy thinking. You can ask, 'are you still thinking?' Children in informal and more structured discussions often like the notion of 'our thinking time'.

- Think about your own open-ended questions and sometimes hold back on the correct answer or explanation – but obviously not to the point where it frustrates children. Useful questions might be phrases like, 'is it true that…. ? how could we find out?', 'I wonder whether…', 'can you tell why… happened?' or 'what makes you say that…?'.

Jennie Lindon is an experienced independent consultant and author who has written on many aspects of child development.

All children should be encouraged to develop fine control skills and take part in energetic activities and you need the right resources to help you support them. Linzi Pearson offers suggestions

Resources to support: Physical Development

Fine motor development

Jigsaw puzzles

Choose a variety of jigsaws for your setting. You need to have inset puzzles, the ones with lift-out pieces - some with big chunky pieces and some with smaller pieces. Look for jigsaws with interlocking pieces, anything from two-piece puzzles ranging to 30 pieces or more. These can be small table-top jigsaws or larger floor puzzles. There is an extensive range available made from both cardboard and wood. Wooden puzzles are best because they are long lasting and fit together better than cardboard ones. There are lots of puzzles with topic based pictures, so keep this in mind.

Threading and lacing

There is an extensive range of threading and lacing toys on the market. Threading toys include beads, cotton reels, buttons and animals and are cheap to buy. Choose a selection that caters for the varying abilities of children in your setting. Start with a basic threading set with chunky pieces that are easy to handle and have a thick lace to thread the pieces onto. You will need something like cotton reels to thread with as the next step before children move onto smaller beads that take a lot more skill. They can also thread dry penne pasta onto string to make necklaces and bracelets.

Plastic or wooden lacing shapes are more suitable for young children as they are easier to handle and last longer than lacing cards. For children who are still developing their fine motor skills, there are large wooden lacing shapes that have a thick lace with a wooden end to make it much easier to thread.

You can also buy lacing shapes that children can use to practise tying their shoelaces - an important self-help skill.

Construction toys

All construction toys promote fine motor skills. Have a selection of different kits so they can be rotated to keep children interested. Look for sets that fit together in a variety of ways, for example bricks that 'click' together or pieces using nuts, bolts or hinges.

Bead frames and peg boards

Bead frames are simple but extremely popular with children of all abilities who need to use a pincer grip (holding things between their first finger and thumb) to move the beads around the frame. They come in different sizes and some are more complicated than others.

Peg boards also encourage the pincer grip. Some boards come with large chunky pegs which are suitable for younger children before they move onto smaller pegs that are more difficult to pick up.

Playdough

Manipulating playdough strengthens the muscles in the hands and fingers. This is a great way, particularly for younger children, to improve their motor skills. Playdough can be bought but it is easy to make. Give children a selection of rolling pins, cutters and anything that can make an imprint in the dough.

Cutting and sticking

When children are cutting and sticking they are learning to use and control tools, such as scissors. Choose both right- and left-handed scissors and look for easy-to-use scissors for children to practise with. These are available from most educational suppliers.

Fun and games

- Games of skill, for example where children have to carefully remove items like bricks from a stack, encourage motor skills.

- Give the children chopsticks and a variety of small toys to pick up. It is quite difficult, but lots of fun.

- There are lots of action rhymes, ring games and physical games that can be played indoors and outdoors. 'Ring-a-ring 'o roses' and 'The farmer's in his den' get the children active and working together as a group.

- A parachute is a great resource that can be used for ring games. There are lots of activities you can use it for, but if you're stuck for ideas there are plenty of books that are full of suggestions.

Writing skills

To encourage pencil control and the correct grip, you need to provide suitable pencils. Triangular pencils are best, but can be expensive. An alternative is to buy tripod grips that fit onto normal pencils. They are reusable, making them much cheaper.

Provide a selection of activities, like templates and stencils, tracing cards and writing patterns to help children improve their pencil control.

Large play equipment

You should provide a range of large play equipment for children to crawl through, climb and balance on. For example:

- Tunnels
- Slides

- Ball pits
- Climbing frames
- Seesaws
- Soft play shapes
- Balancing beams
- Trampolines

The type of equipment you choose will depend on your setting, taking into account your indoor and outdoor play areas and storage facilities. If storage is an issue, look for equipment that folds down or dismantles easily, such as pop-up tunnels and fold-away slides.

Large equipment can be expensive to buy, so contact your local EYDCP to find out if there are any toy libraries in your area. Most toy libraries have a range of large equipment available for childcare settings to borrow. A cheap option is to use strong cardboard for tunnels or play houses, worn car tyres for crawling through and large logs for climbing on. This type of large equipment can be used to make an obstacle course.

Make sure that the surface the children are using it on is safe. If it is a hard surface, put down safety mats.

If your outdoor space is limited or if you have none at all, look to your local community for suitable places such as parks and sports halls.

Pedal, push and pull-along toys

When choosing bikes or trikes bear in mind the varying heights of children in your setting. Choose some smaller cars or trikes that do not have pedals, so they are easier for smaller children to trundle along on. Sit-in cars are ideal and they are great for imaginative play outdoors as children love to pretend they are driving ambulances or police cars. Three-wheeled trikes are great for young children, as they are more stable. When they feel confident children can move onto small bikes with stabilisers. If you choose two-wheeled bikes, buy some cycle helmets as well.

Two-wheeled scooters can be difficult for young children to master, so look out for three-wheeled versions because they stay upright.

When you buy trikes and scooters it is worth investing in hard-wearing metal ones instead of

the cheaper plastic versions - it is more cost-effective in the long run.

Pushchairs and pull-along carts are quite cheap to buy, but when choosing pushchairs think about where they are going to be stored. If your storage is outdoors in a shed or a garage the material may go mouldy, so plastic ones are best.

Small equipment

Choose a range of small apparatus to encourage skills such as throwing and catching.

- Different sized footballs
- Bats
- Hula hoops
- Quoits
- Bean bags
- Small balls (tennis, plastic or rubber balls)
- Frisbees (look for cloth or rubber ones - they hurt less!)
- Tubes for rolling balls down
- Skittles
- Cones and markers
- Skipping ropes

To encourage skill and control use goal posts, basketball hoops and games like hoopla.

To enhance the experience for children with special needs look for resources that are textured, easy to handle, brightly coloured, scented or that make a noise:

- Scented balls
- Brightly coloured balls
- Glittery or shiny hula hoops
- Hedgehog balls
- Koosh balls (pompons made with elastic bands)
- Balls containing bells
- Tactile tiles to step on

Keeping fit and healthy

Children need to understand the importance of being healthy and the things they need to do to stay that way. This includes healthy eating,

getting enough sleep, exercise and personal hygiene. There is a good range of resources to promote good health, including jigsaw puzzles, games, videos and books.

You can also make your own, for example, cut out pictures of healthy and unhealthy foods from magazines and food packaging. Use these for group discussions and activities. Contact your local health promotions department as they may have staff or contacts, such as a community dentist or dental nurse, who will come and talk to children.

The *Foundation Stage Curriculum Guidance* says that children should be able to recognise the changes that happen to their bodies when they are active. A good way is to do keep-fit sessions. It is easy to make up your own routines. Use movements like stretches and star jumps and include a warm up and warm down in your routine. During the warm up talk to the children about how they are feeling and ask them to feel the pulse in their necks. Repeat this during the warm down and talk about the difference in their pulse and the way they feel.

Resources for children who have little or no mobility

Look for resources and toys that make a sound or light up. This will encourage children to move or reach out to play with them. Also hang toys up to get children to reach for them. Mats, soft play areas and ball pools allow them to move around and explore safely without hurting themselves.

Linzi Pearson, play development adviser, Sure Start Brierley Hill.

Young people need personal space in which to develop their ideas and views. Part of this process will involve testing and pushing boundaries, both at school and home.

Working with Young People 13-16 years

At this time of an individual's life they are nearer to adult hood than childhood, but there will be times when the will appear more childlike than adult!! It can also be a frustrating time for the young person and the adults around them as they attempt to deal with life. It can also be an enjoyable time as young people relax with their friends and plan their futures.

As far as physical development is concerned by the age of 15 or 16 girls will have completed the process of puberty and will have the body of an adult woman. Boys may not have completed puberty by this age. Most boys seem to start puberty around the age of 14 and it can take up to three years to complete. This can be a time of great embarrassment for both boys and girls. Some talk about not feeling in control

Dan, 14 years old, used be a talkative and chatty youngster, but as his voice began to break he admitted that he made a conscious effort to talk less as he was never sure what sound would come out. He found the uncertainty frustrating and was often embarrassed, especially if his classmates laughed at him.

of their own bodies, their voices may not always sound the same, spots and blemishes can appear without warning and often at the most inconvenient time.

It is important to help young people develop healthy and hygienic personal care routines as their bodies develop and change.

Hopefully they will already have a good understanding of their personal care needs as they will have been taught from an early age when to wash their hands for example. Boys especially may find that they sweat more and may need to be encouraged to change their tops and socks, especially after physical activities. Girls need to be aware of safe and hygienic ways of disposing of tampons and sanitary towels during their periods. Healthy eating and a balanced diet are very important and young people need to have information to enable them to make sensible and appropriate choices about what they eat and drink.

Young people need physical exercise; teachers often report that around this age some young people become reluctant to participate, whilst on the other hand some become very skilled and competent. Reasons for being unwilling to participate vary enormously, some may feel embarrassed about they have to wear, or think that the activity is childish or below their skill level, some may feel clumsy and uncoordinated and so be self-conscious. Many young people respond positively to circuit training or fitness routines that they develop independently and so have an element of control.

Children in school are assessed from an early age and hopefully by the time they get to 14 years or so tests may be less stressful. However it is at this time that young people are being to start to think about their futures, make choices which could have an impact on their later career choice and sit important examinations. It also around this time that some young people 'drop put' of school'. Truanting, bullying and inappropriate behaviour in classes increases. For some these avoidance behaviours are ways of coping, or not, with the added pressures that they may face. Some may adopt attitudes that at the best can be described as unco-operative and unhelpful, but this does not mean that the adults around them should not try to be supportive. Adults should be non-judgemental and be prepared to listen to the young person's views and opinions. Adults should be aware of the difficulties and pressures that young people may face, such as peer pressure or bullying.

This is a time when for young people being with friends is more important than being with their family. Many parents find this difficult and it can become a contentious issue. Some young people who do not have a group of friends may feel that they are missing out, are different from everyone else and as a result may become stressed and anxious. This can be difficult for adults to deal with as we can not make friends for our children and young

'Adults need to be supportive and help the young people to develop self-confidence. Offer unconditional praise and encouragement, provide opportunities to develop independence and take control.'

people. Adults need to be supportive and help the young people to develop self-confidence. Offer unconditional praise and encouragement, provide opportunities to develop independence and take control.

Some young people who are not part of a group, or have friends may be targets for bullies. They will be seen as easy targets and they may appear vulnerable and different. Bullying in all forms will have a huge impact on the young person's self – esteem. Sometimes the victim will be very reluctant to disclose the fact that they are being bullied as they think that it will make the problem worse. It is important that young people have the information where they can seek help in confidence. Telephone support services, such as Childline, can be invaluable and many school have counsellors are specially trained staff who will help the young person. Bullying should never be treated lightly, it is serious issue and if not dealt with can have very serious consequences. There have been cases reported in the press of young people committing suicide as a result of bullying. Every child and young person has the right to be safe and protected.

Young people are exploring their own identity, attitudes and opinions. They may develop different tastes in clothes, music and activities to their parents and this again can sometimes cause conflict and disputes with their parents and carers.

Adults need to take opportunities to discuss boundaries with the young people and listen to and respect their views. Taking an unbending stance will not be productive and will only lead to further conflict. Young people need to believe that their views and opinions will be respected and considered and not dismissed out of hand.

Sheila Riddall-Leech, educational consultant and trainer.

Aislee, aged 15 years only wore black clothes, with heavy black boots; she dyed her hair black and wore black make-up. Her parents found this unacceptable and there were frequent heated discussions about Aislee's appearance. Things came to a head when the family was invited to a wedding and Aislee refused to wear anything but black. Eventually mother and daughter went shopping and both agreed to compromise, Aislee wore black clothes but not the boots at the wedding and her mother commented that she thought Aislee looked good.

Chapter 5

CCLD 304, Reflect on and develop practice

About this unit

Working with children and young people is challenging, demanding and a rewarding career. It is a skilled job that requires a love of children and a good understanding of the issues that can affect their lives. You need to be able to change and adapt to the many demands on you, often at very short notice. Being reflective means that you make time to think about your work and how you can change or improve what you do in order to meet the needs of the children.

The term 'reflective practitioner' is relatively new to the childcare profession and it can be quite daunting to some people. Being reflective is a learning process as it helps you to increase your understanding and learning skills. It will mean that you can recognise your strengths, yet at the same time understand and accept that you have weaknesses, or things that you could do better. It also means that you do not 'stand still'; you are open-minded and willing to learn. Your setting might, for example, have been given an outstanding grade by OfSTED (or CSIW in Wales), but that does not mean that you can sit back and become complacent, with the attitude, 'I must be doing everything right otherwise I wouldn't have got this grade'. Life is one long learning process and we all have something to learn and improve upon. This is why it is important that you continue your professional development and take advantage of the training opportunities in your area. Being reflective should result in you offering better provision to the children in your care and their families.

In order to think about what we do and why we do it, we need time. Time is often in short supply for many childcare practitioners, but if you are to take this aspect of your work seriously, you will need to find time to think about and evaluate what you are doing and why.

This unit will help you to understand reflective practice. Have another look at Chapter 2, page 12 [Note to typesetter: you will need to check the page number please] which has several reflective style questions that you may find helpful. Although this is a 'stand alone' unit, you have been encouraged to reflect on your practice throughout all the other units. It has been suggested that you write reflective accounts on a wide variety of topics as evidence of your understanding, and many of these pieces can be cross-referenced to this unit.

This unit has two elements of competence and you must have evidence for both elements in your portfolio. These elements are:

- CCLD 304.1 Reflect on and develop practice
- CCLD 304.2 Take part in continuing professional development

Each one of the elements will be discussed in turn, together with suggested ways to collect and record your evidence.

CCLD 304.1 Reflect on practice

Getting started

A good starting point for this unit would be to do a SWOT analysis. This means looking at your Strengths, Weaknesses, Opportunities and Threats. There are many formats that you could use, and the one example suggested here may not work for you, so you might need to adjust it.

The first thing to think about is your strengths. Some people find this difficult; they might feel a bit boastful writing down that they are well organised or are very creative. If this is how you feel, start by thinking about and listing your achievements, both personally and professionally, over the last year. For example:

- You may have had a new baby in your family, who is content and progressing well. This is an achievement.
- You may have started a new job and coped well with the added demands and responsibilities or the extra travel time that it entails. This is an achievement.
- You may have met a new partner and made a commitment to each other. This is an achievement.
- You may have completed NVQ 2 or another training course. This is an achievement.
- Your setting may have had a good OfSTED report. This is an achievement.

From your list of achievements you should be able to list your strengths, the things that you know or think that you do well. Then move on to your weaknesses. These are things in your life that could be improved, for example your time management, both at work and at home, or maybe you think that your communication skills are not that great and could be improved. You might be able to use a computer to write some of your work.

Opportunities are those things that you think will benefit you, so could include a new training manual being issued by your local authority, giving you the chance to get involved in new training. In the same way, joining a childminding network or local support group could be an opportunity to met new people, share expertise and also gain new ideas.

The last stage is to look at the threats that may be apparent in your working life. For example, are the numbers of children attending your setting falling because they are perhaps going to the after-school club which is based at their school, rather than coming to you? Are colleagues becoming more qualified than you, increasing the likelihood of their getting promotion? Has a new setting opened very close to yours?

Although there is no set number of points that you need to have under each heading, it is good practice to have a minimum of two and probably no more than four. Any more would be unachievable.

You will notice that the example SWOT analysis has a column headed up 'action plan'. Under this heading you think about and write what you are going to do about each point that you have made.

My SWOT analysis and action plan

Any actions that you decide upon should be considered as targets, things to aim for. With this in mind, any target that you set should be:

- **Specific** – Be precise. If you have highlighted communication skills as a weakness, state exactly what aspect of communication skills you want to improve. Is it talking to people, writing reports, spelling and grammar?
- **Measurable** – Can your target be measured? For example, if your strength is that you have no vacancies in your setting, your target could be to establish a waiting list; this is measurable as you either do or you don't.
- **Achievable** – Are your targets possible and feasible? For example, if you see going on training courses as an opportunity, is it possible to be out of your setting one weekday every week for the next three months?
- **Realistic** – You may have decided that your record keeping is a weakness, so you decide that your action is to get it organised in the next two weeks. Ask yourself whether this is realistic and achievable.
- **Have a Time frame** – Any target should have a time frame so that you can measure and achieve it realistically.

These points are often referred to as **'SMART'**.

This element has six PCs and you must provide evidence for all of them. In this unit you are aiming to show that you:
- monitor processes, practices and outcomes from your own work.
- evaluate your own performance (achievements, strengths and weaknesses) using best practice benchmarks.
- reflect on your interactions with others.
- share your reflections with others and use their feedback to improve your own evaluation.
- use reflection to solve problems.
- use reflection to improve practice.

Key Issues

Working with children and young people is a huge responsibility and you owe it to them to do absolutely the best you can. This means that you should reflect on what you are doing all the time. You should use your reflections and conclusions to develop and extend your practice. Not only will you benefit from greater job

STRENGTHS	ACTION (include timescale)
• • •	• • •
WEAKNESSES (or area for development)	**ACTION** (include timescale)
• • •	• • •
OPPORTUNITIES	**ACTION** (include timescale)
• • •	• • •
THREATS	**ACTION** (include timescale)
• • •	• • •

satisfaction by doing this, but you will also find that the children and their families will benefit as the service and provision that you offer will be better (CCLD 304.1.1).

As mentioned before, working with children and young people is a dynamic profession, so what is considered good practice can evolve and develop over time. You should evaluate and assess your own practice against current best practice benchmarks. These are standards which are widely agreed as providing the most up-to-date and advanced thinking and practice. Best practice benchmarks are not minimum standards which you have to achieve in your work. These benchmarks can arise from statutory or new regulatory measures or can be based on new research or other requirements. You can use these to measure and assess what you are doing (CCLD 304.1.2).

Unit 301 has elements which relate to how you communicate. You will find that you will be able to cross-reference some of this evidence to help you reflect on your interactions with others; this includes children, their families, your colleagues and other professionals with whom you may come into contact. Interactions are also about making sure that what you say is actually what you do; this may seem very simplistic and obvious, but it is surprising how many people say one thing and then do something else (CCLD304.1.3).

Whatever setting you work in, it is important that you think about and reflect upon your work with colleagues. Even if you are working in your own home, or the child's home, you will still meet other professionals like yourself, for example at childminder 'drop-in' sessions, or nanny 'get-togethers'. As well as being social experiences, such meetings can help you think about how you interact with others, the impact those interactions have on others and the service that you offer (CCLD 304.1.4).

It is also important to talk to parents and get their honest feedback, opinions and views on the service that you or your setting offers. You can do this in various ways such as:
- devising a questionnaire
- during a parents' evening or interview
- face to face conversations
- home/setting diaries
- sharing observations
- social events which include parents

You will probably find that some of the evidence that you gathered for Unit 301.4, Communicate with Adults, can be cross-referenced for this element.

Problem solving is a skill which we can all develop and learn. Skilled problem solvers know that it can take time and thought, in other words you have to be reflective. It also involves being proactive and making things work in ways that will benefit everyone, including the children.

No-one works in isolation, we are all working with others in some way. If you want to change and develop what you do, you will need to consult others, including the children and young people with whom you work. It is true that being reflective and asking the views and opinions of others can sometimes be difficult for you to deal with. You might get some feedback that you would rather not have had and that might challenge you. You might find this undermines your confidence. If this is the case, you may find it helpful to discuss your feelings with a trusted work colleague, friend or your assessor (CCLD 304.1.6).

Suggested activities and experiences
- Carry out a SWOT analysis and subsequent action plan.
- Plan an activity or experience that you have already carried out with the children or young people, one that you know has been successful. Then draw up a list of questions that you could use to reflect on why this activity is successful. Some suggested questions to start you off are listed below:
  - Were most of the children interested in this activity?
  - Why do think this was?
  - How much involvement did you have in this activity?

'I usually go to the local childminder 'drop-in' session each week and take two of the children that I care for with me. One childminder never speaks to anyone when she arrives; she comes in and gets a coffee, leaving the children to play, and no other childminders really bothered with her. I realised that I thought of her as being a bit stand-offish and so left her alone. When I really thought about it, she wasn't stand-offish at all, she was shy; so the next time I spoke to her first and we got chatting; others came and joined us and we ended up having a really good discussion about faddy eaters. I suppose if I hadn't had been reflective I wouldn't have got to know the other childminder or learnt quite a bit about feeding issues. I wrote this up as a reflective account for my portfolio.'

NVQ candidate

- What was the nature of your involvement?
- What did the children learn from the activity?
- How do you know what they learned?
- How could you extend this learning?
- How might you adapt this activity for a different group of children, or different stage of development?
- Did you have sufficient resources?
- Find out if there are any support groups, such as 'drop-in' sessions, in your area.
- Make time to share some of your reflections with others and get their feedback and opinions.
- When you have responded to children's behaviour that may have cause for concern, reflect on how you reacted to the child and to those around at the time. Think about how you felt and ask yourself whether you are meeting this child's needs. You might find it helpful to make a log or note of the following things:
  - How often you had positive interactions with this child, before and after the behavioural incident?
  - What was the child doing before the behavioural incident?

- What happened immediately afterwards?
- Is the child more likely to show unwanted behaviour in certain situations?
- Are you aware of certain activities that the child prefers to others?
- Are you aware of how the child responds to other children and adults? Does he appear to have references?
- Are you meeting this child's needs?

- After an activity has taken place, ask the children or young people involved to give you feedback. Ask them about what they enjoyed the most, what they least enjoyed and why. Ask them to think about how things could be changed and why the changes would be beneficial.

Types of evidence

It may not be practical for your assessor to observe you being reflective, but he could observe you being involved in reflective discussions with colleagues and children or young people (Key letter A). All such discussions should be recorded and noted in some form and then you can use the content to develop reflective accounts (Key letter F). This unit may also provide good opportunities for witness testimonies (Key letter C) from your colleagues and parents as you seek feedback on your practice. This element also lends itself well to case studies (Key letter E). For example, you could write a case study about a behavioural issue and how reflective practice enabled the situation or incident to be positively managed.

CCLD 304.2 Take part in continuing professional development

Getting started

The childcare profession is very dynamic; it is changing and responding to legislation and government initiatives, not to mention children's individual needs. It is for these reasons that you cannot afford to be complacent. The way in which we work with and care for children has changed over the years. There is now a curriculum to follow. Assessment and record keeping are part and parcel of the job. Plans are well-developed to provide wrap-around care, for example before- and after-school clubs, holiday clubs, and this means that those who work in the profession must be ready to develop and adapt. In order to do this effectively and provide the best possible care at all times, it is important that you are reflective about what you do and how you do it. You should be prepared to be open-minded and willing to accept changes.

This element has four performance criteria and you must have evidence for all of them in your portfolio. You must show that you can:

- identify areas in your knowledge, understanding and skills where you could develop further.
- develop and negotiate a plan to increase your knowledge, skills and understanding further.
- seek out and access opportunities for continuing professional development as part of this plan.
- use continuing professional development to improve your practice.

Key Issues

As mentioned before, this is a dynamic profession and therefore we have a professional responsibility to keep up-to-date in both our knowledge and skills. The development of these skills is your responsibility, so you do need to be very aware of your own strengths, weaknesses and consequent areas for development. A common way of doing this across many professions is to draw up a personal development plan. However, such a plan should not be just another piece of evidence for your portfolio; it should be meaningful and realistic. Once you have put together this plan and followed the suggested pattern, you will find that you should have evidence for all the performance criteria of CCLD 304.2.

A personal development plan requires time, thought and effort and involves six processes:

- Reflecting on your skills, experience, strengths and weaknesses.
- You may have already done this as part of the SWOT analysis suggested earlier in this chapter. In addition to the SWOT analysis, you should try to rate your skills. This will make it very clear to you which skills need further development. Many people use a rating of 1 to 5, with 1 being low, therefore needing development, and 5 being high (CCLD 304.2.1).
- Using the ratings that you have given your skills, decide which ones need further development. Remember that not all your skills are job-specific. Some skills, such as using a computer, are transferable to other professions, but maybe if you were to develop this skill it would make your job, such as recording observations, writing reflective accounts, easier and quicker (CCLD 304.2.1).
- Draw up a plan with sensible and realistic timescales. Remember SMART as mentioned earlier (CCLD 304.2.2). A suggested sample plan is given over the page.
- It is important that you discuss your plan with other people who will be affected by it. These could be other members of your family, as the training that you plan may impact on your childcare arrangements, or other people with whom you work. As a result of these discussions you may have to revise your plan or timescales (CCLD 304.2.2).
- This stage is actually putting your plan into action. If you have taken time to find out what training opportunities are available to you, this should not be a long or involved part of the process (CCLD 304.2.3).
- The final part of the personal development plan is reviewing what you have achieved and the impact this has had on your practice and on others. You will also need to think about any changes in circumstances. For example, you may not have any vacancies in your setting; someone may have left and so created a job opportunity for you. A review should be undertaken at frequent intervals to make sure that your plan is a meaningful document and not just another bit of paper. Most people review their plan at least every six months (CCLD 304.2.4).

Suggested activities and experiences
- Draw up a personal development plan following the process outlined above. Think about what you would like to be doing professionally in three or five years' time. This may help you to rate your skills if you are finding this difficult.
- Find out if there are any other settings or people in your area with similar areas for development. See if you can talk to or visit

Skill	Rating	Why?	How to achieve it	When will I achieve it?	Progress and update
Planning, assessment and record keeping	1	This was an area for development following our OFSTED inspection	Go on a training course arranged by local authority. Talk to other colleagues and see how they do it	By the end of this term	

them to discuss their work and how they are going to address their areas for development.

Types of evidence

Make sure you keep all certificates of attendance that you are given if you attend a training event. If the trainer does not provide a certificate, then politely ask if you can have one for your portfolio. These certificates could provide the basis for further reflective accounts on the training event and your assessor may be able to use the evidence to prove prior learning (Key letters F and J). Such evidence could lead to professional discussions (Key letter G) about the training content, what you have learned from it and how that knowledge can be used effectively in your setting.

Your personal development plan should be written in a clear legible style or computer-generated. Remember, in this instance it will need to be read by other people. Your personal development plan could provide the starting point for oral and written questions (Key letter B) and professional discussions (Key letter G).

Key words and concepts relating to CCLD 304

best practice benchmarks - these are standards that are widely agreed and accepted as providing the most advanced, up-to-date thinking and practice against which you can measure and assess what you are doing in your work. Benchmarks are not minimum standards and can be regulatory, statutory or based on other research or requirements

continuing professional development - refers to ongoing training which you can become involved in so that you can improve and update your practice and skills

monitor - to check, keep an eye on

personal development plan - a working document that sets out your skills, strengths and weaknesses, areas for development and ways to implement your ideas; it usually has six steps for you to follow

perspective - a different view or outlook from your own

reflective practice - the process of thinking about and critically analysing your actions with the aim of changing or improving your work

SWOT analysis - a detailed consideration of your strengths, weaknesses, opportunities and threats

Suggested further reading and useful addresses

Tassoni, P. et al (2005) Children's Care, Learning and Development, Heinemann.

www.cache.org.uk

www.cityandguilds.org.uk

www.edexcel.org.uk

www.openuniversity.co.uk/education

Your local authority's continuing professional development guide

Early years practitioners have always been encouraged to think about and try to improve on what they do. But now that Ofsted has introduced an element of self-evaluation into its inspection process, it's more important than ever to be a reflective practitioner

What makes a reflective practitioner?

Do you talk regularly with your colleagues, highlighting what went well that day and what needs changing? Do you identify with the practitioner who said 'The more I learn the less I think I know'? Do you worry that what you do is not good enough? If you answered yes to these questions you are probably a reflective practitioner.

On the other hand, if you say things like 'Tell me whether I'm doing it right' or 'What does Ofsted want us to do?' or 'Ofsted gave us no key issues, so we're fine' you are a dependent practitioner.

What is a reflective practitioner?

In a nutshell, reflective practitioners think deeply about their practice. They:

- Observe and listen carefully to children and adults.

- Raise questions (particularly 'why' questions) about their practice, alone and with colleagues.

- Analyse their practice and consider how things could be done differently.

- Welcome new ideas, but proceed with change cautiously.

- Identify strengths, but also recognise there will always be aspects of practice which need to be developed.

- Are not afraid to be self-critical – in fact they are often their own worst critics!

- Are never complacent about their practice.

Reflective practitioners will have little to fear from the new Ofsted framework, which places great emphasis on self-evaluation.

Why do you need to be reflective?

Over the past ten years, there have been many nationally imposed changes which have influenced early years work, as well as a wealth of new research evidence, which has clear implications for practice. The profession needs practitioners who are capable of reflecting and acting on the implications of these initiatives.

The needs of children and families are also changing (for example, more working parents needing full daycare for their children) and settings may need to adapt their approach accordingly. In the 21st century, there is no place for practitioners who are not willing to be, and who are not capable of being, reflective.

What do you need to reflect on?

There are four main topics which provide a focus for reflective practitioners. These are:

- **Families using the setting**

Each group of children you teach is similar to, but also different from, the last. They will respond differently to the environment, experiences and adults in your setting. You need to keep your practice under review to make sure needs, interests and learning styles are being catered for.

What is working well with the current group may not address the needs of the next group. For example, an increase in the number of boys one year encouraged one team to strengthen their outdoor curriculum to provide

the more active approach to learning that some boys need.

Similarly, one nursery started admitting more children who were not yet three years old, following changes to the local authority admissions policy. The team observed that the children used resources differently – they carried them to all corners of the nursery – and realised that they had too much equipment available. They decided to reduce the amount of choice temporarily and reintroduce equipment when the children were more used to tidying up.

Family structures and lifestyles also impact on settings. Some children may experience their carers' relationship breakdown and key workers may need to plan to provide more emotional support for them. You may need to organise flexible care patterns to meet the needs of working parents.

In full daycare settings, the challenge of planning to meet the needs of children who attend every day, alongside the needs of children who attend for a few sessions each week, should not be underestimated. You need to reflect on your observations of each child's

'In the 21st century, there is no place for practitioners who are not willing to be, and who are not capable of being, reflective.'

interests and needs when planning your weekly and daily programme.

■ National requirements and practice guidelines

There have been a number of helpful but challenging Government initiatives. In England the *Curriculum Guidance for the Foundation Stage* was introduced in 2000 and became statutory in 2002 for all practitioners working with children from three to the end of the Reception year.

You need to use the first 25 pages as an evaluative tool to check that your practice is consistent with this statutory guidance.

The common features of good practice set out in the bullet points on pages 12-16 of the folder should be used to highlight existing strengths and areas for development.

Similarly, the bullet points on pages 20-24, which show what effective learning involves and what effective teaching requires, should be used to address the question 'Is this what learning and teaching look like in our setting?'

Reception teachers need to consider the implications for their practice of the statutory Foundation Stage Profile, which has to be completed at the end of the Reception year.

In the future, Ofsted will require settings to evaluate their own practice against the framework provided by *Every Child Matters* (see www.everychildmatters.gov.uk), so teams need to begin reflecting on how their existing practice achieves the aims of this initiative.

■ Recent research evidence

It is the responsibility of team leaders to keep up to date with the growing body of research evidence relevant to young children and share the key messages with their teams.

The Department for Education and Skills (DfES) has funded two Effective Pedagogy projects, which researched the features of effective Foundation Stage settings and practitioners, and the Effective Provision of Pre-school Education (EPPE) project, which has tracked children over time to discover the effects of different types of pre-school provision on later behaviour and achievement.

The main findings from both of these projects can be downloaded from the DfES website (www.dfes.gov.uk) and should provide food for thought. For example, it was found that in excellent settings there tends to be an equal balance between child-initiated and adult-led experiences, and that, within these child-initiated experiences, intellectual challenge was greater when adults supported and extended learning. This has implications for the way practitioners manage their time – too often they spend too much time directing activities.

■ Team functioning

Effective practice relies on a team which functions professionally and efficiently. Teams rely on having inspiring leaders, but every team member has a role to play. One practitioner who is complacent or negative can have a damaging effect on other team members who are enthusiastic and wish to move forward. It is therefore essential to keep the functioning of your whole team under review. Key questions to address include:

■ Do you have a shared philosophy and vision for your practice?

■ Have you developed professional, supportive relationships with each other?

■ Are all members clear about their role and responsibilities within the team?

■ Are you able to cope positively with change and development?

■ Do you have a plan which sets out clearly both long- and short-term aims for practice development?

Individual team members need to ask themselves whether they are a positive, enthusiastic influence or a negative, energy-sapping colleague.

Reflective practitioners are self and setting aware and consequently take control of their own practice. This is empowering. They do not fear the views of others because they know their own strengths and weaknesses and have plans for addressing the latter. They are outward looking and thrive on new challenges. Above all, they enjoy and are committed to their work. Young children and their families deserve nothing less.

Margaret Edgington, early years consultant and author.

Research

Researching Effective Pedagogy in the Early Years (REPEY): Project led by Professor Iram Siraj-Blatchford. The REPEY team made observations in early years settings identified as having good practice from the Effective Provision of Pre-School Education (EPPE) project.

The EPPE project is the first major European longitudinal study of a national sample of young children's development between the ages of three and seven. EPPE has shown the beneficial effects of high quality pre-school provision on children's intellectual and social/behavioural development.

The Study of Pedagogical Effectiveness in Early Learning (SPEEL) project was designed to investigate Foundation Stage practitioners' perceptions and understanding of effective pedagogy with a view to producing a framework that could be used alongside the Curriculum Guidance.

Details can be found on the DfES website at: www.dfes.gov.uk/research

Did you know that funding is now available to help childcarers pay for training? The Government is investing £250 million in the Transformation Fund for the period from April 2006 until August 2008 - and you could be entitled to a share of this. Here's how to apply

The Transformation Fund: a guide

Whether you're managing a chain of nurseries or working on your own as a childminder, you need to invest in training if you're to deliver a high quality service and remain competitive. But how do you pay for it and still balance the books?

The Transformation Fund aims to make it easier for you to recruit and retain people with the right qualifications without risking affordability for parents or the sustainability of your business.

The Government is investing £250 million in the Transformation Fund over the next two years.

By 2015, they want every full day care setting to employ an Early Years Professional (EYP) trained to graduate level in a relevant qualification. And they want a much higher proportion of professionals in childcare to be qualified to Level 3 (A level equivalent).

They are also providing more funding for training to help staff working with vulnerable children – particularly those with disabilities or special educational needs.

Who is it for?

The Transformation Fund is for anyone who provides professional childcare. How much funding you get will vary, depending on what your training and qualifications needs are.

If you are a nursery in the private or voluntary sector offering full day care, a registered childminder or offer sessional day care for under-fives you can get help towards the costs of:

■ Training for relevant Level 3 (A level equivalent) or higher qualifications – including training towards the Early Years Foundation Degree or to support the new Early Years Foundation Stage from 2008.

■ Training to improve skills working with disabled children and those with special educational needs.

From September 2006, if you run a nursery

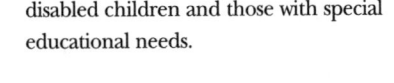

in the private or voluntary sector offering full day care, you can also apply for reimbursement if you've invested money for a new or existing staff member to achieve Early Years Professional status (in other words an Early Years Professional who has a degree-level qualification relevant to early years, a range of early years experience and has gained the recognised status which is being introduced this year).

Nursery schools, children's centres and other settings in the maintained sector are not eligible. This is because one of the main aims of the Transformation Fund is to bring the private, voluntary and independent sectors up to the same recognised skill levels (in terms of quality of the workforce) as the maintained sector.

But there will be support for anyone who works in the maintained sector who wants to train to get EYP status.

If you're a private or voluntary provider that has a partnership with a children's centre or other maintained provider, you're still eligible as long as you haven't received other public money that already covers workforce development, such as from the general Sure Start Grant.

How much is available?

If you already employ a graduate with a degree relevant to working with children you can also apply for a Quality Premium of £5,000 a year (more in London) to spend mainly on additional professional development of any of your staff - or for other quality improvements such as bringing in a nutrition consultant to advise on meals or helping parents support their children's learning and development.

Money for Level 3-5 training:

■ is for any private or voluntary early years setting and for any childminder who looks after children under the age of five.

■ is available for training for full Level 3 (A level equivalent) qualifications or above, including training towards the Early Years Foundation degree.

Money for SEN and disability training:

■ is available for training to support working with children with disabilities or special educational needs, regardless of whether you're working to a particular qualification or not.

The £5,000 Quality Premium:

■ is for any early years settings in the private, voluntary or independent sector that employs a graduate in the role of professional leader.

■ can be spent on additional professional development for all staff that work in that setting.

■ can be spent on bringing in other expertise and enrichment activities – such as a nutrition consultant or activity to get parents involved in their children's learning.

The £3,000 recruitment incentive:

■ is for any early years settings in the private, voluntary or independent sector that employs a graduate professional leader for the first time.

■ is intended to support the additional cost of employing a new graduate, so could be used as a recruitment or retention bonus, or to increase their salary.

If you're taking on a graduate to fill the new role of EYP, you can apply to your local authority for the Quality Premium and a recruitment incentive of £3,000 a year (more in London) towards your extra recruitment and employment costs.

Are there any conditions?

There are no conditions attached to any money you claim for Level 3 to Level 5 training or for training to work with children with special educational needs or disabilities.

But there are conditions attached to both the Quality Premium and the recruitment incentive.

■ The Transformation Fund is available between now and 2008. In that time, a nursery can claim only one Quality Premium and one recruitment incentive per setting.

■ To be eligible, you must offer group based care for more than four hours a day, with a minimum of 20 registered places. You must also have a 'satisfactory' or better Ofsted rating.

If you have not been inspected yet you can still apply. But if a local authority has concerns that you might not be rated as satisfactory or better by Ofsted, they may hold off until after the Ofsted assessment before considering your application. Similarly, if after you've received payments from the Transformation Fund you are then rated by Ofsted as unsatisfactory, the local authority may choose to stop your payments.

■ If you charge parents fees of more than £175 (£205 in London) per week (a full week being 30 hours childcare) you will not be eligible.

■ You must be able to provide evidence that staff attracting the Quality Premium meet the criteria for graduate level qualifications. And the member of staff you appoint as graduate professional leader must gain EYP status within two years of receiving the Quality Premium or the recruitment incentive.

■ You must agree to monitor and provide data on how the Quality Premium and the recruitment incentive have been

• • • • • • • • • • • • • • • •
Further information
For guidance on the Transformation Fund, go to www.everychildmatters.gov.uk/ earlyyearsworkforce

To find our more about qualifications, go to the Children's Workforce Development Council (CWDC) website: www.cwdcouncil. org.uk

To find out more about the Government's plans for the children's workforce, go to www.everychildmatters.gov.uk
• • • • • • • • • • • • • • • •

used if asked.

What are you expected to spend the money on?

The Quality Premium and recruitment incentive is payable to your setting, not the individual that makes you eligible for it. But it is intended to support the additional cost of employing a new graduate.

It's up to you to decide exactly how you use the incentive. The only condition attached is that the majority of it should be used to fund staff professional development, particularly in preparation for the Early Years Foundation Stage, supported by local authority early years advisers. This can be for any of your staff not just the graduate professional leader.

If the EYP status accredited graduate you employ then leaves, you won't have to pay back the Quality Premium. But you will have to recruit a graduate who is able to attain EYP status to replace the one that's left. How long you have to find a replacement will be at your local authority's discretion.

How to apply

Your local authority will be able to give you details of how to apply. The best place to start is by contacting your local authority early years adviser.

What's the deadline?

There's no deadline as such, but as local authorities are currently planning their allocations, you should contact them as soon as possible.

Information supplied by the DfES

Reflective practice - looking carefully at what you do and why you do it - can help you improve the way you deliver services to children and families. The new quality assurance (QA) schemes are designed to encourage childcare providers and early years practitioners to be reflective

Words you need to know:
Quality assurance

The development of high quality childcare and early education services is one of the key elements of the Government's Sure Start agenda. Research has shown that effective quality assurance (QA) schemes can improve the quality of childcare and education. QA schemes support practitioners through mentoring and advice.

In March 2002, the Department for Education and Skills (DfES) consulted with childcare providers, local authorities, quality assurance schemes and professional organisations.

There were two clear messages. Firstly, parents wanted more information about the quality of provision on offer and secondly, childcare providers recognised effective quality assurance as a way of enabling them to raise standards.

Endorsed schemes

It was decided that the Investors in Children (IiC) initiative would be used to endorse QA schemes by assessment against ten rigorous criteria (see box). There are more than 60

'Parents can see that a provider who has taken part in an Investors in Children endorsed quality assurance scheme has shown that they take the quality of the care they provide seriously and that they are working towards providing the best possible service they can.'

A good quality assurance scheme encourages providers to do three things:

- Look critically at the quality of their service for themselves;

- Compare their practices with what is known about best practice;

- Get further training to make sure they are delivering best practice.

QA schemes and these were all given the opportunity to apply for endorsement. During June 2003, a panel of six independent experts met to assess the first tranche of applications. Results were announced in November 2003, and 25 QA schemes were accredited.

Another panel sat in February 2004 and a further 25 schemes were endorsed in July 2004, bringing the total number to 50. A further panel is planned for 2005. A full list of endorsed schemes with contact details can be found at: http://www.surestart.gov.uk/ensuringquality/investorsinchildren/endorsedqualityassuranceschemes/

High standards

There is no obligation for a provider to seek accreditation from a quality assurance scheme. All childcare and early years education providers are required to meet national standards that have been determined by the Department for Education and Skills and are inspected by Ofsted. However, taking part in a quality assurance scheme builds on these standards and indicates to parents that the provider is striving to deliver high standards and good quality services.

Providers apply for accreditation from their chosen quality assurance scheme. Some local authorities (LA) have their own scheme and

will support providers with accreditation, often in terms of finance or training, only for their chosen scheme. Others support several schemes but in different ways. It is important that providers contact their own LA with enquiries about the levels of support and funding available.

QA schemes vary in terms of cost, evidence required, support and completion times. It is highly unlikely that a provider will receive accreditation from any scheme in less than six months, and some schemes can take up to three years to complete. The Sure Start Unit suggests that

Investors in Children criteria

The DfES has ten criteria which schemes have to meet. QA schemes wishing to be part of the Investors in Children initiative should:

- Be based on research evidence
- Build on the national standards
- Include materials for peer observations of adult-child interactions and support self-reflective practice
- Address management practices
- Develop guidelines for accreditation readiness
- Be consistent with the principles of equal opportunity and anti-discriminatory practice
- Have consistent procedures for re-accreditation
- Ensure providers have access to adequate mentoring and support
- Include arrangements for external validation and appeals
- Review paper-based assessment of accreditation criteria

From: www.surestart.gov.uk

between one and two years is the average time for completion. Once a provider is granted accreditation, it will often be for three years. Some schemes offer spot checks in the third year and an extension of accreditation. Others require providers to produce additional, up-to-date evidence at the end of the first accreditation period to extend accreditation. All endorsed QA schemes must have clear, consistent procedures for re-accreditation.

There are a number of different types of endorsed QA schemes. Some are aimed at specific parts of the childcare sector. For example, the Montessori Education QA scheme only provides accreditation for settings 'offering a high standard of education that embraces the Montessori method in theory and practice'. Others cater for all types of provision. For example, the Sheffield Kitemark has been developed to meet the needs of providers in early years group settings, childminders and those working in after-school clubs. The scheme clearly indicates which evidence applies to which sorts of providers.

Strength in diversity

One of the strengths of the endorsed QA schemes is its diversity. It means that providers can choose a scheme which best meets their own needs. But there are also key elements which run through the schemes. All comply with the criteria set by the DfES, which ensure effectiveness. The schemes include self-assessment, which includes the development of a portfolio of evidence. This may include: photos; policies and procedures; parental contracts; questionnaires; reports; staff rotas, staff meeting minutes and other documentary evidence of good practice.

All schemes require staff in group settings to put time aside, preferably on a weekly basis, so that all staff are involved in the process.

Providers are assigned a mentor who supports them in understanding the process and developing the portfolio and also makes independent assessments which will include observation. This is to ensure that practitioners are doing what they say they are, and that the practice reflects the theory! In some QA schemes the mentor's role includes assessment, others involve a separate assessor.

QA schemes also involve external verification. The verifier's role is to check the evidence and make further observations, if necessary, to confirm the mentor's assessments. Although roles in individual schemes may vary, all QA schemes are clear about the roles of their own mentors, assessors and verifiers and provide training at all levels. All endorsed QA schemes include arrangements for external validation and have agreed appeals procedures.

Supporting reflective practice

One essential element of QA schemes is the use of peer observations of adult-child interactions to support self-reflective practice. This means that practitioners working together plan time in which they observe each other at work. These observations lead to feedback and shared discussions which identify elements of good practice and help practitioners to reflect on the quality of the service they provide. QA schemes provide materials and training which support staff through this process. This is one aspect which some practitioners find difficult at first, but often later see as an essential and useful element of the self-evaluation process.

QA schemes are generally modular, which allows providers to focus on specific aspects of practice at different times. The number of modules vary in name, quantity and content, but generally cover:

■ Developing high quality provision, indoors and outdoors;
■ Management practices;
■ Staff development and training;
■ Teamwork and managing change;
■ Welcoming and developing relationships with parents and carers;
■ Meeting diverse needs within an inclusive environment.

Parents can see that a provider who has taken part in an Investors in Children endorsed quality assurance scheme has shown that they take the quality of the care they provide seriously and that they are working towards providing the best possible service they can. This means that parents can make a more informed choice when deciding where to entrust their child's care and early education.

Judith Stevens, early years adviser, Lewisham Education.

Investors in Children

Investors in Children is a programme designed to help parents find the best childcare. It gives a mark of endorsement to quality assurance schemes that accredit individual childcare providers.

Quality assurance schemes must meet a set of rigorous criteria and be recommended for endorsement by an independent panel of experts in quality assurance and early years and childcare. Endorsement lasts for three years.

A childcare provider accredited to an Investors in Children endorsed quality assurance scheme can display a badge indicating its status. Parents and carers who see this badge can be confident that the setting is committed to providing a high quality service to their child.

http://www.surestart.gov.uk/ ensuringquality/investorsinchildren

Ofsted has introduced a self-evaluation form which all childcare providers must fill in as part of the inspection process. But the idea of self-evaluation can be daunting, especially if you work alone. Miranda Walker explains what it involves

Self-evaluation: what it means and how to do it

The terms 'self-evaluation' and 'reflective practitioner' are the language of quality assurance (QA) schemes which set the benchmark standards within the sector. Ofsted has introduced an element of self-evaluation into the inspection process and the new NVQ 3 in Children's Care, Learning and Development dedicates a unit to reflecting on and developing practice.

So the process looks set to become not just part of providing high quality provision, but part of not falling below the minimum standards.

Making time to think

Reflecting (or thinking back) on what you do as an individual practitioner, how you do it and what you achieve, helps you to see how well you are working. Reflection requires adequate non-contact time – you cannot analyse your practice at the same time as working with children.

It is helpful to consider one element of your practice at a time. This enables you to focus on the detail, something you may not have done before. You should reflect on all elements of your practice over time, but you might choose the order in response to external factors, such as:

■ **Feedback** – received either informally (by way of a comment perhaps) or formally (in an assessment or an appraisal).

■ **Naturally occurring events** – when you have done something for the first time, or when you think you have performed particularly well or badly.

■ **Training** – it often makes sense to reflect on an area you are studying.

Organisational self-evaluation is slightly different. This refers to the process whereby a setting considers its current practice, policies and procedures against a set of selected standards. These could be Ofsted's minimum standards or a QA scheme's benchmark standards of quality.

However, practitioners are part of an organisation and their own reflections will impact on, and inform, the overall practice of a setting. Therefore, areas for organisational self-evaluation, as well as individual reflection, may both be selected for these reasons:

■ **Quality assurance** – QA schemes may guide practitioners through areas of reflection in turn.

■ **New regulations** – changes to regulations may make examining particular practices a priority.

■ **Organisational reviews** – existing fixed dates for reviews of a setting's policies and procedures. It's important to consider how well an individual's practice promotes the setting's policies – self-evaluation sometimes reveals that we do not always do as we, or our policies, say we do.

How to analyse

Once you've chosen a subject, the next step is to decide how to analyse how well you or the setting works in this area.

There are a number of methods, known as techniques of reflective analysis. It is usual to use an appropriate combination. Various experts and QA schemes have different names for these techniques, but when you

The benefits
The process of reflection and self-evaluation benefits practitioners and settings by providing opportunities to:

■ Think about what you actually do

■ Consider how and why you do things

■ Identify the impact of your actions

■ Identify your strengths and weaknesses

■ Consider alternatives to existing practice

■ Identify gaps in existing knowledge and skills

■ Plan improvement

■ Actively improve

■ Monitor progress

get down to the nuts and bolts of each, they tend to be similar.

Essentially, you should think carefully about your existing practice in the chosen area. You should then begin to evaluate how successful your current approach is, by thinking about the impact that it has. You might identify particular strengths, weaknesses, advantages and disadvantages. Then consider the subject from new angles, considering new approaches or strategies, thinking about the impact that they may have.

The draft National Occupational Standards of the new NVQ 3 in Children's Care, Learning and Development contain a unit called 'Reflect on and develop practice'. Here the techniques of reflective analysis are identified as:

Help from the professional organisations

Techniques of reflective analysis are new to many practitioners, and it can be difficult to strike a balance between being too critical and not being critical enough.

■ Michael Freeston, Training and QA Director of the Pre-School Learning Alliance says, 'Although self-evaluation is a key element of the increasing professionalism that the Government wishes to see introduced into the sector, it shouldn't be thought of as an innate skill that everyone automatically has. The Alliance is offering training, support and continual professional development for staff, so that they're in a position to actually undertake this activity successfully.' The PLA also offers the Aiming for Quality accreditation scheme.

■ Maggie Walker, of 4Children, says 'Our scheme, Aiming High, is based on self-evaluation techniques, which out-of-school services use to improve their practice. It enables practitioners to reflect on how they are delivering services and providing good quality care for both parents and children.' She anticipates that the scheme, '…will work well with Ofsted's new proposals for self-evaluation'.

■ Lesley Cann, National Childminding Association Development Manager, understands that childminders working alone may find self-evaluation daunting, but says, 'The NCMA offers plenty of support and assistance'. Reflective practice is embedded in its Quality First scheme, and Lesley echoes the words of the portfolio when she tells childminders, 'Quality assurance through self-assessment is part of a dynamic and developing process, not just a one-off assessment, so it is certainly worth embracing'.

■ The National Day Nurseries Association's scheme, Quality Counts, guides settings through a process of self-evaluation. It provides helpful formative questions prompting reflection. A dedicated QA support line is available.

Alternative schemes are also available – contact your local Early Years Development Childcare Partnership for details.

■ Keeping an open mind;

■ Viewing from different perspectives;

■ Thinking about consequences;

■ Testing ideas through comparing and contrasting;

■ Asking 'What if?';

■ Synthesising ideas (In other words, taking your own ideas and blending them with other people's in a cohesive way. Ideas could come from many sources, including books, articles or colleagues.)

■ Seeking, identifying and resolving problems.

Looking to the future

The whole point of reflective practice and self-evaluation is development, so once the process of analysis is complete, it is important to weigh up your thoughts, draw conclusions and decide how to act upon them. This provides the way forward, and without this step, practice is unlikely to improve.

You may decide to try a different approach, for instance evaluating its impact at a later date. Alternatively, you may realise that you would benefit from learning new information or skills, and decide to look for external guidance or further training. (A training or development need may be identified over a period of time as a pattern or theme emerges.) The action to be taken may be influenced by a particular target that you or your setting is aiming towards, perhaps one related to a programme of study or a personal goal, or a clear standard expressed in a QA scheme.

Keeping track

Reflection and self-evaluation should be thought of as an ongoing process, central to continual professional and organisational development. Records of reflection should be kept because:

■ Writing notes helps you to crystallise your thoughts and keep track of them.

'The whole point of reflective practice and self-evaluation is development, so once the process of analysis is complete, it is important to weigh up your thoughts, draw conclusions and decide how to act upon them.'

■ Reading notes enables you to easily pick up where you left off.

■ A deeper insight into a situation can sometimes be gained when you come back to your written thoughts later, often with a different perspective.

■ You can notice patterns emerging in your conclusions, which could be informative.

■ Written reflections can be shared with colleagues, assessors, tutors and inspectors.

■ Over time a record of progress is built.

Some practitioners design their own reflection forms, while others prefer to use a notebook as their reflective journal. It's important to date entries, recording the subject of reflection, initial thoughts about existing practice, notes on analysis (including which techniques are used), conclusions drawn and a plan of action.

A time to review progress should be set, and updates recorded. Some QA schemes provide their own forms and check-lists for these purposes.

Miranda Walker is an early years and playwork writer, trainer and speaker. She owns her own daycare settings in Devon.

Helen Renouf outlines some ways you can work with other providers in the community to give your children the best possible care.

Working in partnership

All childcare settings need to be pro-active in selling their services – but not just to parents and potential service users, they need to create relationships and awareness with other provision in their local area to create a seamless care and education environment for children, and this involves working in partnership with other settings in the local community.

From a business point of view, it is about sustainability – your business will continue to thrive and grow if other professionals are aware of your services, the hours you operate, the age range you cater for, the facilities you offer and how to contact you. If they have a family whose childcare needs are specific and you offer that service they will be able to refer families to you and even perhaps recommend you.

Your local school

Are the local schools aware of your services? Have you been into school and introduced yourself to the school staff, asked them to advertise your services on their parent notice board and told them about the hours you are available? Part of their remit is to create links with the local community – so you can help them do this by getting more involved.

As a childminder with Foundation age children, you could ask to go into school and watch any Easter productions they are holding (perhaps a dress rehearsal), or maybe they are having a theatre production, or a puppet show – perhaps you could watch that too? You are then preparing the children in your care for

school, making the school more aware of your services, and establishing a professional link.

If the school is part of a cluster group with pre-school and nursery staff meeting regularly, ask if you can come along and share information too, or have a copy of the minutes, so that you are informed about local issues.

Local pre-schools and nurseries

A childminder may be collecting children to and from pre-school or day nurseries, again get involved – do you know something that will enhance this term's topic, can you share a skill with them? Making these settings aware may mean that they recommend you to a family who want to return to work, have younger children, or who want someone to take care of their children in the holidays. It may also mean that they become aware of your knowledge and talk to you about your experience in certain situations. It is good practice to share information about children you both care for – and good practice should start with you!

A full-time nursery needs to be able to give parents informed support when children leave to start school – working parents worry about wrap-around care, school holidays and occasional days. If a professional and pro-active relationship has already been established with an after-school facility or a childminder, the parents can feel much more confident about their child moving on.

Childminders

Join or start a local group for childminders – together you have a bigger voice in the community, you can share resources, exchange ideas, refer vacancies, access services together and make the wider community more aware of you. A group of childminders could be on hand to meet new parents prior to starting school to tell them about childcare provision in the local area, or attend a community event and hand out leaflets. They can also celebrate their achievements and their fundraising events through press-cuttings in the local paper.

After school care

By working with other settings in the community you can build up stronger links with the schools you serve and therefore can plan to open to cover occasional days for parents. You can introduce yourself to potential customers by sharing activities with the rising reception children in pre-school and nursery settings and you can have knowledge about what other services are available for the families, and what experiences the children may have had so far.

A family who regularly struggles to collect on time or a child who falls asleep daily after school may be more suited to a childminding setting – yet at time a ten-year-old finding it difficult being around pre-schoolers may find an after school care setting more suitable. It is about knowing what is best for the children and being professional about supporting children the best way we can, and you can only do this with knowledge of other professionals in your local area.

Health visitors and doctors

Health visitors and doctors are the first point of call for advice regarding children. They make recommendations to parents about where they will be getting their foundation stage education as the child develops, inform parents about deadlines regarding applying to school and have numerous patients on their books – but are they aware of your services?

There are numerous ways to involve them, perhaps by asking them to provide a training session for a group of childminders or your staff, inviting them along to visit when you do a relevant topic or simply introducing yourself if you are taking a baby along to baby clinic.

Inclusive services

I attended a Special Needs support group recently as a childminder and several parents were surprised to discover that childminders could and would look after children with specific needs. The parents told me that once their child was diagnosed they were directed to certain services for support, but hadn't considered what the main stream could offer.

It is important to create links with all sections of community, if you can't accommodate everyone, you can plan to accommodate joint events, work together to share ideas and offer some integrated play opportunities. Alternatively others may have the specialist knowledge that you need to access to ensure each child has the best possible care.

The library

The library allows all registered childcare settings to take out a reasonable number of books to share with the children, but they also provide unbiased information to parents. Parents can access information about what is on in the local community, access the children's information service via computers and the library offers specific sessions for children.

Invite the library along to your setting or childminding group to share some stories – so they can see first-hand what you offer and the children can discover more about the library. By talking to the staff you can perhaps agree to share your expertise and skills by putting up a display that shows children's art work. Not only does it brighten up the library on an overcast Spring Day, but it brings joy to the community, makes the children feel good and increases awareness of your setting.

Children's centres

With the Government planning 3,500 children's centres by 2010 – one in every community – it is no good sitting back and worrying about how the children's centre is going to include your services. It is about getting involved in the foundations of your local children's centre and working with them to ensure that you are involved and that your services are an integral part of what the centre offers.

It is about making time now to be involved, asking the team to change meeting times so you can make it and ensuring that your interests are represented. If you would like your children's centre to be aware that there is already after school provision for 60 children, but the demand is only for 50% of that, or you want to see more evening training for childcare provisions that your staff can attend together, or as a childminder you would like to meet regularly with other minders in the community – you need to say.

Settings around each children's centres are essential in sharing existing community information, they know what is needed locally, and who the local contacts are. If you sit back and wait to be included, you may be forgotten about and your ideas remain just ideas, whereas coming forward as a professional with expertise in a wide range of areas, you will be consulted, respected and shape the future of young people in your community.

National organisations

National organisations such as National Day Nursery Association (NDNA), Pre-school Learning Alliance (PLA), and the National Childminding Association (NCMA) not only represent your field's interests nationally but can often be involved in changes much closer to home. The early education childcare unit in your county will be consulting with representatives across the childcare industry and they in turn give the views of the local members. Unless you have got involved, met with other professionals from your sector and exchanged ideas, then they are unaware of the changes you would like to see happen.

It does take time to volunteer and it takes courage to stand up for what you feel passionate about, but with enough passion and enough enthusiasm you can make changes on a local and national level. Your views do count.

The same goal

For some professionals it is easy to meet others, to share expertise and ideas but others feel they are very isolated, either because of where they are situated, the hours their work involves or their other commitments. but if you do begin to talk and share ideas with another setting you will perhaps be amazed to discover that all childcare professionals are working towards the same goal.

We all want the best for the children in our care, we want to be recognised and valued for the job that we do, we want access to training, we want to know about local issues as well as national ones, we want respect and understanding about our particular service and we want to be consulted about changes that may affect us.

Get out there and introduce yourself and share some of your good practice, you may even find that people become envious of the job you do.

Helen Renouf
Advanced Diploma in Childcare and Education (ADCE)

Building regular reviews and self-evaluation into your everyday practice is essential if you are to keep up with the demands of inspection and improve your provision, says Lin Marsh

The value of self-appraisal

Self-appraisal is a process of review, reflection and evaluation through which you become aware of the strengths and weaknesses in your provision, your skills and abilities and your goals for the future. It is a way of assessing, prioritising and planning improvements in your practice and your provision.

It may seem like yet another thing you are being encouraged to do, which you think will include a lot of time and paperwork, when you feel you are already stretched to the limit. But it does not have to be like that. With a little bit of careful planning and thought, and by identifying the areas you need to concentrate on, it will help you to achieve better practice in the long run.

'By getting into the habit of regularly appraising your own practice, you will find that action planning becomes easier, improvement is evident and preparation for subsequent inspections or assessments is less stressful and more effective.'

How can it help?

Self-appraisal has many benefits and it is important to see it as part of the development of your practice and your provision. By assessing and reviewing your practice regularly, and that of your team if you have one, you can emphasise the strengths you identify and begin to work on any weaknesses you find. This, coupled with the strengths and weaknesses identified during any Ofsted inspection or independent accreditation assessment, will enable you to continually strive for and achieve improvement.

When you need to write an action plan following an inspection or accreditation assessment, you will get an even better picture if you are already used to looking at your own practice and provision regularly and can have some constructive and evidence based input. Being able to look back at self-appraisal notes and review them alongside your action plan will also help you to understand the process of continually evaluating the quality of your provision whatever type it may be.

Self-appraisal can inform your action plan by helping you decide how you will set targets for improvement and providing you with a time scale of actions against which you can plot your progress. If you review your progress frequently, this will act as a reminder as well as an evaluation of how far you have got with your actions and how much progress you are making in implementing them.

By getting into the habit of regularly appraising your own practice, you will find that action planning becomes easier, improvement is evident and preparation for subsequent inspections or assessments is less stressful and more effective.

If you are working on your own as a childminder, then self-appraisal is particularly important because you will not always have the advantage of regular discussions with colleagues and peers.

Strengths and weaknesses

Self-appraisal is a never-ending process during which your awareness is raised. It helps you keep track of the skills and practice you, and others around you, are developing. Think about the following points and ask yourself (and any staff you may be working with):

- What are your (or your provision's) greatest strengths? What do you do well as an individual or as a team? What makes your setting a good place in which children can develop and learn? Do you have evidence from parents and other carers, or inspection or accreditation, that your practice and provision is good?
- What are your weaknesses and what are you doing about them? It is sometimes difficult to admit to having weaknesses but, if you are honest with yourself, then think about anything that could be done in a more focused, different or changed way for the better. Look for indications in inspection or accreditation reports. What about feedback from parents and carers, and from the children in your care?
- How do you feel about teamwork (where appropriate)? If you are in some sort of group provision such as a nursery, school or pre-school, this might mean thinking about the people you work with on a day-to-day or occasional basis. Relationships are built up over time with people you work with on a daily basis but you may need to consider the role you play when you team up with people you have

never met before - on a short-term project, perhaps. If you work on your own you might see your partnership with parents or other carers as teamwork you want to consider and explore.

■ How will you know you are making improvements? You need to gather evidence of improvement so think about how you will identify the sort of evidence you need to show that things are actually improving. What might that evidence look like? What will you measure these improvements against?

If you are looking at self-appraisal linked to some sort of inspection or accreditation scheme, the previous report will highlight the strengths and weaknesses of your provision but you might think of a few more to do with the general day-to-day running of things as you implement your action plan and review your practice.

If you work with other people, does your practice reflect genuine teamwork? Does your team influence a much bigger team such as it might in schools or large nurseries? Does every member of your team have an equal opportunity to discuss practice, skills and staff development, for example? Some people are forthcoming about what they think their particular weaknesses are but may be modest and hold back on identifying their strengths. Others may be clearer about their strengths but not want to admit to having any weaknesses. You can help them to appraise their own practice within the team, as well as individually, by raising their confidence so that they feel they are a valued and an integrated member of the team.

Nobody likes criticism so it is important for you to have constructive discussions about what is done well and what needs to be improved. Staff are not always given enough praise for the things they do well. Some people focus on what went wrong in a situation rather than what went right. Everyone needs encouragement in their role so that they understand how important it is to keep up good practice,

and work on getting the things that need to be improved right, given time and appropriate support. By assessing and reviewing practice regularly, you will see if improvements are being made and whether these improvements are making a difference to the quality of the provision.

Self-appraisal helps you learn how to articulate your achievements and goals. When you get used to regular self-appraisal, you will become more aware of why you are doing what you are doing. This, in turn, should give you the confidence to be able to talk freely to an inspector, adviser, parent or other interested party, about your provision. You are more likely to appear knowledgeable, committed, positive and assertive.

The purposes of self-appraisal

Self-appraisal helps you to judge whether you can meet and maintain the conditions, set out by the DfES and monitored by Ofsted, to receive the nursery education grant. It also helps you to review and reflect on your practice and assess any need for change or development.

You will always need to consider whether your educational provision for three- and four-year-olds is appropriate in promoting children's learning towards the Early Learning Goals. Inspection is one process that helps you set and maintain standards. Other ways may include assessment and approval under an independent accreditation scheme where self-appraisal, which includes reflection, review and evaluation of your practice, can play a big part.

In schools, self-appraisal is often an integral part of support and professional development for staff, and is usually linked to supervision and annual staff appraisal. As with nursery education, school inspections focus, in particular, on management, curriculum, the quality of teaching and learning, and children's progress. Reports set out where the standards are met and identify where

'When you get used to doing regular self-appraisal, you will become more aware of why you are doing what you are doing.'

they are not. Action plans support development but only where targets are realistic, appropriate and relevant. Action plans are living documents that should be reviewed and worked on regularly, in accordance with the school's policy, and linked to self-appraisal. If you work in a school environment then you play a significant part in the provision within your department and within the whole school. Looking at your own practice and how that influences the provision you work in is important in that context.

In day care self-appraisal is encouraged to support practice and help people develop a realistic approach to inspection or accreditation.

Your role as manager

If you are involved in running some form of group provision, it is important to review your role as a manager. Look at your staffing levels and opportunities for staff development and training, where and when appropriate. Look at the management of the provision, the quality assurance procedures and any other relevant practice. Revisit your policies for special educational needs, anti-bias/anti-discriminatory practice, premises and equipment, children's welfare and your partnership with parents and carers. Make sure they are up to date and relevant. Then you are ready to look at your part in supporting children's development and learning.

Lin Marsh has considerable experience as an Ofsted registered nursery education inspector, and is a freelance early years trainer, assessor and consultant.

Self-appraisal is necessary to make sure that improvement is a continuous process, not just a quick burst of energy after inspection to address your action plan. Identifying good practice and noting areas for improvement will help you improve quality in the long term

How to carry out self-appraisal

Whether you are writing your very first action plan, working through one linked to inspection or accreditation, perhaps, or simply want to make sure that your practice and provision is the best you can make it, taking the decision to start self-appraisal is an important one.

If you work on your own then only you will know when is the best time to start. If you work as part of a team then talk about it with your colleagues. It will help you to understand the things you do well and the things that need some improvement, making your provision a better place in which children can learn and develop to their best potential.

Getting started

Whether you work alone or with a team, make sure you have a copy of the main areas to deal with ready and the template (provided later) on which to make your notes. Set yourself some time away from any distractions - maybe on a day off (if you can make time) or when you are not working with the children. You need to give yourself, and your team where necessary, enough time to think through the process first before you start.

To help make the whole task easier, here is some more detail on the main areas you need to be aware of and keep brief notes on.

Your aims and objectives

What do you aim to achieve in your provision to enable you to support children's learning and development appropriately? What are your plans to make sure those aims are met? Are they realistic and achievable? Ask yourself who is involved in the arrangements of setting aims and objectives. Who has overall responsibility for making sure those aims are met?

The way you involve parents and carers in supporting and taking an active role in your provision is also important, and a particular area for regular review.

Activities and learning opportunities for children

Early years providers plan their programme of activities in many different ways. You may be the only person who does all the planning or you may use a team approach. How you plan and what particular guidance you use to help you will depend on the age and stage of the children you work with.

You may choose to use one or a combination of curriculum guidance if, for example, you offer care and education and have under-threes and/or over-fives in your provision,

'It will help you to understand the things you do well and the things that need improvement, making your provision a better place in which children can learn and develop to their best potential.'

as well as three- and four-year-olds, receiving nursery education grants. In other words, you may use the Early Learning Goals, Desirable Outcomes (Wales), Scottish Curriculum Framework for Children Three

to Five (Scotland), Curricular Guidance for Pre-School Education (Northern Ireland), Birth to Three Matters, or choose to use an approach specific to organisations such as High/Scope, Montessori, Steiner or Portage.

How well activities promote learning

You should already be evaluating the programme of activities and learning opportunities for children regularly to see if it is appropriate and meets each child's individual learning needs. Reviewing, or appraising, this evaluation is essential to make sure that the programme of activities works well, is effective and that any difficulties or gaps are addressed.

Look at the records of progress and attainment for the children. They will

'You must be frank and honest with yourself about your practice and its impact on your provision. Take on board what inspectors, assessors, parents and children have to say.'

give you some insight into the quality of your educational programme and whether it is challenging yet flexible enough to meet the needs of every child and support their progress.

The knowledge and expertise of people working with young children

For anyone to work effectively with young children in early years provision, they need to be knowledgeable, preferably well trained, experienced and have regular opportunities to update their professional development. The quality of teaching (anything you do with the children to support their learning experiences and development) and learning (this means the children's learning) within any provision is of paramount importance. If the quality of teaching is not of a good standard then children's learning will suffer. If you find, or the inspector or an assessor finds, the teaching or learning in your provision to be less than good, you may need to review your procedures for recruitment, induction, supervision and support for staff.

Policies, procedures, welfare and accommodation

A regular review of all policies and procedures is important to ensure that you safeguard the welfare of the children and promote good practice. Anti-discriminatory and anti-bias practice is

essential, but how do you make sure that it happens? Looking at your indoor and outdoor accommodation, for example, and resources, will help to highlight any areas needing change or development.

Have you had difficulty in providing enough opportunities and space for children to practise and develop some of their physical skills? Are there enough opportunities for them to explore their local environment and learn about the natural world and the community in which they live? These are just a couple of questions that you need to look at regularly and address so that you can explain to an inspector, assessor or other interested body, such as a parent or carer, exactly what you do to support children's learning in these areas.

Partnership with parents

Parents have a unique knowledge of their children – they know them best. You need to respect that and make sure that you invite parents and carers to work alongside you in supporting the learning and development of their children. That need not mean that parents have to come in and help on a day-to-day basis. They can help in other ways behind the scenes if they prefer.

Make sure that during self-appraisal of the quality of your partnership with parents and carers, you take this into account. Ask yourself how you involve parents in their children's learning.

- What do you tell them about your provision before their children enrol?
- How do you give them information about the curriculum and the attainment and progress of their children?
- How do you ensure such information reaches parents and carers who might have difficulty understanding the language you use, or are physically unable to visit the provision for some reason?
- Are you receptive to information that parents and carers want to give you about their children's learning outside of your provision?

Making self-appraisal notes

It is important to keep some notes about self-appraisal so that you can refer to them and incorporate them, where appropriate, into your action plan (if you are formulating and working with one). These notes do not need to be long or too detailed. Simply keep a note of what you are reviewing, what you discover (strengths and weaknesses) and steps you will take to improve practice. Like an action plan, it is useful to give yourself a realistic timescale for achievement.

If you are doing self-appraisal for yourself, you will keep your own notes up to date and accessible to you. If you are doing self-appraisal as a team then either you need to elect someone to take the notes or, if you manage the provision yourself on a daily basis, then you can be the note-taker if everyone else agrees. Either way, everyone in the team should have sight of the notes and agree that they are a true record of what was discussed and what actions were agreed

Self-appraisal notes should not be locked away, but be accessible so that they can be amended and reviewed as necessary, and as improvements are made. It might be a good idea to keep them alongside action plans if you have them, as they are interlinked. How long you keep self-appraisal notes will depend on the nature of improvements you identified and the timescale you gave yourself to complete them.

You will need to keep your self-appraisal notes handy until the next inspection, assessment or staff appraisal (where appropriate). You may find the template provided overleaf useful as a guide.

How often should you be doing self-appraisal?

Once you start self-appraisal it is generally a good thing to review things after about six months to begin with. If you have identified specific dates for achieving particular targets before then, by all means, review the process and do another self-appraisal earlier than that. Every type of early years provision is different.

Schools, nursery schools and most pre-schools work to the academic year and may wish to appraise their practice on a termly or annual basis, depending on their usual programme of supervision and staff appraisal.

On the other hand, provision that runs all year round may wish to introduce quarterly or biannual (six monthly) opportunities for self-appraisal. When provision is offered on an occasional basis, self-appraisal may be introduced after each group of sessions, but before the next sessions begin. This gives everyone a chance to work on improving practice where necessary, and for activities to be observed and assessed during the subsequent sessions.

If you are working to a formal action plan following inspection or accreditation, then self-appraisal needs to tie in with continuous improvement. Your first self-appraisal should be completed before your very first inspection or accreditation assessment. For those of you who have already had several inspections or accreditation assessments, you need to weave in the self-appraisal regularly as you work through and review your action plans. Like an action plan, amend your self-appraisal notes as necessary when you complete improvements.

Being objective

You must be frank and honest with yourself, and your team if you have one, about your practice and its impact on your provision. Take on board what inspectors, assessors, parents and children have to say. Think of it as constructive feedback that can help you to identify improvements you should make.

Inspection outcomes are important, too, because the strengths as well as the improvements necessary are clearly stated in the inspection report. You should include both the strengths and the weaknesses in your self-appraisal.

Timescales for improvements

Depending on what improvements you need to make, try to be realistic. Can you achieve what you set out to do within six months? Will it take a whole school term before you can see any improvements in the classroom? Whatever targets you set for yourself or your team need to be achievable.

Think about the availability of local training opportunities and resources if you are going to need them. Give yourself enough time to make improvements but review how you are getting on during that time. All improvements will have an impact on the quality of the provision for children so although you need to get them right, you do not want to take too long doing them.

Reflection, review and evaluation of your practice and provision – that's self-appraisal. It is a necessary and worthwhile process to support your practice, strengthen the quality of your provision, and enhance the learning opportunities and experiences for the children in your care.

Lin Marsh has considerable experience as an Ofsted registered nursery education inspector, and is a freelance early years trainer, assessor and consultant.

'Like an action plan, amend your self-appraisal notes as necessary when you complete improvements.'

Use this chart to keep a note of what you discover and the steps you will take to improve practice. Keep it up to date and accessible.

Self-appraisal notes

Area of provision	Strengths	Weaknesses	What I need to do to improve	Time scale	Link to action plan (if any)
Aims and objectives					
Programme of activities					
How well activities promote children's learning					
Knowledge and expertise of staff					
Policies and procedures					
Children's welfare and accommodation					
Partnership with parents and carers					

Some people say that attitude is as important as ability, others that attitude is even more important. One thing is for sure, it is attitude that, in a whole range of different contexts, can make a crucial difference between success and failure. Ros Bayley explains

Creating a 'can do' culture

It was Henry Ford who said, 'Whether you think you can, or whether you think you can't – you're absolutely right!' Pause for a moment and think of all the people you know who have achieved things against all the odds. Even when people told them they could never do it, they did. So, if this attitude is so important, how can you help children to develop a 'can do' attitude, and why is it so important?

A fast changing world

The world is changing at an ever-accelerating pace and life is getting faster, more complex and more uncertain. If children are to cope with these demands, they will need to be able to learn quickly and think creatively, and a 'can do' attitude is going to be more important than it's ever been. But what are the essential characteristics of a 'can do' attitude?

Taking risks and making mistakes

To be able to take a risk and cope with things going wrong is fundamental to a 'can do' attitude, and this is not easy in a world that has become so 'right answer orientated'. However, if you are to cultivate a 'can do' approach you must be prepared to dare to get things wrong! You must also have the resilience to keep going when things don't turn out the way you want them to.

'People with a 'can do' attitude believe in themselves and know that they can achieve results.'

Whether you can do this or not depends entirely on how you regard failure. For a person with a 'can do' attitude there is no such thing as failure – there is simply an outcome or a result, and if that outcome or result is not the one they want, they learn from their mistake and do something different until they get a different outcome. If that outcome is not the one they want they do something different again to get another outcome, and they keep doing this until they get the outcome they want.

Good communication skills

The ability to get on with other people and communicate effectively is an essential element of a 'can do' attitude. When things go wrong and there are problems to be sorted and conflicts to be resolved, good communication is at a premium as it enables you to negotiate your way through all manner of difficulties. Without these skills you can flounder, so good assertive communication is an absolute must.

Self-belief

People with a 'can do' attitude believe in themselves and know that they can achieve results. This does not mean that they are arrogant and conceited or that they do not doubt themselves some of the time. What they do know is that if they keep going they can get there in the end. They have passion, purpose and strategies for achieving results, and as an early years practitioner, if you want children to have a 'can do' attitude, you need to make sure that you cultivate these qualities in yourself!

Let's take each of these essential elements and look at how they may be cultivated in your setting.

Risk and resilience

It is only through taking well-calculated risks that you develop resilience, and unless children spend their time with over protective adults who fill them with fear, they are naturally good at risk taking.

You need to trust children's natural instincts. Generally speaking, they know their limitations and rarely go beyond them. Think back to your own childhood and you will soon realise that you only climbed as high as you felt comfortable with and, having run into a patch of stinging nettles once, you soon learned to solve the problem!

In play, particularly outside, children need to be allowed to carry out their own risk assessments, and as long as you have done the same, you should be able to let them, confident in the knowledge that you have taken 'reasonable care' to ensure their safety.

> Anyone in any doubt about how to plan so that children can take risks in an appropriate environment should consult Jennie Lindon's excellent book *Too Safe For Their Own Good.*

It's only natural that you want to protect children from hurt and disappointment, but unless they experience these things they will never become resilient. Your role should be one of support – of helping them to cope when things fail to work out for them. When the model collapses or the game doesn't work out, you should be there to acknowledge their feelings and encourage them to find new ways in which to try again, because when they finally do succeed they will realise how capable they are and their self-esteem will benefit enormously.

Teaching assertive communication

Children often find themselves in conflict situations, and these provide a wonderful context in which they can develop 'can do' attitudes. When children fall out over friends, space or resources, this is an excellent opportunity for teaching conflict resolution skills, and when children know they have strategies for resolving conflicts, they feel powerful indeed. However, they will never learn these skills if adults constantly solve their problems for them. Instead you need to model the process by:

- Acknowledging the feelings of all parties involved in the conflict;

- Gathering information about what has taken place;

- Reflecting the information back for clarification;

- Encouraging children to generate possible solutions;

- Supporting both/all parties to choose a solution together;

- Offering follow-up support.

Once you have taken children through this process a few times they soon begin to use it for themselves and, in so doing, acquire a really important life skill.

> For anyone wanting to know more about supporting children to resolve conflicts there is an excellent video published by High/Scope 020 8676 0220.

Nurturing self-belief

Self-belief comes from the knowledge that we are personally powerful. In other words, we feel that we have the ability to 'take action'.

If children are to develop this belief they need to have experiences in which they can practise thinking for themselves and acting independently, and this has implications for the way you organise your setting and structure our daily routines. For example, how much responsibility do children have for getting things out and putting things away again? Have you organised your setting, both inside and out, so that there is a place for everything and everything is in its place?

Unless you have, it is difficult for children to take responsibility for their own resources. Only by being given responsibility will children learn to be responsible, and only by acting independently will children become independent.

Do you have a consistent daily routine that enables children to make sense of time and plan their time effectively, and do you encourage them to think ahead to the consequences of their plans and reflect back on what they have achieved?

What about the way in which you feedback to children; the way you offer encouragement and praise? Have you thought carefully enough about how you can do this in ways that promote a 'can do' attitude?

We are often told that children need lots of praise and, of course, they do, but you should be careful that they do not become so dependent on your praise that they only believe they have done well if you tell them that they have. So instead of being evaluative ('Good boy, that was brilliant!') try being descriptive ('Look at that painting you've just done. I can see red, yellow and blue circles and lots of black dots!') Then ask the child if they like their painting. If they say they do, you can then agree with them and add your praise. The important thing here is that you have allowed the child to make up their own mind about what they think and allowed them to make their own judgement.

Skills for life

Supporting children to develop a 'can do' attitude requires time, thought and attention but it is well worth it, as attitudes acquired in the early years are inclined to endure for life.

Gaining a 'can do' attitude is important for all children, and especially for children who may be judged to be 'at risk' in some way. In the United Kingdom we still have one in three children living on or below the poverty line and, for them, the ability to solve problems, high self-esteem and autonomy and good communication skills are real protective factors against the circumstances in which they find themselves.

Ros Bayley, early years consultant and trainer, Walsall.

'It's only natural that you want to protect children from hurt and disappointment, but unless they experience these things they will never become resilient.'

Chapter 6

CCLD 305, Protect and promote children's rights

About this unit

This unit is about protecting and promoting the rights of children. This is a fundamental part of your work and you must be very aware and have deep understanding of how these rights impact and influence practice. All children have the right to have a voice and be protected. You must be aware of the individual needs of all children and their families with whom you work and of the ways in which you can meet those needs. You must also be fully aware of how to protect and safeguard children from all forms of abuse and know what procedures you should follow if you suspect that a child is need of protection.

Much of the legislation covering children's rights originates from the United Nations Convention on the Rights of the Child (UNCRC), which is an international treaty developed at the end of the 1980s and ratified by the UK in 1991. This means that British governments are committed to ensuring that policy, practice and laws are in agreement with the convention. The convention itself is not statutory, but laws that stem from it are.

This unit has three elements of competence and you must have evidence for all of them in your portfolio. These elements are:

- CCLD 305.1 Support equality of access
- CCLD 305.2 Implement strategies, policies, procedures and practice for inclusion
- CCLD 305.3 Maintain and follow policies and procedures for protecting and safe guarding children

Each element will be discussed in turn, together with suggested ways to collect and record your evidence.

CCLD 305.1
Support equality of access

Getting started
There is a huge amount of legislation relating to equal opportunities and diversity that impacts upon children and young people, and you should try to be familiar with most of it. Your setting should have a policy for equality of access, but it may not be called exactly that. Regardless of what it is called, it should support diversity, equality and children's rights.

This element is about how you can support equality of access in your setting. This means that you should be a positive role model at all times, challenge discrimination and stereotypical attitudes. To do this effectively you will need to be assertive but calm, communicate well but do not patronise. Also, of course, be reflective about what you say and do. Look again at Unit 304 Reflect on and develop practice.

In the resource section of this chapter there is an article on promoting children's rights. You might find this helps you to understand how children's rights are built into good practice.

This element has seven PCs and you must provide evidence for all of them. In this unit you are aiming to show that you:

- provide information for children, families and communities that promotes participation and equality of access.
- implement transparent procedures and information about access to provision to meet the needs of all children.
- welcome children from all backgrounds, ensuring that barriers to participation are identified and removed.
- seek and respect the views and preferences of children, adapting your practice to the child's age, needs and abilities.
- involve all relevant local community groups in the setting or service and provide information on local community resources.
- find appropriate ways to provide information about equality of access to children and families who have found services hard to access.
- provide information to children about their rights and responsibilities in the context of your setting.

Key Issues
There are many factors which can hinder participation and equality of access, such as poverty or geographical location. This can however give a rather simplistic impression of what can be a complex issue. Giving someone a leaflet or putting up a display on equality of access may be effective for some, but not for others, so you may have to be inventive and resourceful to meet element CCLD 305.1.1. You may find it helpful to talk to other NVQ candidates and your assessor about how other people have provided evidence. The evidence that you provide, other than direct observation, will very much depend on the community in which you are working. How you present the information to families and children will vary on the type of community. One of the biggest problems facing many childcare practitioners is how to reach children and families who find services difficult to access. It is almost a 'Catch 22' situation, because if they are difficult to reach they do not access the services, so we may not know about them. Again you will need to be inventive, not just rely on translations

of leaflets or similar actions, if you are to find appropriate ways to provide information (CCLD 305.1.6).

We all recognize that it is good practice to have policies that clearly state what staff should do in certain situations. But that is not necessarily enough. The implementation of these policies, in other words how they are carried out, must be clear, understandable to all involved, including children, apparent and observable. It is simple to state in a policy that all children will have equal access to all activities, while in practice girls are not allowed to play football (CCLD 305.1.2).

In Unit 301 element 1 we discussed developing relationships with children in ways that make them feel welcomed and valued. Look again at both the section in Chapter 2 and the evidence that you have used to support this PC; you may find that some of it can be cross-referenced to this element.

Barriers to participation can vary enormously across communities and areas; what may be a barrier for one family, such as childcare costs, may not be a barrier to another family who actually want flexible childcare and for whom cost is not such an issue. You will need to take a very objective look at your area and think about what barriers are evident (CCLD 305.1.3).

Article 12 of the UNCRC gives children the right to express their views and have those views taken into account, in keeping with their age and stage of development. This means that you should listen to children, take into account their opinions, consider their feelings and ideas and help them have a say in decisions that affect them (CCLD 305.1.4).

Most communities have a range of services offered to support children and their families. This can vary depending on the nature of the community, but usually focuses on education, health and social care. SureStart programmes are nationwide and you should make sure that you are familiar with the provision in your area, so that you support and inform families and children (CCLD 305.1.5).

Having rights as adults and children brings responsibilities. Part of your responsibilities with children is to help them become aware of their rights and also how they must show consideration and respect for the rights of others. This will have to take into consideration the age and stage of development of the children, and may affect how you organise and plan activities and experiences, whether these are group or individual actions (CCLD 305.1.7).

Suggested activities and experiences
- Look at your setting's policies for equality, diversity and children's rights. Ask yourself whether they really meet all children's needs and those of their families in your community. If the answer is no, what can you do about it?
- What are the barriers to participation in your area and community? Ask yourself:
- What can be done to improve the situation? (Remember SMART from the last chapter and make sure that your answer is achievable and realistic.)
- What could be the first thing you and those you work with could do?
- Find out what sources of information there are for children and families in your area and how accessible this information is.

'One child rarely joined in messy play activities and when she did, she seemed to be almost fearful. During a small group circle time we talked about getting 'messy' and 'dirty' hands. This child again did not join in until a trusted adult asked her what she thought. The child said that she didn't like the feel of messy things on her hands and didn't like these activities. As she was four years three months old, she couldn't really explain what it was she didn't actually like. We have now taken her views into account and respect the fact that she does not want to participate in these activities.'

NVQ candidate

- Begin an information file or box for parents of resources and materials about services that are available in your community. Make sure that you include contact details. You might also want to think about a separate section or even another file for voluntary organisations and charities
- Undertake a survey of your setting and make notes checking whether:
- all areas are accessible, taking into consideration health and safety requirements.
- if some areas are inaccessible to certain children or adults why is this?
- this be dealt with so that some children or adults are not disadvantaged?
- all resources and equipment are accessible to all children
- all activities and experiences are available to all children?
- During circle time or during a discussion session, make sure that you actively listen to what children are saying. Ask open-ended questions, such as 'How do you feel about…?', 'What can we do about…?' to encourage greater involvement.
- Organise open childcare sessions, advertised in as many different locations and ways that you can, to reach as many families as possible. These could be themed, such as 'healthy eating', 'information on immunisations', 'come and have a coffee or other beverage' or 'bring a friend'.

Types of evidence

Legislation covering children's rights, laws covering equality and inclusion, and the UN Convention on the Rights of the Child (knowledge specifications K3P233 and K3P234) may not be especially easy for your assessor to observe, so you might find it easier to **write an assignment** on how your setting ensures that it meets current legislation **(Key letter E)**.

Write an assessment plan that includes either a circle time or discussion session, depending on the age of the children, which your assessor can **observe (Key letter A)**. Provide opportunities for children to freely express their feeling, views and opinions and ask a colleague to observe you; you can then use this as the basis of a **reflective account (Key letter F)**. Your colleague's observation could provide part of a **witness testimony (Key letter C)**.

You could also plan circle time or discussion sessions to help children become aware of their rights and those of others. Again, direct observation of the activity by your assessor, witness testimony and reflective accounts can be sources of evidence.

Your assessor may ask you **questions, either verbal or written**, to check your knowledge **(Key letter B)**. Think about how you could answer some of these questions:

- What could be some of the possible effects of discrimination on children and their families in this community? (K3P235)
- How are inequalities embedded in our society and what might be the negative effects of inequalities on children? (K3P236 and K3D237)
- How can you reach children and families who have difficulty accessing service and provision? What could be done to improve the services offered? (K3C238)
- What are the barriers to participation in your community, and how might they be removed? (K3D239)
- What kinds of community services, resources, information and support are offered in your area? (3D240)

CCLD 305.2 Implement strategies, policies, procedures and practice for inclusion

Getting started

What does inclusive practice actually mean to you? You can probably give a definition, indeed there is such a definition at the end of this chapter. Inclusive means wide-ranging, comprehensive and all-encompassing, all good words but it still does not answer that first question. An inclusive setting helps the development of all children and meets individual needs. This means that children and young people who have learning difficulties or disabilities, and those who do not, are valued, respected and offered support appropriate to their individual needs. Inclusive education is a human right and there is legislation to support that right. You should make sure that you are familiar with all legislation and especially the Disability Discrimination Act 1995, (DDA).

This element has seven PCs and you must provide evidence for all of them. In this unit you are aiming to show that you:

- use inclusive and anti-discriminatory practice in planning and delivery of provision, according to current practice.
- provide an environment, activities and experiences that promote positive images of children and reflect the wider society.
- assess and contribute to meeting the individual needs of children.
- organise the provision of facilitated access and participation for disabled children and children with special educational needs.
- promote all children's entitlement to the full range of activities and learning experiences.
- monitor by collecting relevant data, evaluate how effective your provision is in implementing inclusive practice and implement change to improve the service you offer.
- ensure confidentiality and privacy for children, except where their well-being is at stake.

Key Issues

If your practice is to be inclusive and anti-discriminatory according to current guidance, it makes sense that you know what the current guidance is. The Disability Discrimination Act 1995, The National Standards – Standard 10, the Special Educational Needs and Disability Act 2001 (SENDA) and the Children Act 2004 are the most important pieces of legislation relating to inclusion and you have a working knowledge of these. Remember, if you treat a child or young person less favourably because of their disability or difficulty without good reason, you may be breaking the law (CCLD 305.2.1).

The environment in which you work should promote safety, health, growth and development in all areas and you should be able to describe it as positive, helpful and encouraging. This environment will help to shape children's attitudes and views on society and so it is crucial that the images and resources presented to the children are also positive, enabling them to develop pro-social values and altruistic behaviours (CCLD 305.2.2).

There are two contrasting views of disability:

- The social model which considers that problems arising from a disability are formed by society. If a wheel chair user cannot access a building because there are no ramps, the problem is not with the wheel chair but with the fact that 'society' has not provided appropriate access for all people to the building.
- The medical model regards the disability or difficulty as the problem and considers that people with disabilities or difficulties can not lead normal lives.

We must all actively work towards the social model, because by doing so we will meet the individual needs of all children and so allow all to reach their full potential. This may mean that the setting in which we work and the resources and equipment used should be accessible to all. In order to achieve this you will have to assess and consider the individual and specific needs of children, through observation and discussion. It will take time to do this properly but it is part of your professional responsibilities (CCLD 305.2.3 and 305.2.3.4).

It is sometimes necessary to adapt activities and equipment to allow all children to participate, or adapt the way activities are organised;

for example, a child who has difficulties controlling arm, hand and finger movements may struggle with a modelling activity. You could sit alongside the child and put your hand over his to guide his movements, praising his achievements frequently (CCLD 305.2.5).

In order that you can evaluate how inclusive your setting is and what changes you may need to make, you will need to collect data and relevant information. You should always tell people why you are asking for information. Any data that you collect to help your setting offer an inclusive provision must be available to anyone. This also means that such information is freely available from the Office for National Statistics. You will need to find data on:

- the catchment area of your setting, the ethnic mix, rural/urban mix, social class.
- where the children and young people live in relation to your setting.
- the number of children with registered disabilities.
- the ethnic status of children and young people in the catchment area.
- the number of single parents in the catchment area.

From this information you should be able to see if your provision is really representative of the area in which it operates. If not, you will be able to implement changes to improve the situation (CCLD 305.2.6).

Confidentiality has been discussed several times in this book and it is an important issue that can not be stressed enough. Confidentiality is the basis of respect and trust. If people believe that any information given to you or your setting will not be disclosed to any other person, unless the well-being of the child is threatened, they are more likely to give you open and honest dialogue (CCLD 305.2.7).

Suggested activities and experiences
- Does your setting have a policy that is up-to-date and in line with SENDA to make sure that there is no discrimination?
- Find out how your setting deals with discrimination by staff or other adults.
- Find out if your setting has a complaints policy, when it was last implemented and by whom. What action, if any, was taken?
- Imagine you have a disability that means that you have to use a wheelchair or walking frame. Go around your setting and identify which areas are accessible to you and which are not.
- Look at your book corner. Do all your books promote positive images of children and do they reflect the wider society in which the children and families from your setting live? Do the same with other resources that are used by the children and adults in your setting, including computer programmes.
- Find out if your local authority is offering training for the requirements of SENDA. If you have not had this training, you should attend. Look out for courses on ways to work with children with specific conditions such as autism or cerebral palsy. Learning Makaton will help you communicate more effectively with some children and young people.
- Devise a questionnaire which will enable you to collect information to help monitor the effectiveness of your setting and provision.
- Make sure that you ask unambiguous questions.
- Make sure that the language use is clear and in plain English.
- Get your questionnaire translated into other languages, ncluding Braille. Your local Children's Information Service (or Bureau, or Family Service) will be able to help you with this.

- Remember that a questionnaire may not be the most effective way of reaching some people, as it assumes that all people can read. Think of different ways to get the information you require, such as face-to-face interviews where you ask the questions and record the responses.

Types of evidence
Your assessor will be able to **observe inclusive** practice and should be able to gather evidence on every visit **(Key letter A)**. Inclusive practice and procedures should be included in all your assessment plans. Use your setting's policies to help you write a **reflective account (Key letter F)** on how your setting uses inclusive and anti-discriminatory practice in planning.

This unit could lend itself to several **case studies (Key letter E)** of how practice, provision and delivery have allowed a child, young person or family to access services. (Remember that the individuals in the case study should not be identified by their real names, due to confidentiality issues.) These could also include before and after photographs, of perhaps, for example, a doorway that was not accessible by wheel chairs or a walking frame, but now has a temporary ramp.

Your assessor may ask you **verbal** or give you **written questions (Key letter B)** to assess your knowledge of the kinds of community resources and support which are available in your area (K3D240). Questions will also provide evidence for how your setting assesses and plans for children's needs (K3D242) and many of the other knowledge specification statements. Therefore it is important that you read through ALL the knowledge specifications for each unit. If you do not understand what is required, you make a note of your query and contact your assessor.

CCLD 305.3 Maintain and follow policies and procedures for protecting and safeguarding children

Getting started
It is every child's right to be protected from all forms of abuse, as stated in the United Nations Convention on the Rights of the Child, Article 19. 'Every Child Matters' which resulted in the Children Act 2004, places importance on child protection as one of the five outcomes in 'Be Safe'. However, it is a distressing fact that the number of children and young people on child protection registers is increasing year on year, despite efforts by government and local authorities to reduce the risk of abuse. The most common reason for children being placed on the register is neglect, followed by physical abuse. A sound understanding of child protection issues is essential for every childcare practitioner, and as such all policies should be updated and reviewed regularly.

Support for vulnerable children and a young person is part of your role and responsibilities. Just being aware of and alert to possible abuse is not enough; you need to know how to offer support and when and how to refer the child to the relevant agency's authorities.

This element has seven PCs and you must provide evidence for all of them. In this unit you are aiming to show that you:

- maintain and follow organisational procedures for the protection and safeguarding of children.
- follow policies and procedures for safeguarding children in your local area.
- recognise indicators of possible child abuse.
- help children to protect themselves from abuse.
- respond sensitively to a child's disclosure of abuse.
- promote an environment of openness and trust, allowing children to express themselves in their chosen way.
- follow safe working practices that protect children and practitioners.

Key Issues

Your setting should have a policy for the protection of children and young people. As with all policies, it is essential that it is reviewed and monitored regularly, as contacts and reporting procedures may have changed. The Children Act 2004 has many measures aimed at improving the approach to children protection. One of the measures has been to set up local children's safeguarding boards, often known as LCSB. These boards have statutory powers to make sure that all services work together to protect children and young people. Your setting's policy should include the contact details of the LCSB (CCLD 305.3.1).

Regardless of whether your setting is private, voluntary or state-maintained, it will have to follow the local authority policies and procedures for safeguarding children. If you are a home-based carer, the responsibility for following these policies lies solely with you. If you have concerns about a child you have to report them to the LCSB. In settings where there are several staff, it is quite likely that concerns are passed to the manager, supervisor or officer-in-charge who then has the responsibility to contact the LCSB. Although partnership with parents is regarded as good practice, most local authorities advise settings not to discuss child protection issues with parents or other carers (CCLD 305.3.2).

There are different forms of abuse, which are generally categorized as:

- physical
- sexual
- emotional
- neglect

Bullying is also a form of abuse and can take many different forms, for example verbal, physical, cyber, such as email, text messaging, silent or frequent phone calls.

It is important that you are aware of the signs and symptoms of all forms of abuse. You should remember, however, that not every sign means a child is being abused. Some physical signs can be perfectly harmless, such as birthmarks which may look like bruising, or Mongolian blue spot which can be observed on the lower backs in some Asian or African children. It is more likely that you will become aware of behavioural changes before you observe other signs. It is important that you record your concerns and monitor the child carefully (CCLD 305.3.3).

The reasons for abuse are very complex, but one of the best ways of preventing it is to make sure that parents and carers feel positive about their parenting skills and also that they have support when they need it. Another important aspect of protecting children is to enable children to protect themselves. Children and young people who are assertive, confident and feel good about themselves are less vulnerable. This means that practitioners should provide activities and experiences which promote self-esteem and self-confidence (CCLD 305.3.4).

It is not always easy for abused children or young people to express their feelings. They may feel that they are in some way to blame, or may feel that they are betraying the abuser. It takes a lot of courage and trust to tell another person about abuse. You will need to be sensitive to the child. Do not question him, but take your cues from the child and offer reassurance. Never promise to do something that you know you will not be able to fulfil, and do not ask a child to keep something secret. Secrets can encourage a child to tell untruths and deceive others. Surprises can be good; secrets are not (CCLD 305.3.5).

Disclosures of abuse can happen at anytime, so the child or young person should feel that they can talk in open and honest ways. Some children may not be able to talk about the abuse and it may be more appropriate for the child to draw pictures or use puppets. A child is not likely to talk about this sensitive issue if any other subject is not openly discussed. Simple sessions on how the human body works can help children understand what is normal and what is not. Such sessions and activities should be age- and stage-appropriate (CCLD 305.3.6).

As well as being aware of how to protect children from abuse, you do need to be aware of how to protect yourself from false allegations. One way to do this is to make sure that you always follow safe working practices. Make sure that you always use appropriate language with children, that you allow them privacy and respect the need for privacy. Do not invade a child's space, show respect for children and all the people with whom you work and make sure that all physical contact is appropriate and is not unwanted (CCLD 305.3.7).

Suggested activities and experiences

- Make sure that the contact details of the LCSB are current.
- Make sure that you are aware of the signs, symptoms and behavioural changes which could indicate that a child is being abused.
- Make sure that you give lots of praise and encouragement to help children feel good about themselves.
- Plan and provide activities and experiences which encourage independence and offer real choices, for example instead of asking a young child what he would like to drink, ask him if he would like milk or water. This offer real choices and allows the child to succeed at making an independent decision.
- Be a positive role model and encourage tolerance, co-operation, respect and trust. If children see you praising and rewarding such behaviours in others they are more likely to copy you.
- If a child tells you about abuse, listen very carefully to what he is saying. Try not to show shock or disbelief. Offer reassurance and support that the child is doing the right thing and that you accept what he has told you.

Types of evidence

Because of confidentiality issues, it is very unlikely that your assessor will have opportunities to directly observe you, so **oral** and **written questions (key letter B), professional discussions (Key letter G), assignments (Key letter E)** and possibly **witness testimonies (Key letter C)** will be used. You can use **reflective accounts (Key letter F)** based on your setting's and local area's policy to consider the effectiveness of the procedures. You can also make recommendations for more effective provision.

Key words and concepts relating to CCLD 305

abuse - when a child or young person is suffering or may suffer considerable harm from physical abuse, emotional abuse, sexual abuse, neglect or bullying

access - opportunities for participation

anti–discriminatory practice - taking positive steps to counter and challenge discrimination

child protection - defending the basic right of a child to be protected from abuse

difficulty - a term that is often given to a situation or condition, such as an emotional difficulty, that may be overcome or treated. However, some learning difficulties cannot be overcome

disability - a physical or mental impairment which has a significant and long-term adverse effect on an individual's ability to continue with normal day-to-day activities

disclosure of abuse - when a child or young person tells you that he has been abused

family - a unit that provides a home and care for children and young people

holistic treatment - focuses on the whole person rather than just on the symptoms of an   illness or disability

impairment - a condition that negatively affects the ability to hear, see, walk or co-ordinate actions

inclusion - the process of understanding, identifying and breaking down obstructions to belonging and participation

policies - guidelines that have been agreed by all people working in a setting about what should and should not happen in certain situations

procedures - the ways in which a policy will be carried out

Suggested further reading and useful websites

Tassoni, P. et al (2005) Children's Care, Learning and Development, Heinemann.

www.baspcan.org.uk

www.childcarelink.gov.uk

www.childline.org.uk

www.childrennow.co.uk

www.kidscape.org.uk

www.nspcc.org.uk

www.surestart.gov.uk

www.unicef.org.uk/youthvoice/crc.asp

The United Nations Convention on the Rights of the Child sets out the rights that children all over the world should have. Sue Griffin looks at what this important international agreement means for your day-to-day work with children

Promoting children's rights

The United Nations Convention on the Rights of the Child (UNCRC) is an international treaty which was developed at the end of the 1980s and ratified by the UK in 1991. This means that British governments are committed to making sure that laws, policy and practice in this country are in harmony with the articles of the convention. Every country in the world has signed up to it – except Somalia and the United States.

Promoting human rights starts from a commitment to 'the dignity and worth of the human person', a principle which is familiar and valued in early years and child care. Children need particular protection of their rights because of their immaturity and vulnerability.

Some people in our society are not comfortable with the idea of children having rights. When we talk about children's rights, we acknowledge that they have autonomy as individual human beings, and are not just seen as passively under the control of adults who make decisions on their behalf and organise their lives for them.

The rights set out in the UNCRC can be divided into three main areas:

■ provision (for example, to have access to food, clean water, housing, education and health care);

■ protection (for example, from abuse and discrimination);

■ participation (for example, to have their views heard and participate in making decisions).

The UNCRC applies to all children and young people aged under 18.

If you look at some of the significant Articles of UNCRC, you can see how this international treaty is linked to your everyday work and how much you do to promote children's rights.

Article 2
Article 2 requires that children are protected against all forms of discrimination.
When you:

■ show children that you value their individuality and aim to treat each child with equal concern so you meet their individual needs;

■ operate anti-discriminatory practice such as avoiding stereotypes, offering all children equal opportunities to achieve, and celebrating diversity;

■ challenge prejudice and discrimination; you are promoting article 2.

Callum's mother approached Coombe Valley Pre-school and told them how Callum had been asked to leave the nursery in the nearby town because of his disruptive behaviour associated with his learning difficulties. The pre-school used their knowledge of sources of local funding to pay for an extra member of staff to support Callum at the pre-school and help him learn ways of behaving in a group of other children.

Article 3
Article 3 declares that the best interests of the child should be paramount.
When you:

■ do your best to put the interests of

the child first, before other people's interests, especially if issues of protecting children from abuse arise;

you are promoting article 3.

Shahila, a childminder, felt great sympathy for the mental health problems faced by Freya's mother, but became so concerned about the neglect the little girl was experiencing, she decided she had to take action to safeguard the child and share her concerns with social services.

Article 12
Article 12 assures children of the right to express their views and have them taken into account, according to their age and maturity.

When you:

■ listen to what children can tell you about their ideas and feelings;

■ take account of their opinions;

■ help them to have a say in decisions which affect them;

you are promoting article 12.

Seven-year-old William's parents have recently separated and his mother cut off all contact with his father's family. He poured out his heart to his nanny, Emma, about how much he missed seeing his father's parents. She helped him to find the words to express his feelings to his mother in a way that made her realise how important it was for him to keep in touch with his grandparents.

Kathryn works in the baby room of a nursery. She pays close attention to the likes and dislikes of the babies she works with, and quickly learned that although Megan liked to be held and cuddled as she dropped off to sleep, George would only go to sleep when he was put in his cot with a blanket wrapped firmly round.

Article 16
Article 16 sets out children's right to privacy.
When you:

■ take care to protect children's dignity and privacy;

■ maintain confidentiality about information you hold about children;

you are promoting article 16.

When the Highertown holiday playscheme agreed to take a disabled child, eight-year-old Shelley, they made careful arrangements for her nappy changing away from the play area so that her privacy could be maintained.

Beth is a community childminder and often cared for children whose parents have complex problems. She has to take great care to resist the pressures put on her to gossip about the families when she's waiting for the children to come out of school.

Article 23
Article 23 provides that disabled children require special care.
When you:

■ use your knowledge of the social model of disability as the basis of your work with disabled children, seeing the child as a child first, not just defined by their disability;

■ devise ways of supporting disabled children in their play and learning so they can participate alongside other children and be fully included in your setting;

you are promoting article 23.

Hazelgrove Nursery wanted to be sure that three-year-old Elliott who had difficulty sitting up could join in with all the activities such as painting and water play. They borrowed some foam shapes from the local toy library to provide his back with the support he needed.

Article 28
Article 28 describes children's right to education and health care.
When you:

■ provide experiences and play activities for the children you care for which interest them and motivate them to learn;

■ promote their health and well-being through their diet, exercise and rest;

you are promoting article 28.

Caryn, a nanny, took three under-fives to the city farm, and followed up the visit by sharing books about animals she had borrowed from the library. The children painted pictures of the animals they had seen.

Gladstone Road Pre-school have created a drinks bar so children can help themselves to drinking water whenever they want to during the session.

Article 29
Article 29 provides that the aim of education is to develop the child's personality, talents and mental and physical abilities to their fullest potential.
When you:

■ observe children carefully, assess the stage of development they have reached (what they have achieved, what they can do, what they can almost do), and learn about their interests – and then use all of this information to help you plan for experiences and activities for them;

you are promoting article 29.

Bushra, a childminder, used the knowledge she had gained on a training course to carry out observations of each of the children she cared for. She felt confident assessing their stage of development and identifying their interests and, with the support of her network co-ordinator, developed plans of what she would do with the children over the next month to help them progress in various aspects of their development.

Article 31
Article 31 recognises children's right to play, rest and leisure.
When you:

■ plan your time with children to make sure they have time for learning, but also for play they choose and direct themselves, and build in quiet and restful periods;

you are promoting article 31.

Zigzag After-school Club designed the layout of their rooms so that there are comfortable areas where children can rest and relax, and not feel pressurised to take part in the craft activities laid out in other areas. They offer a range of play facilities outdoors, but keep the organisation of the children's play to a minimum, letting them explore the potential of the play area for themselves.

Having rights always brings responsibilities, so part of your role with children is also to help them become aware of how they must respect the rights of others.

Sue Griffin, early years trainer and consultant.

Where to find out more
You can find out more about the UNCRC from www.unicef.org.uk/youthvoice/crc.asp or by contacting:
Unicef
Africa House
64–78 Kingsway
London WC2B 6NB.
Tel: 0870 606 3377

Some children will already have been identified as having a special educational need (SEN) when they come to you but there is a chance that you (or a member of your team if you are in group provision) may be the first to identify it. Are you confident about what this might mean? Sue Fisher explains

Words you need to know:
Special needs and statements

The term 'special needs' is generally used to describe any child who requires additional support. In general, these special needs fit into four broad areas:

- learning difficulties;
- behavioural, emotional and social difficulties;
- communication and interaction difficulties;
- physical and sensory difficulties.

Each area covers a wide range and level of need, for example communication and interaction difficulties obviously includes children with limited speech and vocabulary but also includes autistic spectrum disorders and children who have difficulty in understanding the meaning of spoken language and in following instructions.

Often, the term used for children who fall into one of these categories is special educational needs as their difficulty means

that special educational provision has to be made for them. For example, a child with cerebral palsy may need special equipment or resources to enable them to access the curriculum or a child with Asperger syndrome may need a support worker to encourage communication and involvement with others.

Special educational needs is therefore ultimately an educational definition, but one that is used generally, as all children with special needs will eventually enter the education system.

Meeting the needs of children with special educational needs

There has been a move away from specialised segregated provision to inclusive practice where children play and learn alongside each other, regardless of their need or disability.

A growing number of childminders, playgroups, nurseries and out-of-school clubs are now caring for children with special needs. Some of these children need a lot of additional support but for many it will be possible to differentiate activities so that each child can join in.

Often it's just a case of breaking tasks down into smaller parts or providing additional support. It may mean providing extra or different resources, for example paint brushes with fatter or softer handles for children with a weak grasp or poor motor

control, and larger than usual pieces of paper for creative expression. Remember, each child is different and it is crucial to have a full understanding of their needs to provide appropriately for them - a child with poor motor control may benefit from larger than usual paper but a timid, reserved child may find it daunting! Treat each child as an individual and value their contributions.

You will also need to make sure that the physical environment, routine and resources do not discriminate against individual children and enables them to develop independence.

Early intervention
Some children who come to you will already have been identified as having special educational needs (SEN), for example children with Down's syndrome or a physical disability.

Occasionally, however, it may be you, along

What is the SEN Code of Practice?
Whenever schools and LEAs decide what they should do for children with special educational needs, and whenever health services and social services help schools and LEAs take action on behalf of such children, they must consider what the Code of Practice says. The Code gives them practical advice on carrying out their statutory duties to identify, assess and make provision for children's special educational needs.

A revised Code of Practice came into force on 1 January 2002. This revision includes new rights and duties introduced by the SEN and Disability Act 2001.

with the child's parents, who are the first to suspect that a child may have special needs. This is particularly likely with children who have communication and interaction difficulties or behavioural difficulties, as these are likely to become more apparent as the child gets older and also when they are introduced into a group situation.

Through your knowledge of child development it will become apparent when a child has a delay in development of communication or when a child is not behaving as you would expect. By identifying such needs early, you will be giving the child a greater opportunity to come to terms with their difficulties and to provide support or help overcome these where possible.

Supporting children with SEN

Settings in receipt of government funding for early years education are expected to draw up Individual Education Plans (IEPs) for children with special needs, identifying targets to work towards and strategies for doing this.

This is good practice for anyone working with a child with special needs, including out-of-school clubs, although it is likely that clubs would call it a play plan or care plan. If a child has health needs it is important that everyone caring for them has access to the information on their care and medication. This could range from keeping an inhaler for an asthmatic child to administering medication for children with epilepsy or diabetes.

External specialists such as speech and language therapists or the Portage service may also be supporting the child. Working together and recording the guidance they give will help you make sure the child receives the best possible support.

All plans should be reviewed regularly (usually termly) and updated and amended as necessary. This will help to provide a useful and meaningful working document.

Statements of special educational needs

The SEN Code of Practice states 'for a

very few children the help given by the early education setting through Early Years Action Plus (*IEP plus support from external specialists*) will not be sufficiently effective to enable the child to progress satisfactorily.

'It will then be necessary for the setting in consultation with the parents and any external agencies already involved to consider whether a statutory multi-disciplinary assessment may be appropriate.'

There will always be a small number of children who need more support than can normally be provided without additional human and/or financial resources. For these children a statement of special educational needs may be sought.

To apply for a statement of special educational needs for a child, a request for a statutory assessment of the child's needs must be made to the local education authority (LEA). This request can be made by the child's parent(s), an agency involved with the child (such as a consultant or speech and language therapist) or it could be made by you.

Such a request would need to include evidence clearly illustrating the child's difficulties, such as IEPs and the views of the child's parents. The LEA would inform you of what should be included but remember to provide details of your setting and the provision you are currently making in working towards the child's special needs, including information on the progress the child has made in any area (if any) and the lack of progress despite intervention.

For some childminders, nannies and playgroups, the educational provision for the child may be being provided by another setting the child also attends, but your views are still important and should form part of the assessment process.

The LEA has six weeks to decide whether they feel a statutory assessment is necessary, then ten more weeks to carry out the assessment and make a decision whether or not to issue a statement.

During this time, they will gather information from everyone involved with the child to help them make a decision. If the LEA feels that a statement is necessary, this will be drawn up and will include:

- The provision the child will need to make progress;

- The support offered under the statement;

- The name of the setting where this provision will be made.

The statement will identify the amount of hours a week of one-to-one support that the LEA will fund. This can differ greatly depending on the needs of the child, and the clarity and detail of information given by groups and individuals working with the child will have a strong effect on the final decision.

Informal assessment and reviews of the child's progress will take place regularly, but the statement itself will only be reviewed annually. Generally, the responsibility for organising and carrying out this review is attributed to the setting identified on the statement. This is an opportunity for all parties involved with the child to meet and assess how effective the provisions of the statement have been in meeting the needs of the child.

Sue Fisher, early years training consultant, Hull.

If you want to know more

Special Educational Needs Code of Practice and *SEN Toolkit* (DfES 2001)

Special Educational Needs (SEN): A Guide for Parents and Carers (DfES 2001)

All available (free) from: DfES Publications, PO Box 5050, Sherwood Park, Annesley, Nottingham NG15 0DJ. Tel: 0845 6022260

Special Educational Needs in Practice (Step Forward Publishing £11.50) Tel: 01926 420046

Kidsactive (formerly HAPA), Pryor's Bank, Bishop's Park, London SW6 3LA Tel: 020 7736 4443

Childminders have a lot to offer in terms of looking after a child with special needs, so it is important to make parents, health visitors and local organisations aware of what you can do. Helen Renouf gives advice on training, funding pathways, special needs support, childminder referrals and the Disability Discrimination Act.

Working with special needs

Childminders are often overlooked in the area of special needs. There are many childminders who do care for children with specific needs, happy to offer children care in a small home-from-home environment, often offering a unique integrated setting. These childminders have undertaken extra training, and there are many who would offer this kind of care if families asked for it.

It is quite often the case that families with specific needs do not consider a childminder as their first choice of care, unless they are already familiar with one. They assume we are unable to offer care, and worry about our ability to cope, yet at the same time we may be prepared to offer flexible care – possibly overnight or at weekends – to fulfil a family's requirements.

All children with specific needs have different requirements and really need a specialist service tapered to these. Childminding has the distinct advantage of shaping its service around the needs of individual children.

How can we make families aware of what childminders can offer?

Families can be made aware of your services if you advertise in doctors' surgeries, health clinics, parent and toddler groups, and libraries. If you have particular skills or experience, then highlighting these on your advertising material can make parents aware of any specialist services that you offer.

It would also be good practice to familiarise yourself with any local support groups for families. If you

know what their role is and how they support families locally, then you have useful information you can use to support the families in your care. At the same time you in turn can introduce yourself and tell them about the services you offer, and then they may be able to refer families to you.

It is very much about raising your profile and highlighting what childminders in your area can do really well. This includes providing opportunities for children across a large age range, with different abilities, to mix and socialise together through childminding groups, children's centres and local support networks. By sharing what you do well you are making others more aware of the service you offer.

Working with other agencies

All agencies should be working together for the child's best interests. Sometimes you do have to take a stand and say that you are a professional childcarer caring for the child, and that you are an important part of the child's life, especially if you are overlooked in a child's care plan. But as a childminder, you may well be involved by having specialist agencies, such as speech and language therapists, portage workers and physiotherapists coming into your home-setting. You may also be one of the key figures providing continuity for the children over a period of several years.

What support is available to childminders if they take on a specific child?

Support varies from area to area; the parents are the number one place

to go to for support. They know the child best and what their particular needs are and often the best way to encourage the child to develop further. They may already have access to services and specialist equipment that they can share with you and they can probably advise you on where to go for further information.

Support should also be available via a Childminding Support worker in your county, who will know what support you can access. This can include financial support for the family, or equipment that may be hired or loaned through lending libraries of specialist equipment.

Can I access specialist training?

If you need training and specialist equipment to help you care for a child, your local inclusion officer should be able to help point you in the right direction – the best way to find out how to contact this person is through your local early education and childcare unit.

Some of these courses may be funded through the Early Education and Childcare Unit, others may be available at a subsided cost, or you may be eligible for a training grant. The Gail Memorial Fund can help NCMA members, who have not been able to access funding through other means, to learn the skills they need to care for children with specific needs. More information on this can be found at www.ncma.org.uk

Can we refuse a child because of their needs?

No, you can't refuse anyone on their specific needs, that would be discriminatory.

How does the Disability Discrimination Act (DDA) affect me as a Childminder?

Childminders cannot discriminate against disabled children and they do have to make reasonable adjustment to their homes to make them accessible to families if they are asked. This may mean placing a temporary ramp over the threshold for a wheelchair user, but it won't mean that the childminder needs to do major building work to ensure that the downstairs toilet can allow full access for a wheelchair.

It also means that a childminder can charge

extra if they need to employ more staff or limit their provision to fewer children to ensure that child's needs are met, but only for the extra costs incurred. There may be some funding to offset these costs in some areas, through local inclusion workers. It is simply a case of investigating each individual case.

If I think a child in my care has a specific need, can I do anything about it?

Yes you can, and you have a duty of care to the child to ensure that his/her specific needs are met.

The first step is often the hardest bit – you need to talk to the parents about your concern and see whether they also have similar concerns. It is best to do this when you have time to sit and talk to the parents, tell them some of the achievements that their child has made, and then ask them how they are getting on at home. Share with them some observations that you have

recorded about their child and ask whether they have noticed the same.

You can then monitor and review the situation, perhaps deciding together how you can help the child progress, and then how you will access the appropriate support – for under-fives this would be via your local inclusion coordinator, or the child's health visitor.

If you have concerns about how to approach the situation, or are unsure of anything, then you can always seek advice from an inclusion worker, without naming the child.

If you are a childminder or nanny who is part of a network, or who has established links with a children's centre, then you may already know by sight the inclusion worker in your area.

Helen Renouf
Advanced Diploma in Childcare and Education
(ADCE)

When the Childcare Act 2006 became law, the Minister for Children, Beverley Hughes, called it 'an historic and radical piece of legislation - the first solely dedicated to early years and childcare - that redraws the boundaries of the welfare state'. Sue Griffin explains the key elements of this important new law

The Childcare Act 2006: a guide

The Government intends the Children Act to transform childcare and early years services in England for generations to come, as part of its *Every Child Matters* policies and the ten year strategy. This means that it will affect every early years and childcare setting and practitioner in England over the coming years.

The main provisions of the Childcare Act 2006 (which are expected to come into effect in 2008) are:

■ **a new set of duties for local authorities who will have to**

- improve the five *Every Child Matters* outcomes of all children aged under five;

- make sure that

- there is sufficient childcare provision in its area to meet the needs of working parents;
- young children's views are taken into account when strategic decisions are made;
- free early education and care is offered to three- and four-year-olds;
- information and advice is available for parents on all aspects of looking after their children;
- information, advice and training is available to childcare providers.

■ **the introduction of the Early Years Foundation Stage;**
■ **a reformed and simplified regulation and inspection framework.**

Duties of local authorities
Every Child Matters
The *Every Child Matters* outcomes aim to

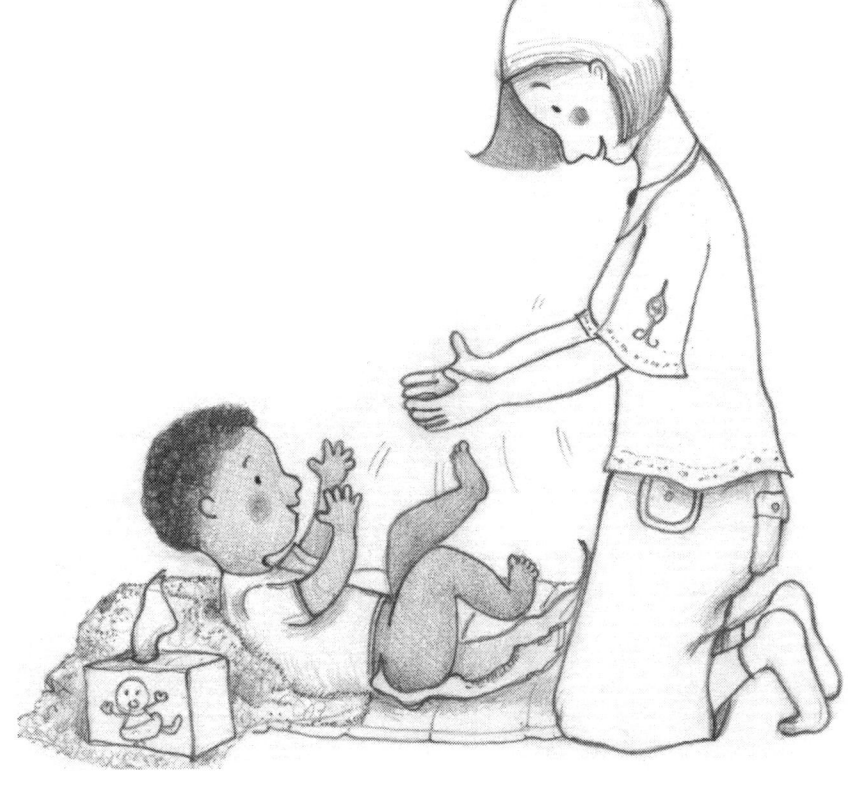

ensure that every child can:
- Be healthy
- Stay safe
- Enjoy and achieve
- Make a positive contribution
- Achieve economic well-being.

Some young children are not faring as well as others in terms of these outcomes. Local authorities will have a duty to reduce these inequalities, narrowing the gap between the most vulnerable children for whom the outcomes are least favourable and other children.

To achieve this, they must make sure that families have access to good quality early childhood services.

The aim to create a children's centre in every community is seen as a central pillar of this part of the Act. Efforts must be made to reach out to families and encourage them to use the services.

The views of parents, children and existing providers and professionals about these early childhood services must be sought, and the local authority must work in partnership with other relevant agencies.

Childcare for working parents
Local authorities will not normally be expected to provide childcare direct, but they are required to work with local private, voluntary and independent sector providers to make sure that the provision of childcare is sufficient to meet the needs

of parents in the area who work or are training for work.

The test of whether there is 'sufficient' provision will be whether there are enough childcare places for children up to 14, but especially for families on lower incomes and those with disabled children (for whom there must be care up to 18).

The role of local authorities will be strategic – they will have to:•
at least once every three years, assess how well provision in the local childcare market is already meeting demand;
- identify what additional provision is needed;
- help to develop childcare provision by, for example, offering support like business advice, access to training and start-up funding.

If parents can't find the childcare they require, they can complain to their local authority which must take strategic action to fill the gaps this reveals. (But they are not obliged to meet the precise individual needs of every family!)

Early education and care

The Act restates the duty of local authorities to make sure that enough places are available to provide the minimum amount of free early learning and care for all three- and four-year-olds whose parents want it, currently operating at 12.5 hours per week for 38 weeks per year.

Information for parents

The Act extends local authorities' duty to provide information to parents. Parents and prospective parents must have access to the full range of information and advice they may need to help them care for their children right through to their 20th birthday.

Local authorities will be required to provide this service to all parents and must be pro-active in reaching parents who might have difficulty getting access to current information services. In particular, information must be provided about childcare for parents of disabled children.

Advice, information and training to childcare providers

Local authorities will be required to provide advice, information and training to childcare providers, but they will have the power to charge for this.

Local authorities in Wales are also required to ensure sufficient childcare provision to meet the requirements of working parents, and to provide information and advice to parents, but the rest of the Act does not apply in Wales.

Early Years Foundation Stage

The Act requires all registered early years providers to promote the Early Years Foundation Stage (EYFS). The EYFS brings together the *Curriculum Guidance for the Foundation Stage*, *Birth to Three Matters* and the national standards for registration and inspection of sessional and full-time group care and childminders into a single 'quality framework'. This is an important step in integrating care and education provision in the early years.

The EYFS will set Early Learning Goals for the knowledge, skills and understanding a child will be expected to have acquired by the September following their fifth birthday, in the areas of learning of:

- Personal, social and emotional development
- Communication, language and literacy
- Problem solving, reasoning and numeracy
- Knowledge and understanding of the world
- Physical development
- Creative development.

The consultation on this framework took place earlier this year, and the final version should be available by the end of 2006. The hope is that this will allow time for settings to become familiar with the content of the new framework and for practitioners to be offered the training they will need to be ready for implementation in September 2008.

Within the new framework will be 'welfare requirements' which echo many of the existing standards for registration and inspection of group and home-based provision, covering aspects of health and safety linked to suitability of premises, qualifications of practitioners, and safeguarding children.

Regulation and inspection

The Act aims to make sure that the regulation of childcare and early education is carried out in a framework which reduces bureaucracy and focuses on raising quality and standards.

The new framework will end the distinction between care and education, each with different regulatory and inspection requirements. Integrated care and education provision will be inspected as a single entity and there will be a single judgment about the quality of the provision.

All providers caring for children up to the age of five will be required to register on the early years register and deliver the Early Years Foundation Stage.

Childcare settings providing for school age children will be judged against a 'streamlined' set of Ofsted childcare register standards. Meeting these standards will be compulsory for all settings caring for children under eight, and other providers will be able to join the register if they wish to.

The details of these proposals have also been consulted on this year, and final versions should be available in 2007.

The coming year will see many of the details of this Act fleshed out, and all settings and practitioners will need to be alert to how it will affect them, and prepare thoroughly so that they are able to meet its requirements and play their part in offering ever-improving services to the nation's youngest children.

Sue Griffin, early years trainer and consultant.

If you are involved in, witness or overhear a racial incident, you must judge how best to deal with it - you may respond to it immediately, there may be wider issues that you need to address. But you cannot ignore it. Eve Cook and Jane Lane outline some clear procedures

Dealing with racial incidents

How you would deal with an incident that has clear racist implications is likely to be different from one where the motive or intention is not clear. Some incidents involve children personally and others involve children playing together and using racist terminology not directed at anyone present.

An incident may be:

■ Overtly racist (for example, where a child refuses to sit next to another child because he is black).

■ Covertly racist but with unconscious racist intentions or implications (for example, where a child calls another by a racist name but may not understand that it is racist or why).

■ Due to personality differences with no racist intention (for example, where a black child refuses to hold a white child's hand because they have had a previous personal disagreement).

You need to be very sensitive when deciding how to deal with situations in a way that is appropriate to the circumstances. There are, however, certain principles that apply to almost all situations where racial prejudice or discrimination is clearly involved. For example:

■ Ensuring that any child who has been on

'Recognise and accept that the incident and follow-up work may reveal the need for work to be done with all the children about equally valuing and respecting one another, even if there are no children from minority ethnic groups in the setting.'

the receiving end of any racist incident is sensitively supported, making sure that it is clear that they are not responsible for the incident, that nothing they have said or done has caused it.

■ Ensuring that the child who has behaved in a racist way is also dealt with sensitively and that it is clear that any concern is about what they have said or done and not about them personally.

■ Ensuring that any observers/bystanders are noted so that action is taken to address what they may have seen or heard as soon as possible.

■ Encouraging children to listen and give opinions.

■ Reflecting on what action, if any, should be taken with the children and colleagues in the setting to address the issues raised by the incident.

■ Working together with family members wherever possible in supporting these principles.

■ Being continually positive about difference and diversity.

■ Reflecting on our own attitudes to racial equality.

What would you do?

It is difficult to decide how best to respond to an incident involving racial concerns in an early years setting unless you know the circumstances - the ethos of the setting, whether they have any policies on equality, the understanding, knowledge and training of the practitioners, individual knowledge of the particular child(ren) involved and possibly their family as well as whether there have been any other racial incidents in the past. However, you might find it helpful to discuss, as a team, the following

incident, which took place in 2000.

A playgroup in the largely white suburb of a country town decides to buy some 'multicultural resources' to help deliver the Foundation Stage. Two four-year-old white girls are having a lovely time stirring their food in a wok. When asked what they are doing, one replies by saying: 'We're playing Pakis and we're cooking poo'. This is not said in an obviously negative way but as an apparent description of what they are doing.

The following suggestions explore the principles of addressing such an apparently covert incident.

■ Consider whether the immediate response might be to the use of the term 'Paki' by saying something about people who come from Pakistan and that 'Paki' is an unkind word. The negative side of this situation might be too complex for a child to understand all at once and too simplistic a reaction may not cover some of the important issues it raises.

■ Be aware that other children may have overheard what was said and decide whether they, too, need to be included in any discussion or whether there needs to be follow-up work.

■ Make sure that any response addresses what the child(ren) has said or done, not the child himself/herself personally

■ Be sensitive to the child's feelings and self-esteem.

■ Be careful to ensure that the child does not feel the need to react in a defensive manner.

■ Be aware that the child who said this may have no negative intent but is just repeating something she has heard. On the other hand, be alert to any knowledge of the negative aspects of what she said.

- Be careful not to imply that the child's family is 'wrong' if they are implicated in the child's reply as this would set up conflict in the child.

- Do not deal with the situation by saying something like: 'That's not a very nice thing to say - I love curry' or diverting the scene to another topic.

If appropriate, be careful not to appear to be moralising or 'holier than thou':

- Try to find out more about the terms used - whether the child knows what the term 'Paki' means and understands and knows that it is offensive; the association in the child's mind between the term 'Paki' and 'poo' and any reasons for this.

- Try to find out, if possible, the origins of the statement.

- Find out, or pursue information that arises from the conversation with the children, anything further that might clarify or throw light on what happened.

When the information and background have been collected, you can deal with the situation according to what has been ascertained. This might include:

- Pointing out that using the term 'Paki' is hurtful, that it is an unkind way of describing people, that people from Pakistan are called Pakistanis, that because it is hurtful they do not like being called 'Pakis', that neither does anyone else like being called a 'Paki' and

that sometimes people call anyone who has a skin colour other than white a 'Paki'.

- Making sure that the discussion does not fall into the trap of allowing people from countries other than Pakistan (for example India) to disassociate themselves from being called Paki or not being concerned about the use of the term because they are from India.

- Explaining that lots of people in England like the food that people from Pakistan eat (it might be a good idea to use the wider term Asia or South Asia). Some of it is called curry, but there are lots of different foods that people eat from all over the world and that it is fun to try different foods even though we may not like all of them equally.

- Explaining that it is not kind to describe the food that anyone eats as 'poo'.

- Explaining that it is unkind and not respectful of others if we make fun of them and what they do. This would need to be a general point, applying to a variety of things.

- Explaining that the world we live in is full of different and exciting things - some are interesting for us to learn about, some we don't like as much as others, but we might miss out on the good things if we don't try them in the first place.

- Explaining that it is always a good idea to think about what we are going to say before we say it, if this is possible, because we don't want to hurt people's feelings.

Make sure that these conversations are appropriate to the situation. They might take place over a period of time. Words like 'respect', 'Asia', 'Pakistan' and 'curry' might need to be explored. The word 'unkind' that is used here may need to be replaced by another word that expresses the hurt someone may feel.

Recognise and accept that the incident and follow-up work may reveal the need for

work to be done with all the children about equally valuing and respecting one another, even if there are no children from minority ethnic groups in the setting.

Find out what children really think and encourage them to listen and to give their opinions. Remember to plan this aspect of the curriculum. Think in advance about the planning stage to explain and emphasise diversity issues, using the *QCA Curriculum Guidance for the Foundation Stage in England.* Follow up work done and evaluate it over time.

These principles are only suggestions for what might be done. According to the people involved there would be a variety of responses.

The issues that this incident raises in terms of whether the setting was adequately prepared to include the new multicultural resources would also need to be considered. For example, developing a policy for equality that addresses issues of antiracist practice and any training implications would include considerations of such incidents and why they might occur.

Eve Cook (trustee) and Jane Lane (policy director), Early Years Equality. This is a version of an article that was first published in the Early Years Equality newsletter.

Further reading

A Policy for Excellence: Developing a Policy for Equality in Early Years Settings, Understanding the Past, Thinking About the Present, Planning for the Future, A Practical Handbook for Early Years Workers (price £7). This guide provides a step-by-step approach for practitioners to follow. The DfES has sent a copy to all EYDCPs.

Action for Racial Equality in the Early Years (price £13) by Jane Lane, published by NEYN and available from NCB or EYE (details below). This practical handbook looks at issues of fairness, equality, prejudice and racism and how how to help children and adults promote and enjoy differences between people.

These and other titles can be ordered from: Early Years Equality, PO Box 28, Wallasey, CH45 9NP Tel/fax: 0151 639 1778
Email: eyequality@tiscali.co.uk

Are you worried about what words to use for fear of being thought racist? Do you try to do what is seen as politically correct? Jane Lane takes some examples of terminology in common usage and explores the issues that arise from using them

Promoting racial equality: What words should you use?

It is sometimes difficult to know what words to use when talking about racial equality and to be confident about using them. Some people feel anxious or unsure about using the 'right' words or terms and, as a result, avoid using them at all. They may feel uncomfortable about using some of the words they hear.

There are no right or wrong words, so unless it is someone's intention to hurt, discriminate or abuse, we need to be sensitive about our approach to those who we believe use unacceptable or inappropriate words. It is important to recognise that everyone comes from a particular ethnic, language, gender, cultural, socio-economic, family and belief background that influences their actions.

> *'There are no right or wrong words, so unless it is someone's intention to hurt, discriminate or abuse, we need to be sensitive about our approach to those who we believe use unacceptable or inappropriate words.'*

You are unlikely to hear people who work with young children using offensive and racist words, but some may, unwittingly, use terms that others find unacceptable or inappropriate. They may use words without thinking about what they mean or realising that they do not make sense.

You might choose to talk with the person afterwards about this or you may feel you have to deal with it there and then, because not saying anything might be interpreted by others present as meaning the word is acceptable.

You shouldn't blame or criticise someone because of the terminology they use - it won't encourage them to join in discussion. So the problem is how to address such a sensitive issue without making the person feel bad about themselves, apprehensive about using terms at all and even avoid being involved in anything to do with thinking about racism? Most people are afraid of being accused of being racist and will do anything to avoid it. This is an important issue that requires careful thought and practice.

Terminology is always changing. What may have been acceptable at one time may no longer be so. That's why we all, both black and white people, need to talk about the words/terms we use. We need to be open, receptive to questioning and change and really reflect on and consider their meanings and how they are used.

We need to recognise that other people may have different understandings. We should not allow ourselves to get diverted from this by notions of what is 'politically correct' (often

called 'pc') – such discussions are usually triggered by people who are unwilling to listen to those who are affected by the terminology used and not concerned with ensuring everyone is treated equally.

Because there are no definitive rights and wrongs, we should respect people for what they wish to call themselves even if we feel the words are unacceptable. Rather than feeling guilty or apprehensive we should ask those involved or affected what they wish to be called or what words they feel comfortable with. Talking about them together may help to clarify both perspectives.

It is important not just to repeat terms that you have heard without thinking carefully about what they mean.

Words you need to think about

These words or terms are sometimes used incorrectly, confusingly or inappropriately.

Diversity
The word 'diversity' is often used to show that the full range, extent or variety of something is recognised, somehow implying, when associated with equality, that this is a 'good thing'. It indicates that it is important to acknowledge differences as opposed to treating everyone the same.

However, it does not automatically follow that all the diverse aspects are equally valued, respected and treated.

When referring to people it may even imply that there are different species. It often fails to acknowledge or encompass negatives such as racism or discrimination.

It can't be assumed that diversity means equality for all the aspects being described or identified. For example, 'valuing diversity' (usually meaning society and its cultural, linguistic, religious and ethnic diversity), indicates that all these aspects have been identified. It does not mean that they are all equally valued unless this is spelt out. 'Different but equal' needs to be part of the use of the term.

Ethnic

The term 'ethnic' is often used to mean something associated with black people, about black people or people from an 'ethnicity' different from 'ours'. For example, 'ethnic food', 'ethnic clothes', 'ethnic music'. But everyone has an ethnicity, not just black people.

The word is also often associated with other cultural, national, tribal or racial differences from a colonialist perspective, suggesting inferiority.

Normal

While this word could be used to mean the norm – in the sense of 'average' or the 'usual' – it is sometimes used to imply deviation from an ethnocentric perspective. For example, people talk about different foods as Asian, Chinese or 'normal'.

When distinguishing between differences it is important to describe each in its own right and, at the same time, be aware of making assumptions/generalisations. So, for example, it is better to talk about Asian, Chinese or traditional English food.

Hard-to-reach groups

This term is used to describe groups, often minority ethnic groups, that are not statistically represented/reflected according to their numbers among the population under consideration.

It has often been used, perhaps unintentionally, to describe groups that should be represented but, for whatever reason, are not. But it nearly always implies that the reason why they are 'hard to reach' lies with the groups themselves. It tends to see such groups as a problem, as the cause of their apparent exclusion, rather than examining the reasons why they are not yet included.

There are many possible explanations for this – including perceptions of them as being difficult, unfamiliar and requiring precious and limited time and resources. If they are perceived in this way, it is likely to influence the way they are treated and whether they are included on equal terms.

Groups that are usually described in this way are Travellers/Gypsies, refugees/asylum seekers and other minority ethnic groups. Perhaps 'groups not yet included', 'groups not yet reached' or 'unreached' would be better, placing the responsibility firmly on those whose duty it is to 'reach' or 'include'.

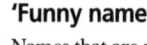

'Funny name'
Names that are unusual to people or difficult for them to pronounce are sometimes called 'funny names'. Names are a fundamental aspect of everyone's persona and should be treated with respect. Correct pronunciation of the full name is an important part of this respect.

Tolerant
This word usually has a positive meaning but often means 'putting up with' rather than being accepted.

Words that are no longer acceptable

Coloured
This word, when used to describe a person, is seldom used in a deliberately negative/offensive way. However, it is inappropriate, harking back to the past and colonialism (see 'Black/black').

Half-caste
This term is sometimes used to describe someone whose parents each have a different ethnic background. You may hear it used negatively or by someone who appears unaware of its implications. If you break down the term, it's easy to identify the origins of hierarchy (caste) and only being 'half'. It is, therefore, unacceptable. Other terms, such as mixed race, dual heritage, mixed parentage or multiple heritage may be used.

Words and phrases that may need explaining

Travellers/Gypsies
Advocates of racial equality argue that both these terms should have a capital initial letter. Traveller has a capital 'T' to distinguish it from other 'travellers' (commercial travellers, travellers on trains) and to ensure that its individual/unique status is acknowledged.

Gypsy has a capital 'G' to designate its status as an ethnic group in the same way as a person of a particular nationality/ ethnic group has a capital letter.

Treating children all the same

Treating people equally does not necessarily mean treating them in the same way. Treating people in different ways may also be treating them equally, depending on their individual needs and circumstances. People who have more than one child in their family will recognise that they are unlikely to treat them in the same way because their needs, personalities and abilities are likely to vary.

Multicultural

This means comprising/including a variety of/many cultures. It is sometimes misused, for example in the phrase 'multicultural doll' or 'multicultural people'. Each doll or person usually has one culture only. However, the word is usually used to mean:

- 'multicultural doll' - a doll which is not white;

- 'multicultural dolls' - dolls reflecting our multicultural society, but perhaps more realistically black dolls, that is, not including white dolls;

- 'multicultural people' - black people.

The term 'multicultural resources' should mean resources reflecting the multicultural nature of our society. It is often used, however, to mean resources only depicting black people and their cultures.

Similarly, 'multicultural education' often excludes the cultures of white people. The original intention was for the cultures of black people to be included in educational provision, but because white people's cultures were not seen as an integral part of multicultural education this created a 'them' and 'us' dichotomy and encouraged the notion that only black people have a culture.

The term 'multicultural' does not usually include the differences and diversity of white people's cultures. It reinforces the idea

that 'white' is unproblematic.

While multiculturalism is important in introducing children to the variety of cultures of people living in Britain today, alone it is insufficient to counter the racism of our society.

Black

In the past, some white people, who were not overtly or intentionally racist, thought that using the term 'Black/black' was insulting. It was, perhaps, because it drew attention to black skin colour which, in the minds of many white people, was wrongly seen as undesirable and unfortunate. The word 'coloured' came into use as a term that was not intentionally insulting and could not be seen as intentionally offending anyone. The term has different origins in the United States and South Africa.

In the United States in the 1960s, there was a campaign, largely by black people, to affirm the term 'black'. They made the phrase 'Black is beautiful' popular and this played a significant role in ensuring that the term came to be used positively, and with pride, in Britain and in the USA.

As well as affirming black as a skin colour, the term 'black' is now widely used to describe people who have a skin colour other than white who share a common experience of racism – it is used as a political term, one of solidarity. However, some minority ethnic groups of people prefer to be defined by their nationality, country of origin or in some other way.

The terms 'Black' and 'black' are used by different people in different ways. Some use Black to mean people of African Caribbean origin. There are continual discussions about this term.

In the eighties, the term 'black' was sometimes used to mean anyone who experienced racism. This became a nonsense when Gypsies, Jewish and Irish people and even some refugees/asylum seekers (who experience racism but have a white skin colour) were described as black. This form of racism can be described as 'xenoracism' – racism against 'foreigners'.

The issue of whether Turkish people, along with Kosovans, Albanians and Chechnyans can be described as white remains a topic for discussion.

'While multiculturalism is important in introducing children to the variety of cultures of people living in Britain today, alone it is insufficient to counter the racism of our society.'

Non-white

The term 'non-white' is generally unacceptable because it suggests that 'white' is the norm and anything else is judged against that. It reinforces a notion of superiority/ inferiority. It is like describing men as 'non-women' or women as 'non-men'.

Words that may have negative meanings

There are some words that, although by a strict dictionary definition appear to be neutral, are actually 'loaded' with negative associations. There are others that have a a pejorative meaning simply because of their association with certain words.

For example, the term 'asylum seeker' becomes negative when associated with 'bogus' or 'influx' so that even when these words are not used the negative association remains. The use of such terms needs to be carefully considered if they are not to have hidden meanings.

Civilised

This may be used to describe people from countries with whom 'we' are familiar. It is seldom used to describe those from countries with whom 'we' are unfamiliar or less like 'us'. These countries tend to include African countries disproportionately. People from such countries are often

Inclusion

Inclusion is a process of identifying, understanding and breaking down the barriers to participation and belonging.

(This definition was devised and agreed by members of the national Early Childhood Forum in 2003.)

At the core of inclusion is an assertion that 'special needs' is not a separate category. All children have needs; no child has the same needs at different stages of their development; all have equal rights to have their needs met in the form of educational provision that gives them a realistic chance of reaching their full potential (Ofsted, LEA strategy for the inclusion of pupils with SEN, 2002).

The term has usually been used to refer to including children with special educational needs (SEN) and disabilities in mainstream education/society. It is used to counter assumptions about such children needing to be educated separately. While this point is important, the definition above takes the issue to a wider perspective and addresses **all** forms of discrimination and disadvantage, both historically and in the present, as being about the achievement of equality for all - including on grounds of sex/gender, ethnicity, skin colour, physical features, language, ability/disability, special educational needs, culture, religion/belief and socio-economic/family background.

The term is often used in official documents to describe issues of community cohesion without addressing the implications of racism (see 'Diversity'). The concern is that issues to do with gender and disability are sometimes given priority while issues of race are marginalised.

described as having a 'culture' in contrast to those who are 'civilised'.

Mud and wattle hut

This description is often used in a negative way, suggesting that people who live in mud huts are naïve, simple and 'primitive'. It may not be recognised that this may be an appropriate way of living according to their circumstances and economic situation, the climate and environment – Nelson Mandela, for example, grew up in a 'mud hut'. Some African countries have cities with skyscrapers. The visual picture for children is thus distorted.

Primitive

This word is often used to describe someone who does not live the same 'advanced' lifestyle as 'us'. In this sense it is negative and value laden, implying simplicity, ignorance and perhaps that they do not have the equivalent human feelings as 'us'. It is often associated with a skin colour that is not white.

Asylum seeker

This is a person who has crossed an international border and is seeking safety in another country. It is often used in a pejorative way. The term 'refugee' is also sometimes used pejoratively. A positive term to describe all people coming to live in Britain - asylum seekers, refugees and migrants, temporarily or permanently - is 'new arrivals'.

Names of pieces of clothing

It is important to use the correct name for all pieces of clothing. For example, the head covering used by some Arab men is a *keffiyeh* (the spelling may vary), not a tea towel and the headscarf worn by many Muslim women is a *hijab*.

Jane Lane, and others working for racial equality in the early years field.

What does it feel like to be a young disabled child in an early years setting today? Mary Dickins unpicks some of the issues surrounding disability and explores what steps you can take to address them

An inclusive approach to disability

The one thing that disabled adults, parents of disabled children and the organisations that work to support them all agree on is that attitude is the biggest problem in our society.

There is no doubt that the life chances of young disabled children are often severely limited by the attitudes and expectations of those around them. It is hard to develop a positive sense of identity and self-worth whilst picking up a clear message that you are seen as a potential problem.

None of us can get through life without accumulating negative personal baggage, opinions and attitudes. Most of us would be horrified at the idea that we might be unwittingly unkind or uncaring to the children in our care. Yet unless we examine our personal and professional attitudes and explore how they influence our policies and practice that is exactly what can happen.

What is disability and where do our attitudes towards it come from?

The quotes in the box above illustrate some of the religious and historical influences that underpin our attitudes. However much we would like to distance ourselves from them, remember that it is only 20 years ago that we segregated disabled people and children in long stay hospitals and provision.

Many disabled adults and children will testify that current attitudes perpetuate some of the prejudice and injustices that they face.

It is important to be clear what we mean by disability. The international Classification of Impairments, Disabilities and Handicaps (CIDH) produced for the World Health Organisation defines it as:

'None of your descendants throughout their generations who has a blemish shall draw near, a man blind or lame, or one who has a mutilated face or a limb too long, or a man who has an injured foot or an injured hand, or a hunch back or a dwarf, or a man with defective sight, or an itching disease or scabs or crushed testicles.'   Leviticus 21 (16-20)

'The unnatural; and increasingly rapid growth of the feebleminded classes, coupled with a steady restriction among all the thrifty, energetic and superior stocks constitutes a race danger. I feel that the source from which the stream of madness is fed should be cut off and sealed before another year has passed.
(Winston Churchill, Home Secretary 1913) from *Inclusion in Early Years* Disability Equality in Education Course Book (2002)

'any restriction or lack (resulting from an impairment) of ability to perform an activity in the manner or within the range considered "normal" for a human being' (*The Way Ahead* Com 917, HMSO January 1990)

This definition was adapted by Disabled Peoples International 1981 as:

'The loss or limitation of the ability to take part in the normal life of the community on an equal level with others, due to physical and social barriers.'

Compare these two definitions and you will see a clear difference. On the one hand, disability is seen as resulting from the impairment or shortcoming of the individual. On the other, it is society's inability to enable its disabled members to lead full and productive lives.

There is no clear boundary between 'disabled' and 'not disabled'. Disability is a continuum ranging from the severe to the slight. Disability is a human issue that will touch all of us in some way during our lifetimes rather than something that happens to other people. Whom we count as disabled will depend on where we draw the line on the

continuum and there are no obvious answers.

Think about your own experience of disability on both a professional and a personal level. For example, have you ever had a disabled friend or colleague? If not, why do you think this is so?

Unfamiliarity with disability can result in fear and discomfort, particularly with physical difference. This is just one of the reasons why inclusion is so important for a healthier society.

What do you really think about disability?

To make any meaningful examination of these issues and how they relate to current attitudes we need to understand the different ways in which all societies, including our own, have tried to explain disability.

■ The religious model

This is the idea that disability is a punishment for evil behaviour. Disabled people and their families are thus stigmatised and avoided. Vestiges of this model still exist in many cultures, including our own. In this model the child is seen as a punishment.

'Inclusion is a process of identifying, understanding and breaking down the barriers to participation and belonging.'

(Early Childhood Forum, June 2003)

■ The medical model

This is the idea that disability is caused by an impairment(s) that professionals must try to cure or alleviate. It is a medical 'problem' which we must 'treat'. The impairment rather than the whole person becomes the focus of attention.

Much of current policy is underpinned by the idea that we must actively intervene as early as possible and that this is always a good thing. But this means we do not distinguish effectively and sensitively enough between those difficulties and impairments that are transient and those that are lifelong and cannot be changed.

To develop the self-esteem and positive identity that underpin later fulfilment in life and the achievement of potential, children need to accept themselves and be accepted and valued by others *as they are*. In this model the child is seen as faulty.

■ The social model

This view is crucial to successful inclusive practice and underpins current legislation such as the Disability Discrimination Act. It means realising that the social, emotional and physical barriers that society creates are the disabling factors in our society. This model enables us to accept and value difference because in this model the child is celebrated and valued.

The media and other influences

Media, such as television, films and books, have tended to stereotype disabled people into nasty or frightening characters (such as the Hunchback of Notre Dame) or brave and courageous individuals that get better in the end (Heidi, Forrest Gump).

Few books are written and published by disabled novelists in mainstream fiction. Television and newspaper stories about disability concentrate on the person as a victim or sufferer. Disability is considered a separate specialised subject, disabled people are singled out as experts in the disability field, rather than accepted and listened to as the capable individuals they are, with different skills and insights. Their social comment is generally not wanted beyond the field of disability.

There are few positive role models for disabled children in the media.

What is inclusion?

Nationally, our progress towards inclusion has been patchy. Part of the problem has been a lack of common understanding of what inclusion is.

The Early Childhood Forum definition (above) sees inclusion as an ongoing process by which all young children may be enabled to receive care and education in mainstream settings and join in as fully as possible with their peers in the curriculum and life of the setting.

This statement recognises that barriers to inclusion and equality are to be found at individual and institutional levels. In practical terms this means a whole team approach and openness to new ideas, approaches and systems change. Inclusion involves everybody and everything. The changes and adjustments that we make for the benefit of individual children are likely to enrich the curriculum and ethos of settings and benefit all of the children, parents and staff.

Early years settings do not exist in a vacuum. They reflect and absorb the views and influences of their local communities and the wider society. Through inclusive practice and policies early years workers are becoming agents of positive and historic social change for disabled people, but this change cannot begin in earnest unless we are brave and honest enough to examine ourselves.

All children and families need to feel valued for who they are and the gifts that they bring. Disabled children need to feel ordinary in the sense that their presence amidst the able-bodied community becomes completely unremarkable and just. All they are asking for is to belong.

Mary Dickins, trainer and consultant specialising in equality and inclusion in the early years.

Positive resources
All Equal, All Different – a resource to develop disability equality (Disability Equality in Education) Call 020 7359 2855 or visit www.diseed.org.uk

Letterbox Library sells children's books that reflect positive images of disability. Tel: 0207 503 4801

The charity Action for Leisure provides information, training and resources. Tel: 01926 650195 or visit www.actionforleisure.org.uk

Persona dolls are an effective way of working on equality issues. Visit: www.persona-doll-training.org

Training
All Together Training and Consultancy (Tel: 020 7482 1165)

Disability Equality in Education (Tel: 020 7359 2855)

Useful books
Early Years and the Disability Discrimination Act 1995: what service providers need to know (Council for Disabled Children/Sure Start/ National Children's Bureau). This leaflet explains how the Disability Discrimination Act 1995 applies to early years settings.

All Together: How to Create Inclusive Services for Disabled Children and their Families M Dickins and J Denziloe (National Children's Bureau). A handbook for early years workers.

Dealing with parents who are separated or divorced can be problematic. Sometimes, the parent's relationship deteriorates and you may find yourself caught up in the dispute. Ashlie Prescott, a solicitor, examines the legal issues and offers advice

Family law:
Child contact disputes

What would you do if a parent who does not live with their child (the non-resident parent) arrived to collect or take their child away - and you knew that this was against the wishes of the parent with whom the child resides (the resident parent)? It's a situation you could easily find yourself in.

That's why it is important for you to understand the legal position regarding the rights that each parent has in relation to their children. The legal term is parental responsibility (PR). PR gives a parent the responsibility for taking the important decisions in their child's life, for example, to do with education and medical care.

Note: I will refer to the non-resident parent as the father and the resident parent as the mother. However, the advice is the same where the circumstances are reversed.

Who has parental responsibility?
The mother, whether married or unmarried, will always have PR but will never have a piece of paper to show this.

'The most important factor for you to consider is the welfare and safety of the child. This supercedes any rights that a parent asserts, no matter how aggressively.'

The law draws a distinction between married and unmarried fathers. An unmarried father does not automatically have PR. He may acquire it by the mother giving it to him or by the Court granting it to him. If the unmarried father has acquired parental responsibility he will have a piece of paper to prove it.

Married fathers, like mothers, automatically have parental responsibility and will not have a piece of paper to prove this. A married father does not lose his parental responsibility in the event of the parents separating or divorcing.

Good practice
You should make sure that all children's record sheets indicate whether the father has parental responsibility, even if the parents are together.

If the parents are not estranged at the time of enrolling the child with you, then it is usual for both parents to be named as persons who may collect the child. If the parents are separated when the child is enrolled, the record sheet should ask a specific question of the mother as to whether she consents to the father collecting the child. It is advisable for the contracts between you and the parents to include a clause that states that the mother is responsible for informing you of any change to her consent for the father to collect the child.

Where the parents have separated or divorced you should make sure that your contract is with the resident parent. This means that if the father originally enrolled the child when the parents were together and the father is now the non-resident

parent, the contract should be renewed with the mother as the resident parent.

It is especially problematic when you are put in the position of having to decide whether or not to release a child to a non-resident parent who has turned up to collect their child unannounced. It can be difficult to know what to do, especially if the father starts to become awkward.

The most important factor for you to consider is the welfare and safety of the child. This supercedes any rights that a parent asserts, no matter how aggressively. The advice below will apply in any of the following circumstances:

■ If the father is not on the list of persons authorised to collect the child; or

■ If the father was on the list at one time but has since been removed; or

■ If you have been advised by the mother or are aware of a possible problem but the father has not yet been removed from the list.

In these circumstances, the following procedure should be followed:

1. If the father is not known to you already, adequate steps should be taken to establish the identity of the person alleging to be the father. Nothing less than photographic ID, such as a photographic driver's licence or passport should be accepted. If the father cannot produce such ID, you should inform him immediately that the child will remain on the premises and that he must leave straight away. If he refuses, you should call the police.

2. If the ID is produced and you are satisfied that the man is the father of the child, you should keep the child on the premises until such time as you have been able to telephone the mother to inform her of the father's presence and his wish to remove the child.

3. If the mother states that she does not want the father to leave with the child, she should be asked to attend the nursery herself or arrange for one of the other authorised persons on the list to collect the child immediately. This will enable you to keep the child until the mother or her appointed person arrives to collect the child. The father should be informed that the mother or another authorised person is collecting the child instead and he should be asked to leave. If he refuses, you can either call the police or wait until the mother/authorised person arrives in the hope that he then leaves at that point. When the mother/ authorised person collects the child they should be asked not to return the child to the nursery until the problem with the father has been resolved.

4. In the event that the mother states that she does not want the father to remove the child and she is not able to arrange to collect the child herself or for another authorised person to do so, my advice is to keep the child on the premises and not allow the child to be released to the father. If the father becomes aggressive, call the police.

Court orders

There may be occasions when a father produces a court order which states that he is to have contact with the child at certain times and those times coincide with the nursery or school session. The court order may even go as far to say that the father can collect the child from nursery or school for the purposes of exercising such contact. You should be extremely cautious when dealing with court orders.

The court has the power to make a range of orders in relation to children and has the power to revoke an existing order. On rare occasions an order may be made on one day, allowing contact between the father and the child, and on the very next day a different court order

What should you do if a non-resident father tries to pick up their child and remove them from the premises?

It is your responsibility to make sure that the father does not get close enough to the child to allow this to happen. You would not allow a stranger to come in and simply pick up the child and remove them and the same approach should be adopted with a non-resident parent who is no longer authorised to collect their child without the authority of the resident parent.

The first and easiest step is, of course, to refuse the father entry into the building. It is important for any negotiations with the father to take place outside the building. This is not only to prevent the child from witnessing the incident and to prevent the child being forcibly removed but also to safeguard the welfare of the other children on site and your staff. You do not want children witnesssing outbursts of aggression and hearing potentially foul language from an angry parent.

If, for any reason, the father has entered the building to speak with staff, steps should be taken to make sure that he is confined to the reception area. There should be a further security system in place inside the premises to isolate the children from the reception area, in other words a facility to lock the door leading to the area(s) where the children are. Ultimately the same measures which are used to stop strangers coming in should be adopted for an unauthorised parent. The child's safety has to take precedence.

Your staff will not know what kind of risk, if any, the father is to the child. Is he going to abduct the child? Has he been adjudged by a court recently to be a danger to the child and therefore not allowed to have any contact? Staff will not know the answers to these questions and it is not fair to expect them to have discretion as to whether the child should go or not.

If a non-resident father with a grievance does manage to gain access to your premises and remove a child, call the police and the mother immediately.

may be made revoking contact altogether.

A court will only normally order that there be no contact between a father and a child if the father potentially poses some kind of risk to the child. The father will likely only show you the order that states he can have contact and not the later one which may have revoked it. Therefore, if a father does produce such a court order, you should follow the steps detailed above.

There is no doubt that you are placed in a difficult position when dealing with some of the issues that arise from separated parents. However, provided you have taken every step to safeguard the safety and welfare of the child placed in your care no one could justifiably raise any criticism. Provided the practical guidance above is followed, Ofsted would find it very difficult to uphold any complaint that either parent may make against you.

Ashlie Prescott is a solicitor at Gosschalks Solicitors, Hull who specialise in nursery law.

Contracts and fees

Renewing a contract can be difficult if the resident parent is not paying the fees. You have no comeback on non-payment, for example, if your contract is with the mother and the father refuses to pay the bill, which is quite a common negotiating tool used between warring parents. So what can you do?

The person responsible for payment should be the person with whom you have a contract. The contract must clearly state that the person enrolling the child and signing the contract is responsible for payment. If the contract is changed so that it is now with the resident parent, the contract is binding on the resident parent and that includes payment of fees. If the non-resident parent chooses to make payment on behalf of the resident parent, then that is a matter for the parents. It does not negate responsibility upon the resident parent to be primarily responsible for the fees.

What is autism? How do you know if a child in your care has autism? Who can offer support to you, the child and their family? Lindy Hardcastle looks at autistic spectrum disorders and answers these questions for you

Words you need to know: Autistic spectrum disorder

The term autistic spectrum disorder (ASD) reflects the wide range of ability and disability in children who are autistic. The most severely affected children have little or no speech and no apparent response to the people or things around them. They live entirely within themselves and are difficult to reach. At the other end of the spectrum are intelligent, highly articulate children who nevertheless have great difficulty relating to other people and understanding what society requires of them. Children at the more able end of the spectrum are sometimes described as having Asperger syndrome.

Of course, many children fall somewhere between these two extremes. To complicate matters, many ASD children also have either dyslexia, dyspraxia or attention deficit hyperactive disorder (ADHD) – sometimes all of them.

What is autism?

Whatever the severity of the autism, there are three common characteristic difficulties.

- **Communication:** Children have limited use of language. Some appear fluent, but they are often echoing or parroting things they have heard without understanding. They have difficulty using and interpreting facial expressions, body language and non-literal speech; they avoid eye contact.

- **Relationships:** Children have no empathy: they cannot understand other people's thoughts and feelings. They don't pick up social skills – they need to be taught. They often want to join in with other children but don't know how; their behaviour is inappropriate and they are often excluded from social groups.

- **Rigidity/lack of imagination:** Because they have such difficulty understanding their environment, ASD children cling on to anything familiar. They resist change, preferring to eat the same food, play with the same toys, wear the same clothes and stick to a rigid routine. They do not engage in imaginative play and they may have an obsessive interest – for some as yet unexplained reason, washing machines, vacuum cleaners and other domestic appliances are popular!

Clearly, the frustration arising from an inability to communicate, make relationships and cope with change can trigger tantrums and challenging behaviour, which is often the most obvious sign that something is amiss. But it should also be recognised that some ASD children will become withdrawn, silent and isolated.

The autism 'epidemic'

The diagnosis of ASD has increased tenfold in the last ten years. This huge rise in numbers, together with growing media interest, means that most people will know someone who is affected. From being a fairly rare condition, it has become relatively common. Estimates of prevalence vary, but a figure of one child in every hundred is generally accepted, meaning that most primary schools could expect to have two or three autistic children at any time. The Government is now undertaking research into the autistic children born in the 1990s to try to determine the causes.

Part of the reason for the rapid increase is better diagnosis, with more recognition that children of normal or high intelligence can also be on the autistic spectrum; but it is also probable that there is some environmental factor or factors triggering the autism 'epidemic'.

MMR – can it cause autism?

It is generally agreed that some children have a genetic predisposition to autism and that it is triggered by some trauma at birth or shortly afterwards. Some children with autism appear to be affected from birth; others seem to be developing normally and then regress at about 18 months to two years old, losing their speech and social skills. It is this regression that leads parents to suspect that the MMR vaccination, which children are given around that age, may be to blame. There is no direct medical proof of this, but anecdotal evidence is worrying. Parents with a family history of autism or who are particularly concerned should certainly be encouraged to seek separate vaccinations for their children rather than not have them vaccinated at all.

What to look out for

As a childcarer, you are in a good position to spot autistic spectrum disorders. You have the opportunity to observe the child alongside others the same age and you will notice problems with communication, social interaction and play which the parent, particularly of a first or only child, may not be aware of.

You may notice that the child does not seem to relate to the other children in your care, or that his responses are inappropriate. Sharing and taking turns will be difficult concepts for the child to grasp. He (boys outnumber girls by at least four to one) will play with the same toys every day in the same way, typically lining up toys in an unvarying order. You may also notice the child tiptoe walking, spinning objects and rocking. Many children with ASD react badly to noise.

Sharing your concerns

If you think a child in your care may be on the autistic spectrum, you need to share this information with the parents. Early diagnosis and support can make an enormous difference to the child's development and opportunities.

It is essential that there is good communication between you and the parents: a few minutes at the beginning and end of each day and, if at all possible, a longer meeting every few months, to discuss the child's progress. Every parent wants their child to be healthy and 'normal' and it is never easy to tell them that there may be a lifelong problem rather than a temporary difficulty.

Tread gently, outlining some of the warning signs you have observed. You may well find the parents are already worried and will welcome the opportunity to share their concerns. Be ready with some basic information and positive suggestions, like contacting a specialist health visitor or a local support group, and reassure them that you will continue to support them and their child.

If parents are not ready to acknowledge the problem, return to the subject every few months. You may have to accept that, having alerted them, you will have to let them come to terms with their child's difficulty in their own time.

Getting a diagnosis

Autistic spectrum disorders are difficult to diagnose. There are no blood tests or brain scans, so diagnosis is based on the child's case history as reported by parents and observation of the child, preferably in a variety of settings. Specialist health visitors can support parents through the process and GPs will refer the child to an appropriate paediatrician or child psychiatrist. Parents will sometimes encounter delays and an unwillingness by professionals to make a firm diagnosis. They will need to be persistent both in seeking a diagnosis and getting appropriate support.

Supporting the child in your home

All children do best if their parents and carers are communicating well with each other and providing a consistent approach to behaviour management.

Children with ASD need routine and predictability. Use a visual timetable with interchangeable symbols for meals, drinks, television, story time, outdoor play, rest time and other daily activities, so the child knows what is going to happen next. Children with little speech can learn to use pictures to communicate with their parents and carers. They are visual learners and may respond well to jigsaw puzzles and simple sorting and matching activities. They can be gently encouraged to try new activities and join in with other children, but beware of treating autism as a character defect which can be corrected. It is a serious disability which needs careful, expert intervention: get all the help you can.

Lindy Hardcastle, childminder, Leicestershire.

Information and support

The National Autistic Society (NAS) can provide advice, information and support for parents. Telephone the helpline (0207 903 3555) or visit their website www.nas.org.uk. The NAS will also be able to provide contact details for a local group; it is invaluable for parents to meet others who have encountered the same problems and can advise on local provision.

The NAS Earlybird scheme provides support for pre-school children and their families in their homes and pre-school settings. As the child's carer, you should be involved in this programme. Local education authorities can provide pre-school teachers and speech therapy may also be appropriate. If a child is likely to need support in school, the parents should request a statutory assessment of the child's special needs so that a statement can be in place when the child starts school. The child may also be eligible for Disability Living Allowance and Mobility Allowance.

One of the cornerstones of central government policy for children and families in England is now children's centres. Sue Griffin explains the aims and aspirations of this policy, and raises some of the uncertainties surrounding it

Words you need to know:
Children's centres

The concept of children's centres is an exciting and promising one, and if enough resources can be put into them, they have the potential to offer children and families excellent services.

What is a children's centre?

A children's centre is a 'one-stop centre' which offers:

■ early education integrated with childcare;

■ health services for children and families (including ante-natal services);

■ support and information for parents and families, both on parenting and on training and getting into work.

All children's centres must:

■ have a suitably qualified teacher

leading the learning provided for the children;

■ be the base for a childminding network so parents have choices about whether their child is educated and cared for in a centre or a home base;

■ provide services for disabled children and children with special educational needs, and for their families.

Children's centres are part of the Government's vision for the future for children and families. This vision also includes extended parental leave (so fewer babies and under-twos would need childcare places, as has already happened in Sweden).

Earlier this summer the Chancellor announced funding for 2,500 centres by 2008. These centres will be in the 30

'Children's centres are part of the Government's vision for the future for children and families.'

per cent most disadvantaged areas. The long-term goal of government policy is that there should be a children's centre in every community, serving all children and families wherever they live. That aim is in the future – maybe a fairly distant future.

It seems that the development of children's centres will start from existing provision, so all Sure Start projects, all Early Excellence Centres, all Neighbourhood Nurseries and, eventually, all nursery schools, will be looked at as the basis of the children's centre for their area.

Education and care

Children's centres will offer good quality early education combined with full day, all year round childcare. All early years practitioners will agree that it is not possible to care for a child without being involved in their learning and education, or to educate a child without contributing to their care. So the integrated approach makes a lot of sense, certainly more sense than the experience that some children currently have, where their education and their care (as wrap-around) are seen as happening in different places, at different times and with different adults.

Children don't experience their lives in this divided-up way, so services for them should aim to provide education and care in a coordinated way. This offers children continuity in their day and week, and creates a stable and secure environment for them, helping them to develop well emotionally and socially.

Some children still experience their early education in five separate two-hour blocks, for only some weeks in the year. This approach needs to change, to acknowledge that children are learning throughout their day, week and year (whether or not the adults they're with are consciously trying to teach them).

In integrated provision, it would be difficult to say whether care or education is happening for the child – from their point of view, these are not separate experiences.

The Government's aims also include the development of a new framework of integrated education and care for children from birth to six years old, drawing on all that is best in the birth to three and Foundation Stage frameworks. This will be an exciting development. The birth to three framework has shown us how sensitive guidance can help

But what about ...?

Other questions which will have to be addressed in the development of children's centres include

■ What part can the VIP (voluntary, independent and private) sectors play in this? How could children's centres be based on community pre-schools and private nurseries?

■ How can this be made to work in rural as well as urban areas? There is talk of 'virtual' centres – a range of integrated services spread across the countryside, rather than a centre in a particular place. How could that be made effective?

practitioners plan and practise in ways which meet the youngest children's needs, and which don't separate the ideas of care and learning.

Interesting times

There is always a period of waiting after announcements by ministers when civil servants work out the details of how ambitious plans can be put into action. So we wait to see how the challenges and questions which surround children's centres are worked out.

It seems that the experiences of change that everyone in the early years and childcare field has learned to live with will continue. For the concept of integration to really take hold and become reality, there will have to be changes on several fronts.

■ Knowledge and skills of the workforce – training and qualifications.

■ Professional boundaries between those who are currently seen as educating and those who are seen as caring – roles and responsibilities, pay and conditions.

■ Leadership and management of teams of practitioners from different backgrounds.

■ Regulation and inspection – the current parallel systems of inspection of care settings and education settings is due for a shake-up, as we saw in last year's consultation document from Ofsted.

Practitioners will need broad knowledge and skills, across the old education/ care divide, and across age ranges. The development of the new National Occupational Standards (on which NVQs and other qualifications are based) has tackled this challenge and made radical changes. The drive to increase numbers of people in the early years and childcare workforce has had only limited success. The basic problems here are the pay and status of the work, which make it less attractive than it might be. The development of children's

'The long-term goal of government policy is that there should be a children's centre in every community, serving all children and families wherever they live.'

centres will need more practitioners, so recruitment campaigns need to be re-thought if they are to have the necessary impact.

There is logic in targeting disadvantaged areas – you have to use limited resources to focus on the greatest needs. But not all disadvantaged families live in disadvantaged areas. There are pockets of deprivation in affluent areas - 44 per cent of people on the lowest incomes don't live in areas of disadvantage. Until a children's centre is available in every community, these families will go on losing out.

And, of course, the biggest question is – as ever – who pays? The current nursery education grant keeps education separate and paid for out of the public purse. Tax credits are a roundabout way of the state contributing to childcare, which is still seen in this country mainly as the responsibility of parents.

Sue Griffin, early years and childcare consultant, Wiltshire.

The phrase Sure Start was coined six years ago but its meaning has changed since then. It originally stood for a concept, a new way of delivering services for families through local programmes but it now covers all registered childcare as well and has even been adopted as the name of a Government unit

Words you need to know: Sure Start

Sure Start is the name of the Government unit for early years and childcare up to the age of 14. It brings together policy and services on early education, childcare, health and family support and is the result of different departments working together in an approach the Government likes to call 'joined up thinking'.

The Sure Start Unit was created in 2002 -but it's not a new name. It's one the Government has adopted almost as a slogan - or brand - for its goal of providing good quality, affordable childcare for all children and families. It was taken from the Sure Start local programmes that are aimed at improving the health and well-being of families and children from before birth to four in deprived neighbourhoods.

Joined up thinking - where it all began

The first Sure Start local programmes were set up in 1999 as a result of the 1998 Comprehensive Spending Review (CSR). The CSR was formed soon after the Labour government came to power in 1997 to look at the pattern and level of public spending and suggest reforms to take account of the Government's priorities. It was carried out by a group of officials from 11 different departments plus the Number 10 Policy Unit and the Social Exclusion Unit.

The review made a number of findings:

■ The earliest years in life are the most important for child development

■ Multiple disadvantage for young children was a severe and growing problem, increasing the chances of social exclusion later in life

■ The quality of provision for young children and their families varied enormously with uncoordinated and patchy services being the norm in many areas. Services were particularly dislocated for the under fours - an age group which tended

to get missed out by other government programmes.

■ The provision of a comprehensive community-based programme of early intervention and family support which built on existing services could have a good effect, not only on child and family development but also help break the cycle of social exclusion. This could lead to significant long term gain to the Exchequer.

It proposed a programme called Sure Start to upgrade the level of services to young children and their parents. This programme was set out in the White Paper, *Modernising Public Services for Britain*.

A new way of doing things

Once the decision was taken to go ahead with the programme, a Sure Start Unit was set up. It was part of the Department for Education and Skills (then the DfEE) but also consisted of officials seconded

National Sure Start month

National Sure Start month is a chance for you to promote your work with children, raising awareness and increasing understanding by parents of the services available to them in their neighbourhood. Providers are encouraged to celebrate by holding fun events and inviting parents, MPs, local celebrities and the media.

It takes place during June and is organised jointly by the National Day Nurseries Association (NDNA), 4Children (formerly Kids Club Network), Daycare Trust, National Childminding Association (NCMA) and the Pre-School Learning Alliance (PLA).

If you want posters or leaflets to help promote your event, email nssm@ndna.org.uk or call the National Sure Start Month helpline on 0870 774 4308.

from the Treasury, DfES, Department of Health and the Department of Environment, Transport and the Regions.

One of the striking features of the development of Sure Start local programmes was the involvement of people outside central government in designing the policy.

Sure Start local programmes represented a new way of doing things, both in the development of the policy and in its delivery. It was an attempt to put joined up thinking into practice .

Sure Start aims

The policy of Sure Start was set out in a report by the Social Exclusion Unit in 1998. It is aimed at areas of deprivation and based on the belief that investment in early childhood can help later performance at school, prevent truancy and reduce the risk of unemployment,

drug abuse and crime. Its goal is to make sure that all children are ready to learn when they arrive at school.

Sure Start local programmes are delivered by local partnerships with strong parental and community involvement. They should be easily accessible, within pram-pushing distance, and backed up with outreach to offer support in the home. Services include childcare, primary health care, play and support for families, from pregnant mothers to those with children up to 14. They can be based in all sorts of centres from GPs' surgeries to nurseries.

From local programme to Government department

In December 2002, the Government published a review of childcare services, called *Delivering for Children and Families*, which said that there were too many sources of funding and too many different brands of services, from Sure Start to Neighbourhood Nurseries and Early Excellence Centres. It said that the whole scene was difficult for parents and the general public to understand.

So childcare was 'rebranded'. Sure Start got a relaunch at a major national conference and the Government announced that from then on Sure Start would be the name used to describe all policy and services on childcare, early education, health and family support.

The review called for a restructuring of the whole of the services and a beginning was made with the establishment of one single interdepartmental unit under Baroness Ashton, Minister for Sure Start.

The Sure Start Unit has under its control all the early years and childcare departments previously established. It is managed by Naomi Eisenstadt.

The new brand is to help the unit inform people working in the sector and parents that Sure Start is a coherent Government strategy to improve support for children, parents and communities.

Epilepsy is more common than most people realise. Rachel Baker gives some pointers on what to do if you care for a child with epilepsy.

Caring for children with epilepsy

One in every 250 children suffers from epilepsy. So if you work in a nursery there is a strong probability that you will meet a child with epilepsy. It is the most common serious neurological disorder in the UK, yet very little is generally known about it unless you, or someone you know suffers from it.

What is epilepsy?

Epilepsy is the term used to describe recurrent seizures, but there are in fact 40 different seizure types. Seventy per cent of children with epilepsy will grow out of it, and most are controlled by medication, although this might not mean that they are completely fit-free as Dr. Nicolaides of Great Ormond street explains:

'Epilepsy has its natural cycles, so even children with well-managed epilepsy may still fit, so it is important that carers know what to do in an emergency, as fits lasting longer than five minutes can cause damage to the brain.'

Many children have febrile convulsions (fever related fits), but that doesn't mean that they are epileptic. Febrile convulsions occur when a child gets so hot that their bodies effectively shut down. The child will go limp and may lose consciousness. These fits are dealt with differently to epileptic seizures; a child who has epilepsy is 'expected' to have fits, which can be dealt with at home, whereas a child who has never had a fit before would need urgent medical attention. In the case of a febrile convulsion, the child's temperature can be brought down with liquid paracetamol (when they are conscious enough to take it), but they must be seen by a physician as high temperatures are usually the result of an infection which must be administered to.

What do seizures look like?

Epileptic seizures can be divided into two categories; partial and generalised. There are sub-categories for both types, but generally partial seizures affect just one part of the brain and therefore one part of the body, whereas generalised seizures affect the whole brain and therefore the whole body.

Partial seizures can be as simple as the jerking of one limb, while the child remains fully conscious and alert. These are called simple partial seizures (SPS), and can sometimes serve as a warning that another type of seizure is imminent. Complex partial seizures affect more of the brain, so can alter the child's consciousness, causing them to become confused and unresponsive. Secondary generalised seizures are very hard to tell apart from generalised seizures as although they start in one area of the brain, they can spread quickly to involve it all, which results in a loss of consciousness.

Generalised seizures can be altogether more disturbing for both child and carer; the most common seizure type in this category is tonic-clonic, which involves the child losing consciousness, stiffening (tonic stage), then falling to the ground and twitching (clonic stage). This isn't always the case however as absence seizures, which are also common in children, involve just a brief loss of consciousness, which can sometimes go unnoticed as they often last just a few seconds. Also in this category are myclonic seizures which are like simple partial seizures, except that the child will be unconscious, though maybe for just a few seconds. These usually tend to happen upon waking, so a child who is known to suffer with these seizures should be watched carefully after a nap, as any loss of consciousness could indicate a fall.

What should I do if a child fits?

Whatever type of seizure a child has, a record of when it happened, what happened, how long it lasted, and sometimes temperature, should be recorded. The parents/carers will need to know this so that they can inform their physician. If a child has never had a seizure before, or if the fit lasts longer than five minutes, an ambulance should be called. If the child loses consciousness they should be put in a safe place (preferably on something soft) and placed in the recovery position.

Basic first-aid for seizures:

Do
- Stay calm.

- Note the time.

- Protect the child from injury – (remove harmful objects from nearby).

- Cushion their head.

- Be calmly reassuring.

- Stay with the child until recovery is complete.

- Aid breathing by gently placing them in the recovery position (see page six) once the seizure has finished.

Don't
- Restrain the child.

- Put anything in the child's mouth.

- Try to move the child unless they are in danger.

- Give the child anything to eat or drink until they are fully recovered.

- Attempt to bring them round.

Call an ambulance if...
- You know it is the child's first seizure.

- The seizure continues for more than five minutes.

- One tonic-clonic seizure follows another without the child regaining consciousness between seizures.

- The child is injured during the seizure.

- You believe the child needs urgent medical attention.

Treatment
A child's treatment depends on the type of epilepsy they have. You may have to administer drugs already in a solution, or as tablets to crush. Make sure you note exactly how much and at what time to administer them, as epilepsy can be very sensitive to the treatment prescribed for it.

For a few children with hard to manage epilepsy, an alternative to medication is the ketogenic diet. This is a bit like the Atkins diet and works by cutting out carbohydrates. When fat is burned in the body without sufficient carbohydrates to fuel the process ketones are produced, which are thought to prevent seizures. Before the diet was invented fasting was used to control seizures, which also makes the body produce ketones. If a child is on this diet it is especially important never to give them sweets or any other source of carbohydrates, as this will stop them producing ketones, which may cause them to fit.

Effects on children
Children whose epilepsy is easy to manage will rarely have any developmental issues, and will progress 'normally'. Others, whose epilepsy is more complex, may be set back by frequent seizures and high doses of medication. It is important that any child with epilepsy is treated normally, and that no stigma is attached to their condition. Some children may need a little extra help with learning or speech development, but they should never be singled out or be made to feel 'different'.

Activities for children with epilepsy
Children with epilepsy can join in most activities – even swimming. The lifeguard should always be aware that the child has epilepsy, but this is generally a safe activity.

Restrictions apply only when the child may be at risk from a fall, such as riding a bike on the road or climbing trees.

All children love music, so if a child has difficulty concentrating and needs to develop their speech, they may prefer to learn this way. Playing instruments and making noise is also a good way of venting any frustrations they may feel.

Painting is good for co-ordination, and children can express themselves through this medium.

Keeping track
The child's parents will be able to guide you through their routines, and discuss the child's needs. It is important that you work out a 'safety plan' with them for emergency situations, and also establish which activities they feel are suitable for their child. Records should be kept of any drugs administered and at what time, and a seizure 'chart' containing time, duration and presentation may also be useful if the child is fitting frequently.

Looking after a child with epilepsy is as rewarding as looking after any 'normal' child – it's just a case of learning as much about their condition as you can, and knowing what to do in the case of an emergency. Every child is an individual with their own unique character, despite any illness or condition they may have.

For more information on epilepsy training services contact:

The National Society for Epilepsy (NSE): 01494 601 305, www.epilepsynse.org.uk

Rachel Baker

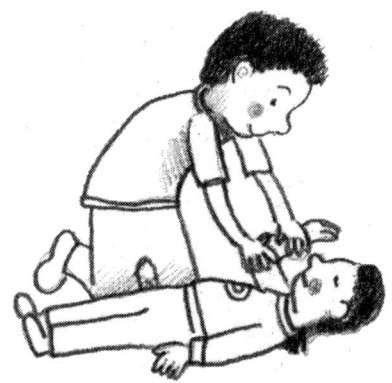

Placing a child in the recovery position.

Helping children to protect themselves is very important. Sheila Riddall-Leach suggests strategies to assist practitioners to enable children develop positive self esteem and self image.

Enabling children to protect themselves

One of the five outcomes of the Children Act 2004 is that children and young people are safe. A child has a right not be to be abused and to be supported when abuse is identified. Therefore one of your main responsibilities, regardless of what setting you are in is to make sure protect children. It is also very important that you give children and young people the skills and strategies to protect themselves. They need to understand that they have the right to be safe and protected. To be able to protect themselves from abuse and bullying children need to feel good about themselves, they need to have a high level of self-esteem and positive self image. Children who are abused often have low self esteem or a negative self image.

Self esteem is how we see ourselves and it has three main features:

- **Worth and significance** - children need to feel accepted, loved and respected by those around them. It is difficult to feel good about yourself if you know that

Jake aged 12 attends a school for children with emotional and social difficulties and he lives in a home run by the local authority. He has never known his father and his mother, a registered drug user, has little contact with him. The staff at school are very award that Jake is subject to bullying by his peers and he spends much of his time being shadowed by a support worker. Jake is very reluctant to learn strategies to help himself and feels safe when in the company of a trusted teacher.

you are not loved or have been rejected by others.

- **Competence** – children need to feel competent and capable. This will encourage them to learn new skills and feel motivated. Obviously competence is limited by a child's age, size and stage of growth and development, but it may also be affected by unrealistic expectations of what a child can achieve. Repeated failure can lead to frustration and dissatisfaction. Consequently, a child will develop negative views of their own competences and have low self-esteem.

- **Control** – the level of an individual's self esteem may be directly affected by the amount of control that they feel that they have got over a situation or their environment. Even young children can gain control over their environment, for example when a baby cries the parent or practitioner comes to find out why. Children quickly learn that when they behave or act in certain way, their actions can produce a change in their environment.

Self-image is related to self-esteem in that a person with low self esteem will also suffer from low self-image. Self-image is how a person sees themselves in relation to others. This also includes physical and mental qualities. A child or young person with a good level of self-esteem and positive self-image will do better in many aspects of their development.

Children who constantly hear criticism or believe that they are useless are very likely to have low self-esteem.

Consequently they will be more likely to engage in activities that challenge, for fear of failure and may have less ambition. These children and young people may also find it more difficult to cope with pressure, be they SATS, disagreements with peers or other adults. Some children and young people with low self-esteem may engage in destructive behaviours, such as drug taking or become involved in abusive relationships.

How to help children develop good self-esteem and positive self-image:

- Offer lots of praise and encouragement, even when the 'achievement' is relatively small. For example saying something like,' what a lovely smile you have', or 'thank you for waiting for me,' can have a positive impact.

- Provide opportunities to encourage independence, to try new things out, but not to fail or achieve.

Jake asked if he could water the seedlings in the school poly tunnel, usually a supervised task as it involved carrying the watering can through a classroom. The teacher trusted Jake to do this independently and he succeeded and returned happily to the group.

- Provide opportunities for children to make real choices. Try not to ask questions such as, 'what would you like to do?' These questions do not offer real choices and the child or young person may not know what the options are and so may not feel confident enough to give you an answer in case they are wrong.

- Provide opportunities for children and young people to express their feelings and wishes. Be available to talk with children and really listen to what they have to say. Don't rush them and take your cues from the child.

- Provide opportunities and activities where children and young people can succeed without fear of failure or 'getting something wrong'

- Plan and offer activities and experiences that appropriate to their needs and age and stage of development, for example age appropriate sessions, linked to other activities on how the body works can help children understand what their bodies can do and help them learn what is normal and what is not.

- Be a positive role model who encourages tolerance, respect and co-operation between children and adults alike.

The charity Kidscape has devised 'The Keepsafe Code' which has nine straightforward pointers to help children to protect themselves, such as saying NO in an assertive way, how to respond to

'It is important that children and young people have factual information so that they can make sound judgments for themselves and so develop strategies about looking after themselves.'

unwanted hugs and kisses, and whether or not to keep secrets. The Keepsafe Code can be accessed form the Kidscape website at www.kidscape.org.uk.

All children and young people need factual information about their rights, sexual behaviour, misuse of their bodies and risks. The older the children the more detailed the information should be. It is good practice to talk about and discuss sexual behaviours related to adults (in accordance with your setting's policy). Give the young people information about the effects of drugs, smoking, alcohol and other substances, HIV and AIDS and sexual transmitted diseases. There are many organisations that can give you fact sheets and information on all these topics, such as NCPCC, Childline and Kidscape.

Children need to understand that they have a right to be safe and feel protected. They also need to have people that they can tell if they are not feeling safe or are being threatened. Schools have developed a citizenship programme which provides opportunities for children and young people to consider and discuss safety, not just about themselves, but also on a wider basis. Having an understanding of the impact of not feeling safe on other can help some children and young people develop their own individual ways to protecting themselves.

We need to think about if we should encourage children and young people to keep secrets. It can be argued that keeping secrets can encourage a child to be cagey and reticent to talk about things. It can be suggested that keeping secrets can encourage dishonesty as the child might not tell the truth in order to keep the secret.

But we also need to consider what do children and young people mean and understand by being safe? What do they consider acceptable behaviours? It is important that children and young people have factual information so that they can make sound judgments for themselves and so develop strategies

'Children need to understand that they have a right to be safe and feel protected.'

about looking after themselves. Children and young people should never feel uncomfortable about someone that they are with or something being done to them. Children and young people need to know that they are valued not for what they can do but simply because they are there. Unconditional acceptance by adults will encourage high self-esteem and positive self-image.

Sheila Riddall-Leech, educational consultant and trainer.

Glossary of key words and concepts

Abuse - when a child or young person is suffering or may suffer considerable harm from physical abuse, emotional abuse, sexual abuse, neglect or bullying

Access - opportunities for participation

Adolescence - the period of social and psychological transition between childhood and adulthood – the teenage years.

Advocate - a supporter, someone who speaks on behalf of another with the needs of that individual in mind

Adults - mature family members, such as parents, grandparents, aunts and uncles, colleagues, other professionals

Agency - an organisation or group of individuals with a specific purpose

Allergy - sensitivity and/or an intolerant reaction to a specific food or substance

Anti-bias practice - Taking positive action to oppose prejudice, stereotypical attitudes and unfair dealings with other individuals; making sure that you meet individual needs

Antibiotics - Medication which kills bacteria

Anti-discriminatory practice - Taking positive action to oppose discrimination in any shape or form; making sure that you respect and have a positive attitude towards differences and similarities between individuals

Appropriate - suitable, fitting, apt for the circumstance, situation and setting

Assertiveness - mental attitude of negotiation and solving problems rather than giving in to emotional urges

Assess - to measure, consider, or weigh up

Assessment - making an informed judgement about something or a measurement of it, for example the development of a specific skill

Attachment - unique emotional bond between an adult and a child

Bacteria - A pathogenic organism that can cause infections

Balance - a skill that requires coordination, but not necessarily from the eyes or ears. The ability to balance is developed by the

body as the movements use information received from the central nervous system

Balanced diet - one that includes a wide range and variety of foods

Behaviour - what an individual does, says or shows, actions, deeds and activities of an individual

Best practice benchmarks - these are standards that are widely agreed and accepted as providing the most advanced, up-to-date thinking and practice against which you can measure and assess what you are doing in your work. Benchmarks are not minimum standards and can be regulatory, statutory or based on other research or requirements

Birth to Three Framework - a framework to support those people working with and caring for babies and young children under three years old

Child protection – defending the basic right of a child to be protected from abuse

Children - the children with whom you work

Chronic illness - A prolonged illness where the signs and symptoms change very little from day to day

Cognitive – also intellectual related to how children think, understand and learn

Colleagues - the people you work with, people working at the same level as yourself or your manager

Common Assessment Framework (CAF) - a standardised approach to assessing children and young people's needs, designed to help practitioners communicate and work together more effectively

Communication - different forms of contact with others in order to give a message or impart meaning

Communicable diseases - diseases that can be communicated or transmitted

Communication - all forms of interactions with another individual or individuals, including body language, facial expressions, gestures, speaking, listening, writing and electronically, e.g. emails, texts

Confidentiality - usually refers to information that should not be disclosed to a third party and refers to the right to privacy of the individual. (Information that would otherwise remain confidential can be disclosed to a third party, if it suspected that a child or young person is in need of protection

Conductive education - very intensive medical treatment that focuses upon a step-by-step approach, encouraging the child to gradually develop movement

Continuing professional development - refers to ongoing training that you can become involved in so that you can improve and update your practice and skills

Coordination skills - of hand, foot and eye and the abilty to combine more than one skill or movement at the same time

Correct procedures - Those that are required by law, inspection agencies and the organisation or setting

COSHH - Control of Hazardous Substances to Health regulations (1994)

Creativity - An individual response; ways in which children can express their own original ideas, children can express creativity in all areas of learning

Creative play - play that encourages and enables children and young people to explore, experiment and discover, in their own unique ways, sometimes called imaginative play

CSIW - the Welsh Assembly department for inspecting childcare and schools in Wales

Curriculum - a set of activities, opportunities and experiences which help and support children's learning and development

Development - ways in which children grow and acquire skills and competences

Developmental needs - those things that are required to enable children to progress and move forward in their development

Difficulty - a term that is often given to a situation or condition, such as an emotional difficulty, that may be overcome or treated. However some learning difficulties cannot be overcome

Disability - a physical or mental impairment which has a significant and long term adverse effect on an individual's ability to continue with normal day to day activities

Disclosure of abuse – when a child or young person tells you that they have been abused

Early Years Foundation Stage - setting standards for learning, development and care for children from birth to five

Effective working relationships - the type of relationship with your colleagues that helps the team to work well and provide a high level of service to the customer. This includes getting along well with your colleagues, being fair, avoiding unnecessary

disagreements or arguments and not letting your personal life influence the way you relate to colleagues

Emergency - an urgent situation, that is unplanned

Empowerment - to give strength, confidence or power to someone

Emotional responses - how children and young people express their feelings

Environment - All aspects of the indoor and outdoor surroundings for which you, the candidate has responsibility.

Equipment - all toys, utensils, furniture, fittings and materials that may be used with or by children

Ethnicities - Refers to a person's identification and recognition with a group that shares some or all of the same culture, way of life, customs, traditions, language, religious beliefs and practices. It can also refer to a geographical region and history. Everyone has an ethnicity

Evaluate - to find out, judge, assess, measure the value of something, look at strengths, weaknesses, positive and negative points

Family - a social unit that includes adults and children and which provides a home and care for children

Fine manipulative skills - small movements that are needed to write or draw

Fine motor skills - small movements of the whole hand

Fitness - levels of agility, suppleness, muscle tone

Formative assessment - Initial and ongoing assessment

Gross motor skills - movements involving all of an arm or leg

Hazard - Something that is likely to cause harm

Health - the physical condition of an individual

Heuristic play - a form of play that encourages babies and young children to explore everyday natural objects through their senses

Holistic - whole or complete development, not looking at specific areas

Holistic treatment – focuses on the whole person rather than just on the symptoms of an illness or disability

HIV - Human immuno-deficiency virus; the virus that causes AIDS

Impairment – a condition that negatively affects the ability to hear, see, walk or co-ordinate actions

Inclusion - the process of recognising, understanding, and overcoming obstructions, or barriers to participation

Independence - allowing a child to have self-autonomy, freedom, self-reliance and therefore undertaking an activity or experience without intervention

Individual Learning Plan (ILP) - can also be called Individual Education Plan (IEP) drawn up by SENCO and/or parents with other professionals who may be working with the child

Individuality - What makes each person unique, the way that everyone is different from everyone else, for example because of their attitudes, appearance, behaviour

Individual needs - The unique requirements and wants of a person that should be met in order for them to reach their full potential

Inclusive - The process of identifying, recognising, understanding and removing barriers to belonging and participation

Infection - a disease, illness, virus or bug

Information Sharing and Assessment (ISA) - the process through which agencies can appropriately share information to better meet the needs of children with whom they are working

Key person - a named member of staff who ahs responsibility for a small group of children or young people

Key Stage - age divisions of the National Curriculum

Learning ways - in which children and young people obtain new knowledge and understanding about something or acquiring a new skills or changing behaviour as a result of experience

Learning style - the way in which we process new information

Literacy - how we use words, either in writing or reading

Local Safeguarding Children Board (LSCB) - is a statutory body responsible for overseeing the safeguarding of children and young people in a local area

Managing - the organisation, supervision, administration and running of a business

Medicine - a remedy, tablet, pill, lotion or liquid that can help alleviate a medical or health problem

Mental health - the well being and strength of the mind

Milestones - clearly defined stages within a sequence of development

Monitor – to check, keep an eye on

Multi-Agency Teams (MAT) - co-located teams of practitioners from different agencies, working together to support children and young people in the area

National Curriculum - a set of learning activities and experiences for children and young people between five and sixteen years of age

Observation - watching, studying, examining, or scrutinising the actions of others

OfSTED - the government department responsible for the inspection of childcare, schools and local education authorities

Oracy - what is said and how it is said

Pattern of development - the sequence of development, what development would be expected to be observes and the rate at which it takes place

Personal development plan - a working document that sets outs your skills, strengths and weaknesses, areas for development and ways to implement your ideas; it usually has six steps for you to follow

Perspective - a different view or outlook to your own

Physical development - how children gain control of their bodies

Plan - to prepare, set up and organise activities and experiences

Policies - guidelines that have been agreed by all people working in a setting about what should and should not happen in certain situations

Positive relationships - dealings, association and contact with others that are beneficial in all ways to children, young people and adults

Potential - the latent capabilities of an individual that will emerge under the right circumstances and situations

Prejudice - narrow-mindedness, bigotry, unfairness, discrimination

Procedures - the ways in which a policy will be carried out

Provision - this includes the physical setting that a child can be in, such as a school, childminder, day nursery or a peripatetic service within the community, such as a playbus, portage

Rate of development - the time frame in which development takes place

Reflective practice - the process of thinking about and critically analysing your actions with the aim of changing, improving your work.

Risk - the danger or seriousness of a hazard and its likelihood to actually cause harm to an individual

Routine - a custom, scheduled event or activity that is usually planned with regularity

Self-image - how a person sees themselves in relation to others

SENCO - the person responsible for coordinating special educational needs provision with a setting

Sequence of development - Order in which development occurs

Setting - Anywhere children's care, learning and development takes place and where children are normally under supervision

Statement - a legal document that outlines a child or young person's special educational needs and the local authority's duty towards the child

Stereotyping - to label, put into artificial categories, to type cast

Structured play - when play is planned by the adults

Summarise assessment - Assessment which summarises, reviews and goes over the main points of findings

Supervision - control, management or command of a situation or other individuals

SWOT analysis - A detailed consideration of your strengths, weaknesses, opportunities and threats

Vigour - energy levels and vitality

Well-being - a positive state of overall good health, both physical and mental

Wrap around care - care for children before and after school and during holidays